Shojo Beat MANGA FROM THE HEART

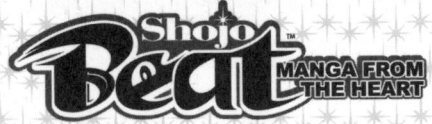

COMPLETE OUR SURVEY AND LET US KNOW WHAT YOU THINK!

☐ Please do NOT send me information about VIZ Media and Shojo Beat products, news and events, special offers, or other information.

☐ Please do NOT send me information from VIZ Media's trusted business partners.

Name: ______________________________

Address: ______________________________

City: ____________ **State:** ______ **Zip:** __________

E-mail: ______________________________

☐ **Male** ☐ **Female** **Date of Birth** (mm/dd/yyyy): ___/___/_____ (Under 13? Parental consent required)

1 Do you purchase *Shojo Beat* magazine?

☐ Yes ☐ No **(if no, skip the next two questions)**

If **YES**, do you subscribe?

☐ Yes ☐ No

If you do **NOT** subscribe, how often do you/will you purchase *Shojo Beat* magazine?

☐ 1-3 issues a year

☐ 4-6 issues a year

☐ more than 7 issues a year

2 Which Shojo Beat Graphic Novel did you purchase? (please check one)

☐ Full Moon ☐ Fushigi Yûgi: Genbu Kaiden ☐ MeruPuri

☐ Ouran High School Host Club ☐ Tokyo Boys & Girls ☐ Ultra Maniac

Will you purchase subsequent volumes?

☐ Yes ☐ No

3 How did you learn about this title? (check all that apply)

☐ Advertisement ☐ Article ☐ Favorite creator/artist

☐ Favorite title ☐ Gift ☐ Recommendation

☐ Read a preview online and wanted to read the rest of the story

☐ Read introduction in *Shojo Beat* magazine ☐ Special offer

☐ Website ☐ Other ______________________________

4 Of the titles that are serialized in *Shojo Beat* magazine, do you plan to purchase the Graphic Novels?

☐ Yes ☐ No

If **YES**, which one(s) do you plan to purchase? (check all that apply)

☐ Absolute Boyfriend ☐ Baby & Me ☐ Crimson Hero
☐ Godchild ☐ Kaze Hikaru ☐ Nana

If **YES**, what are your reasons for purchasing? (please pick up to 3)

☐ Favorite title ☐ Favorite creator/artist
☐ I want to read the full volume(s) all at once ☐ I want to read it over and over again
☐ There are extras that aren't in the magazine ☐ Recommendation
☐ The quality of printing is better than the magazine
☐ Other _____

If **NO**, why would you not purchase it?

☐ I'm happy just reading it in the magazine ☐ It's not worth buying the graphic novel
☐ All the manga pages are in black and white ☐ There are other graphic novels that I prefer
☐ There are too many to collect for each title ☐ It's too small
☐ Other _____

5 Of the titles NOT serialized in the magazine, which ones have you purchased? (check all that apply)

☐ Full Moon ☐ Fushigi Yûgi: Genbu Kaiden ☐ MeruPuri
☐ Ouran High School Host Club ☐ Tokyo Boys & Girls
☐ Ultra Maniac ☐ Other _____

If you did purchase any of the above, what were your reasons for purchase?

☐ Advertisement ☐ Article ☐ Favorite creator/artist
☐ Favorite title ☐ Gift ☐ Recommendation
☐ Read a preview online and wanted to read the rest of the story
☐ Read introduction in *Shojo Beat* magazine ☐ Special offer
☐ Website ☐ Other _____

Will you purchase subsequent volumes?

☐ Yes ☐ No

6 What race/ethnicity do you consider yourself? (please check one)

☐ Asian/Pacific Islander ☐ Black/African American ☐ Hispanic/Latino
☐ Native American/Alaskan Native ☐ White/Caucasian ☐ Other _____

THANK YOU! Please send the completed form to: Shojo Survey
42 Catharine St.
Poughkeepsie, NY 12601

VIZ media

All information provided will be used for internal purposes only. We promise not to sell or otherwise divulge your information.

Full Moon
O Sagashite

1

Story & Art by Arina Tanemura

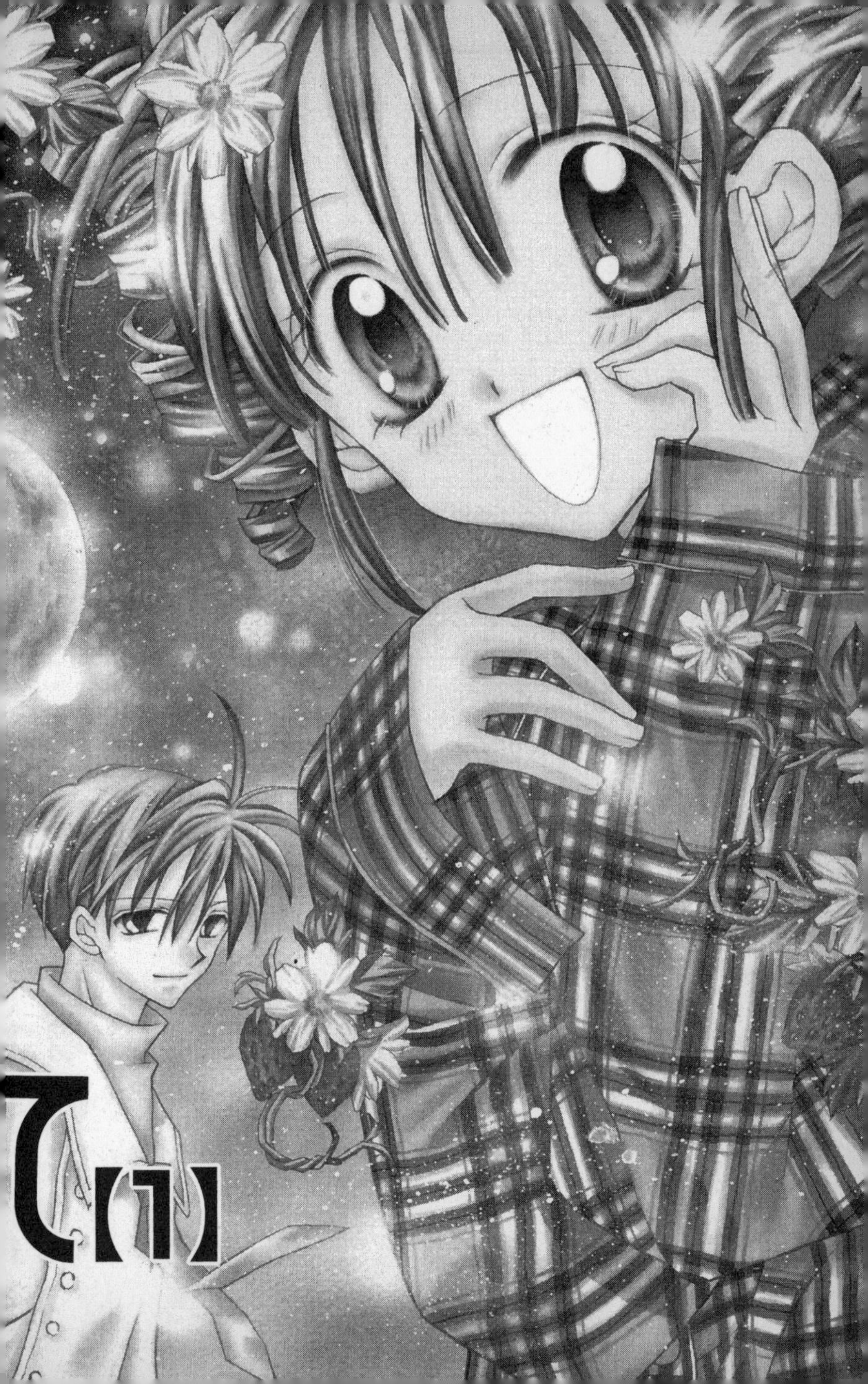

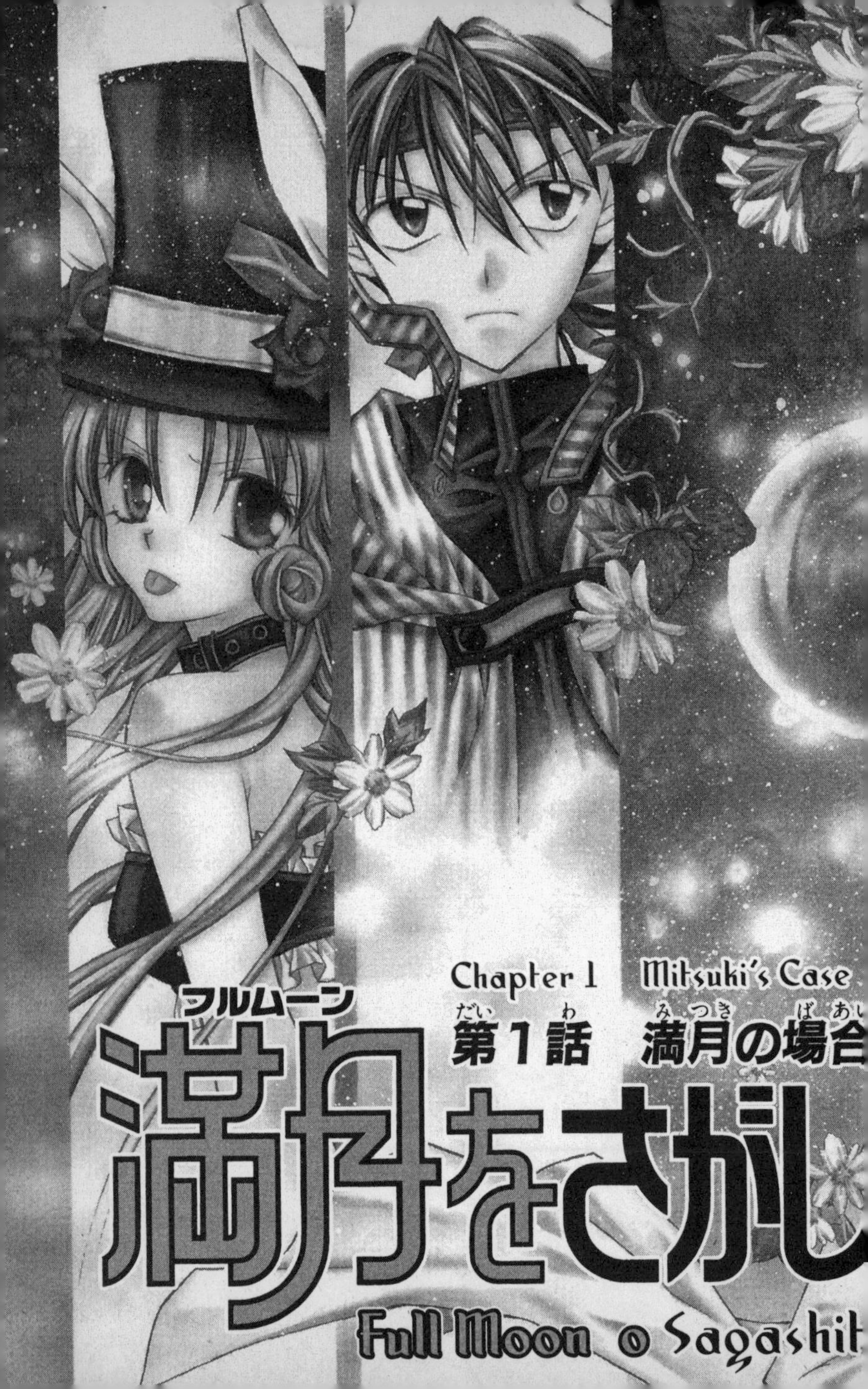
Chapter 1 Mitsuki's Case
第1話 満月の場合
フルムーン
満月をさがし
Full Moon o Sagashit

Table of Contents

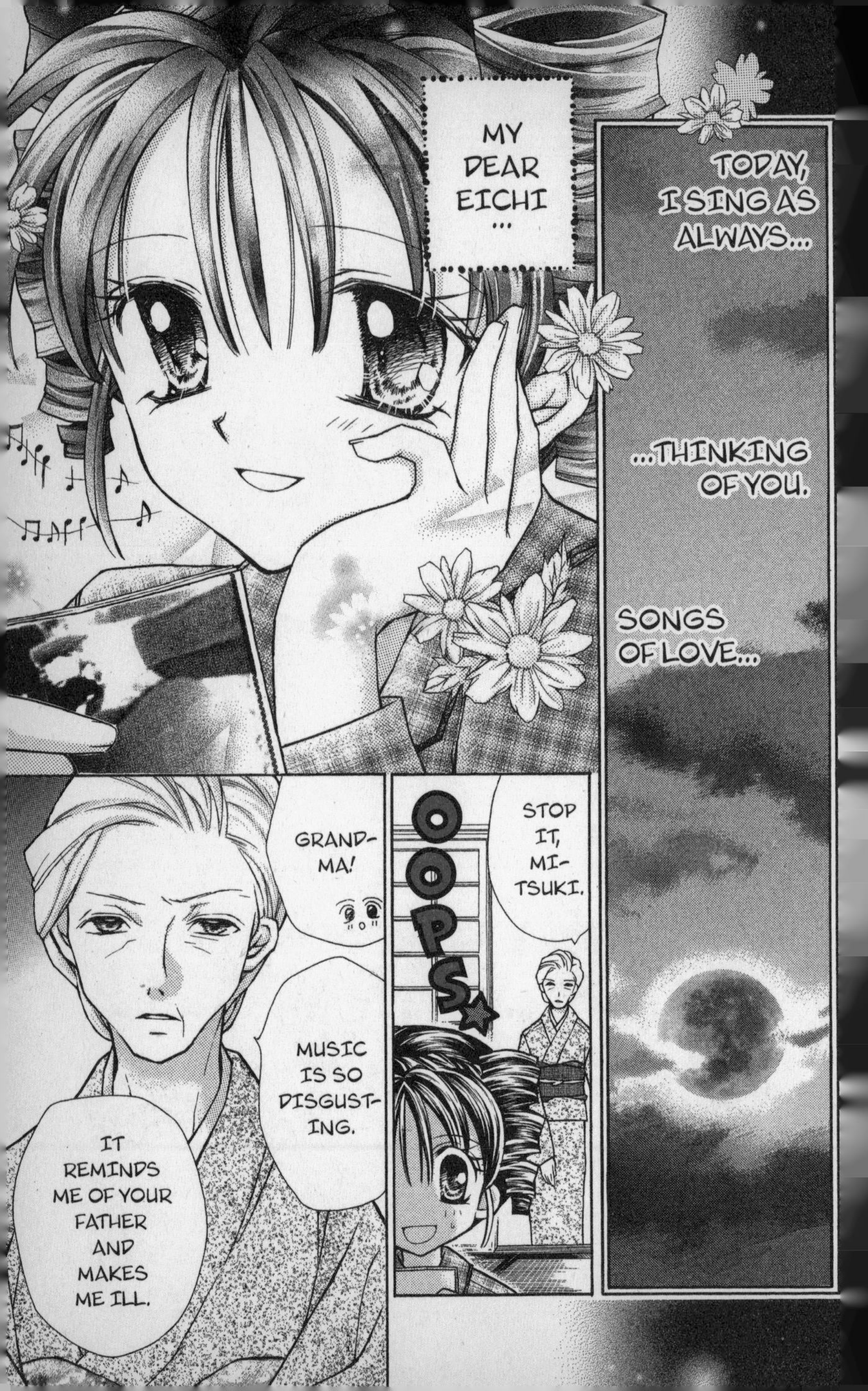
TODAY, I SING AS ALWAYS...
...THINKING OF YOU.
SONGS OF LOVE...
MY DEAR EICHI ...
OOPS
STOP IT, MI-TSUKI.
GRAND-MA!
MUSIC IS SO DISGUST-ING.
IT REMINDS ME OF YOUR FATHER AND MAKES ME ILL.

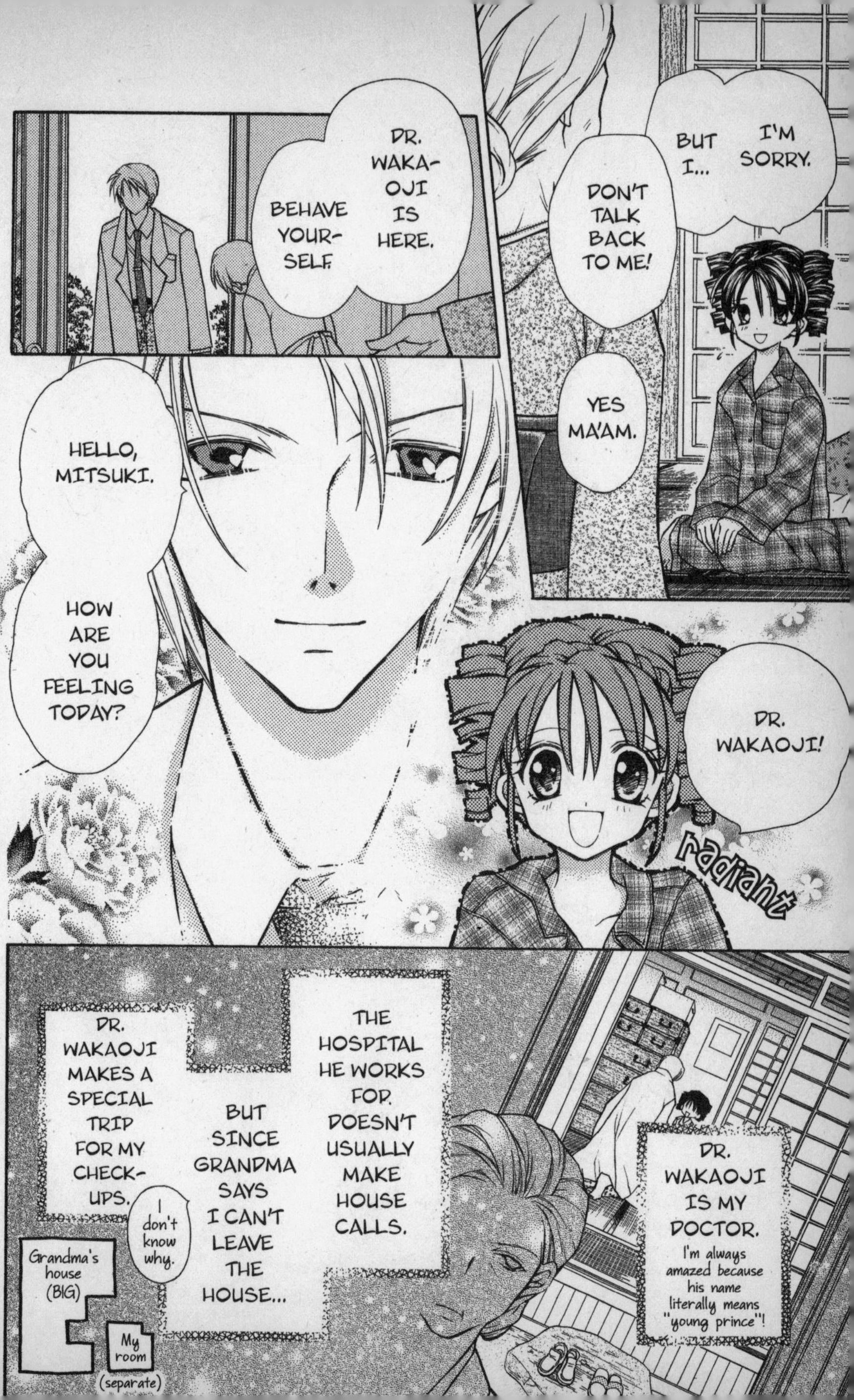
I'M SORRY.
BUT I...
DON'T TALK BACK TO ME!
YES MA'AM.
DR. WAKAOJI IS HERE.
BEHAVE YOURSELF.
DR. WAKAOJI!
radiant
HELLO, MITSUKI.
HOW ARE YOU FEELING TODAY?
DR. WAKAOJI IS MY DOCTOR.
I'm always amazed because his name literally means "young prince"!
THE HOSPITAL HE WORKS FOR DOESN'T USUALLY MAKE HOUSE CALLS.
BUT SINCE GRANDMA SAYS I CAN'T LEAVE THE HOUSE...
DR. WAKAOJI MAKES A SPECIAL TRIP FOR MY CHECK-UPS.
I don't know why.
Grandma's house (BIG)
My room
(separate)

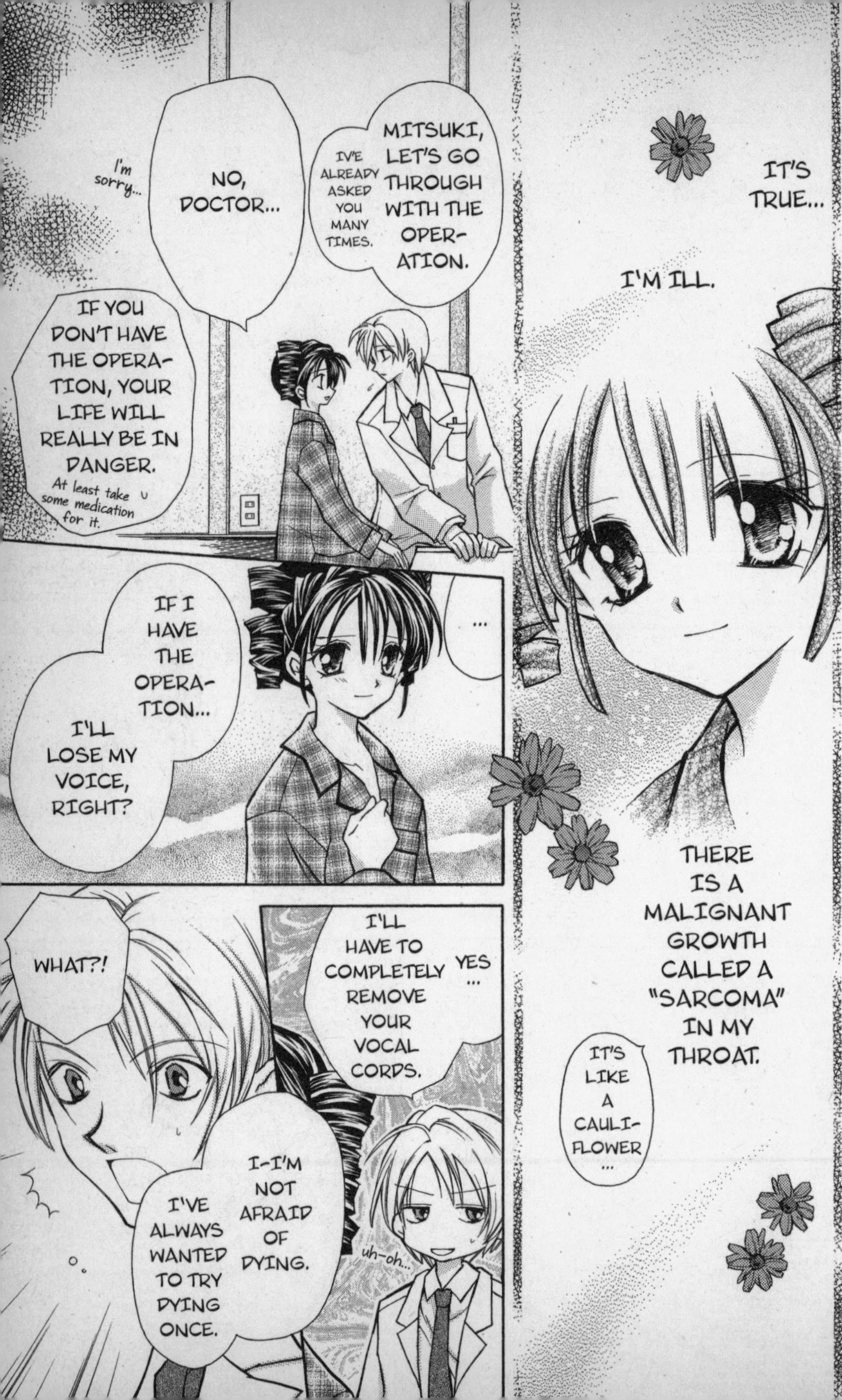
IT'S TRUE...
I'M ILL.
THERE IS A MALIGNANT GROWTH CALLED A "SARCOMA" IN MY THROAT.
IT'S LIKE A CAULIFLOWER...
MITSUKI, LET'S GO THROUGH WITH THE OPERATION.
I'VE ALREADY ASKED YOU MANY TIMES.
NO, DOCTOR...
I'm sorry...
IF YOU DON'T HAVE THE OPERATION, YOUR LIFE WILL REALLY BE IN DANGER.
At least take some medication for it.
...
IF I HAVE THE OPERATION...
I'LL LOSE MY VOICE, RIGHT?
YES...
I'LL HAVE TO COMPLETELY REMOVE YOUR VOCAL CORDS.
WHAT?!
I-I'M NOT AFRAID OF DYING.
I'VE ALWAYS WANTED TO TRY DYING ONCE.
uh-oh...

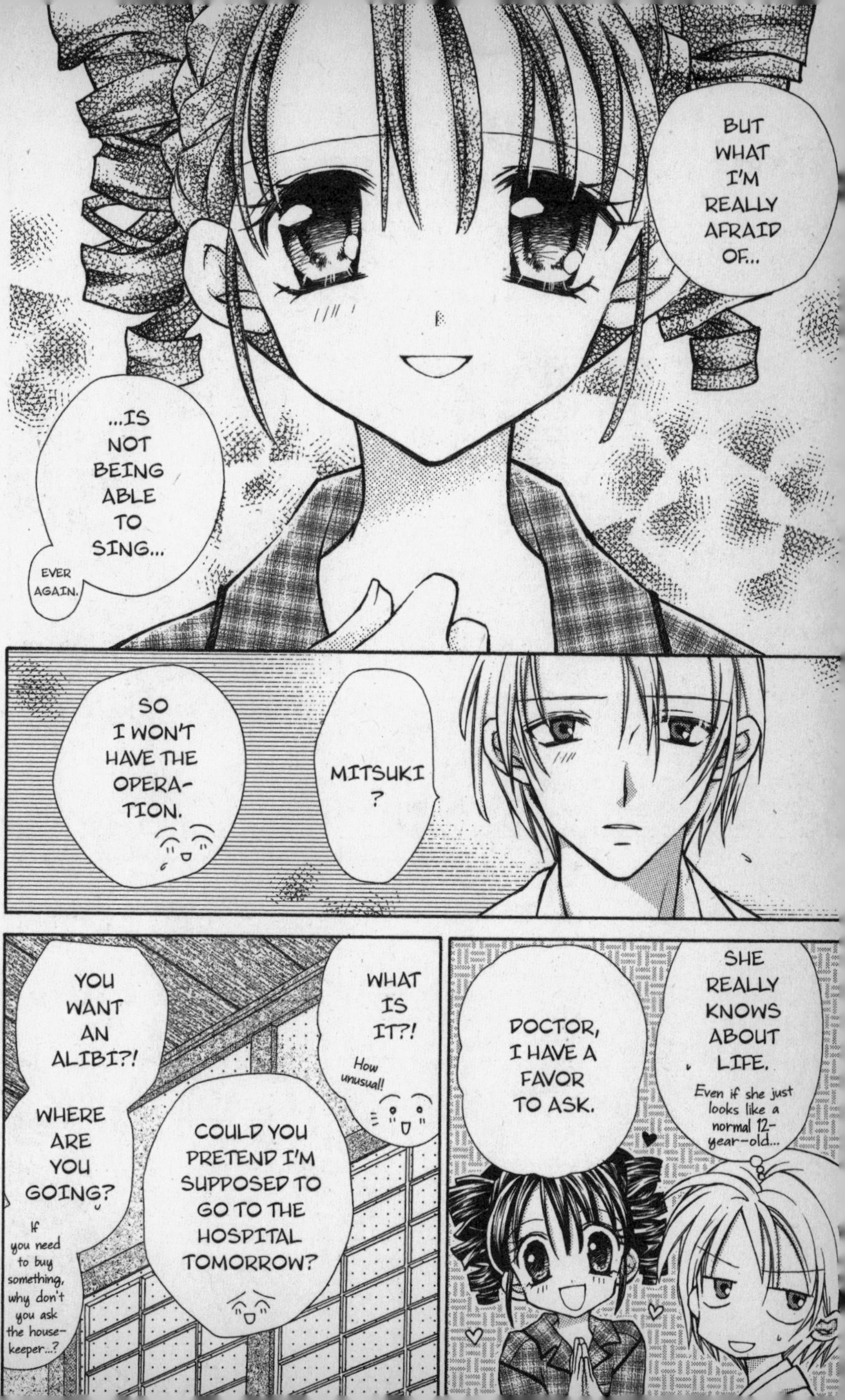
BUT WHAT I'M REALLY AFRAID OF...
...IS NOT BEING ABLE TO SING...
EVER AGAIN.
MITSUKI?
SO I WON'T HAVE THE OPERATION.
SHE REALLY KNOWS ABOUT LIFE.
Even if she just looks like a normal 12-year-old...
DOCTOR, I HAVE A FAVOR TO ASK.
WHAT IS IT?!
How unusual!
COULD YOU PRETEND I'M SUPPOSED TO GO TO THE HOSPITAL TOMORROW?
YOU WANT AN ALIBI?!
WHERE ARE YOU GOING?
If you need to buy something, why don't you ask the house-keeper...?

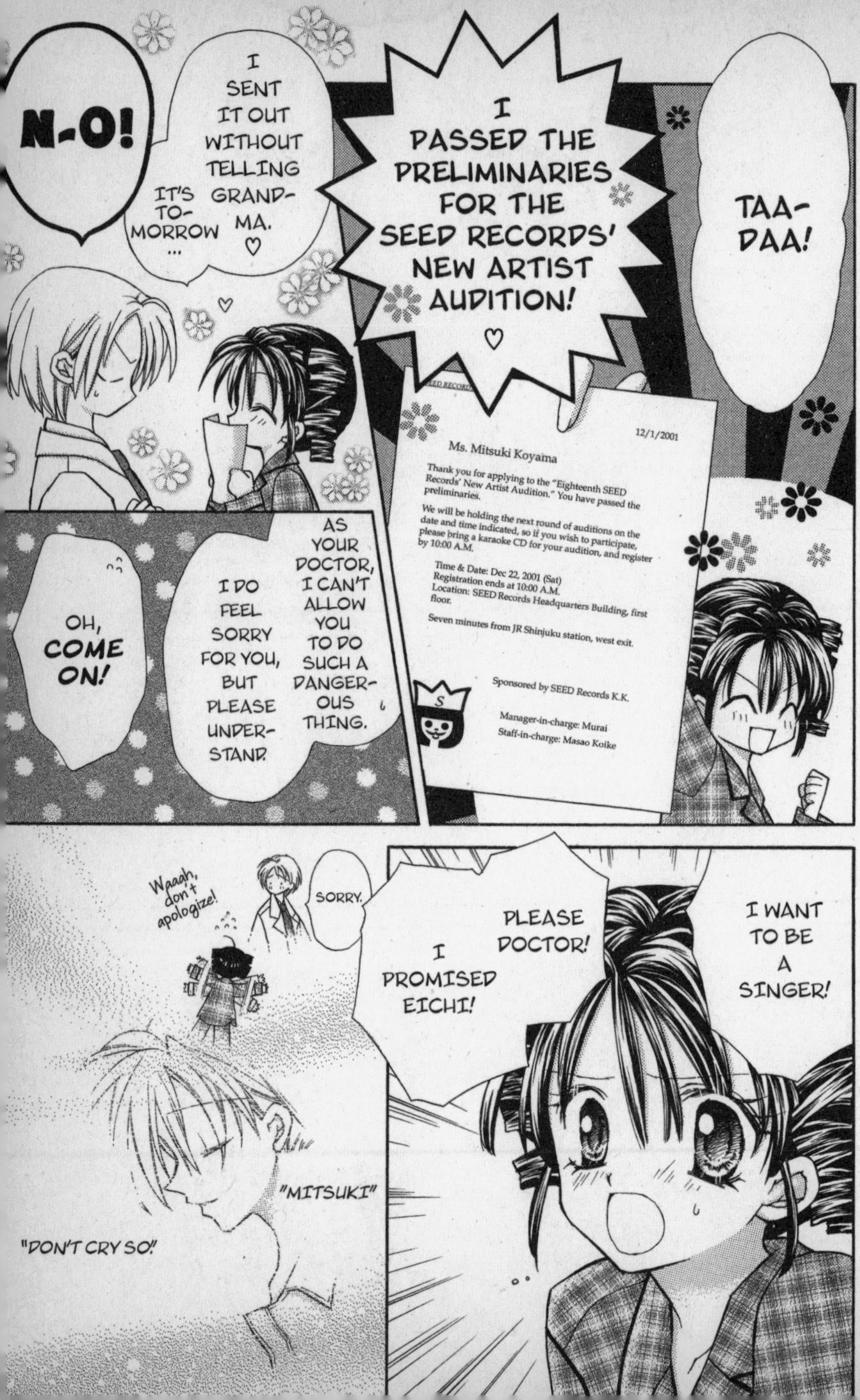
TAA-DAA!
I PASSED THE PRELIMINARIES FOR THE SEED RECORDS' NEW ARTIST AUDITION! ♡
12/1/2001
Ms. Mitsuki Koyama
Thank you for applying to the "Eighteenth SEED Records' New Artist Audition." You have passed the preliminaries.
We will be holding the next round of auditions on the date and time indicated, so if you wish to participate, please bring a karaoke CD for your audition, and register by 10:00 A.M.
Time & Date: Dec 22, 2001 (Sat)
Registration ends at 10:00 A.M.
Location: SEED Records Headquarters Building, first floor.
Seven minutes from JR Shinjuku station, west exit.
Sponsored by SEED Records K.K.
Manager-in-charge: Murai
Staff-in-charge: Masao Koike
I SENT IT OUT WITHOUT TELLING GRAND-MA. ♡
IT'S TO-MORROW ...
N-O!
AS YOUR DOCTOR, I CAN'T ALLOW YOU TO DO SUCH A DANGER-OUS THING.
I DO FEEL SORRY FOR YOU, BUT PLEASE UNDER-STAND.
OH, COME ON!
I WANT TO BE A SINGER!
PLEASE DOCTOR!
I PROMISED EICHI!
SORRY.
Waaah, don't apologize!
"MITSUKI"
"DON'T CRY SO!"

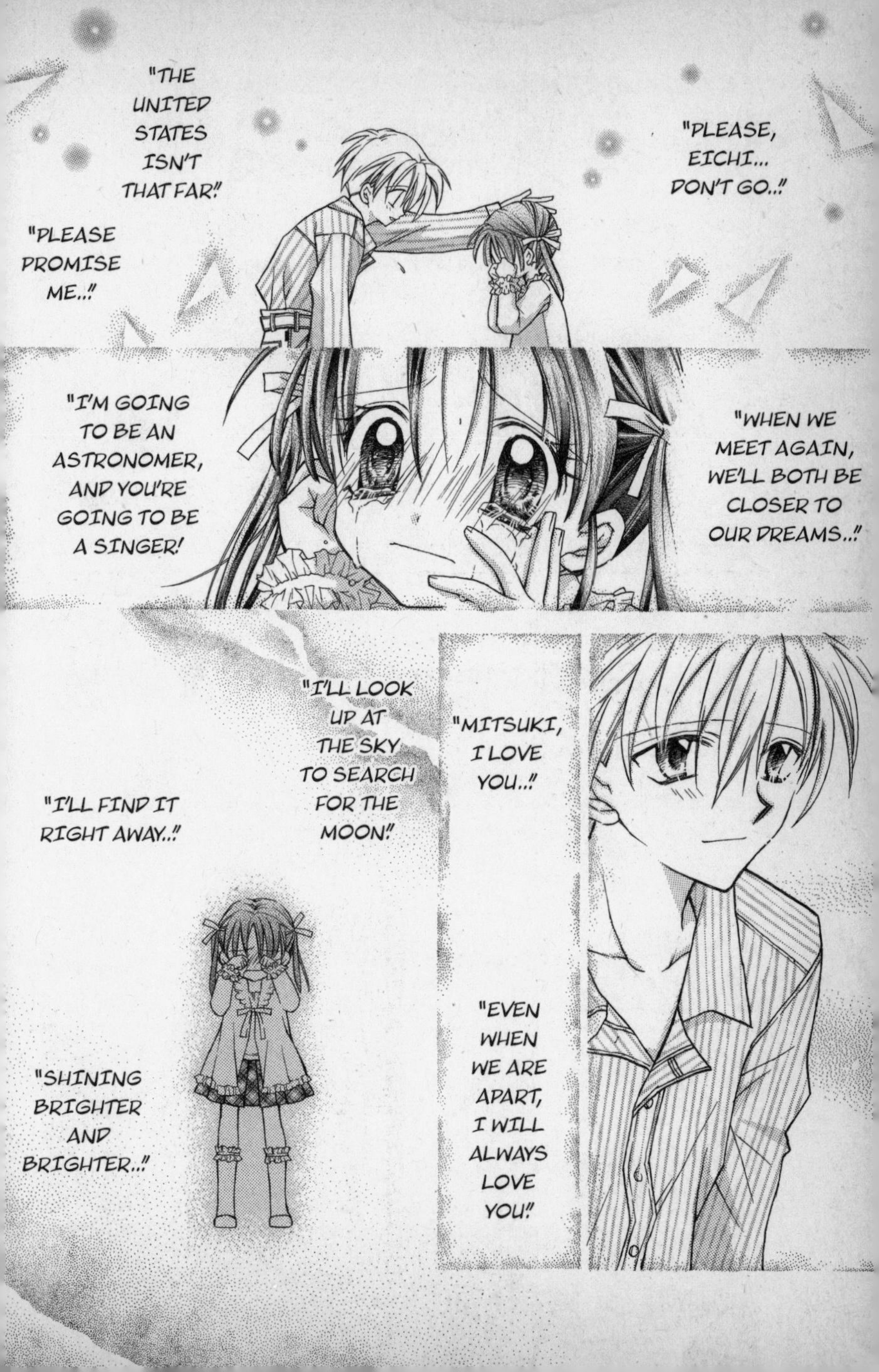
"PLEASE, EICHI... DON'T GO..!"
"THE UNITED STATES ISN'T THAT FAR!"
"PLEASE PROMISE ME..!"
"WHEN WE MEET AGAIN, WE'LL BOTH BE CLOSER TO OUR DREAMS..!"
"I'M GOING TO BE AN ASTRONOMER, AND YOU'RE GOING TO BE A SINGER!
"MITSUKI, I LOVE YOU..!"
"EVEN WHEN WE ARE APART, I WILL ALWAYS LOVE YOU!"
"I'LL LOOK UP AT THE SKY TO SEARCH FOR THE MOON!"
"I'LL FIND IT RIGHT AWAY..!"
"SHINING BRIGHTER AND BRIGHTER..!"

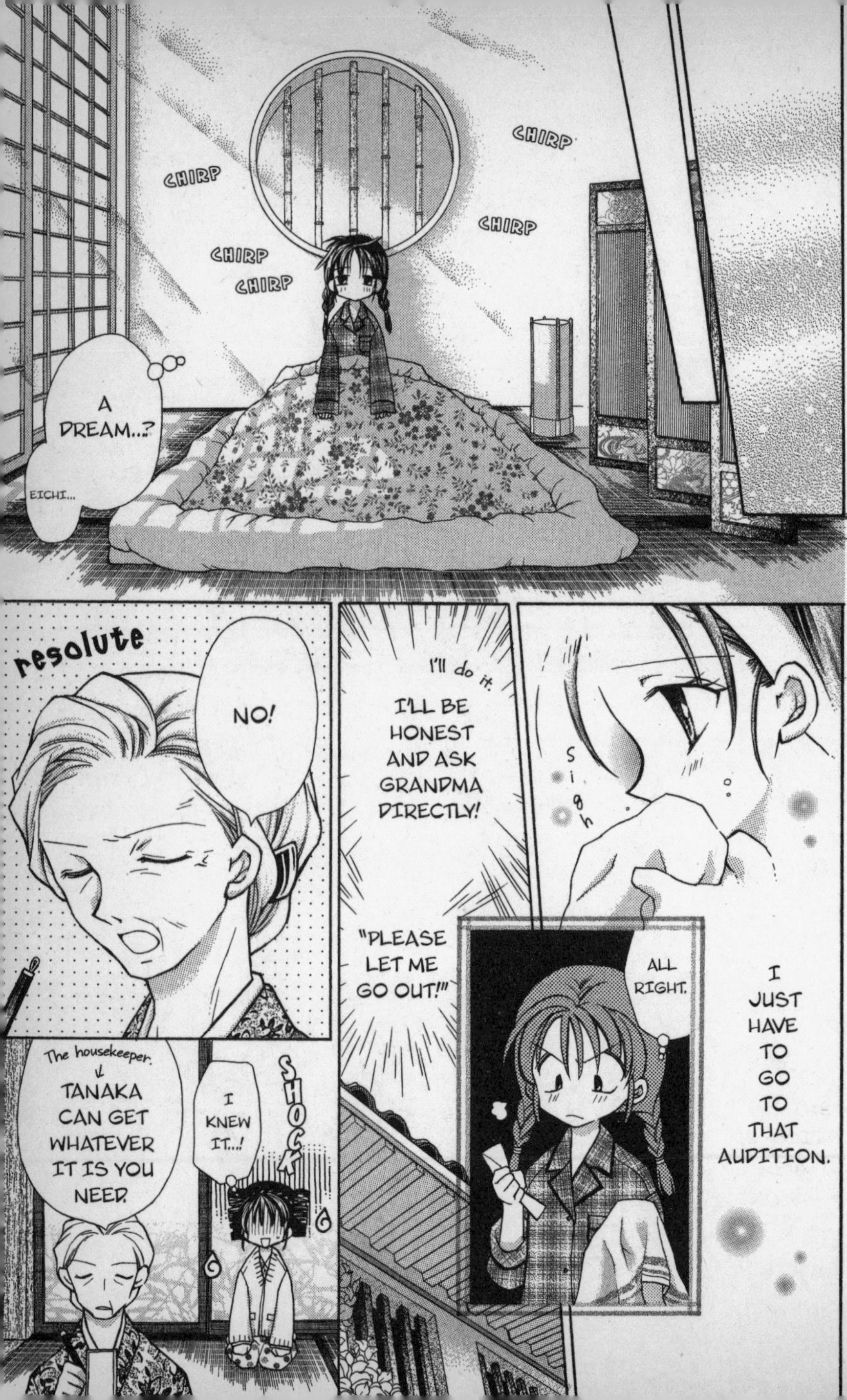
CHIRP
CHIRP
CHIRP
CHIRP
CHIRP
A DREAM...?
EICHI...
S i g h
I JUST HAVE TO GO TO THAT AUDITION.
I'll do it.
I'LL BE HONEST AND ASK GRANDMA DIRECTLY!
"PLEASE LET ME GO OUT!"
ALL RIGHT.
resolute
NO!
The housekeeper.
TANAKA CAN GET WHATEVER IT IS YOU NEED.
SHOCK
I KNEW IT...!

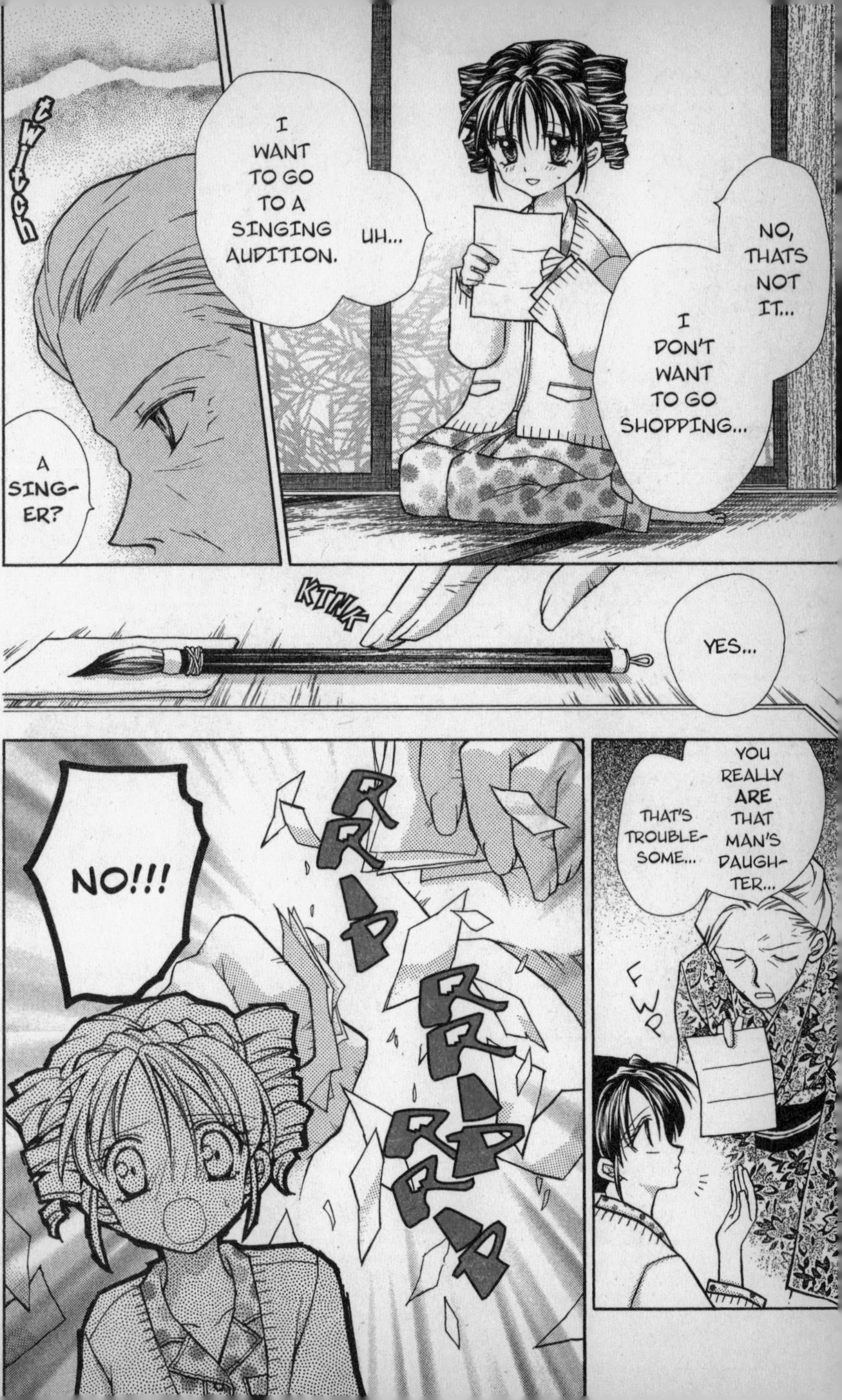
NO, THATS NOT IT...
I DON'T WANT TO GO SHOPPING...
UH...
I WANT TO GO TO A SINGING AUDITION.
twitch
A SINGER?
YES...
KTINK
YOU REALLY ARE THAT MAN'S DAUGHTER...
THAT'S TROUBLESOME...
FWP
RRIP
RRRRIP
NO!!!

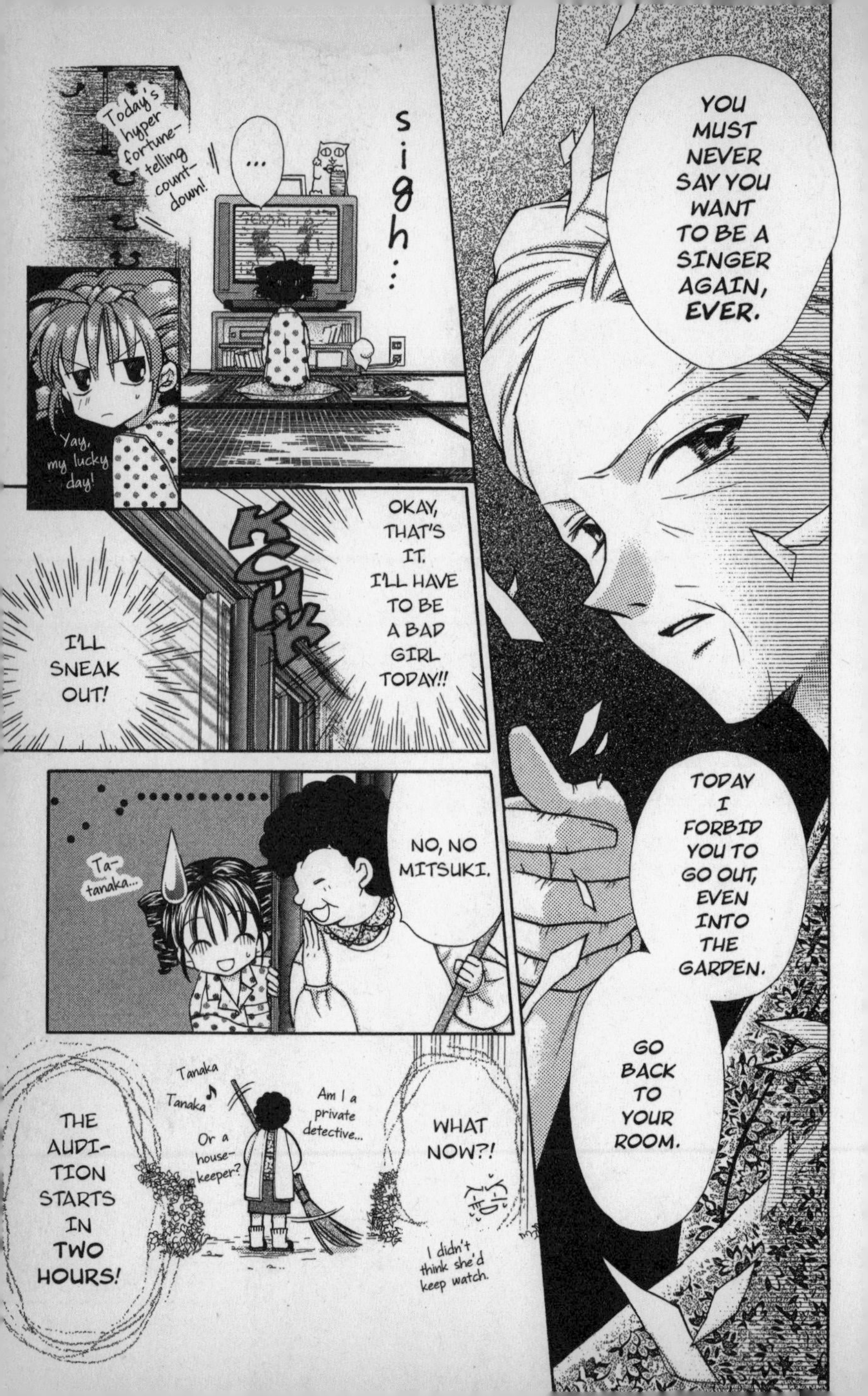
YOU MUST NEVER SAY YOU WANT TO BE A SINGER AGAIN, EVER.
TODAY I FORBID YOU TO GO OUT, EVEN INTO THE GARDEN.
GO BACK TO YOUR ROOM.
sigh...
...
Today's hyper fortune-telling count-down!
Yay, my lucky day!
OKAY, THAT'S IT. I'LL HAVE TO BE A BAD GIRL TODAY!!
I'LL SNEAK OUT!
NO, NO MITSUKI.
Ta-tanaka...
WHAT NOW?!
I didn't think she'd keep watch.
Am I a private detective...
Or a house-keeper?
Tanaka Tanaka ♪
THE AUDI-TION STARTS IN TWO HOURS!

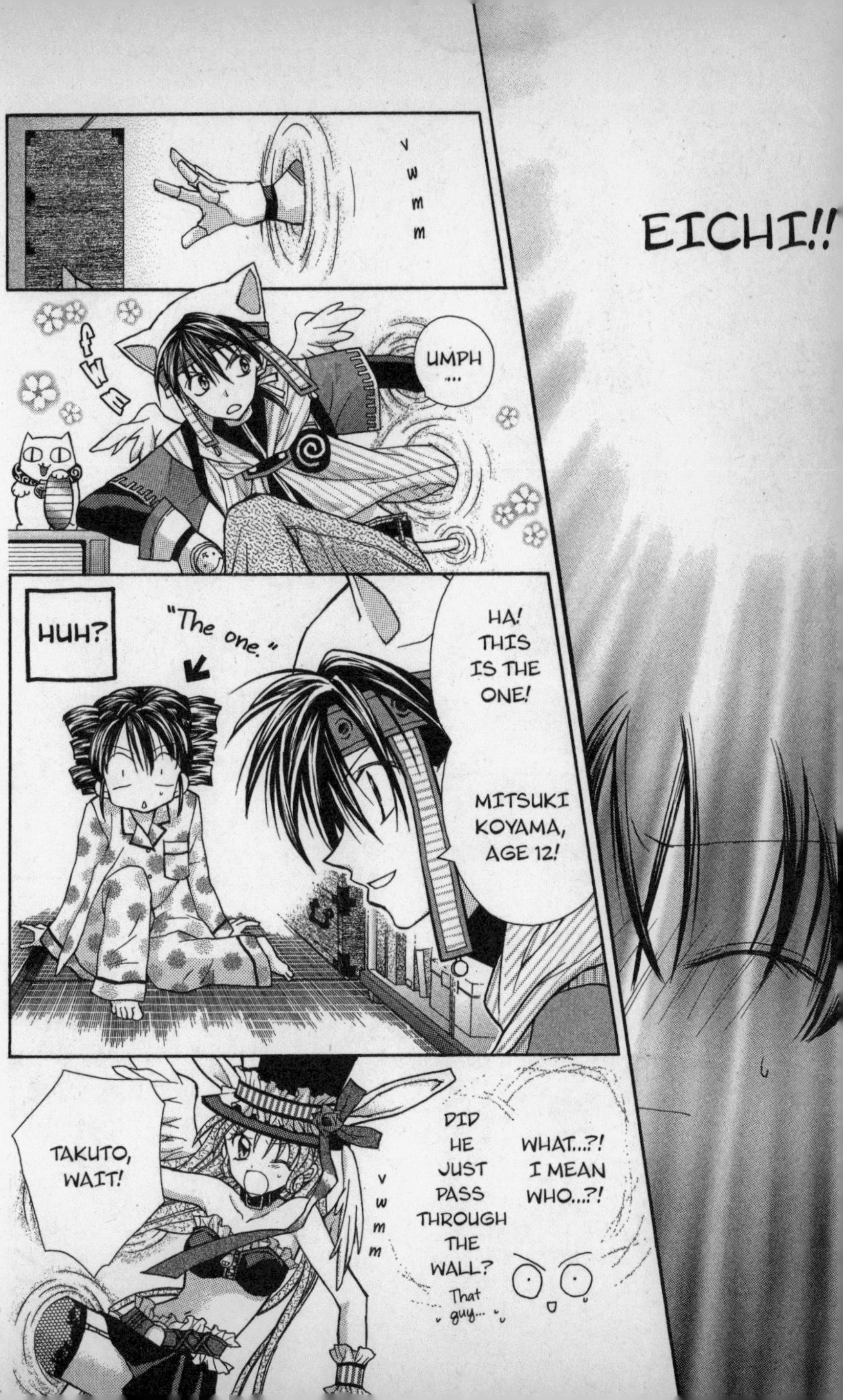

EICHI!!
vwmm
UMPH...
fwee
HA! THIS IS THE ONE!
MITSUKI KOYAMA, AGE 12!
"The one."
HUH?
WHAT...?! I MEAN WHO...?!
DID HE JUST PASS THROUGH THE WALL?
That guy...
vwmm
TAKUTO, WAIT!

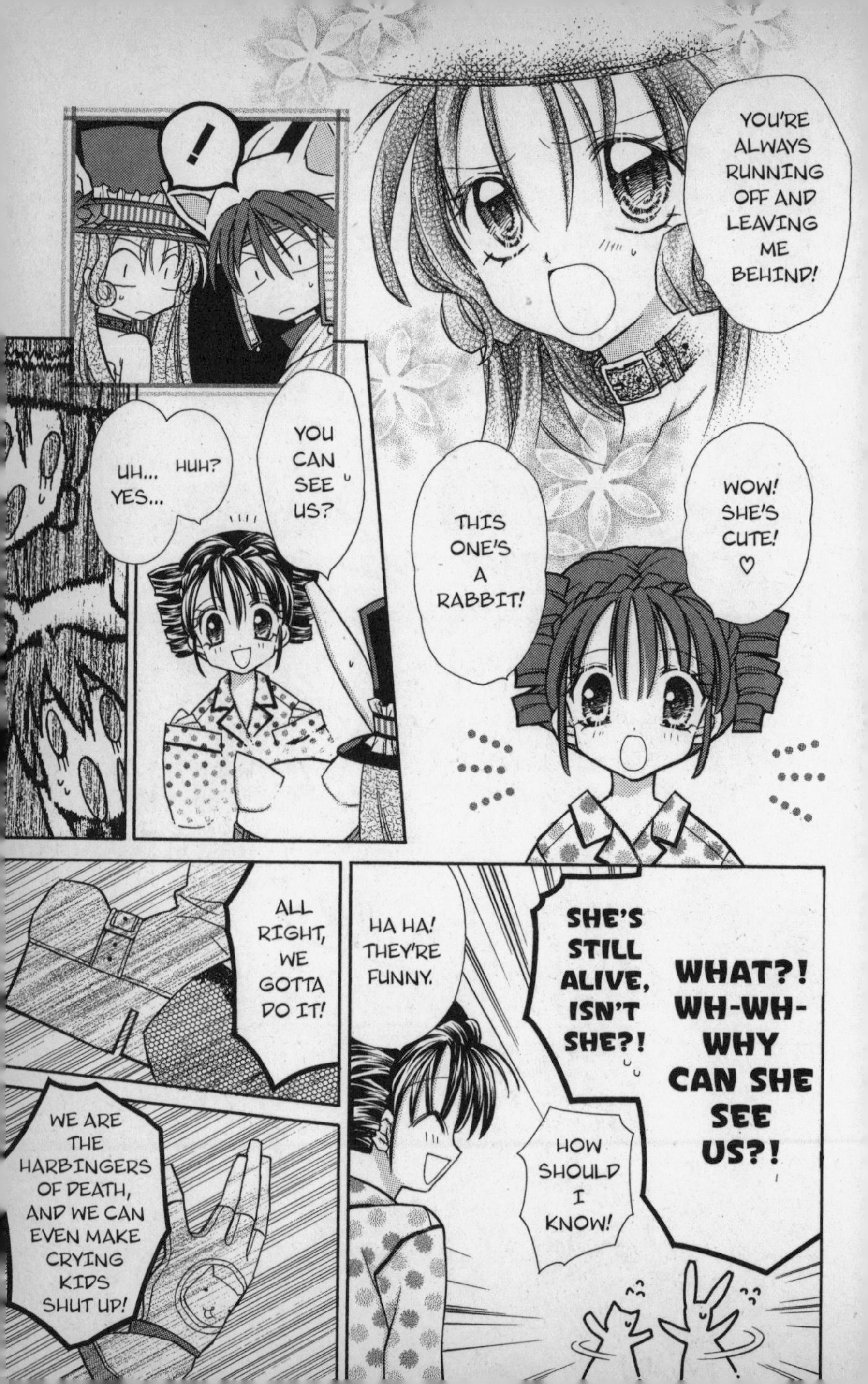
YOU'RE ALWAYS RUNNING OFF AND LEAVING ME BEHIND!
!
WOW! SHE'S CUTE! ♡
THIS ONE'S A RABBIT!
YOU CAN SEE US?
HUH?
UH... YES...
WHAT?! WH-WH-WHY CAN SHE SEE US?!
SHE'S STILL ALIVE, ISN'T SHE?!
HOW SHOULD I KNOW!
HA HA! THEY'RE FUNNY.
ALL RIGHT, WE GOTTA DO IT!
WE ARE THE HARBINGERS OF DEATH, AND WE CAN EVEN MAKE CRYING KIDS SHUT UP!

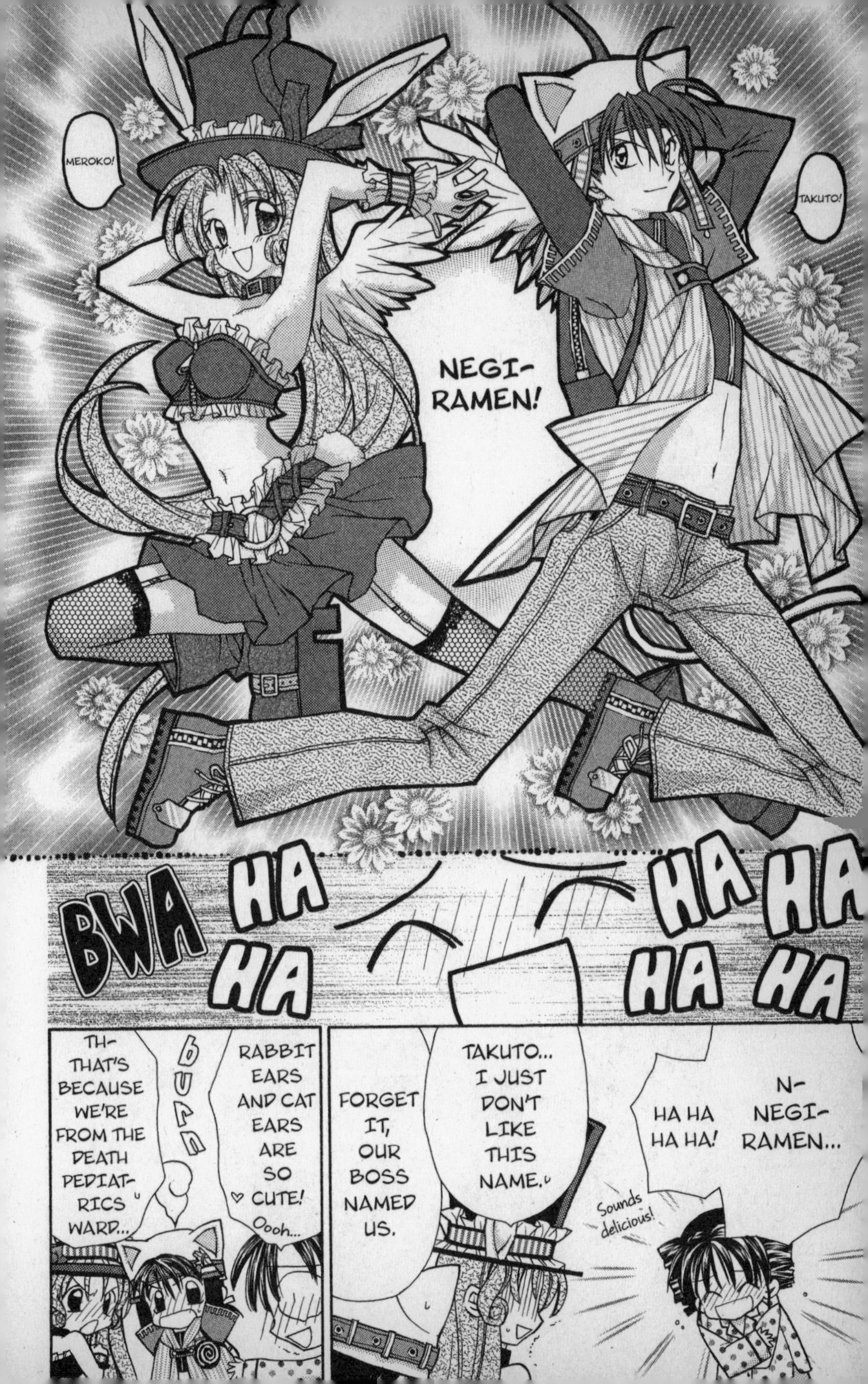
TAKUTO!
MEROKO!
NEGI-RAMEN!
BWA HA HA HA HA HA HA
N-NEGI-RAMEN...
HA HA HA HA!
Sounds delicious!
TAKUTO... I JUST DON'T LIKE THIS NAME.
FORGET IT, OUR BOSS NAMED US.
RABBIT EARS AND CAT EARS ARE SO CUTE!
Oooh...
burn
TH-THAT'S BECAUSE WE'RE FROM THE DEATH PEDIAT-RICS WARD...

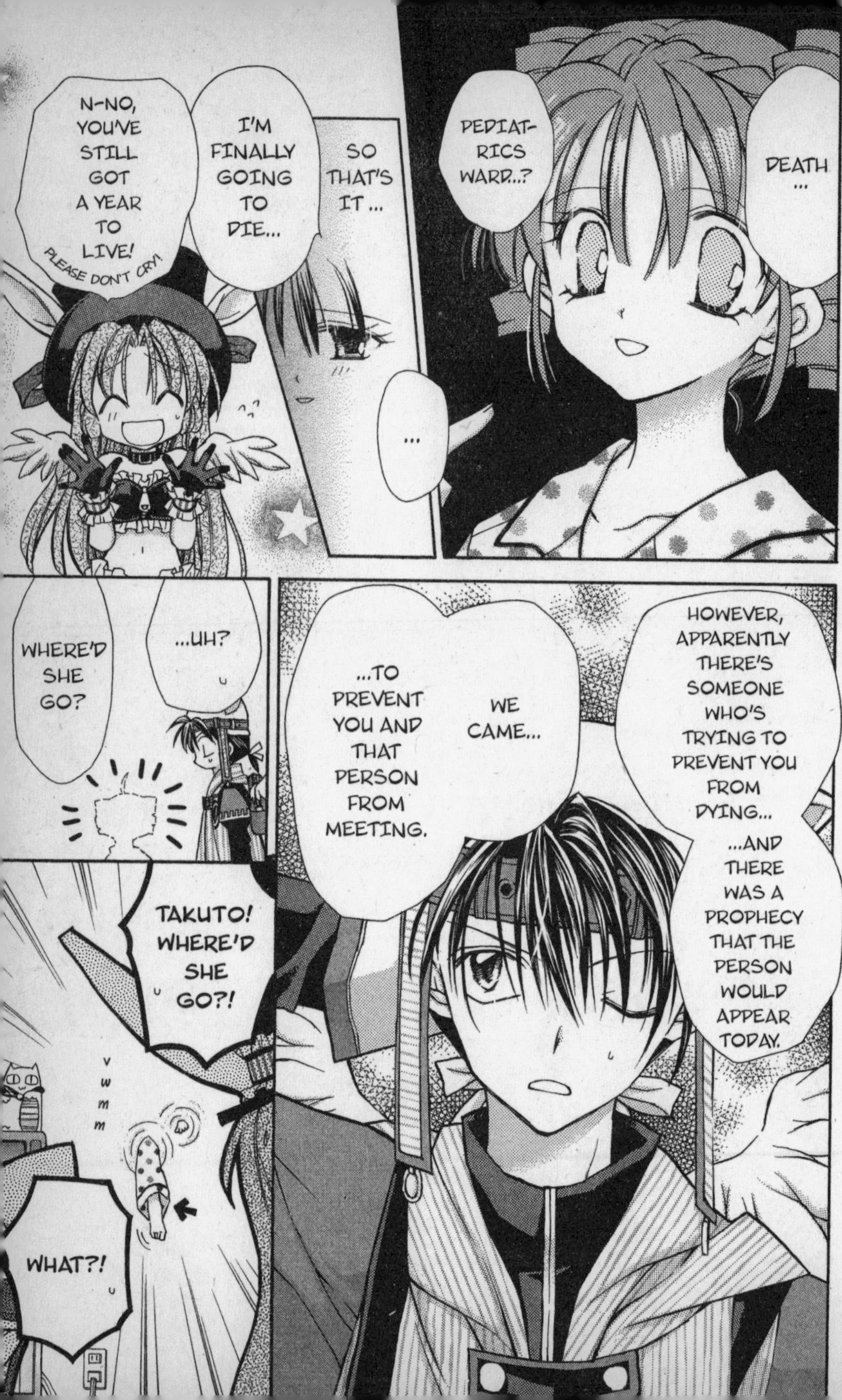
DEATH ...
PEDIATRICS WARD...?
SO THAT'S IT ...
...
I'M FINALLY GOING TO DIE...
N-NO, YOU'VE STILL GOT A YEAR TO LIVE!
PLEASE DON'T CRY!
HOWEVER, APPARENTLY THERE'S SOMEONE WHO'S TRYING TO PREVENT YOU FROM DYING...
...AND THERE WAS A PROPHECY THAT THE PERSON WOULD APPEAR TODAY.
WE CAME...
...TO PREVENT YOU AND THAT PERSON FROM MEETING.
...UH?
WHERE'D SHE GO?
TAKUTO! WHERE'D SHE GO?!
VWMM
WHAT?!

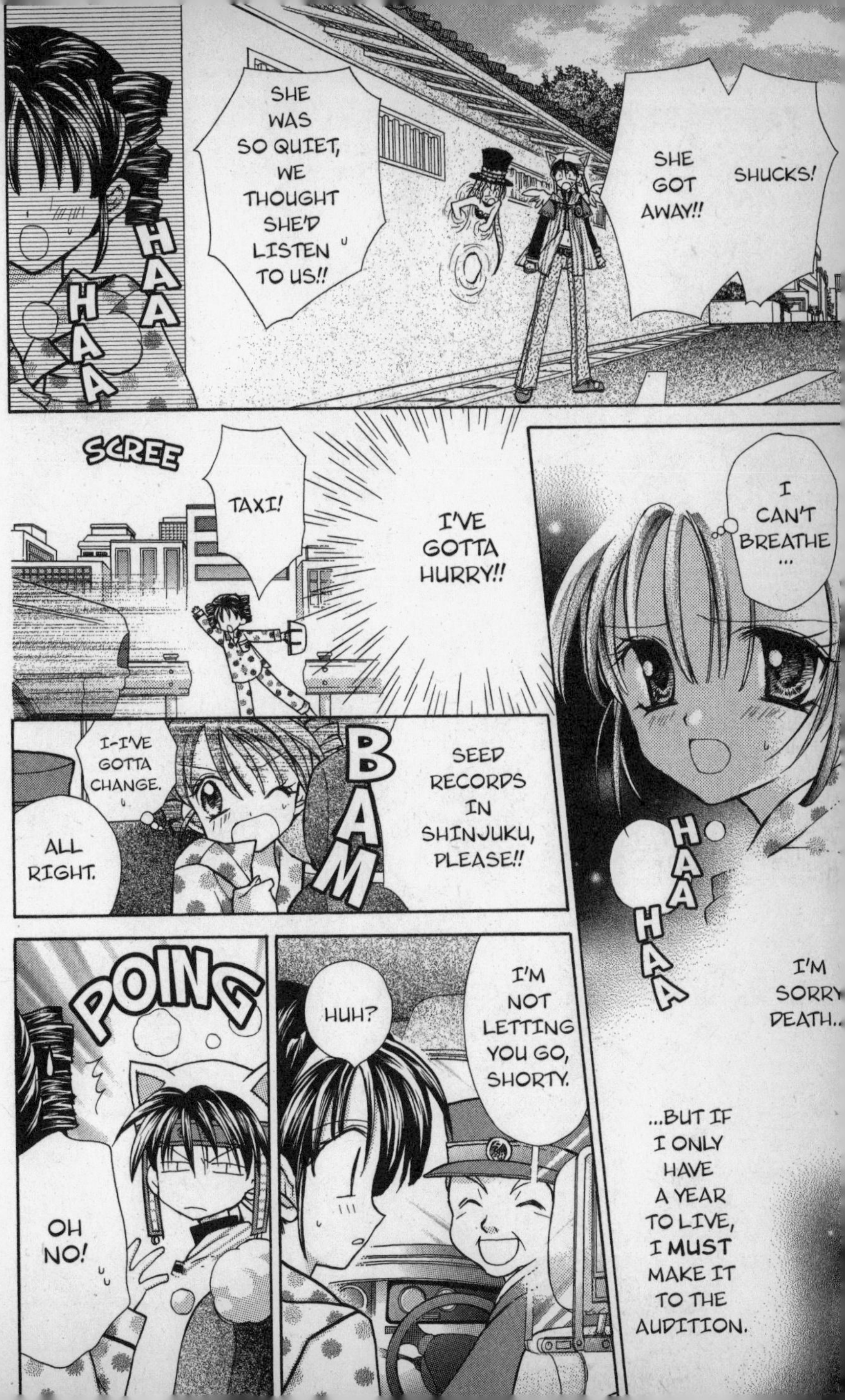
SHUCKS!
SHE GOT AWAY!!
SHE WAS SO QUIET, WE THOUGHT SHE'D LISTEN TO US!!
HAA HAA
I CAN'T BREATHE ...
HAA HAA
I'M SORRY DEATH...
...BUT IF I ONLY HAVE A YEAR TO LIVE, I MUST MAKE IT TO THE AUDITION.
I'VE GOTTA HURRY!!
TAXI!
SCREE
SEED RECORDS IN SHINJUKU, PLEASE!!
BAM
I-I'VE GOTTA CHANGE.
ALL RIGHT.
I'M NOT LETTING YOU GO, SHORTY.
HUH?
POING
OH NO!

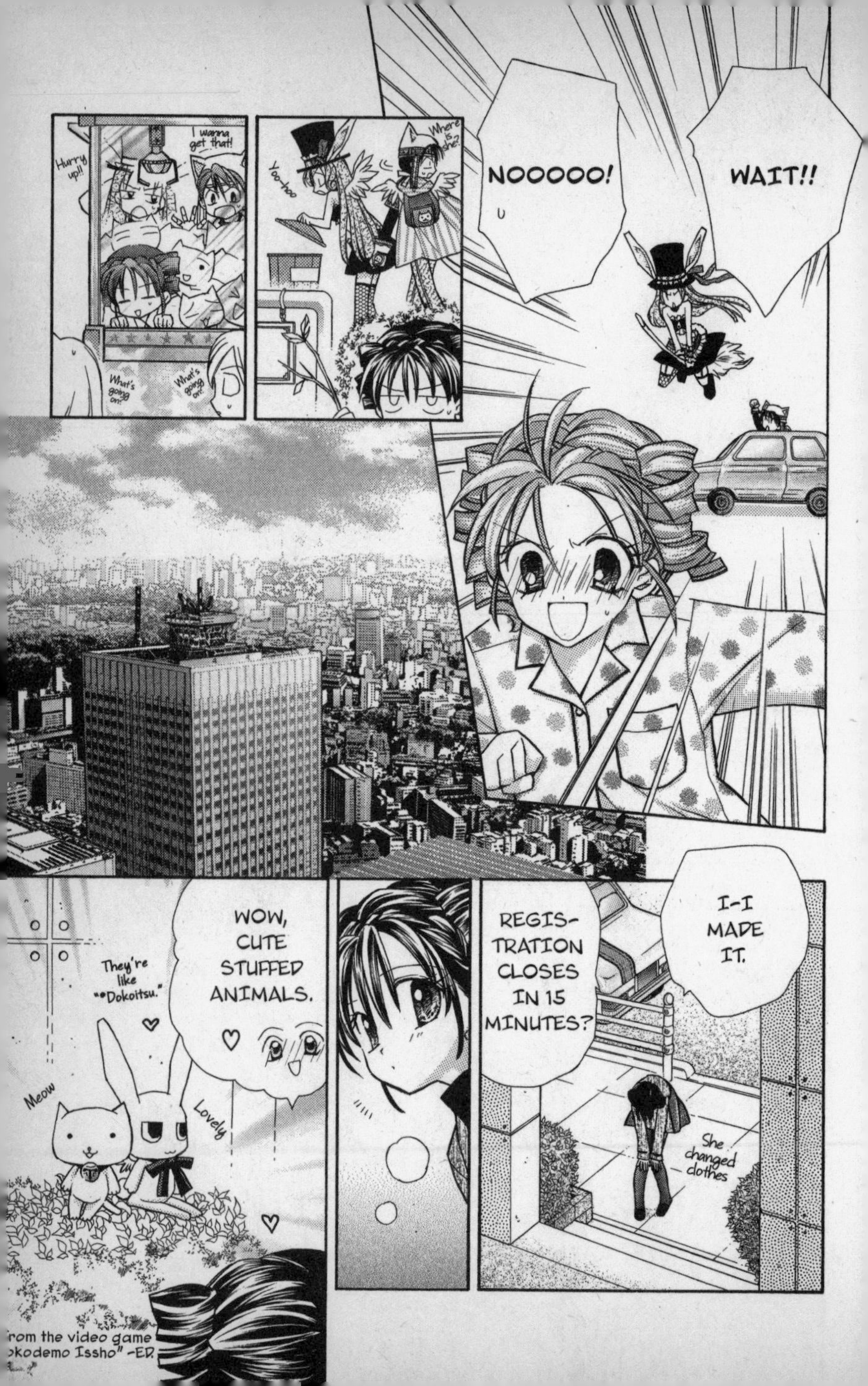
WAIT!!
NOOOOO!
Where is she?
Yoo-hoo
I wanna get that!
Hurry up!!
What's going on?
What's going on!
I-I MADE IT.
REGIS-TRATION CLOSES IN 15 MINUTES?
She changed clothes
WOW, CUTE STUFFED ANIMALS.
They're like "*Dokoitsu."
Lovely
Meow
rom the video game
okodemo Issho" -ED.

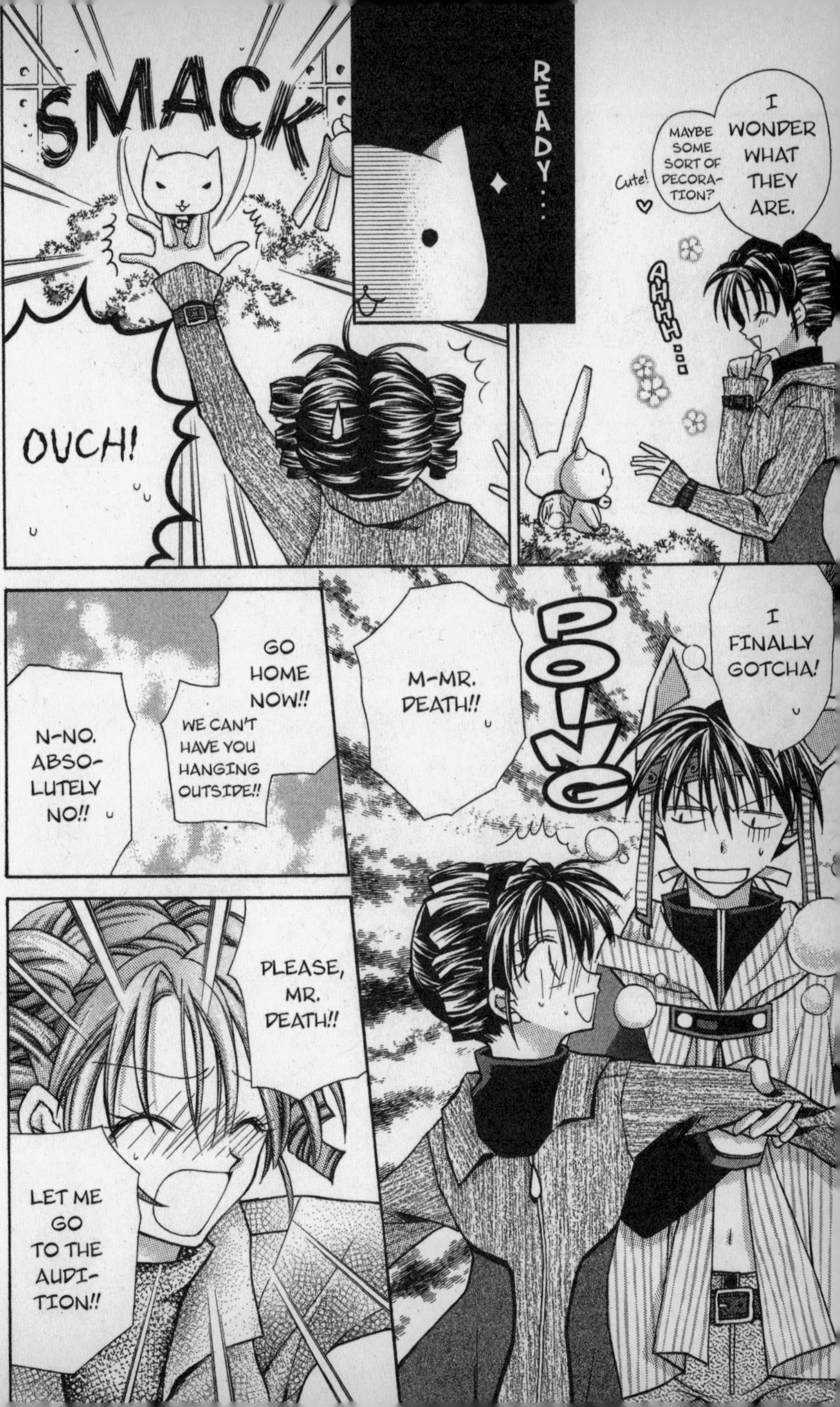
I WONDER WHAT THEY ARE.
MAYBE SOME SORT OF DECORA-TION?
Cute!
AHHH...
READY...
SMACK
OUCH!
I FINALLY GOTCHA!
POING
M-MR. DEATH!!
GO HOME NOW!!
WE CAN'T HAVE YOU HANGING OUTSIDE!!
N-NO. ABSO-LUTELY NO!!
PLEASE, MR. DEATH!!
LET ME GO TO THE AUDI-TION!!

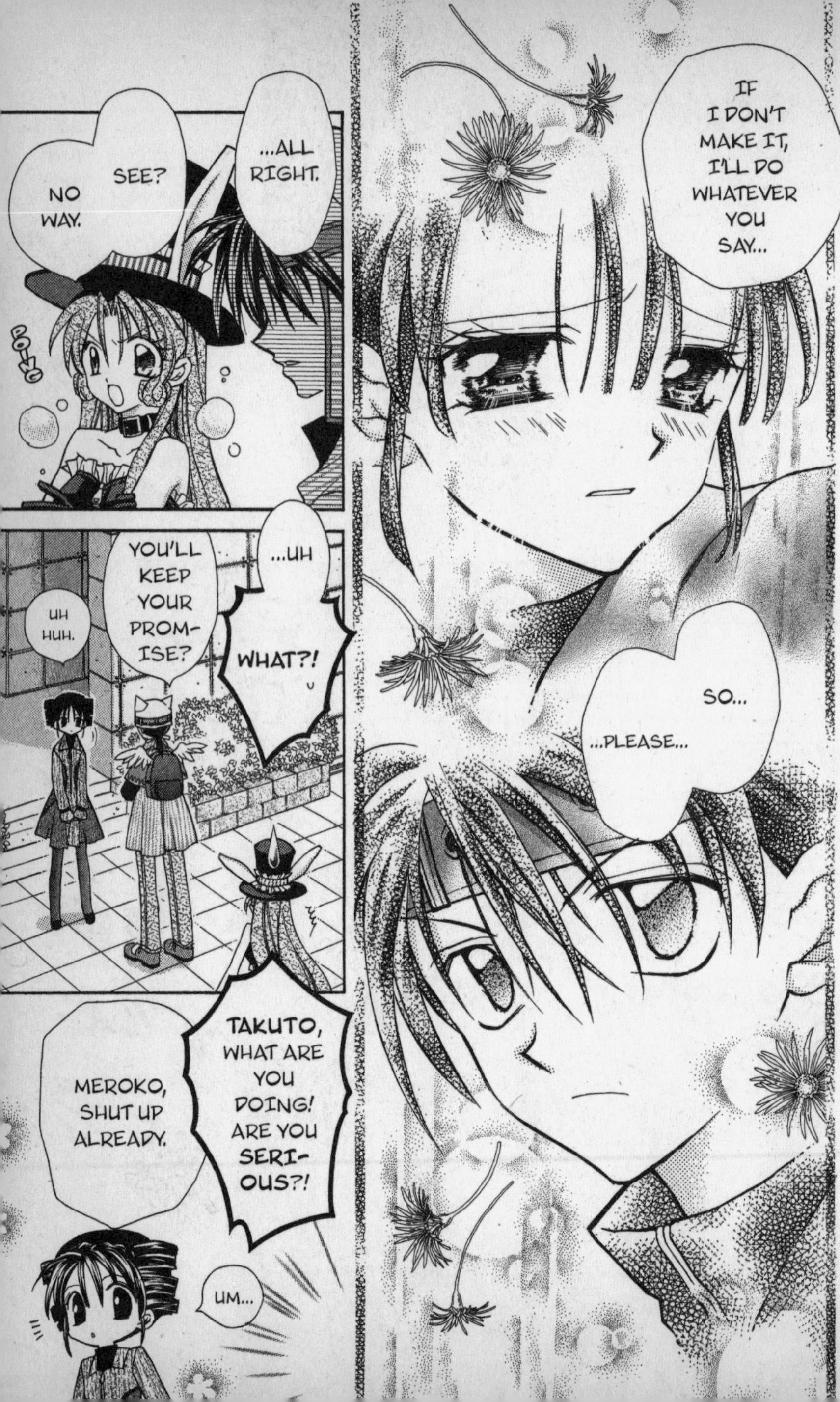
IF I DON'T MAKE IT, I'LL DO WHATEVER YOU SAY...
SO...
...PLEASE...
...ALL RIGHT.
SEE?
NO WAY.
POING
...UH
WHAT?!
YOU'LL KEEP YOUR PROMISE?
UH HUH.
TAKUTO, WHAT ARE YOU DOING! ARE YOU SERIOUS?!
MEROKO, SHUT UP ALREADY.
UM...

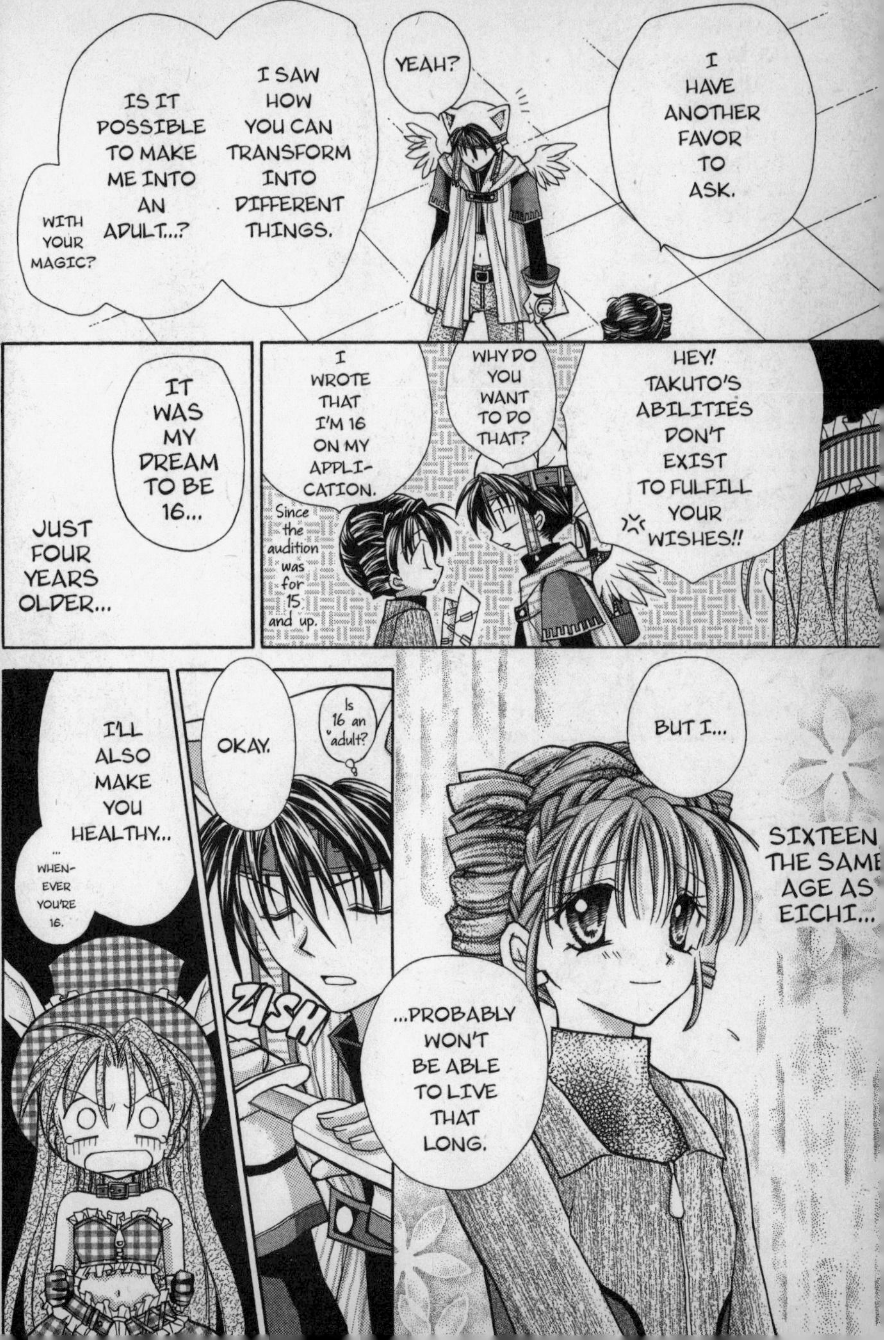
I HAVE ANOTHER FAVOR TO ASK.
YEAH?
I SAW HOW YOU CAN TRANSFORM INTO DIFFERENT THINGS.
IS IT POSSIBLE TO MAKE ME INTO AN ADULT...?
WITH YOUR MAGIC?
HEY! TAKUTO'S ABILITIES DON'T EXIST TO FULFILL YOUR WISHES!!
WHY DO YOU WANT TO DO THAT?
I WROTE THAT I'M 16 ON MY APPLI-CATION.
Since the audition was for 15 and up.
IT WAS MY DREAM TO BE 16...
JUST FOUR YEARS OLDER...
BUT I...
SIXTEEN THE SAME AGE AS EICHI...
...PROBABLY WON'T BE ABLE TO LIVE THAT LONG.
Is 16 an adult?
OKAY.
ZISH
I'LL ALSO MAKE YOU HEALTHY...
...WHEN-EVER YOU'RE 16.

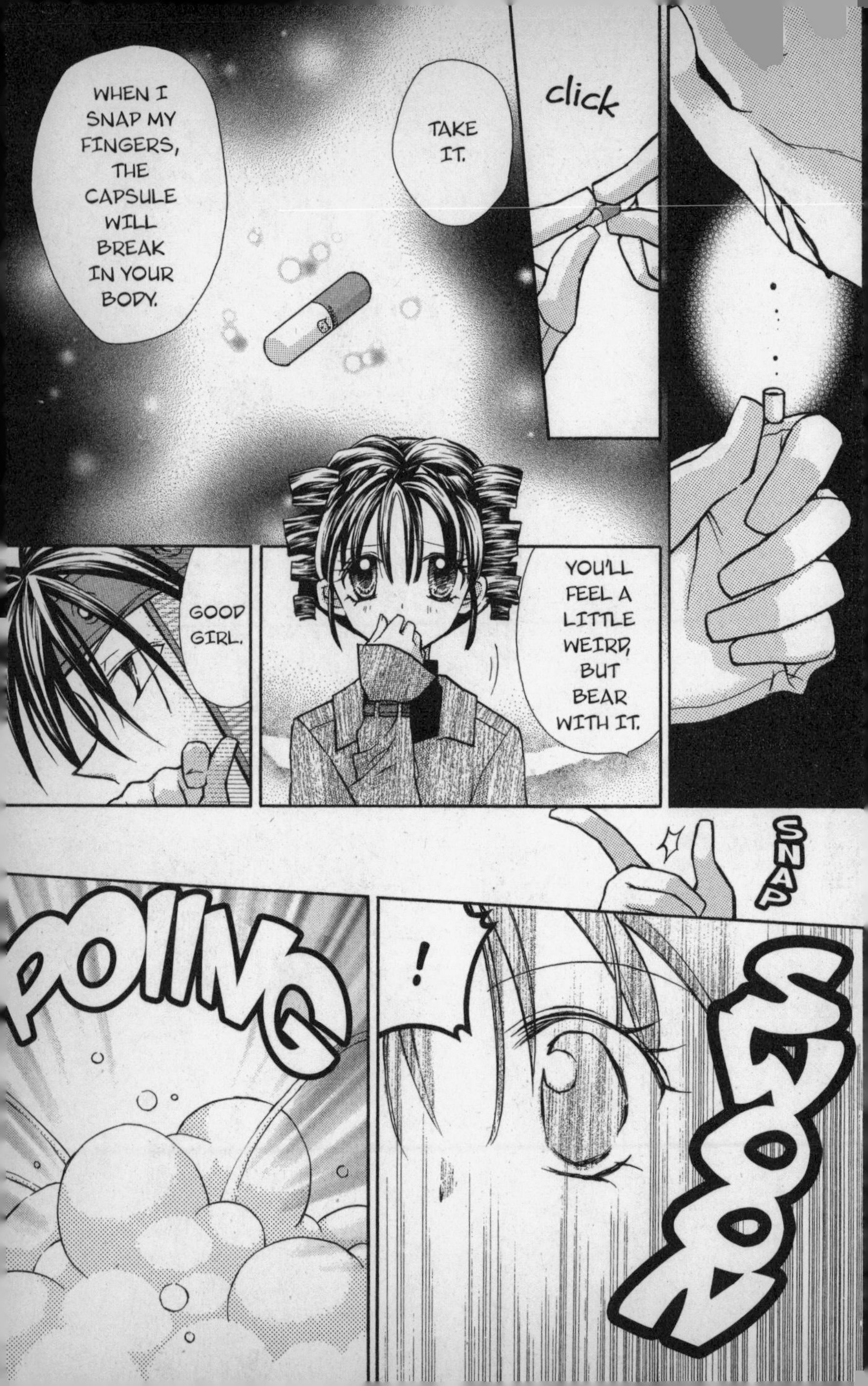
click
TAKE IT.
WHEN I SNAP MY FINGERS, THE CAPSULE WILL BREAK IN YOUR BODY.
YOU'LL FEEL A LITTLE WEIRD, BUT BEAR WITH IT.
GOOD GIRL.
SNAP
!
POIING

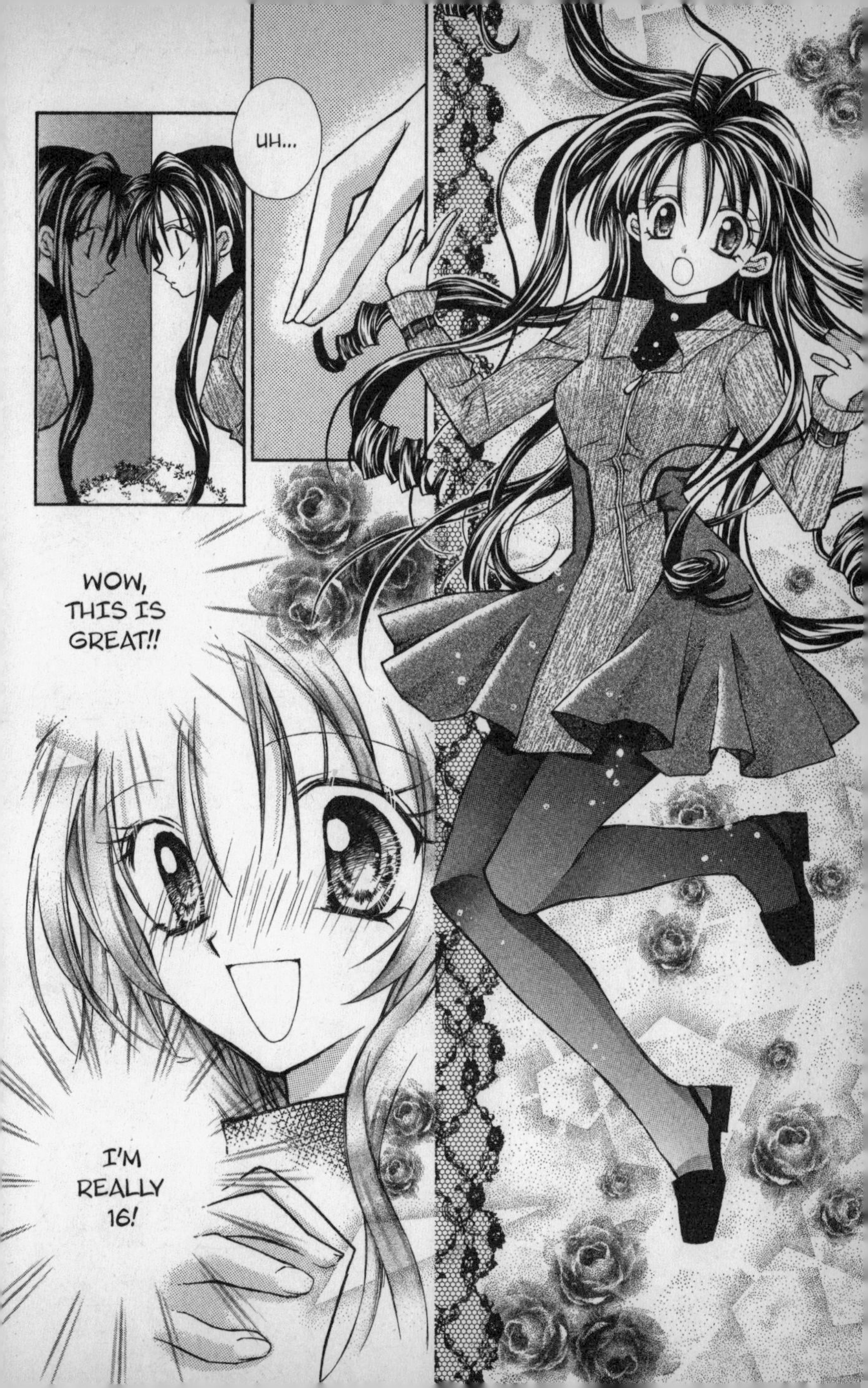
UH...
WOW, THIS IS GREAT!!
I'M REALLY 16!

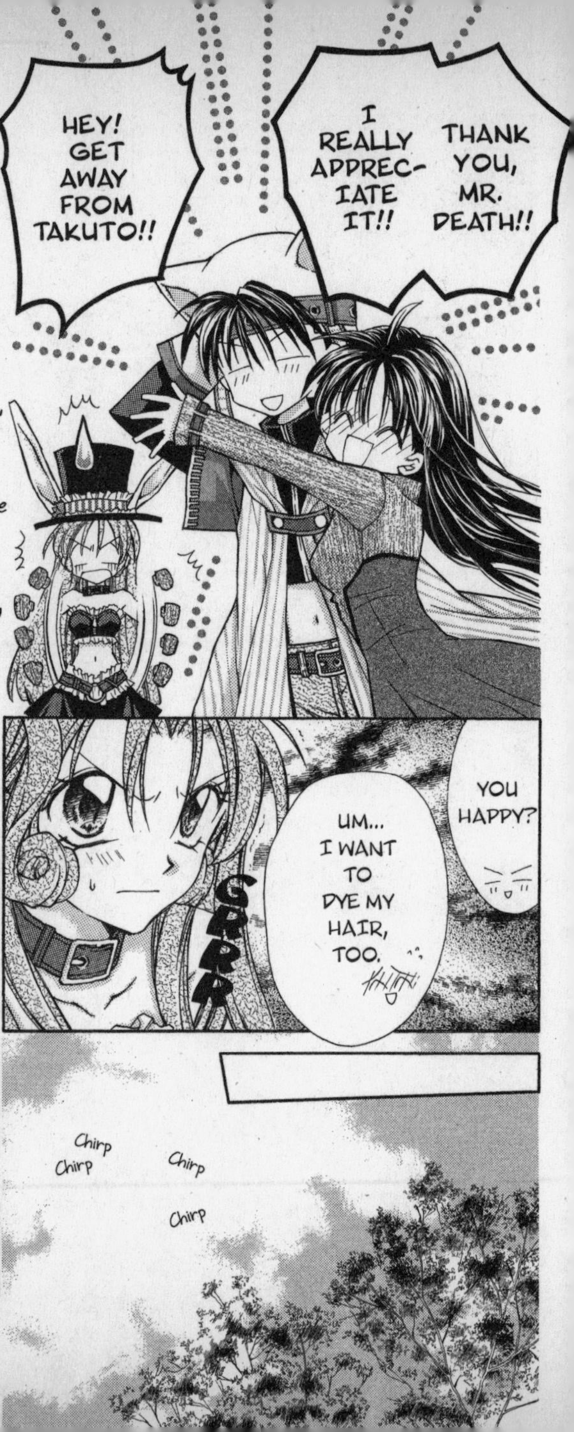
THANK YOU, MR. DEATH!!
I REALLY APPRECIATE IT!!
HEY! GET AWAY FROM TAKUTO!!
YOU HAPPY?
UM... I WANT TO DYE MY HAIR, TOO.
GRRR
Chirp
Chirp
Chirp
Chirp

Hello.

For first-time readers, welcome!

I'm Arina Tanemura. It's been a while since I've had a comic out, so I'm happy the first volume of "Full Moon o Sagashite" is out.

"Full Moon" started in the 2002 January issue of Ribon, but it is already an anime. This was a real surprise. "It's still episode 4!" was what I thought back then.

When it was decided that the story would be turned into an anime, I was confused because I was dealing with the hassles of starting a new series. I would like to make the story interesting by keeping the manga separate from the anime, while still keeping a good connection with the anime.

The anime, "Full Moon o Sagashite" is...

being broadcast on TV Tokyo every Saturday at 7:30AM!

It seems that the staff loves Meroko.

Negi-ramen is all over the screen.

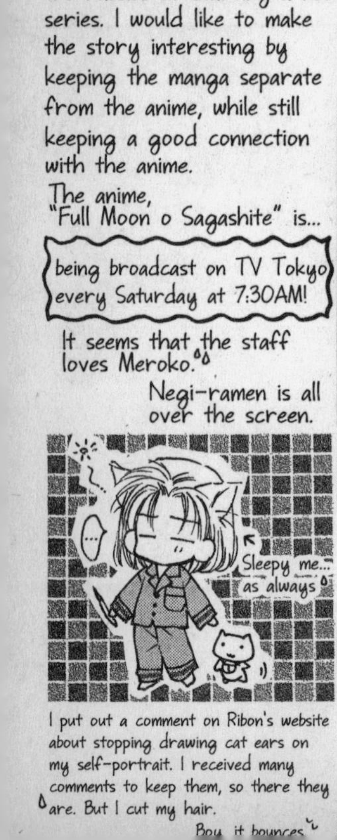
...
Sleepy me... as always

I put out a comment on Ribon's website about stopping drawing cat ears on my self-portrait. I received many comments to keep them, so there they are. But I cut my hair.

Boy, it bounces

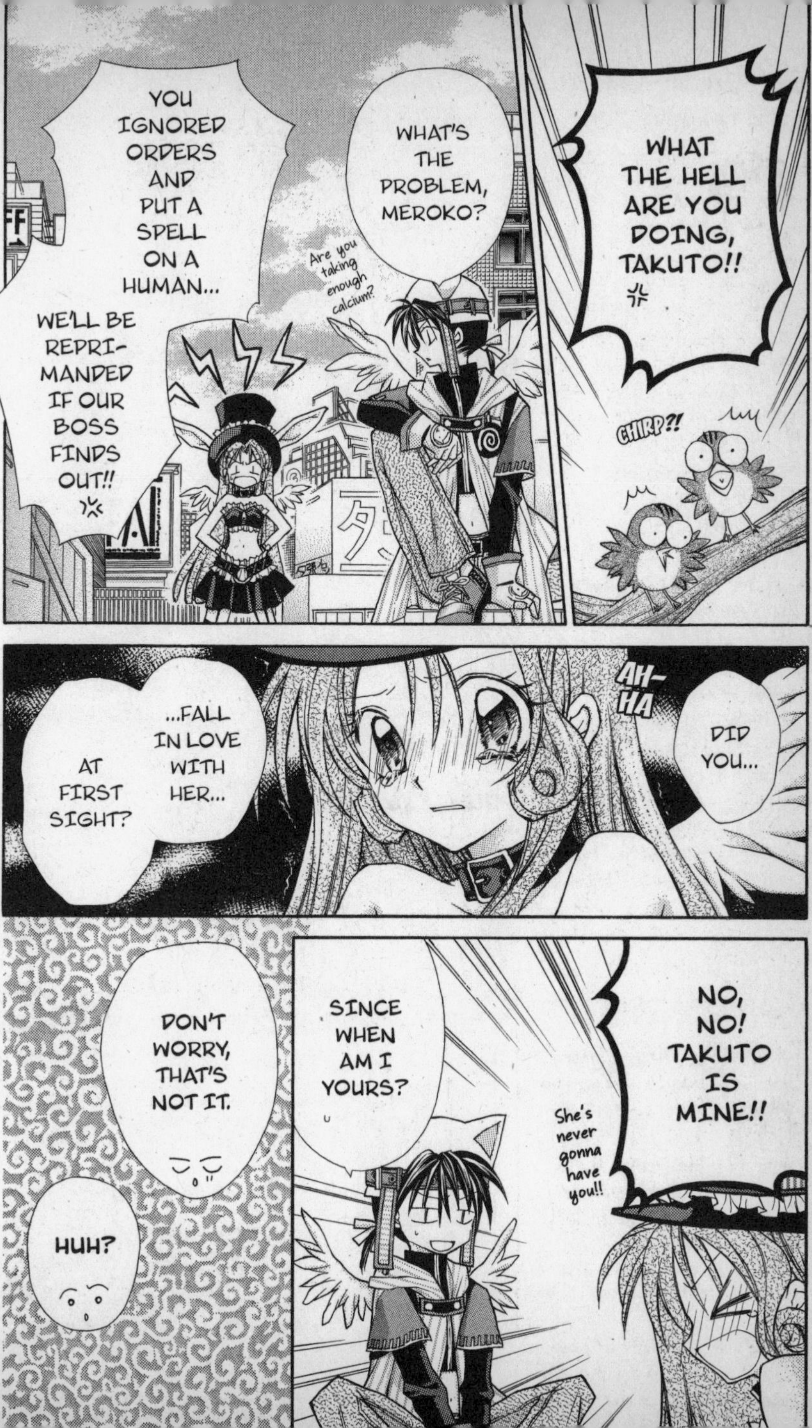
WHAT THE HELL ARE YOU DOING, TAKUTO!!
CHIRP?!
WHAT'S THE PROBLEM, MEROKO?
Are you taking enough calcium?
YOU IGNORED ORDERS AND PUT A SPELL ON A HUMAN...
WE'LL BE REPRI-MANDED IF OUR BOSS FINDS OUT!!
AH-HA
DID YOU...
...FALL IN LOVE WITH HER...
AT FIRST SIGHT?
NO, NO! TAKUTO IS MINE!!
She's never gonna have you!!
SINCE WHEN AM I YOURS?
DON'T WORRY, THAT'S NOT IT.
HUH?

Character Introduction.

- Mitsuki Koyama ☆

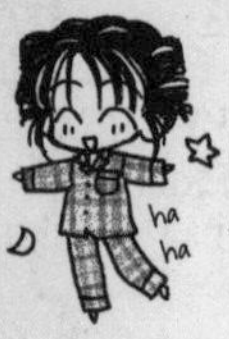

ha
ha

Her hairstyle was taken from Ai Kago of Morning Musume. (I usually don't make models or motifs when I create my characters, though.) Her character model is Airi, my assistant. She's a girl who looks like a grade-schooler, although she's 19. Mitsuki's last name was taken from the producer of voice actress Houko Kuwashima's radio "Club db," without permission. (Sorry, Koyama-sensei.) Mitsuki is 160-degrees different from my own personality (only 20-degrees the same), so it's difficult to pretend to be Mitsuki and draw. (I have to pretend to be the character so the character talks naturally.) (I am always acting when I do the storyboards!) I believe voice actress Yui Horie's songs match Mitsuki's image, so I listen to her songs a lot to get into the mood. ♪ I love the songs "Tsuki no Kikyuu" "Sakura" and "Kosaji Ippai no Yuuki." LOVE I highly recommend them.

- Takuto Kira (Negi-ramen)

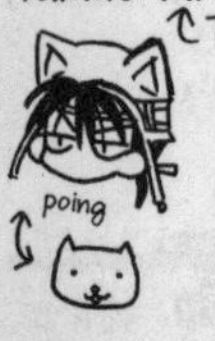

poing

Takuto is his name. He's a Shinigami who talks tough. He wears those clothes because I want him to look like a toy. The cat is that character that I used to draw with my self-portrait. It first appeared in Vol.7 of "Kamikaze Kaitou Jeanne." If you want to be a real maniac, call Takuto the cat "Neko-kun."

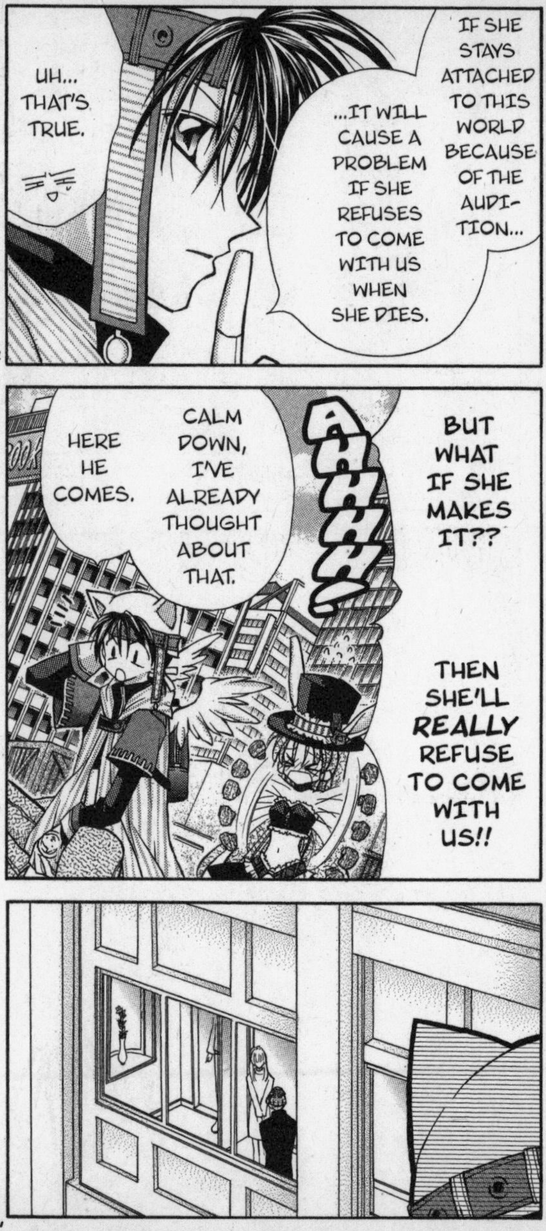

IF SHE STAYS ATTACHED TO THIS WORLD BECAUSE OF THE AUDITION...
...IT WILL CAUSE A PROBLEM IF SHE REFUSES TO COME WITH US WHEN SHE DIES.
UH... THAT'S TRUE.
BUT WHAT IF SHE MAKES IT??
THEN SHE'LL REALLY REFUSE TO COME WITH US!!
AHHHH!
CALM DOWN, I'VE ALREADY THOUGHT ABOUT THAT.
HERE HE COMES.

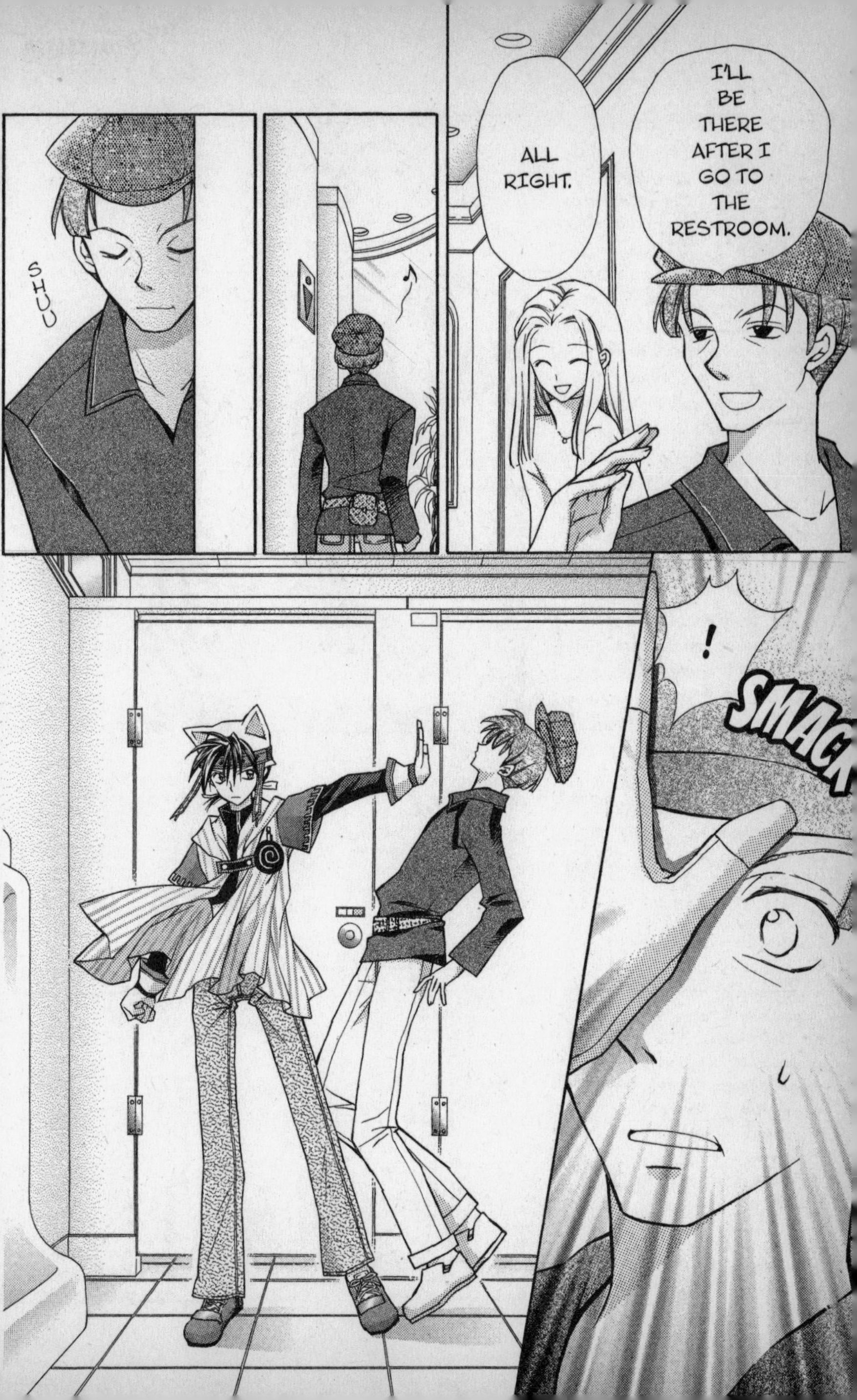
I'LL BE THERE AFTER I GO TO THE RESTROOM.
ALL RIGHT.
SHUU
!
SMACK

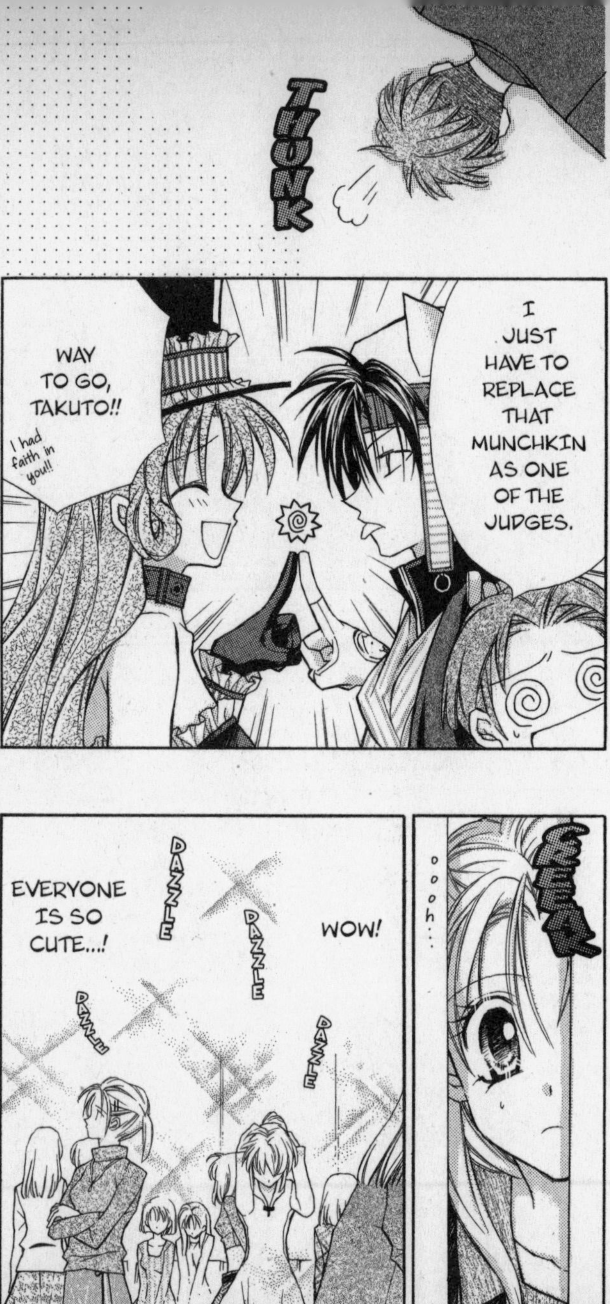
THONK
I JUST HAVE TO REPLACE THAT MUNCHKIN AS ONE OF THE JUDGES.
WAY TO GO, TAKUTO!!
I had faith in you!!
ooh...
WOW!
DAZZLE
DAZZLE
EVERYONE IS SO CUTE...!
DAZZLE
DAZZLE

Arina Tanemura's "little treasure?!" rare item. Back of the box.

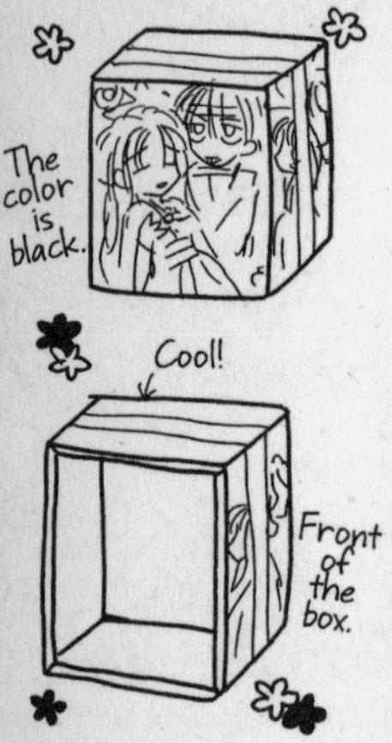
The color is black.
Cool!
Front of the box.

This is a box that can hold all seven volumes of "Kamikaze Kaito Jeanne." My illustrations are printed on the box. A publisher in Denmark (I think) made it. (Apparently, you get it when you buy the seventh volume.) The box is made of hard cardboard, and is of good quality.

For some reason, my manga is popular in Europe (maybe because they broadcast the "Jeanne" anime), especially in Germany. In any case, it was a very welcome gift. If you go to Denmark, please check out the bookstores. (The sizes of tankobons in Denmark are the same as Japanese ones, so you can put the Japanese comics in the box too.) Please make a similar box for "Full Moon o Sagashite," Shueisha!

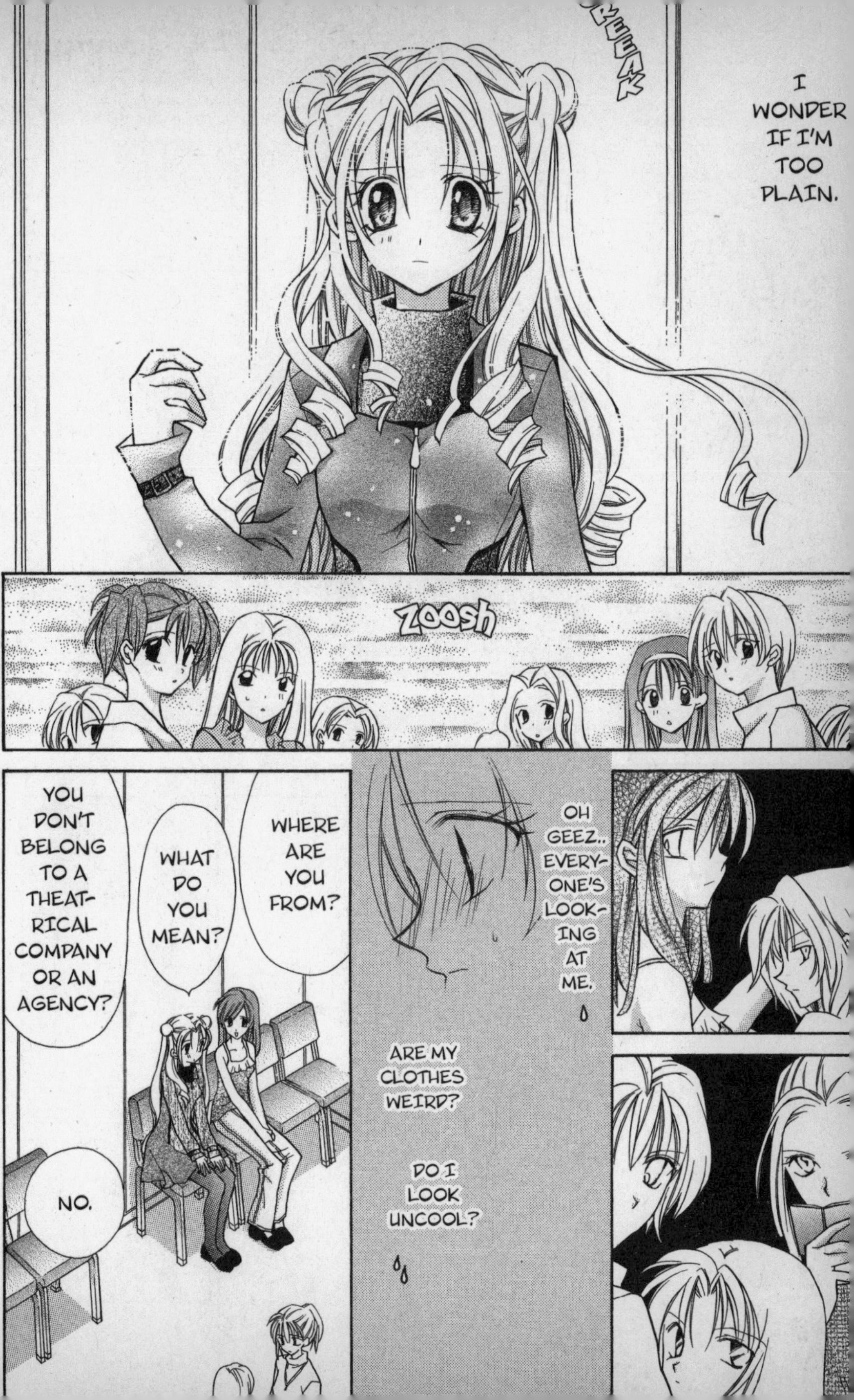
REEAK
I WONDER IF I'M TOO PLAIN.
ZOOSH
OH GEEZ.. EVERYONE'S LOOKING AT ME.
ARE MY CLOTHES WEIRD?
DO I LOOK UNCOOL?
WHERE ARE YOU FROM?
WHAT DO YOU MEAN?
YOU DON'T BELONG TO A THEATRICAL COMPANY OR AN AGENCY?
NO.

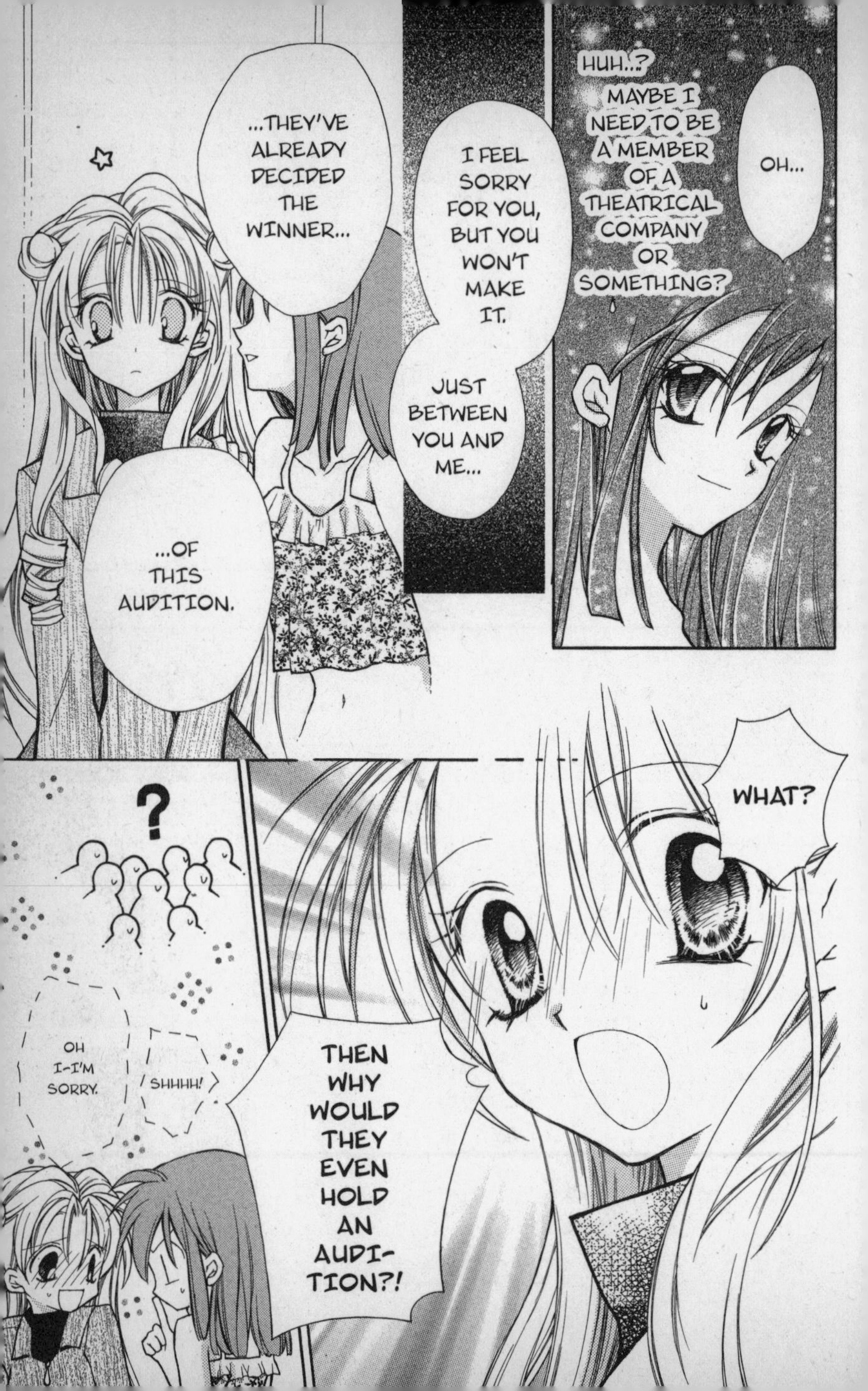
OH...
HUH..? MAYBE I NEED TO BE A MEMBER OF A THEATRICAL COMPANY OR SOMETHING?
I FEEL SORRY FOR YOU, BUT YOU WON'T MAKE IT.
JUST BETWEEN YOU AND ME...
...THEY'VE ALREADY DECIDED THE WINNER...
...OF THIS AUDITION.
WHAT?
THEN WHY WOULD THEY EVEN HOLD AN AUDI-TION?!
?
SHHHH!
OH I-I'M SORRY.

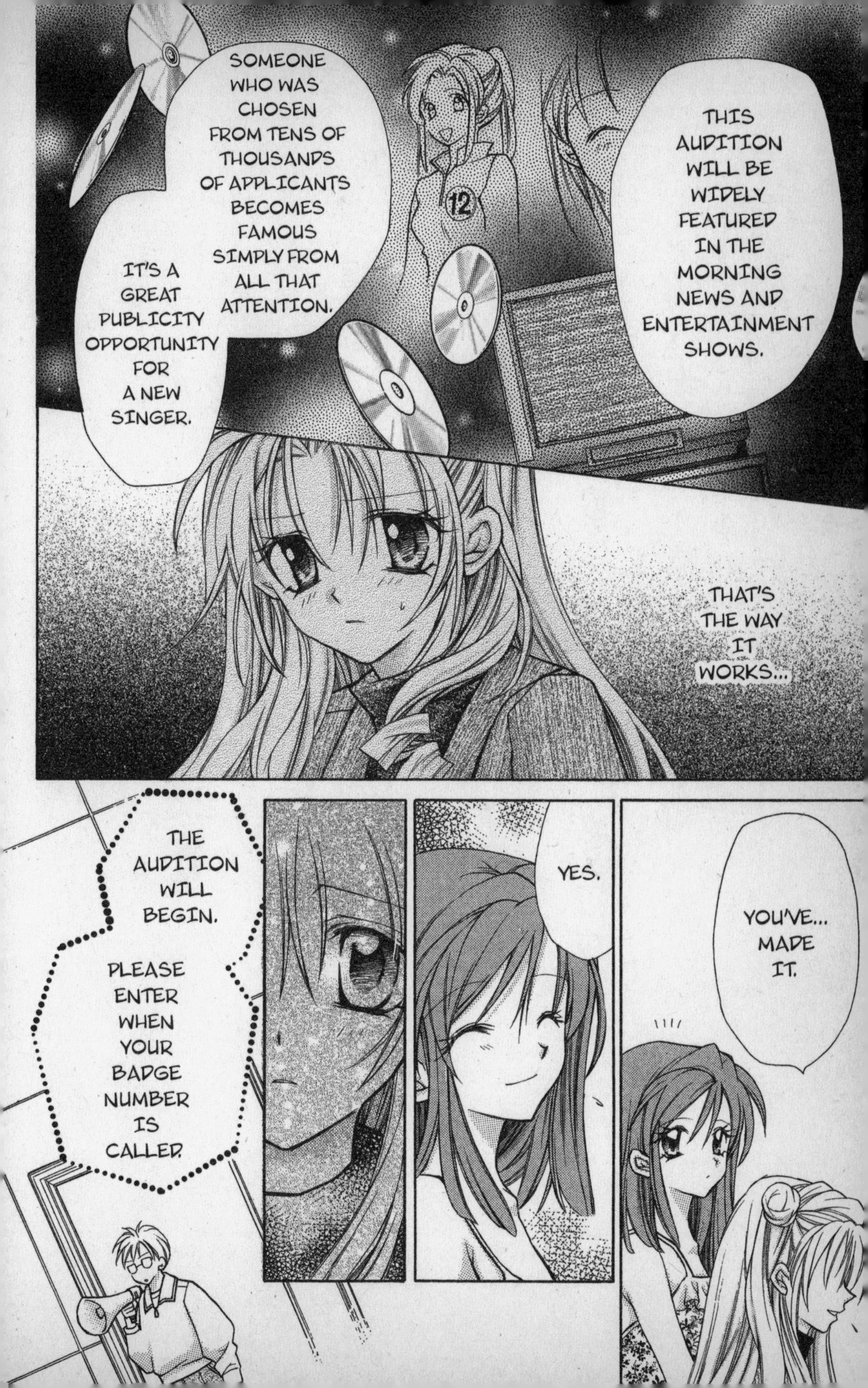
THIS AUDITION WILL BE WIDELY FEATURED IN THE MORNING NEWS AND ENTERTAINMENT SHOWS.
SOMEONE WHO WAS CHOSEN FROM TENS OF THOUSANDS OF APPLICANTS BECOMES FAMOUS SIMPLY FROM ALL THAT ATTENTION.
IT'S A GREAT PUBLICITY OPPORTUNITY FOR A NEW SINGER.
12
THAT'S THE WAY IT WORKS...
YOU'VE... MADE IT.
YES.
THE AUDITION WILL BEGIN.
PLEASE ENTER WHEN YOUR BADGE NUMBER IS CALLED.

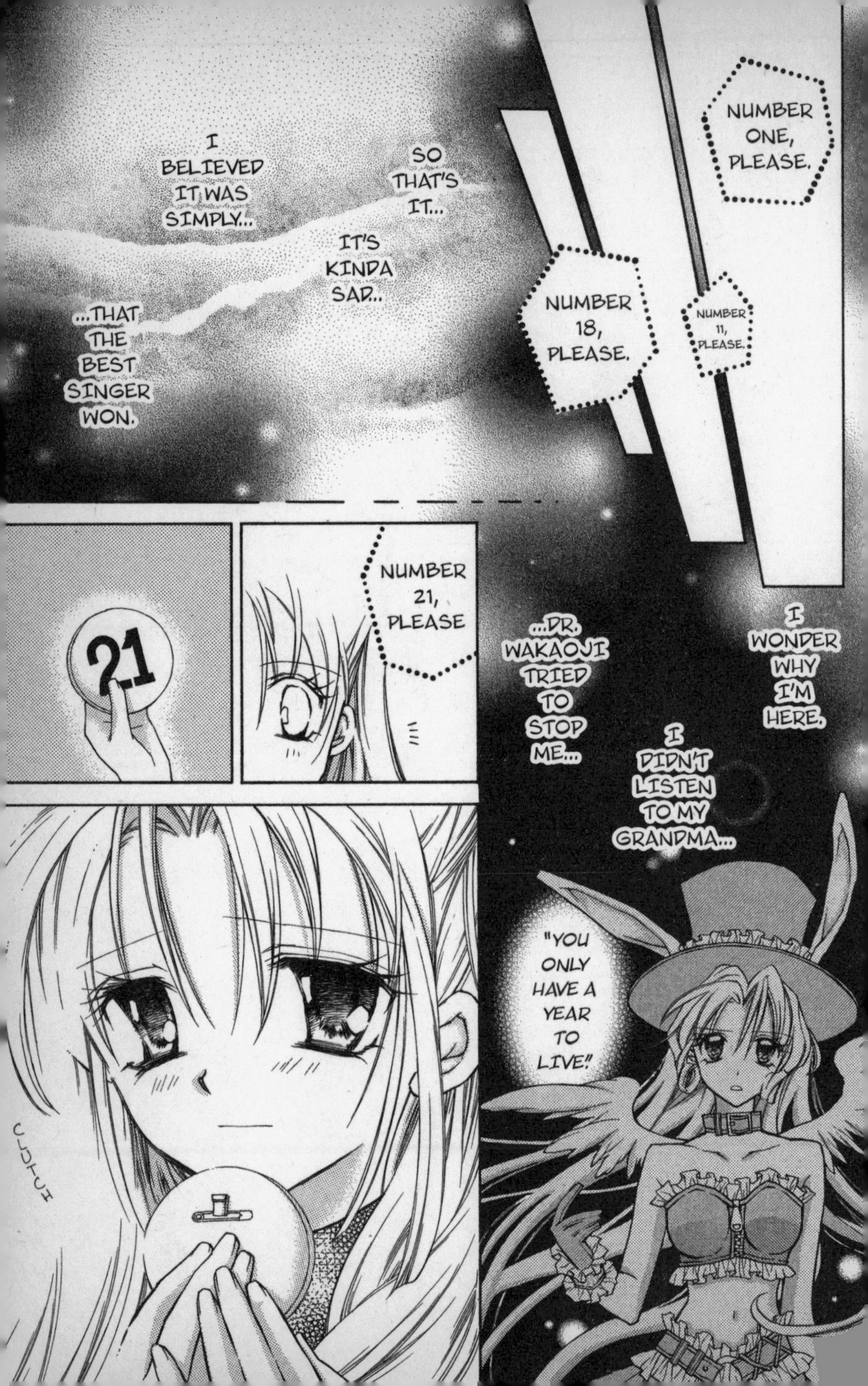
NUMBER ONE, PLEASE.
NUMBER 11, PLEASE.
NUMBER 18, PLEASE.
SO THAT'S IT...
IT'S KINDA SAD...
I BELIEVED IT WAS SIMPLY...
...THAT THE BEST SINGER WON.
I WONDER WHY I'M HERE.
...DR. WAKAOJI TRIED TO STOP ME...
I DIDN'T LISTEN TO MY GRANDMA...
"YOU ONLY HAVE A YEAR TO LIVE!"
NUMBER 21, PLEASE
21
CLUTCH

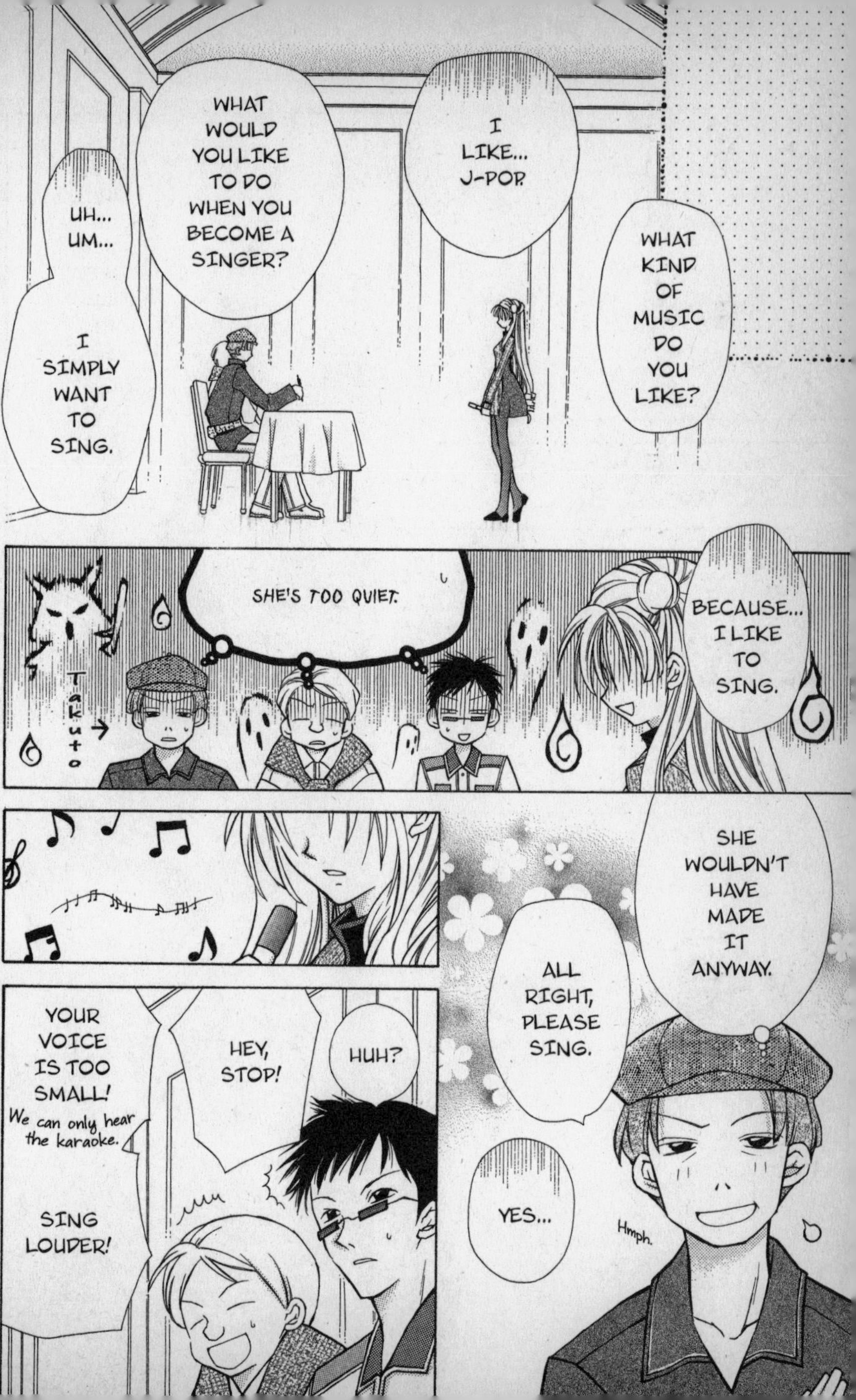
WHAT KIND OF MUSIC DO YOU LIKE?
I LIKE... J-POP.
WHAT WOULD YOU LIKE TO DO WHEN YOU BECOME A SINGER?
UH... UM...
I SIMPLY WANT TO SING.
BECAUSE... I LIKE TO SING.
SHE'S TOO QUIET.
Takuto
SHE WOULDN'T HAVE MADE IT ANYWAY.
ALL RIGHT, PLEASE SING.
YES...
Hmph.
HUH?
HEY, STOP!
YOUR VOICE IS TOO SMALL!
We can only hear the karaoke.
SING LOUDER!

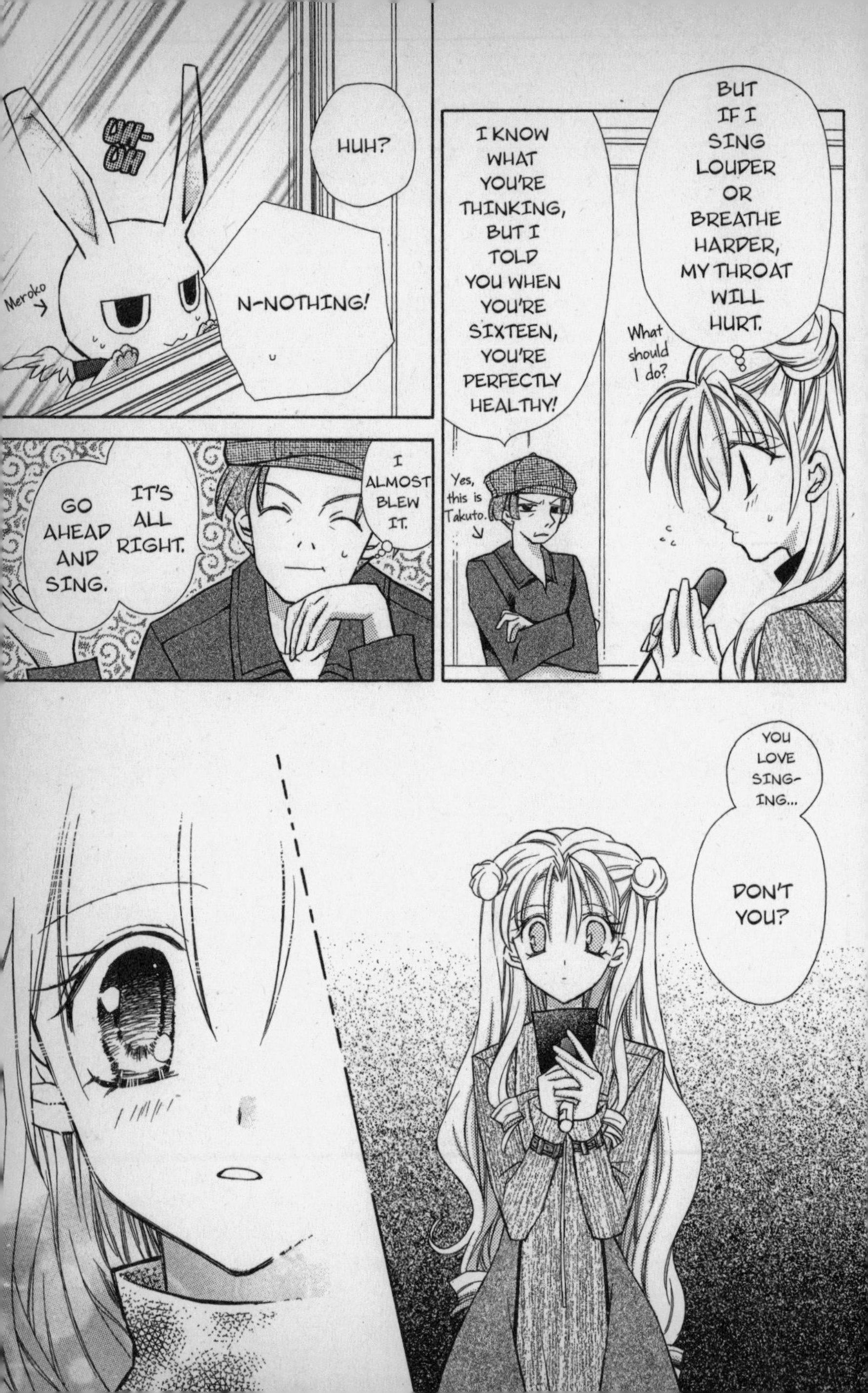
BUT IF I SING LOUDER OR BREATHE HARDER, MY THROAT WILL HURT.
What should I do?
I KNOW WHAT YOU'RE THINKING, BUT I TOLD YOU WHEN YOU'RE SIXTEEN, YOU'RE PERFECTLY HEALTHY!
Yes, this is Takuto.
HUH?
UH-OH
N-NOTHING!
Meroko
I ALMOST BLEW IT.
IT'S ALL RIGHT.
GO AHEAD AND SING.
YOU LOVE SING-ING...
DON'T YOU?

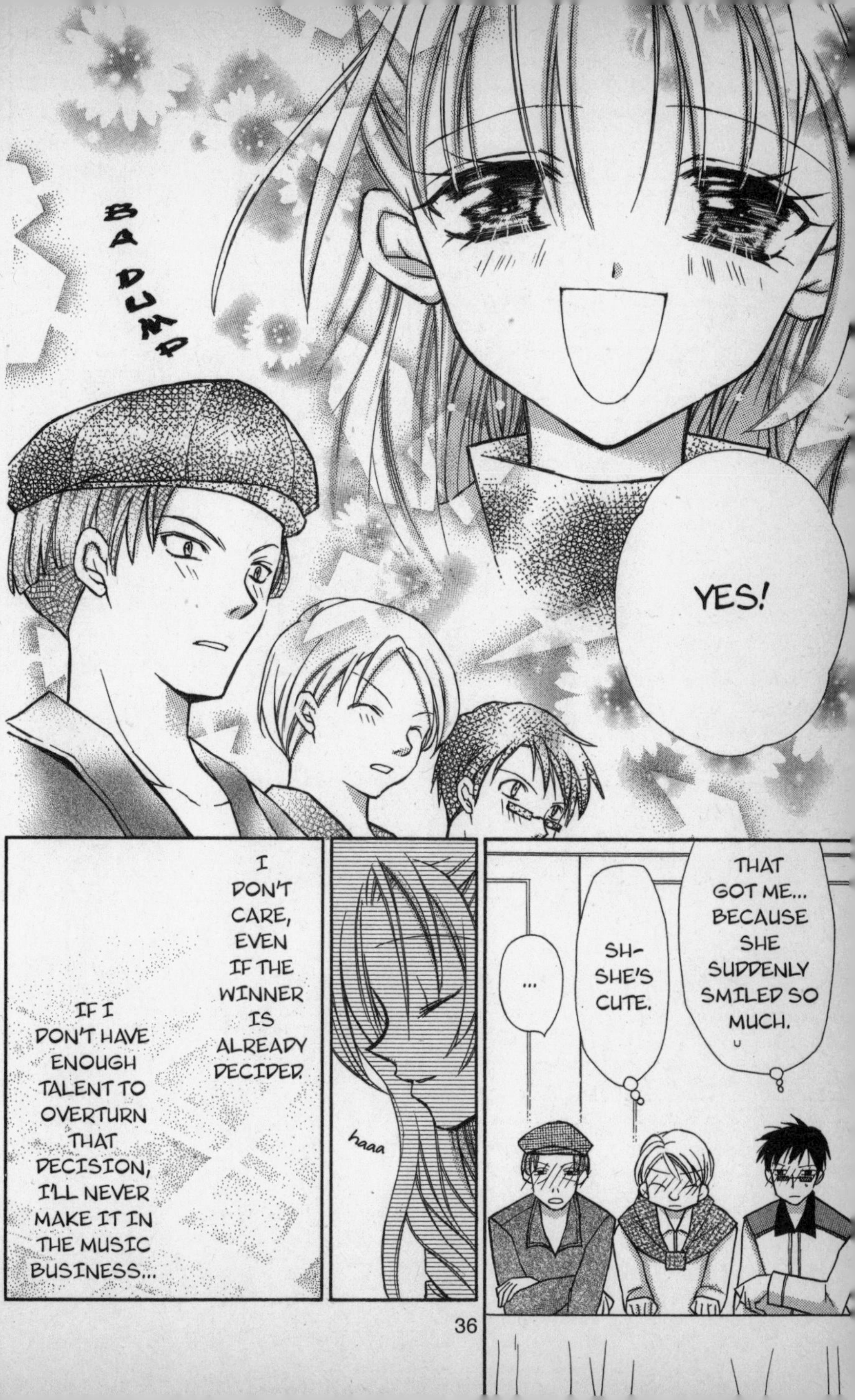
YES!
BA DUMP
THAT GOT ME... BECAUSE SHE SUDDENLY SMILED SO MUCH.
SH-SHE'S CUTE.
...
haaa
I DON'T CARE, EVEN IF THE WINNER IS ALREADY DECIDED.
IF I DON'T HAVE ENOUGH TALENT TO OVERTURN THAT DECISION, I'LL NEVER MAKE IT IN THE MUSIC BUSINESS...

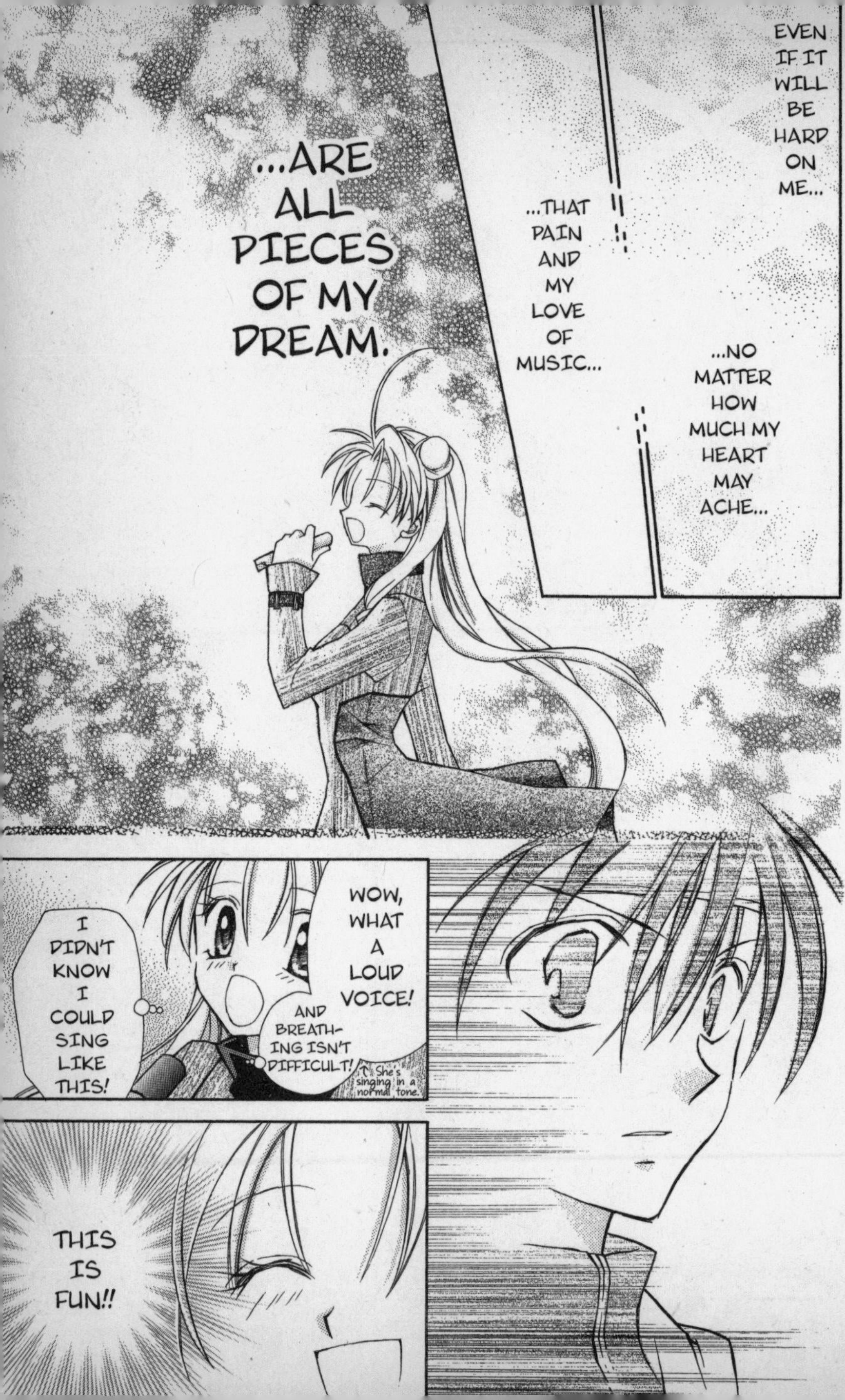
EVEN IF IT WILL BE HARD ON ME...
...NO MATTER HOW MUCH MY HEART MAY ACHE...
...THAT PAIN AND MY LOVE OF MUSIC...
...ARE ALL PIECES OF MY DREAM.
WOW, WHAT A LOUD VOICE!
AND BREATHING ISN'T DIFFICULT!
I DIDN'T KNOW I COULD SING LIKE THIS!
She's singing in a normal tone.
THIS IS FUN!!

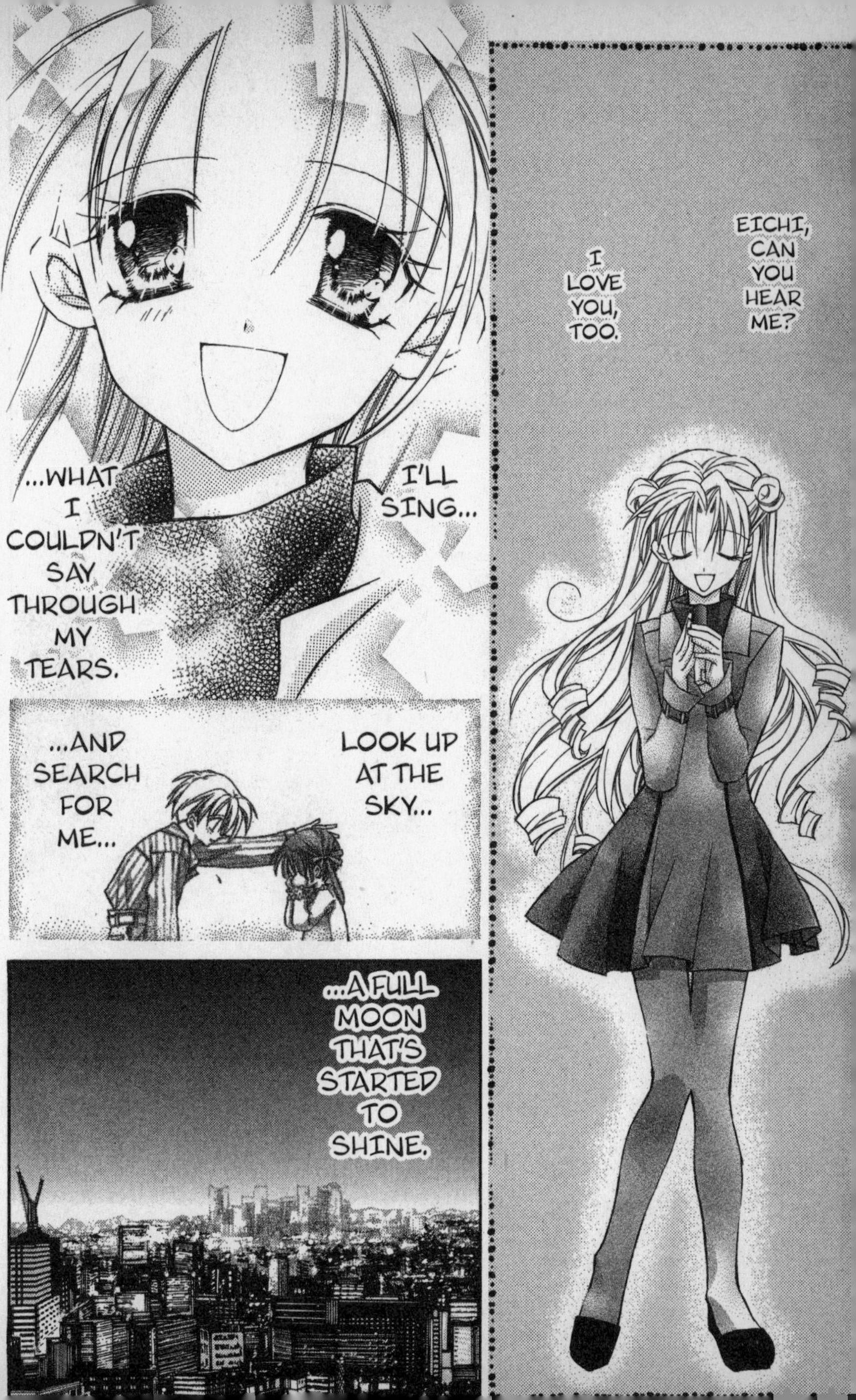
EICHI, CAN YOU HEAR ME?
I LOVE YOU, TOO.
I'LL SING...
...WHAT I COULDN'T SAY THROUGH MY TEARS.
LOOK UP AT THE SKY...
...AND SEARCH FOR ME...
...A FULL MOON THAT'S STARTED TO SHINE.

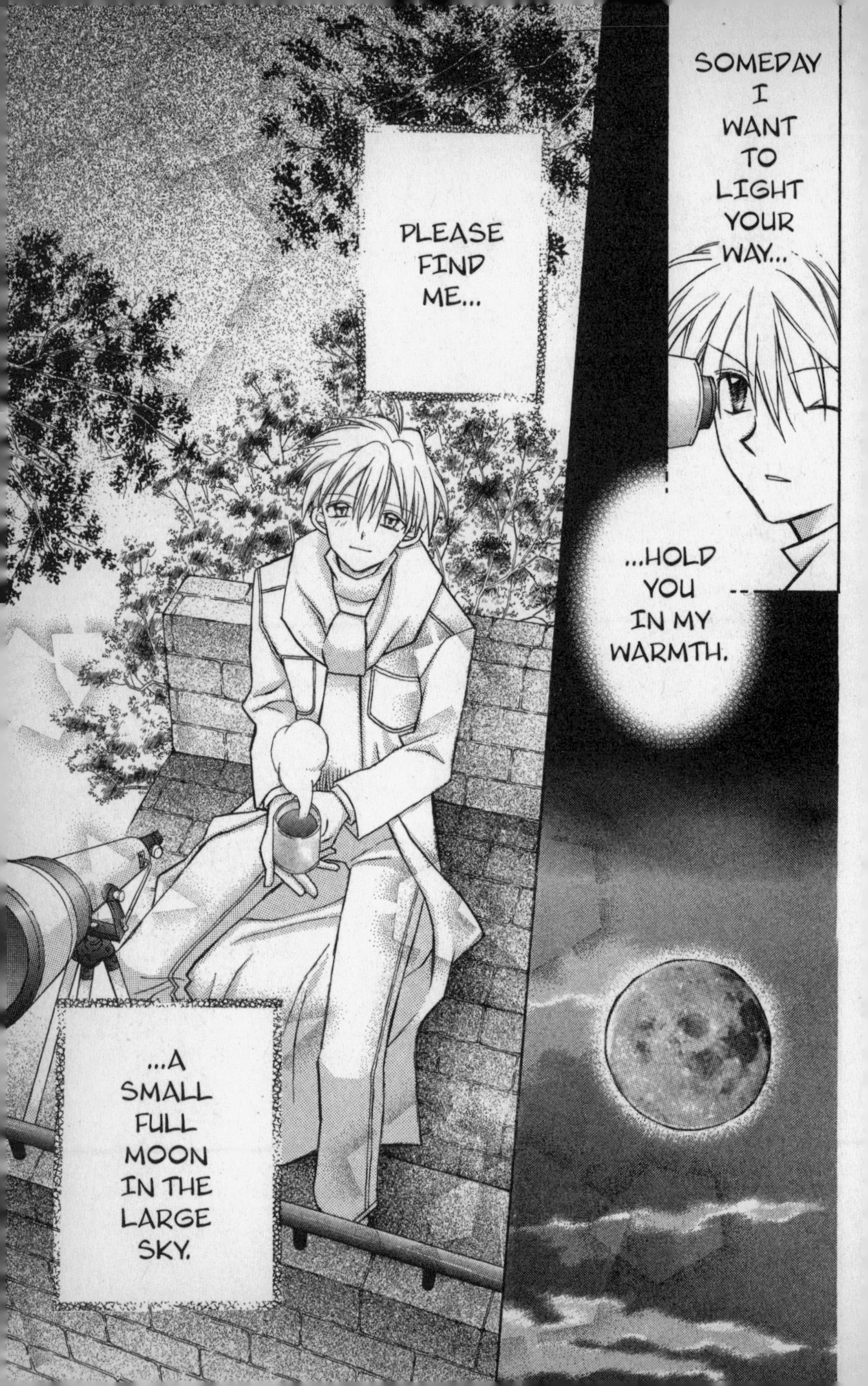
SOMEDAY I WANT TO LIGHT YOUR WAY...
...HOLD YOU IN MY WARMTH.
PLEASE FIND ME...
...A SMALL FULL MOON IN THE LARGE SKY.

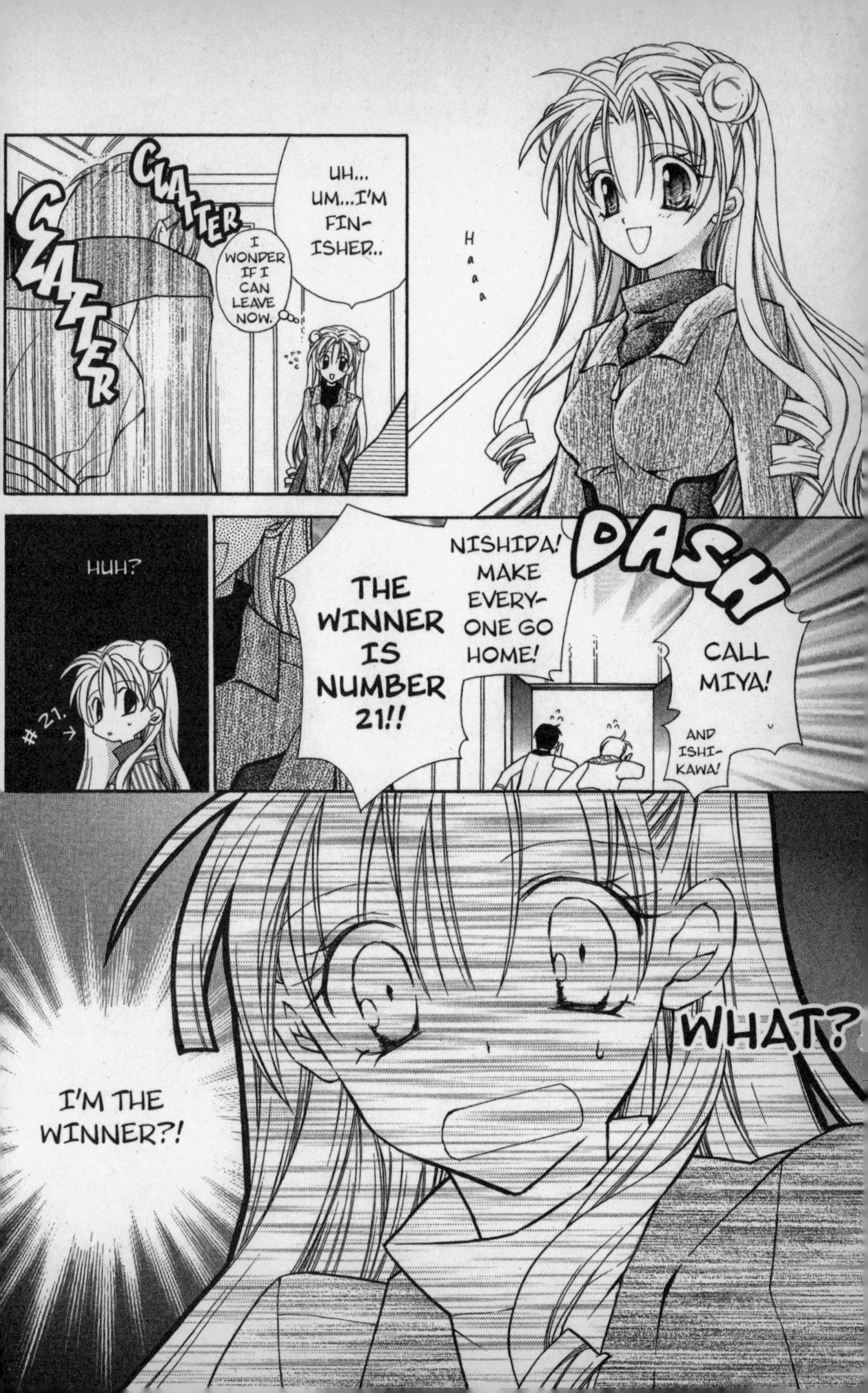
Haaa
UH... UM...I'M FIN-ISHED...
I WONDER IF I CAN LEAVE NOW.
CLATTER
CLATTER
DASH
THE WINNER IS NUMBER 21!!
NISHIDA! MAKE EVERY-ONE GO HOME!
CALL MIYA!
AND ISHI-KAWA!
HUH?
#21.
WHAT?
I'M THE WINNER?!

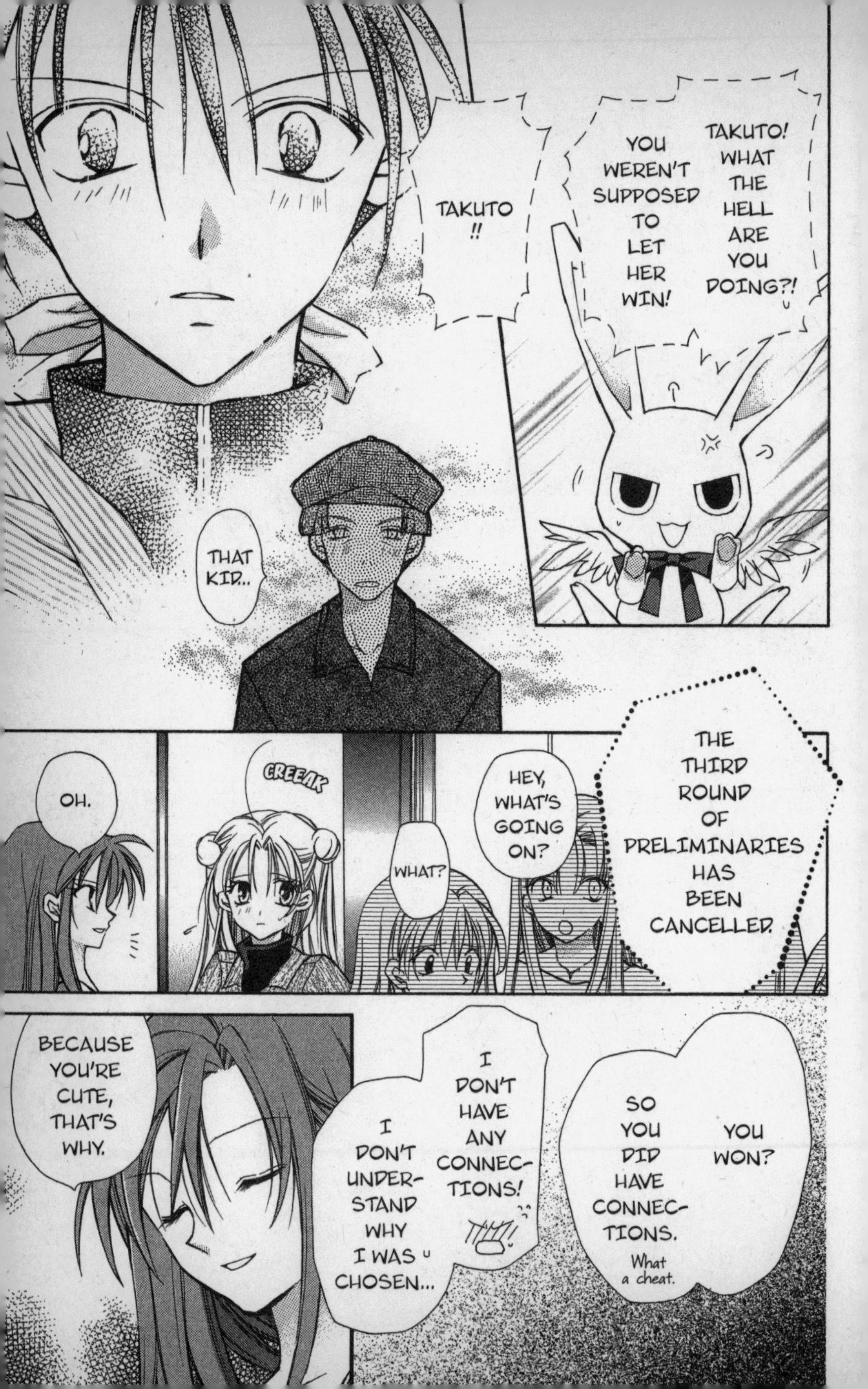
TAKUTO! WHAT THE HELL ARE YOU DOING?!
YOU WEREN'T SUPPOSED TO LET HER WIN!
TAKUTO !!
THAT KID...
THE THIRD ROUND OF PRELIMINARIES HAS BEEN CANCELLED.
HEY, WHAT'S GOING ON?
WHAT?
CREEAK
OH.
YOU WON?
SO YOU DID HAVE CONNECTIONS.
What a cheat.
I DON'T HAVE ANY CONNECTIONS!
I DON'T UNDERSTAND WHY I WAS CHOSEN...
BECAUSE YOU'RE CUTE, THAT'S WHY.

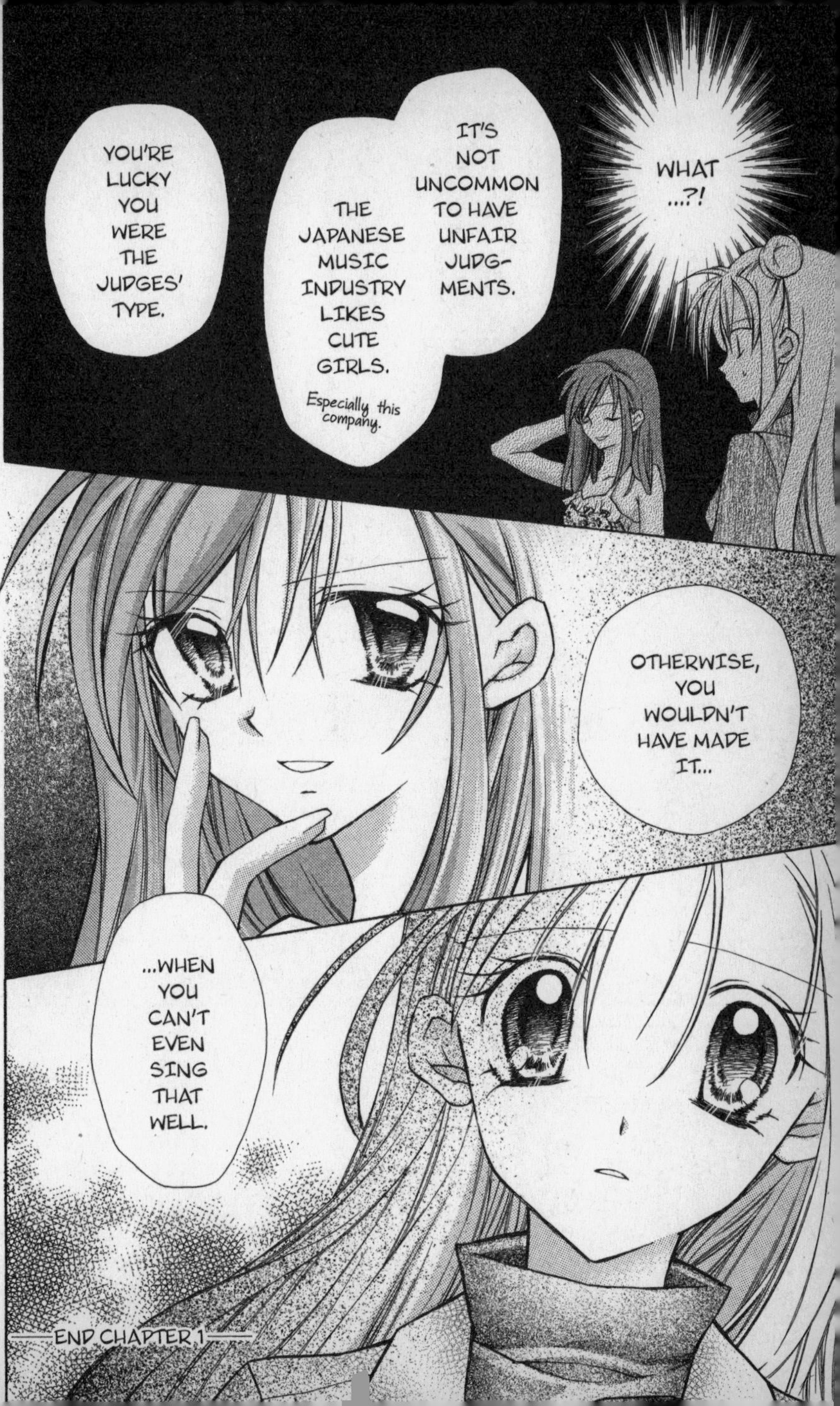
WHAT ...?!
IT'S NOT UNCOMMON TO HAVE UNFAIR JUDG-MENTS.
THE JAPANESE MUSIC INDUSTRY LIKES CUTE GIRLS.
Especially this company.
YOU'RE LUCKY YOU WERE THE JUDGES' TYPE.
OTHERWISE, YOU WOULDN'T HAVE MADE IT...
...WHEN YOU CAN'T EVEN SING THAT WELL.
END CHAPTER 1

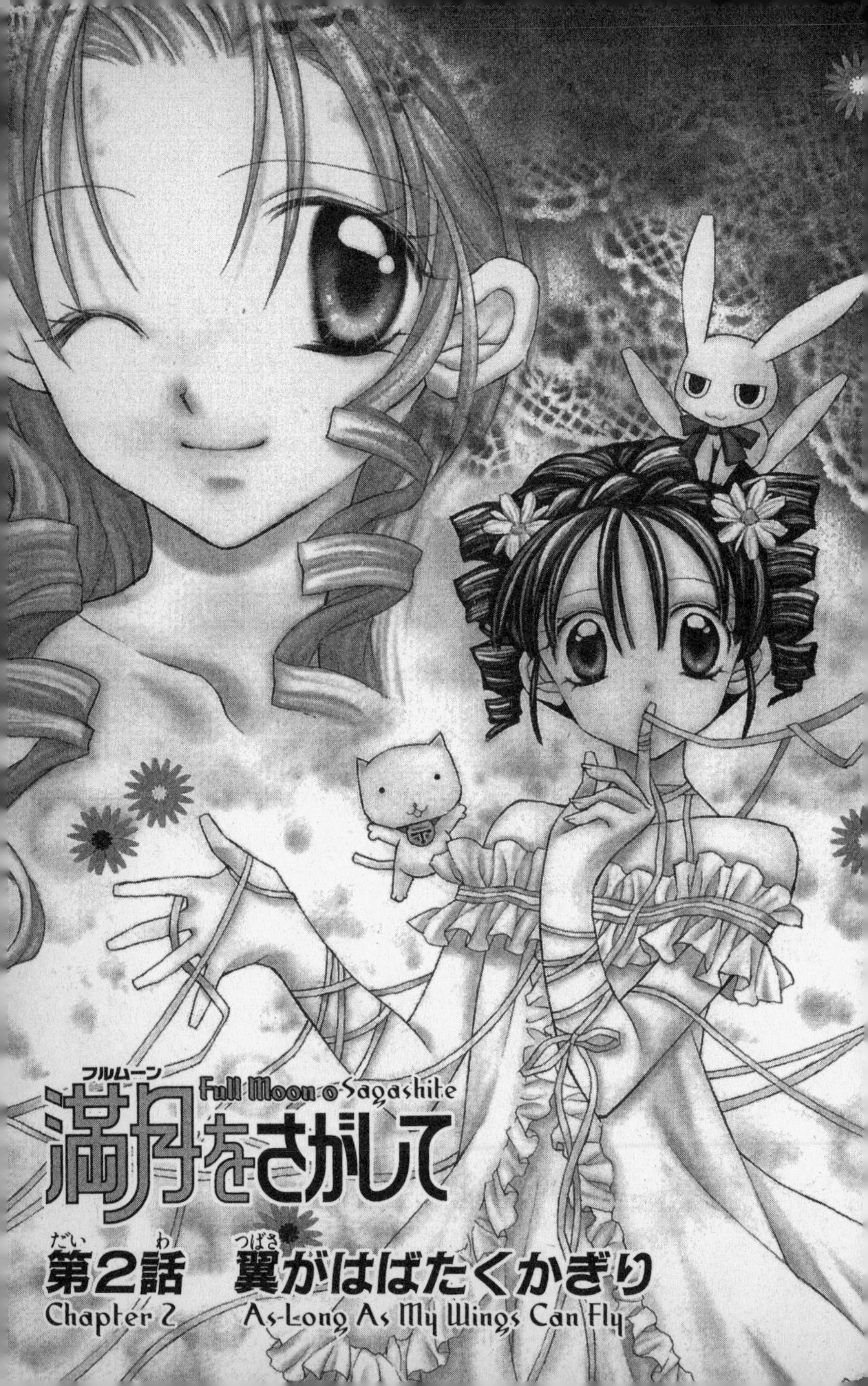
フルムーン
Full Moon o Sagashite
満月をさがして
第2話　翼がはばたくかぎり
Chapter 2　As-Long As My Wings Can Fly

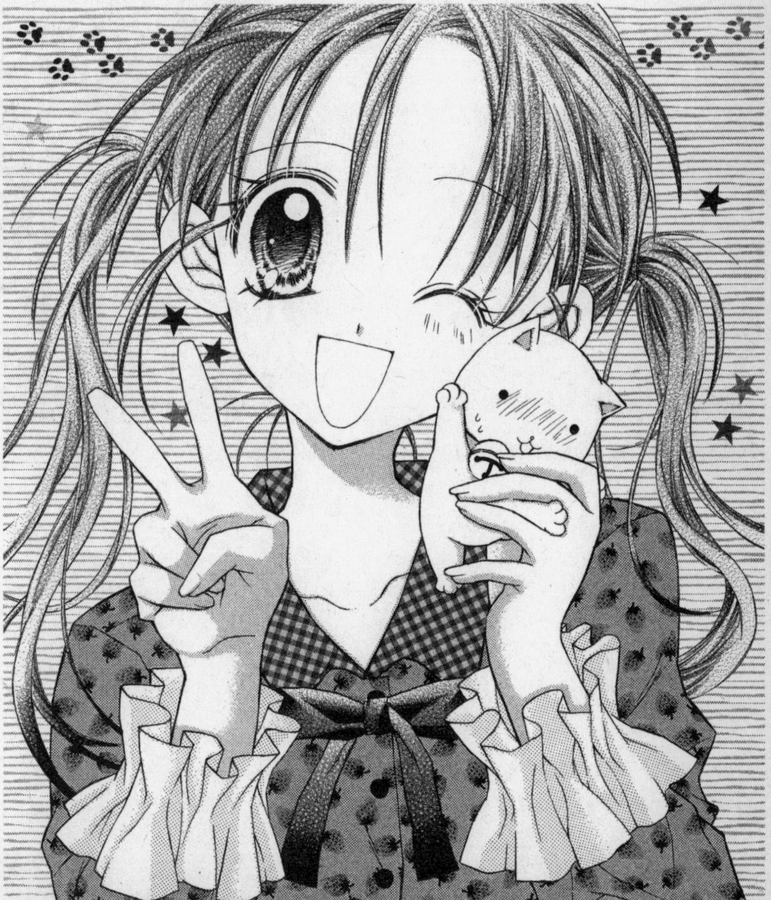

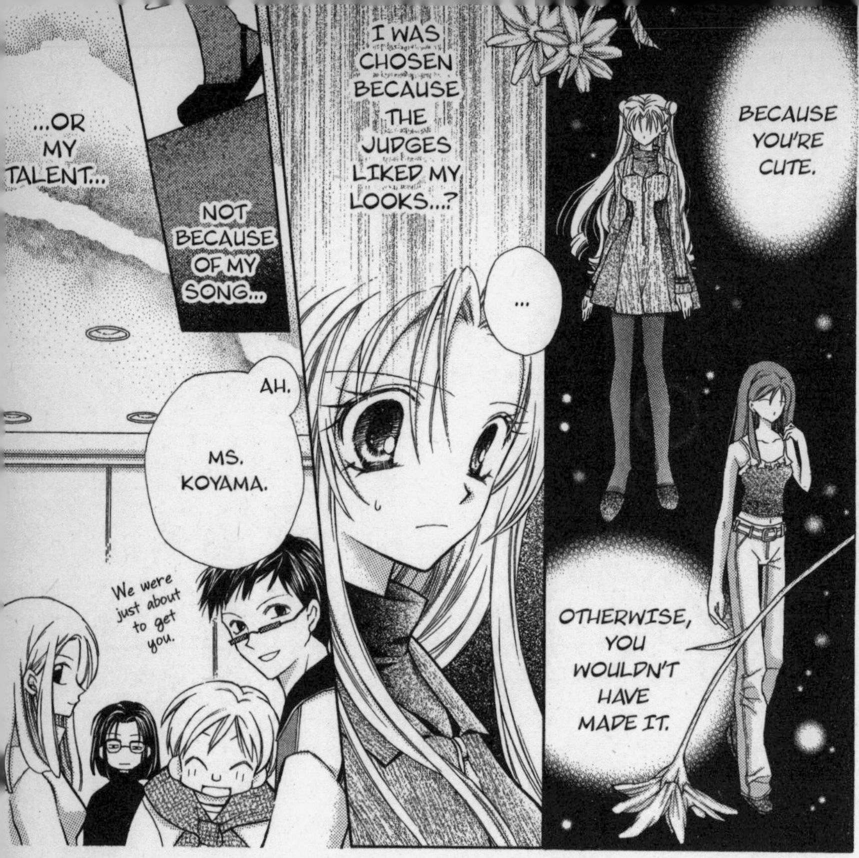
BECAUSE YOU'RE CUTE.
OTHERWISE, YOU WOULDN'T HAVE MADE IT.
I WAS CHOSEN BECAUSE THE JUDGES LIKED MY LOOKS...?
...
NOT BECAUSE OF MY SONG...
...OR MY TALENT...
AH.
MS. KOYAMA.
We were just about to get you.

@Author's Comments about the Cover Illustrations@

Chapter 1 Mitsuki's Case

I don't remember much about this picture~ (I was so busy then). I only remember taking a loooooong time to paint it. And this is how people get old. I don't like it too much. It's...not quite what I had in mind. But I downloaded the wallpaper from Ribon's website by solving the puzzle (though I'm not using it, hehe♥).

Chapter 2 As Long As My Wings Can Fly

Cover Copy → Let's start walking toward the dream...!

Hmmm...I can't bear to look at this picture either. Ouch.

This picture was used as a mousepad for a Ribon giveaway, and for a pencil board for the mail-order stationery set.

Usually I choose the pictures myself, but because of time constraints, my editor chose this picture. I'm sorry Mr. Koike, I'd have preferred a different picture. π.π

But I haven't drawn Full Moon and Mitsuki together in one picture, so this may be a rare one.

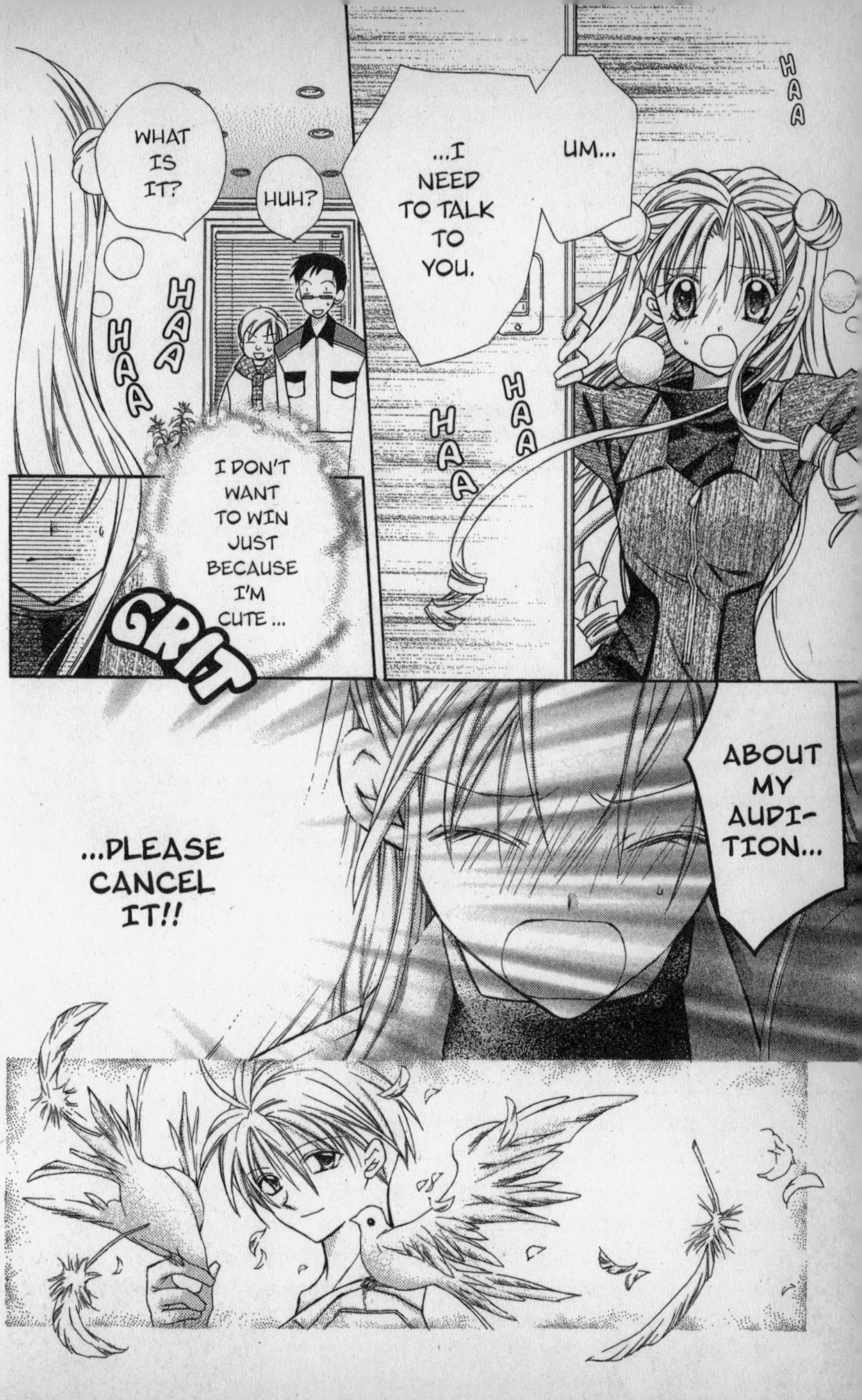
HAA HAA
UM...
...I NEED TO TALK TO YOU.
HAA HAA
HAA HAA
WHAT IS IT?
HUH?
HAA HAA
HAA HAA
I DON'T WANT TO WIN JUST BECAUSE I'M CUTE ...
GRIT
ABOUT MY AUDITION...
...PLEASE CANCEL IT!!

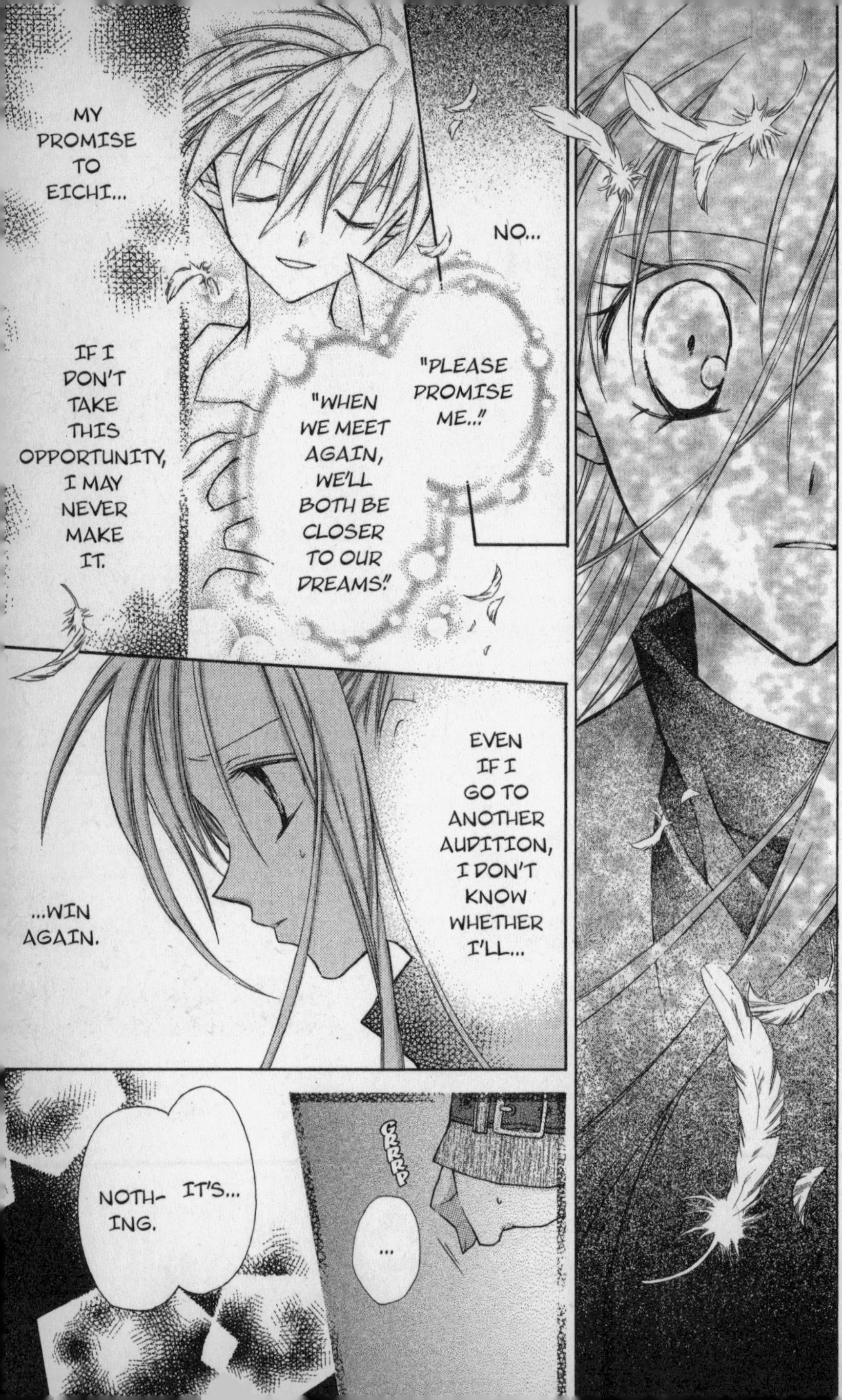
NO...
"PLEASE PROMISE ME..."
"WHEN WE MEET AGAIN, WE'LL BOTH BE CLOSER TO OUR DREAMS!"
MY PROMISE TO EICHI...
IF I DON'T TAKE THIS OPPORTUNITY, I MAY NEVER MAKE IT.
EVEN IF I GO TO ANOTHER AUDITION, I DON'T KNOW WHETHER I'LL...
...WIN AGAIN.
GRRRP
...
IT'S...
NOTH-ING.

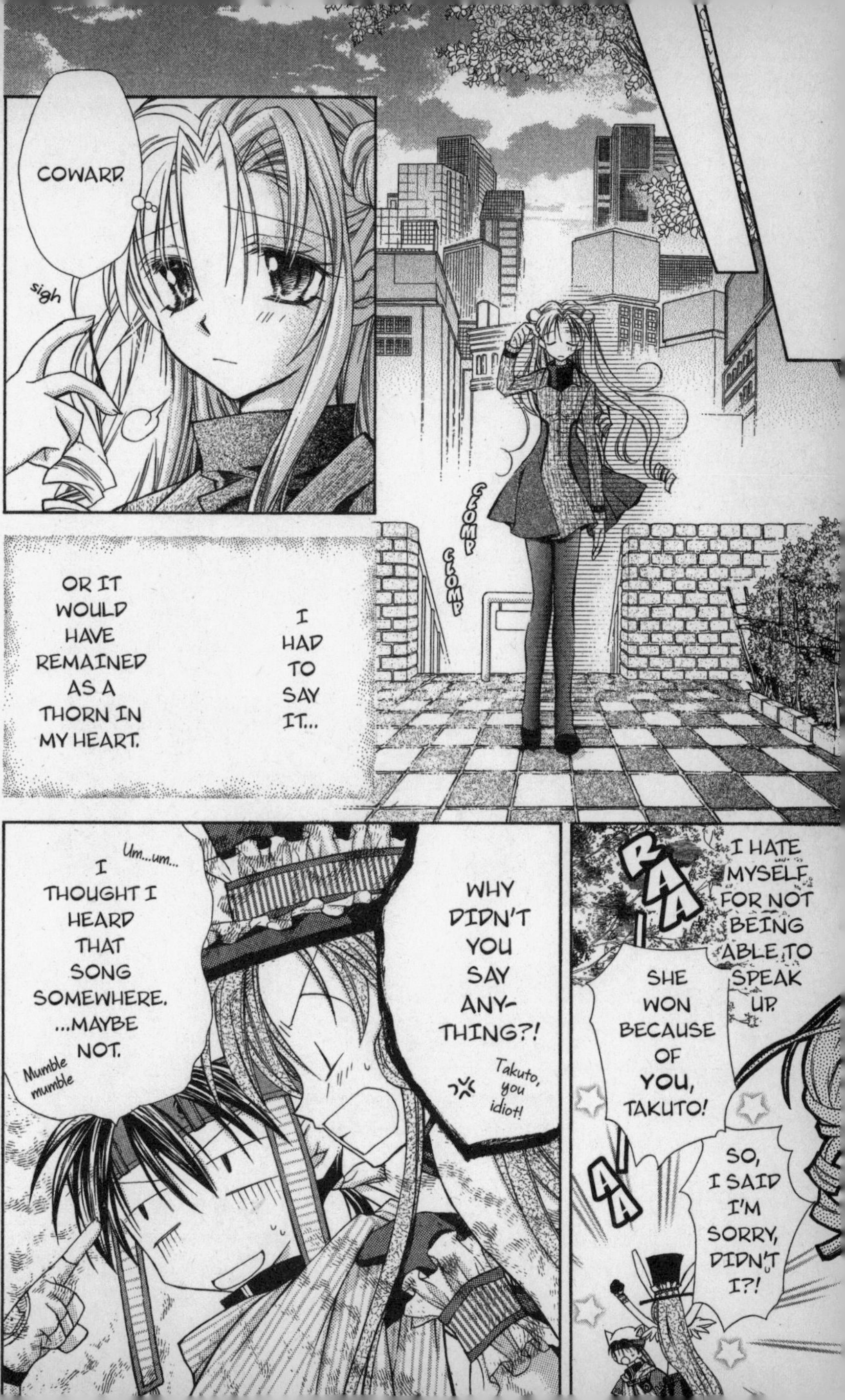
CLOMP
CLOMP
COWARD.
sigh
I HAD TO SAY IT...
OR IT WOULD HAVE REMAINED AS A THORN IN MY HEART.
RAA
I HATE MYSELF FOR NOT BEING ABLE TO SPEAK UP.
SHE WON BECAUSE OF YOU, TAKUTO!
AA
SO, I SAID I'M SORRY, DIDN'T I?!
WHY DIDN'T YOU SAY ANY-THING?!
Takuto, you idiot!
Um...um...
I THOUGHT I HEARD THAT SONG SOMEWHERE. ...MAYBE NOT.
Mumble mumble

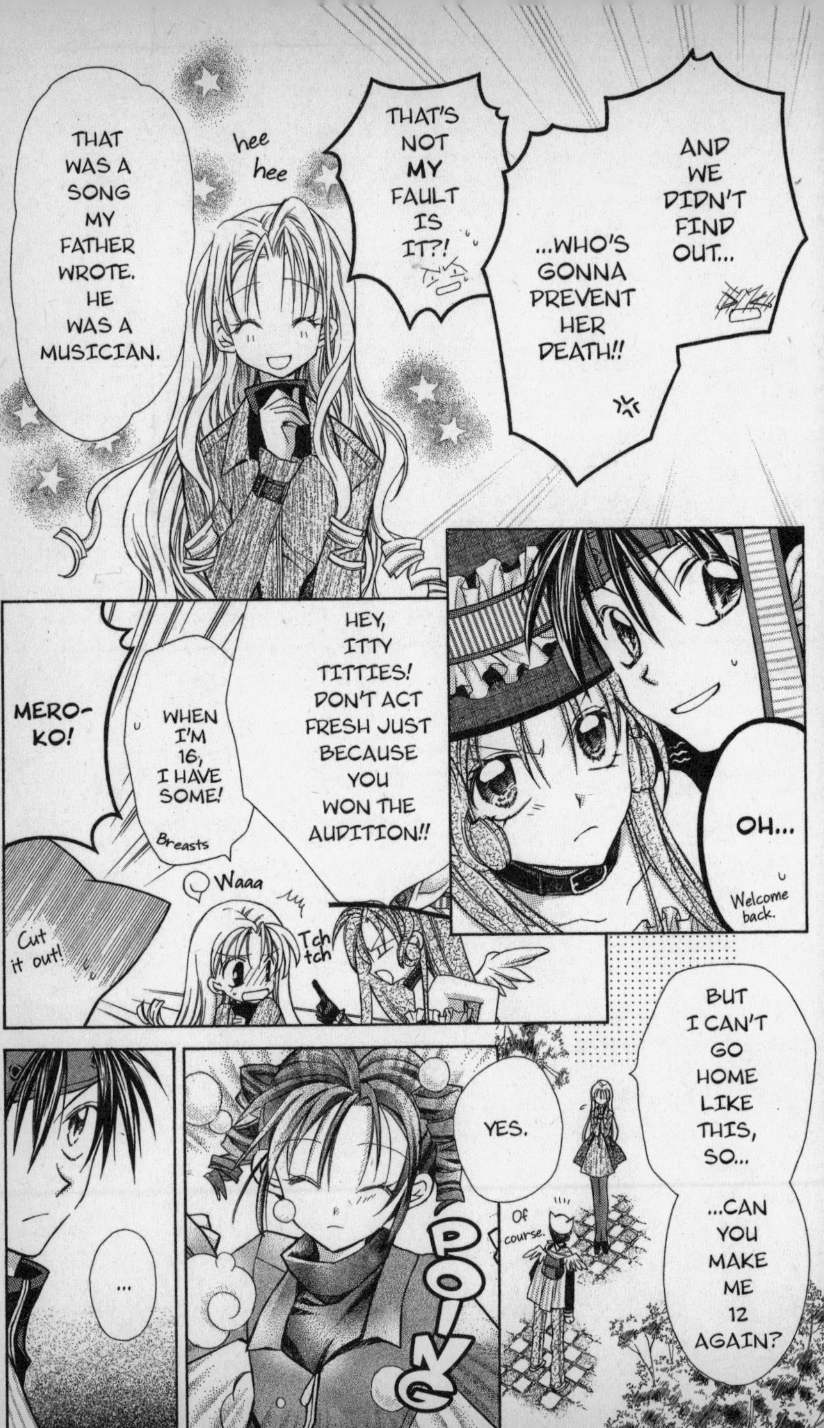
AND WE DIDN'T FIND OUT...
...WHO'S GONNA PREVENT HER DEATH!!
THAT'S NOT MY FAULT IS IT?!
hee hee
THAT WAS A SONG MY FATHER WROTE. HE WAS A MUSICIAN.
OH...
Welcome back.
HEY, ITTY TITTIES! DON'T ACT FRESH JUST BECAUSE YOU WON THE AUDITION!!
WHEN I'M 16, I HAVE SOME!
Breasts
MERO-KO!
Waaa
Tch tch
Cut it out!
BUT I CAN'T GO HOME LIKE THIS, SO...
...CAN YOU MAKE ME 12 AGAIN?
YES.
Of course.
POING
...

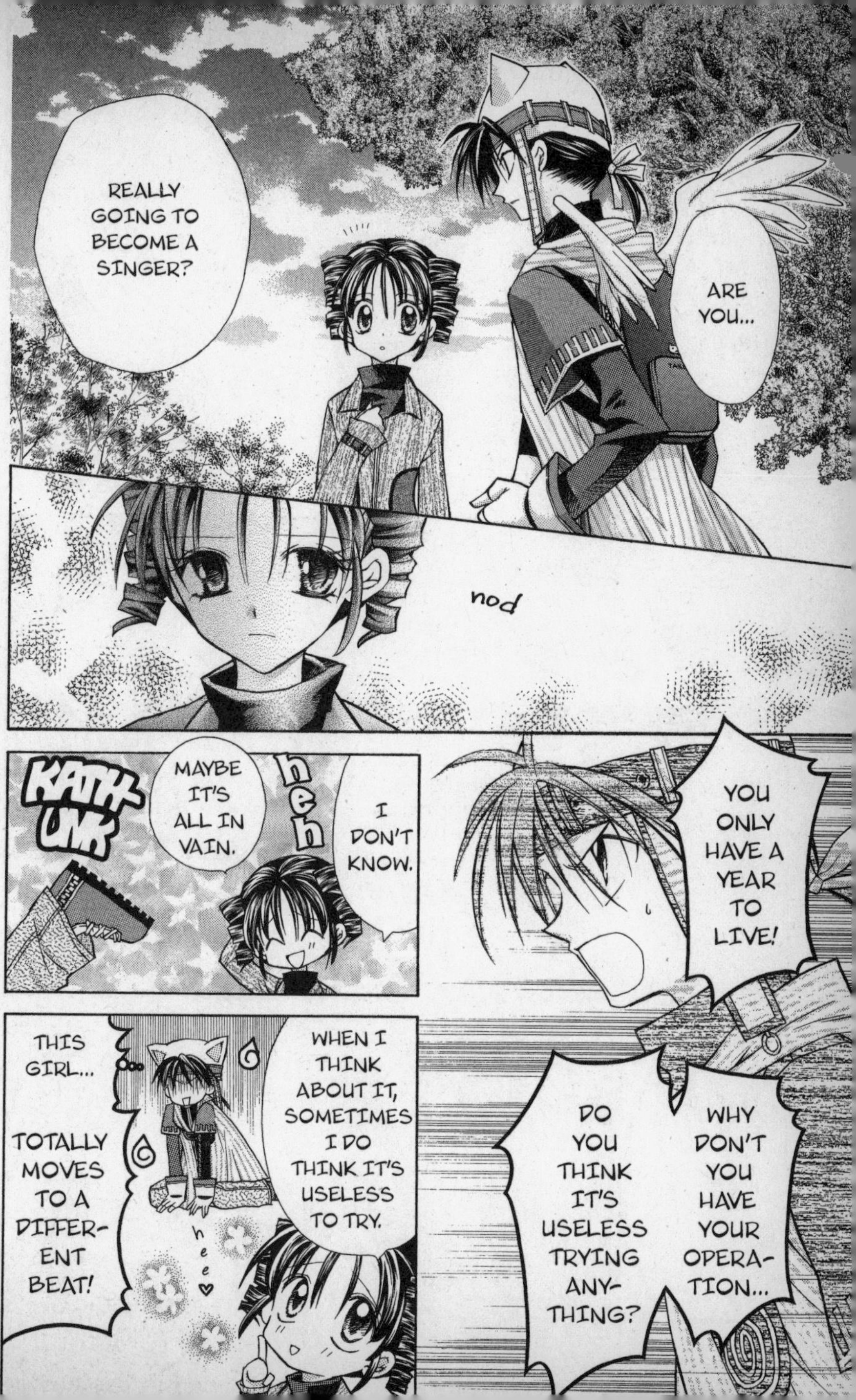
ARE YOU...
REALLY GOING TO BECOME A SINGER?
nod
YOU ONLY HAVE A YEAR TO LIVE!
I DON'T KNOW.
heh
MAYBE IT'S ALL IN VAIN.
KATHUNK
WHY DON'T YOU HAVE YOUR OPERATION...
DO YOU THINK IT'S USELESS TRYING ANYTHING?
WHEN I THINK ABOUT IT, SOMETIMES I DO THINK IT'S USELESS TO TRY.
hee
THIS GIRL...
TOTALLY MOVES TO A DIFFERENT BEAT!

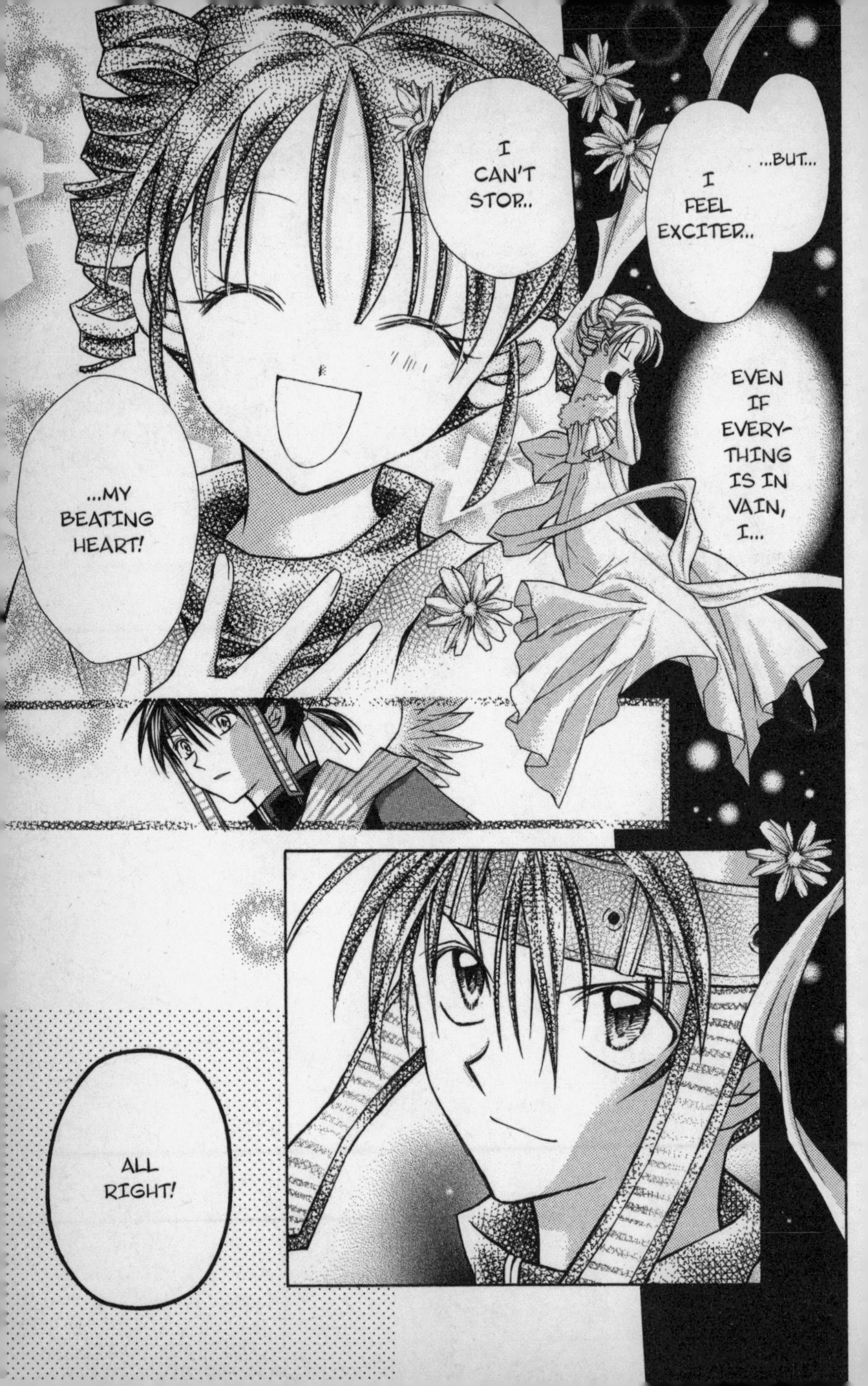
...BUT... I FEEL EXCITED...
I CAN'T STOP..
EVEN IF EVERY-THING IS IN VAIN, I...
...MY BEATING HEART!
ALL RIGHT!

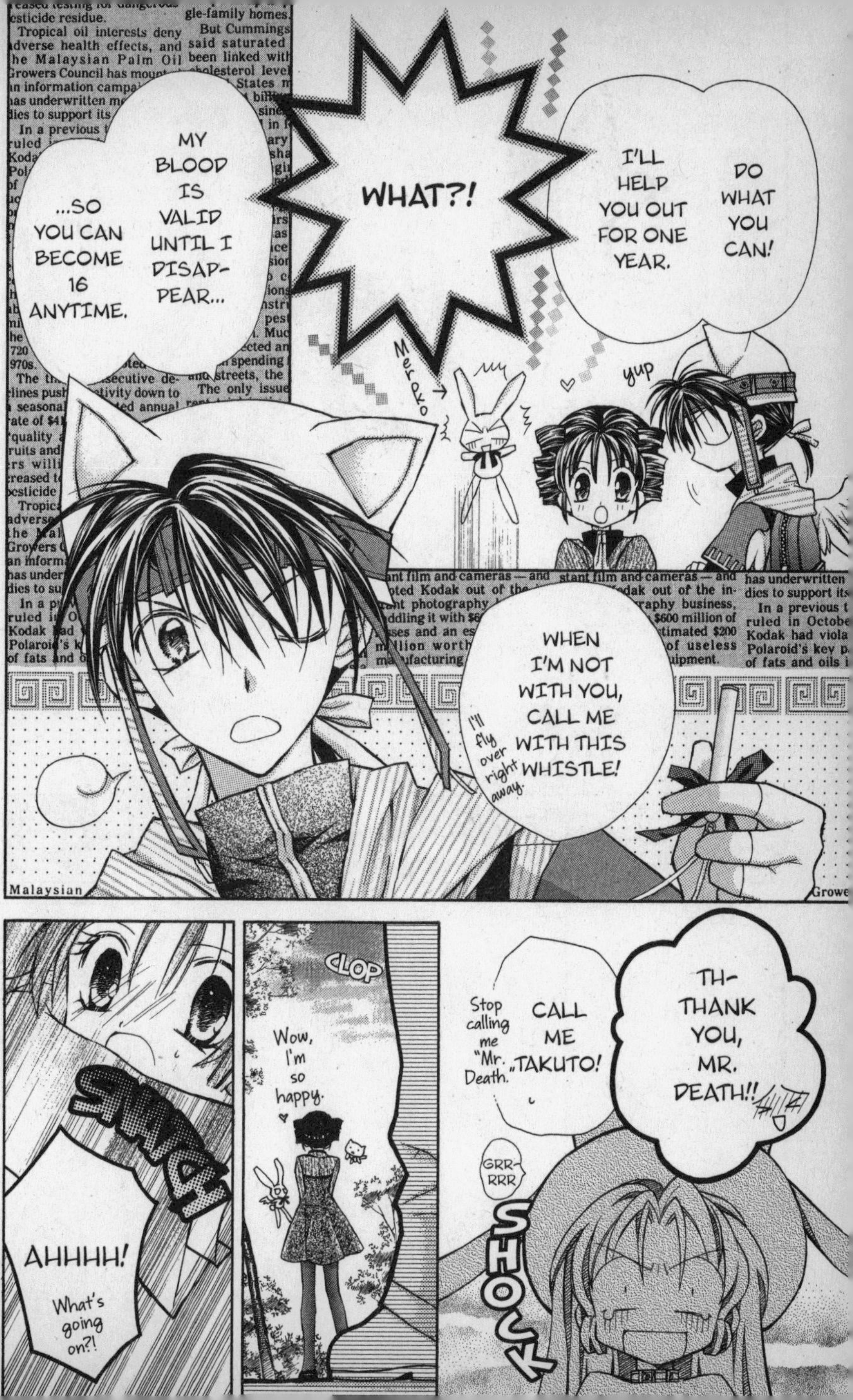
DO WHAT YOU CAN!
I'LL HELP YOU OUT FOR ONE YEAR.
yup
Meroko
WHAT?!
MY BLOOD IS VALID UNTIL I DISAP-PEAR...
...SO YOU CAN BECOME 16 ANYTIME.
WHEN I'M NOT WITH YOU, CALL ME WITH THIS WHISTLE!
I'll fly over right away.
TH-THANK YOU, MR. DEATH!!
CALL ME TAKUTO!
Stop calling me "Mr. Death."
GRR-RRR
SHOCK
CLOP
Wow, I'm so happy.
SMACK
AHHHH!
What's going on?!

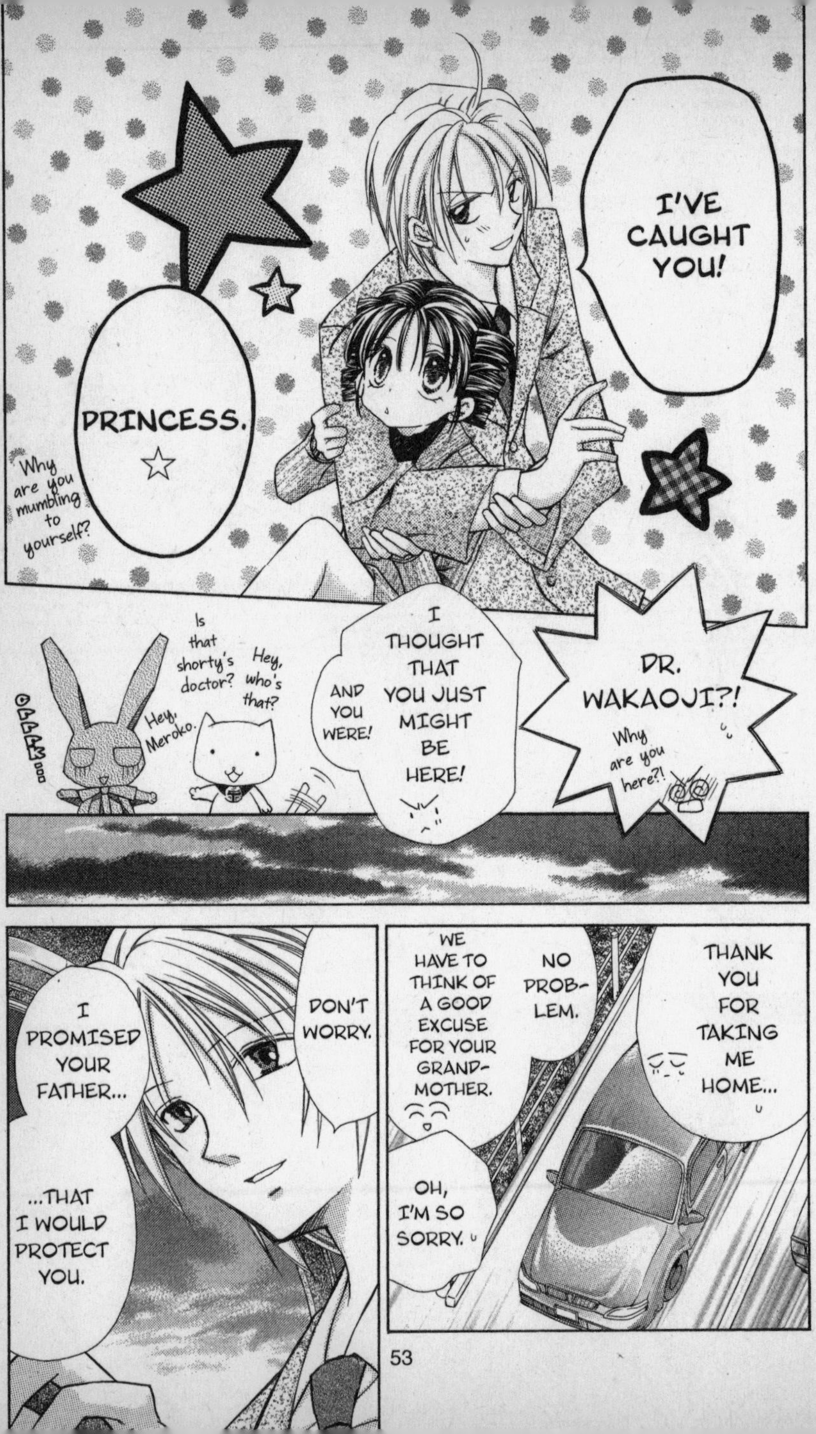
I'VE CAUGHT YOU!
PRINCESS.
Why are you mumbling to yourself?
DR. WAKAOJI?!
Why are you here?!
I THOUGHT THAT YOU JUST MIGHT BE HERE!
AND YOU WERE!
Hey, who's that?
Is that shorty's doctor?
Hey, Meroko.
THANK YOU FOR TAKING ME HOME...
NO PROBLEM.
WE HAVE TO THINK OF A GOOD EXCUSE FOR YOUR GRANDMOTHER.
OH, I'M SO SORRY.
DON'T WORRY.
I PROMISED YOUR FATHER...
...THAT I WOULD PROTECT YOU.

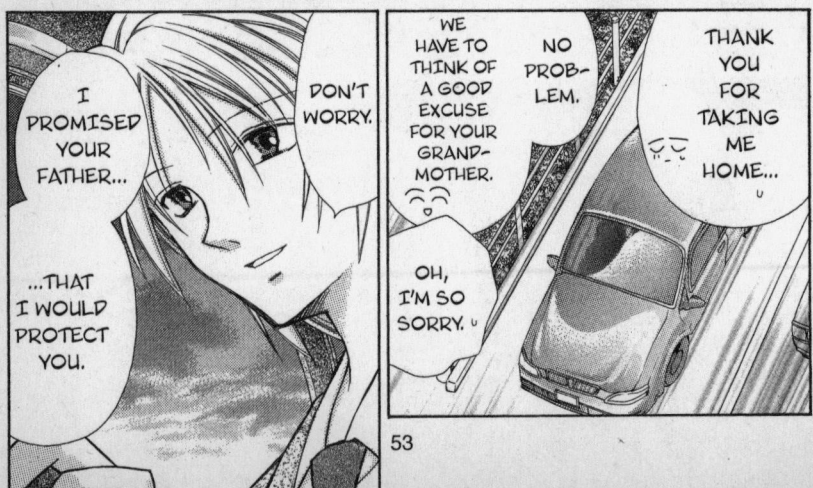

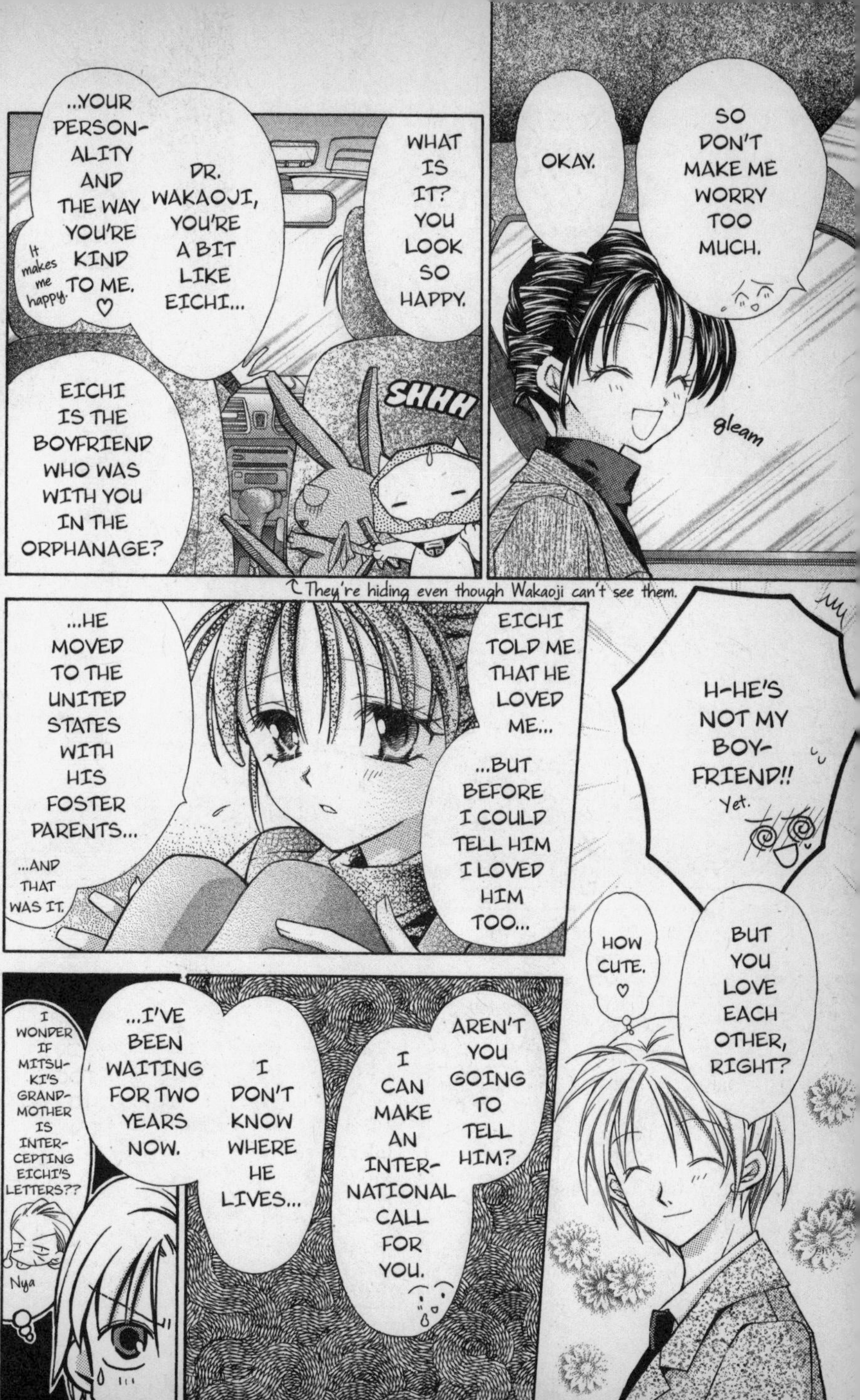
SO DON'T MAKE ME WORRY TOO MUCH.
OKAY.
gleam
WHAT IS IT? YOU LOOK SO HAPPY.
DR. WAKAOJI, YOU'RE A BIT LIKE EICHI...
...YOUR PERSONALITY AND THE WAY YOU'RE KIND TO ME. ♡
It makes me happy.
SHHH
EICHI IS THE BOYFRIEND WHO WAS WITH YOU IN THE ORPHANAGE?
They're hiding even though Wakaoji can't see them.
H-HE'S NOT MY BOY-FRIEND!!
Yet.
BUT YOU LOVE EACH OTHER, RIGHT?
HOW CUTE. ♡
EICHI TOLD ME THAT HE LOVED ME...
...BUT BEFORE I COULD TELL HIM I LOVED HIM TOO...
...HE MOVED TO THE UNITED STATES WITH HIS FOSTER PARENTS...
...AND THAT WAS IT.
AREN'T YOU GOING TO TELL HIM?
I CAN MAKE AN INTER-NATIONAL CALL FOR YOU.
I DON'T KNOW WHERE HE LIVES...
...I'VE BEEN WAITING FOR TWO YEARS NOW.
I WONDER IF MITSU-KI'S GRAND-MOTHER IS INTER-CEPTING EICHI'S LETTERS??
Nya

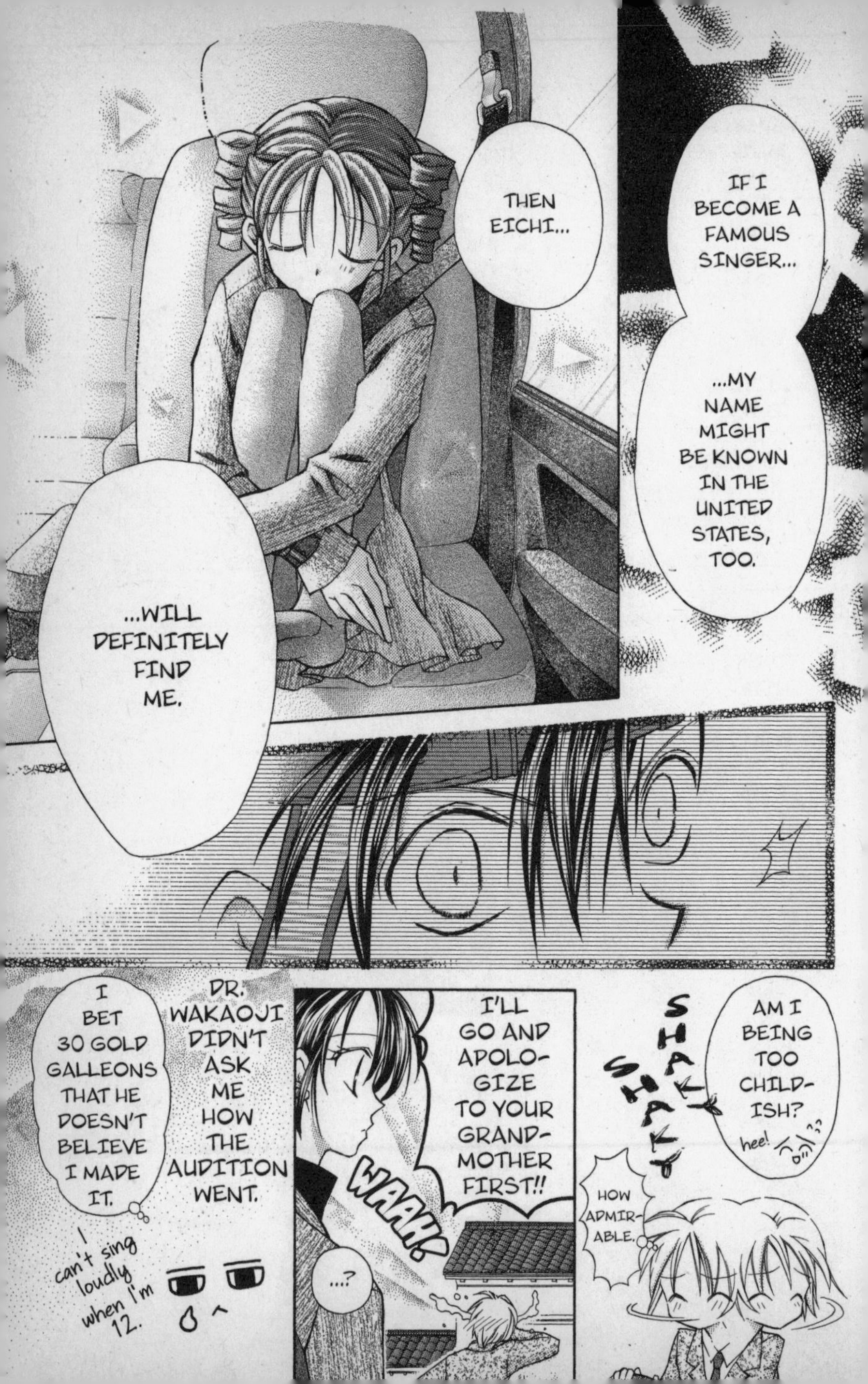
IF I BECOME A FAMOUS SINGER...
...MY NAME MIGHT BE KNOWN IN THE UNITED STATES, TOO.
THEN EICHI...
...WILL DEFINITELY FIND ME.
AM I BEING TOO CHILD-ISH?
hee!
SHAKY SHAKY
HOW ADMIR-ABLE.
I'LL GO AND APOLO-GIZE TO YOUR GRAND-MOTHER FIRST!!
WAAH!
...?
DR. WAKAOJI DIDN'T ASK ME HOW THE AUDITION WENT.
I BET 30 GOLD GALLEONS THAT HE DOESN'T BELIEVE I MADE IT.
I can't sing loudly when I'm 12.

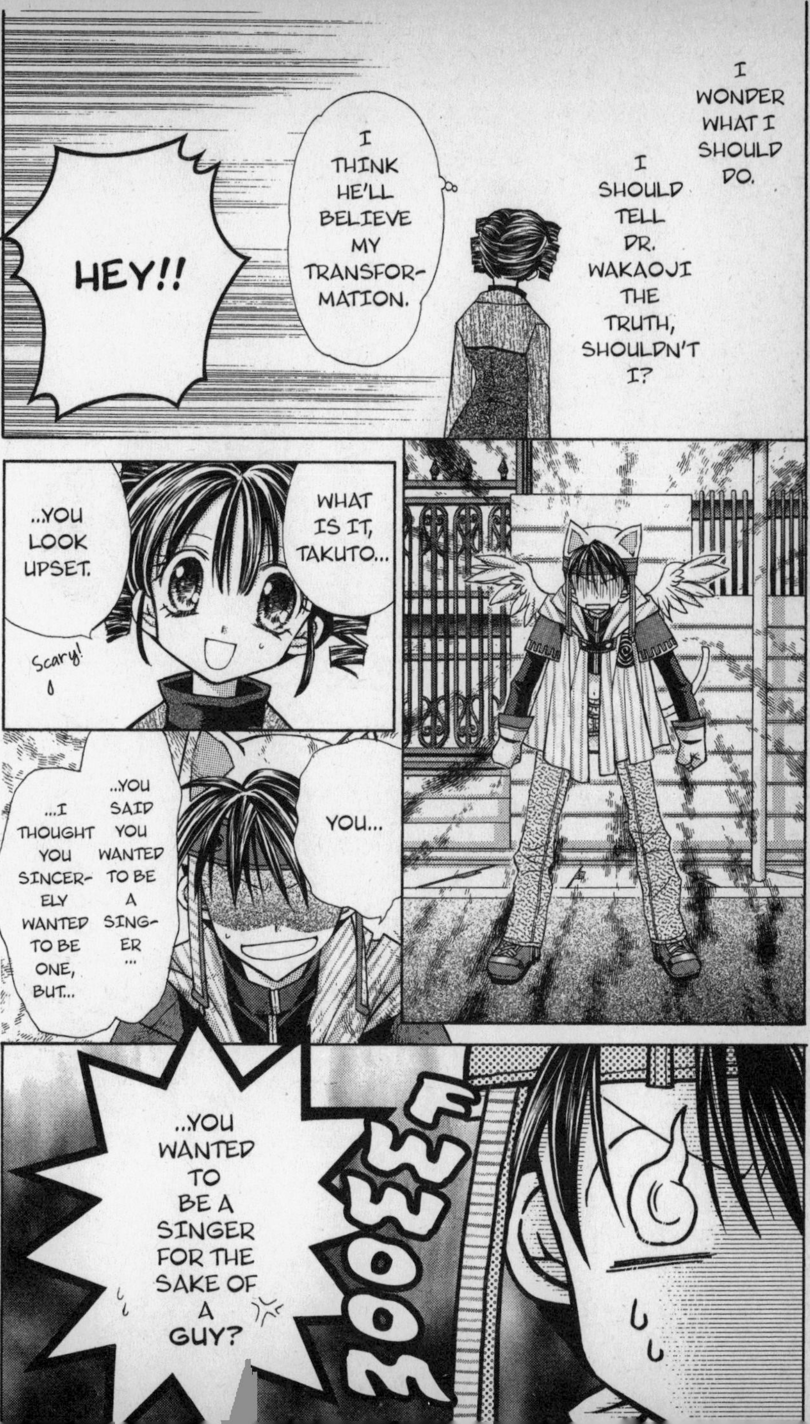
I WONDER WHAT I SHOULD DO.
I SHOULD TELL DR. WAKAOJI THE TRUTH, SHOULDN'T I?
I THINK HE'LL BELIEVE MY TRANSFORMATION.
HEY!!
WHAT IS IT, TAKUTO...
...YOU LOOK UPSET.
Scary!
YOU...
...YOU SAID YOU WANTED TO BE A SINGER...
...I THOUGHT YOU SINCERELY WANTED TO BE ONE, BUT...
FWOOM
...YOU WANTED TO BE A SINGER FOR THE SAKE OF A GUY?

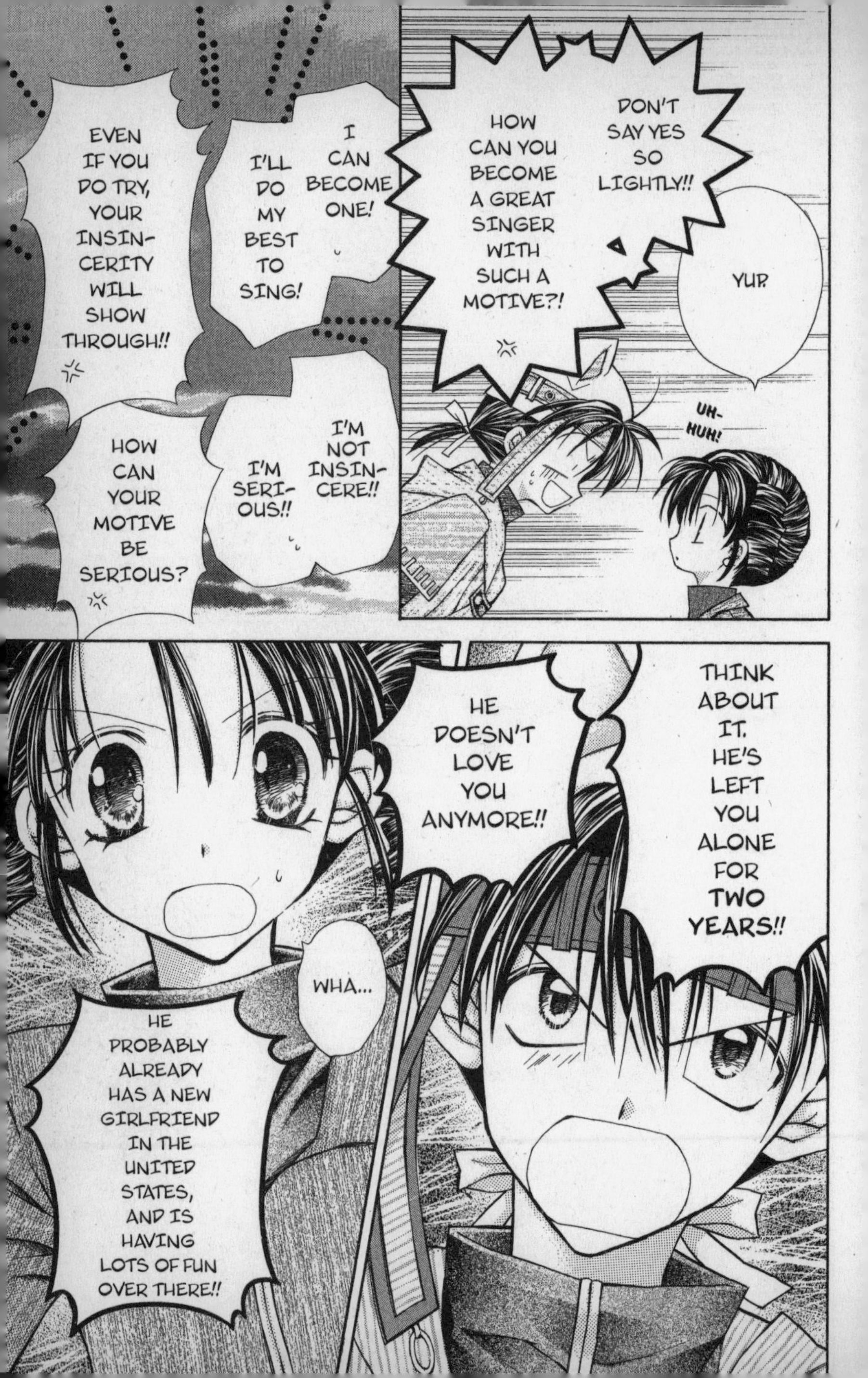
DON'T SAY YES SO LIGHTLY!!
HOW CAN YOU BECOME A GREAT SINGER WITH SUCH A MOTIVE?!
YUP.
UH-HUH!
I CAN BECOME ONE!
I'LL DO MY BEST TO SING!
EVEN IF YOU DO TRY, YOUR INSINCERITY WILL SHOW THROUGH!!
I'M NOT INSINCERE!!
I'M SERIOUS!!
HOW CAN YOUR MOTIVE BE SERIOUS?
THINK ABOUT IT. HE'S LEFT YOU ALONE FOR TWO YEARS!!
HE DOESN'T LOVE YOU ANYMORE!!
WHA...
HE PROBABLY ALREADY HAS A NEW GIRLFRIEND IN THE UNITED STATES, AND IS HAVING LOTS OF FUN OVER THERE!!

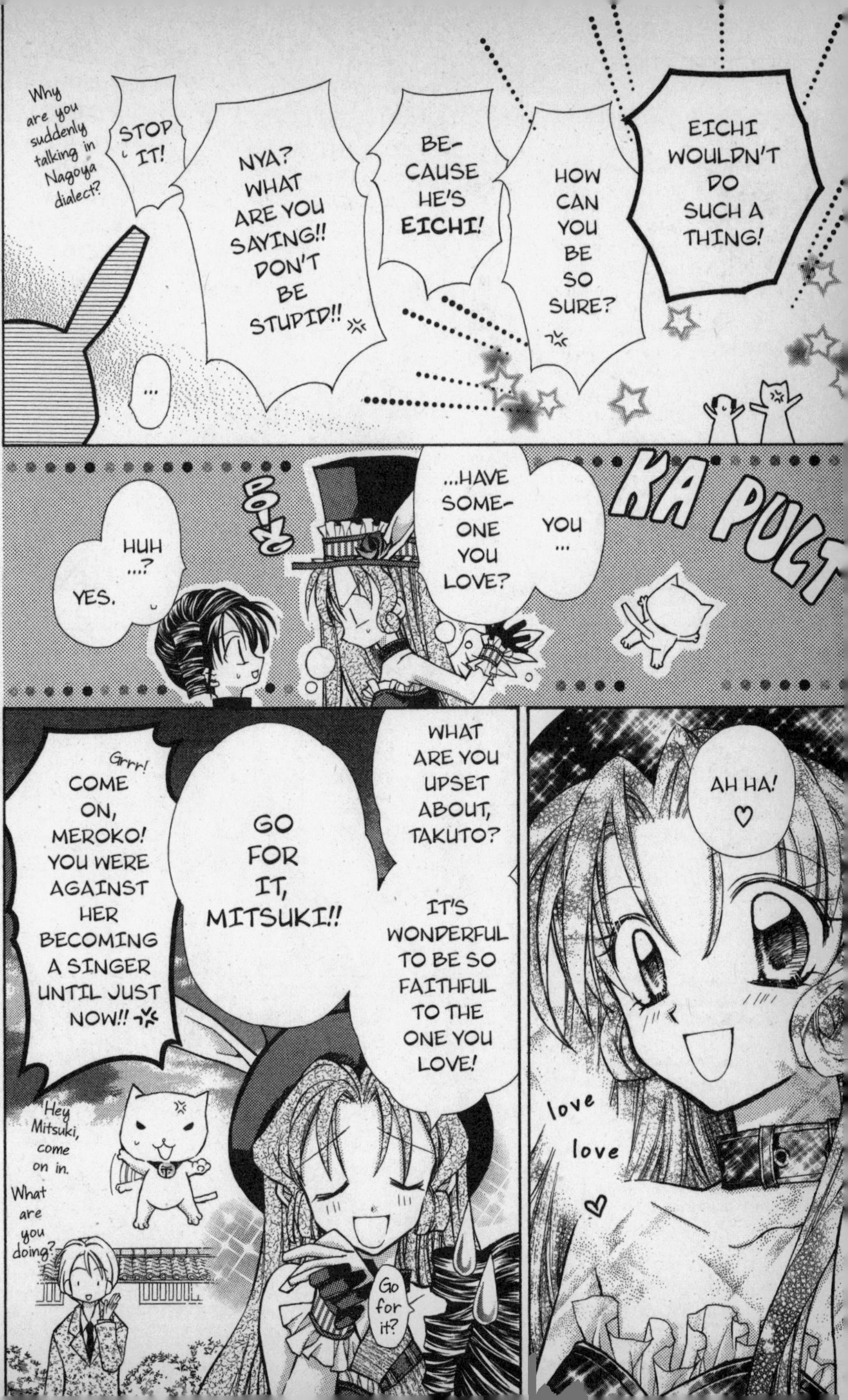
EICHI WOULDN'T DO SUCH A THING!
HOW CAN YOU BE SO SURE?
BE-CAUSE HE'S EICHI!
NYA? WHAT ARE YOU SAYING!! DON'T BE STUPID!!
STOP IT!
Why are you suddenly talking in Nagoya dialect?
...
KA PULT
YOU ...
...HAVE SOME-ONE YOU LOVE?
POING
HUH ...? YES.
AH HA! ♡
love love ♡
WHAT ARE YOU UPSET ABOUT, TAKUTO?
IT'S WONDERFUL TO BE SO FAITHFUL TO THE ONE YOU LOVE!
GO FOR IT, MITSUKI!!
Grrr!
COME ON, MEROKO! YOU WERE AGAINST HER BECOMING A SINGER UNTIL JUST NOW!!
Go for it?
Hey Mitsuki, come on in.
What are you doing?

ABOUT THE CHARACTERS

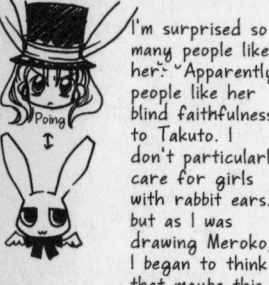

● Meroko Yui
↑Meroko's her name.

Poing

I'm surprised so many people like her. Apparently, people like her blind faithfulness to Takuto. I don't particularly care for girls with rabbit ears... but as I was drawing Meroko, I began to think that maybe this is okay as well.

In the beginning, Meroko looked like a bunny girl. (The reason I put bunny ears on her is so that you could tell which character is which, just by looking at their silhouette.) I also wanted them to look a little like stuffed toys. Meroko changes to a rabbit the way Takuto changes to a cat, and there is a reason why they do this. (I will explain this later in the manga.)

I'm not sure whether I should reveal this, but I received the request for drawing illustrations for the free stationary set that came with the magazine before I started working on the first episode storyboards. For the free gifts, it's better to have non-human characters as mascots, because they're cute. (I get more variations that way, too.) That's why I thought of them. Hehe.

(I could have used those characters just for that letter set, but a series in Ribon has lots of furoku, and I thought the readers will be more happy if the characters were those that appear in the manga.) But I...didn't want something that was too cute, so I made them a little uncool → and with sharp eyes.

What?

Now they've become stuffed toy presents, and cell phone straps, and are all over the place.☆

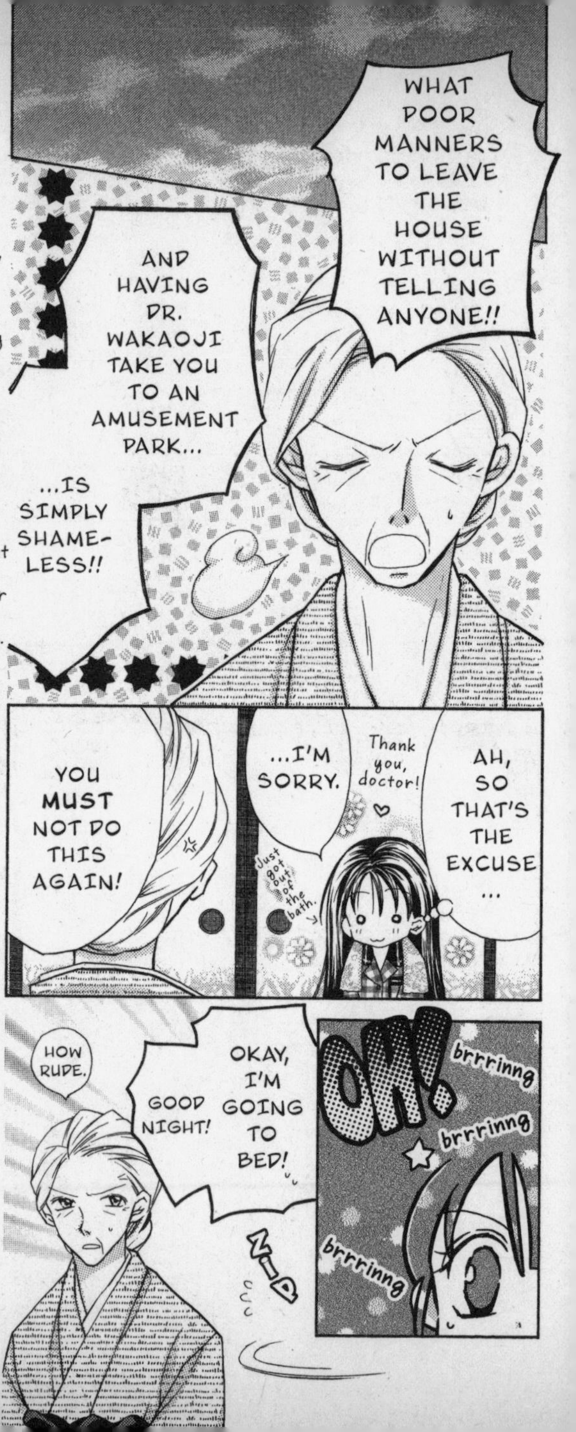
WHAT POOR MANNERS TO LEAVE THE HOUSE WITHOUT TELLING ANYONE!!
AND HAVING DR. WAKAOJI TAKE YOU TO AN AMUSEMENT PARK...
...IS SIMPLY SHAMELESS!!
AH, SO THAT'S THE EXCUSE ...
Thank you, doctor!
...I'M SORRY.
Just got out of the bath.
YOU MUST NOT DO THIS AGAIN!
OH!
brrrinng
brrrinng
brrrinng
OKAY, I'M GOING TO BED!
GOOD NIGHT!
HOW RUDE.
ZIP

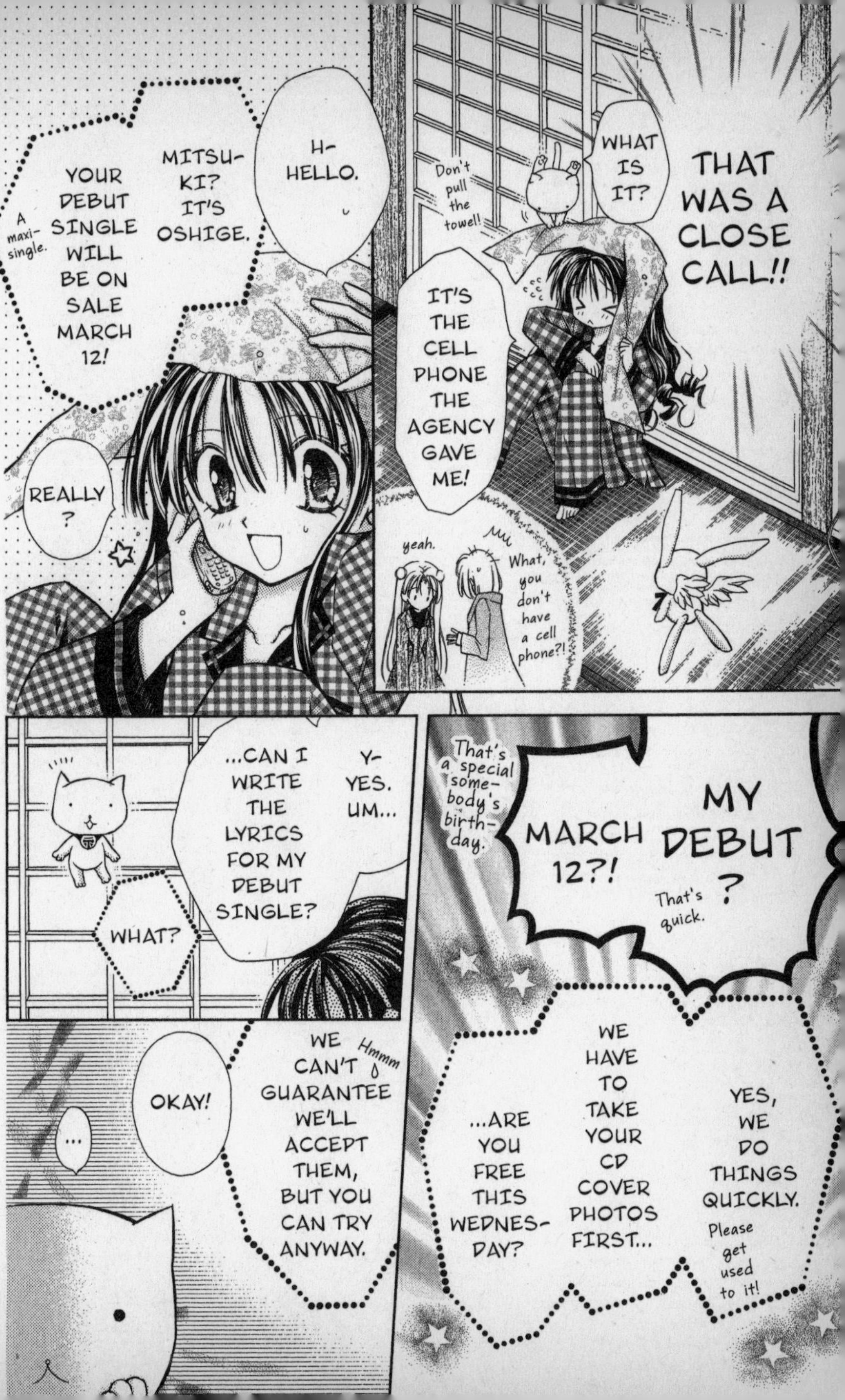
THAT WAS A CLOSE CALL!!
WHAT IS IT?
Don't pull the towel!
IT'S THE CELL PHONE THE AGENCY GAVE ME!
What, you don't have a cell phone?!
yeah.
H-HELLO.
MITSUKI? IT'S OSHIGE.
YOUR DEBUT SINGLE WILL BE ON SALE MARCH 12!
A maxi-single.
REALLY?
MY DEBUT?
That's quick.
MARCH 12?!
That's a special somebody's birthday.
Y-YES. UM...
...CAN I WRITE THE LYRICS FOR MY DEBUT SINGLE?
WHAT?
YES, WE DO THINGS QUICKLY.
Please get used to it!
WE HAVE TO TAKE YOUR CD COVER PHOTOS FIRST...
...ARE YOU FREE THIS WEDNESDAY?
WE CAN'T GUARANTEE WE'LL ACCEPT THEM, BUT YOU CAN TRY ANYWAY.
Hmmm
OKAY!
...

About the Characters

(Spoiler Alert!)

● Eichi Sakurai

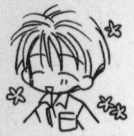

He is a mysterious character, even to me (I'm half serious.) He has an aura, and the air surrounding him is very tender. He looks great in white shirts and with white doves.

● Dr. Wakaoji

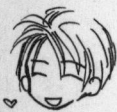

His image is that of Eichi as an adult. They have the same hairstyle!! I was going to write more about him, but because Mitsuki left home earlier than expected, I couldn't. He'll probably appear sometime later.

● Fuzuki Koyama

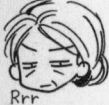

Rrr

Grandma. It was fun drawing her (although it was difficult).

● Madoka Wakamatsu & Gutchan

GU

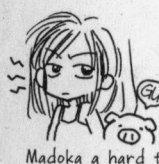

Madoka secretly has lots of fans. (I get scolded by her fans about giving Madoka a hard time. Sorry.) But she's that type of character, so please bear with it. Gutchan...Gutchan is very popular! He loves Madoka so much. I love the way Gutchan is. Gutchan was named from pig's "G" (since there's already a P-chan).

For people only reading the tankobon, here is a spoiler.

The Shinigami pair that appeared in the last episode is:

the boy → Izumi Lio

the ghost → Jonathan

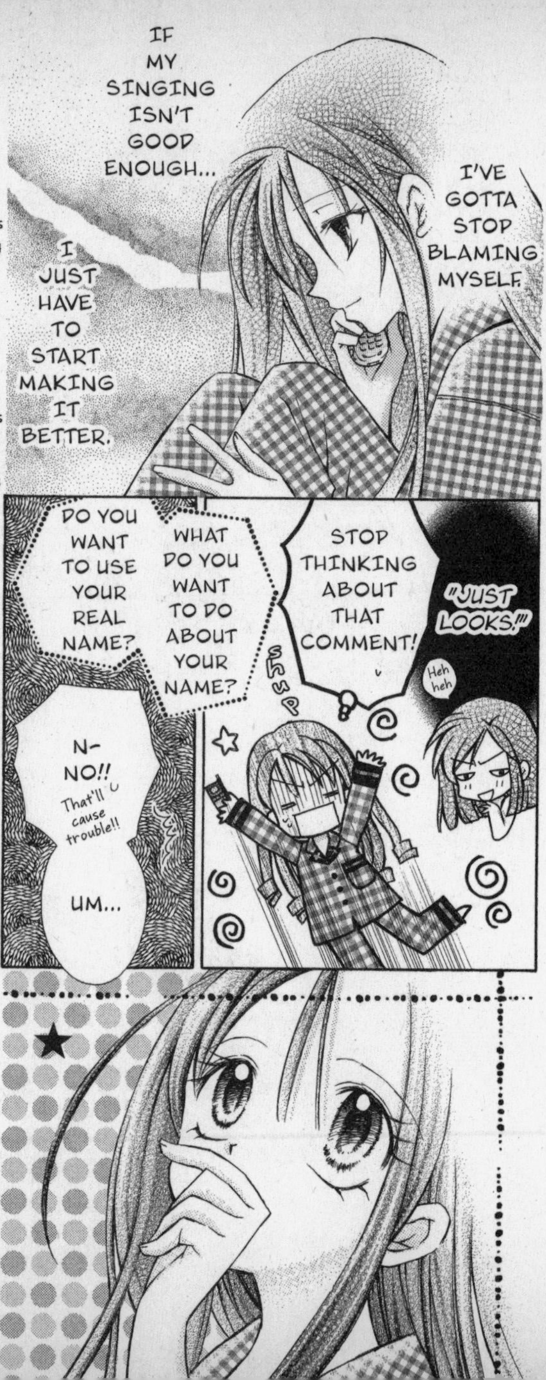
IF MY SINGING ISN'T GOOD ENOUGH...
I'VE GOTTA STOP BLAMING MYSELF.
I JUST HAVE TO START MAKING IT BETTER.
STOP THINKING ABOUT THAT COMMENT!
"JUST LOOKS!"
Heh heh
shup
WHAT DO YOU WANT TO DO ABOUT YOUR NAME?
DO YOU WANT TO USE YOUR REAL NAME?
N-NO!!
That'll cause trouble!!
UM...

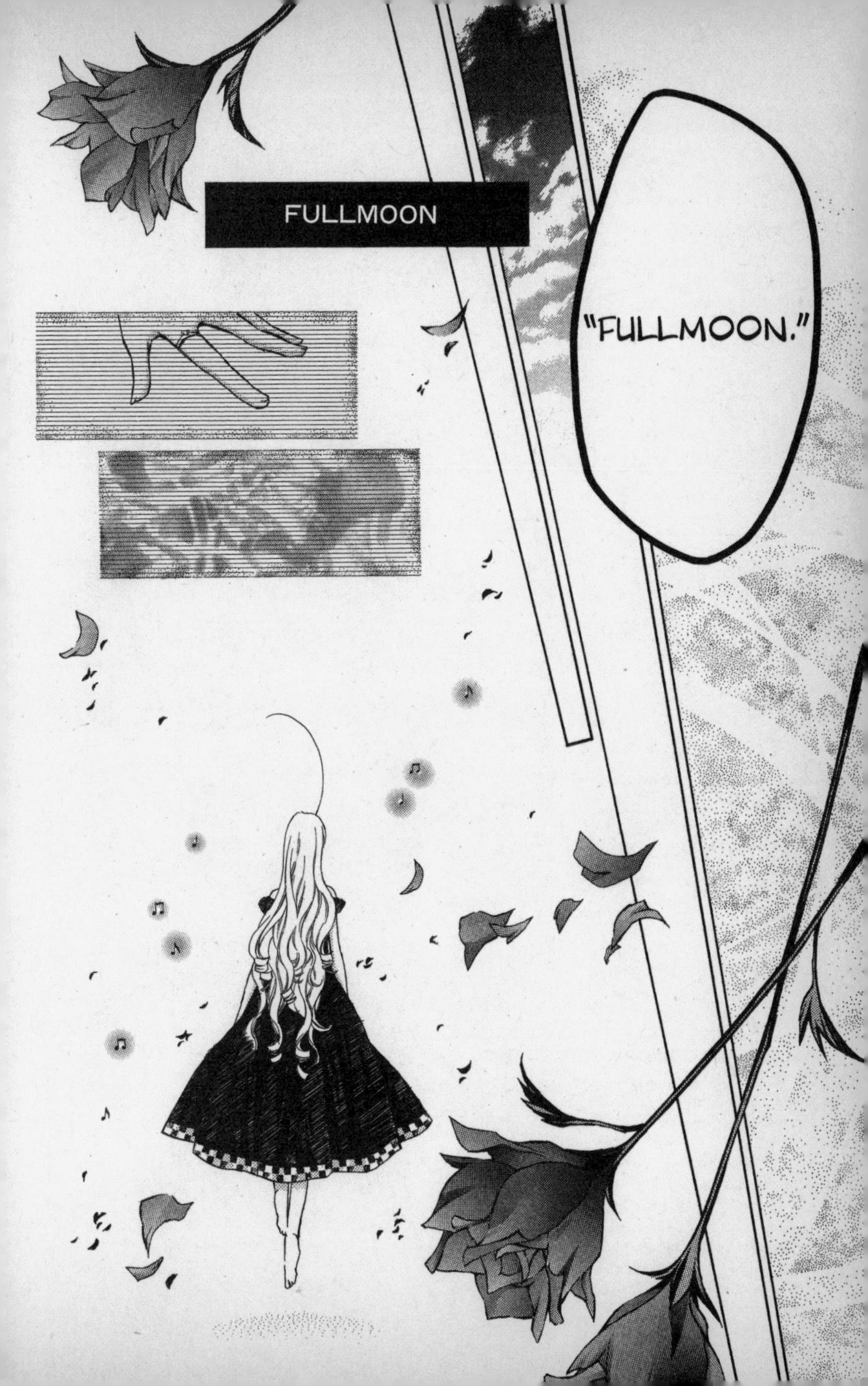
"FULLMOON."
FULLMOON

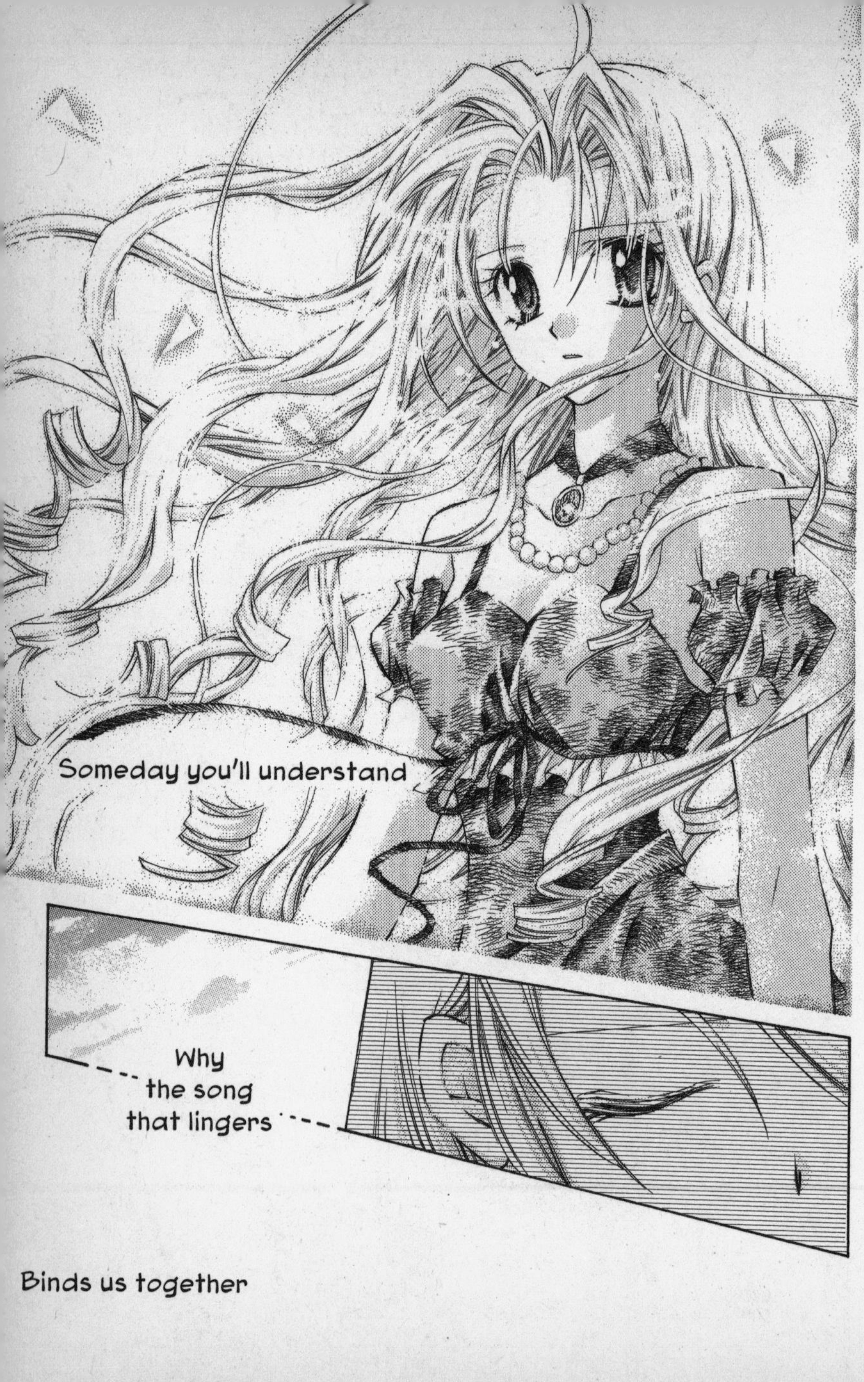
Someday you'll understand
Why
the song
that lingers
Binds us together

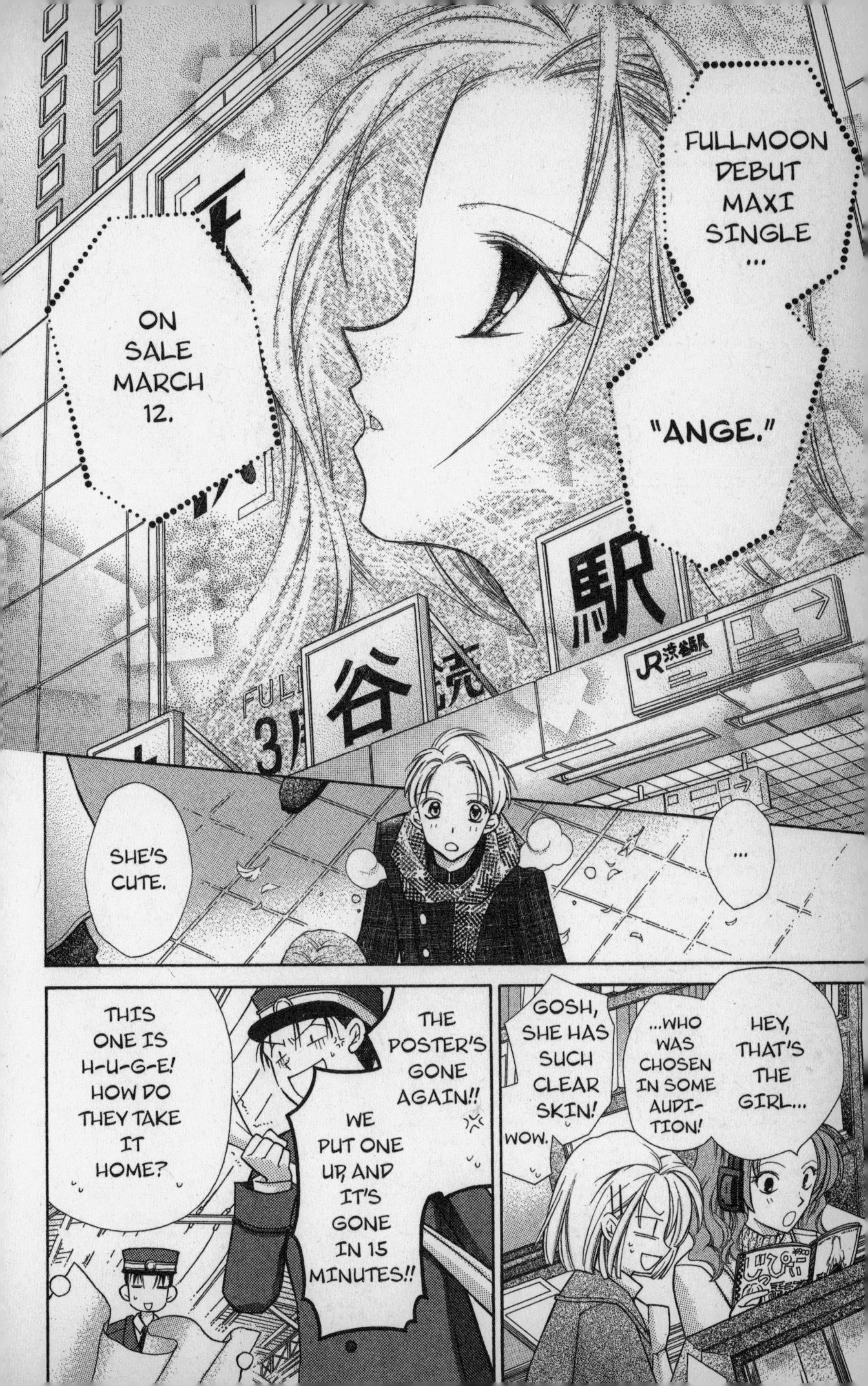
FULLMOON DEBUT MAXI SINGLE ...
"ANGE."
ON SALE MARCH 12.
駅
谷
JR渋谷駅
...
SHE'S CUTE.
HEY, THAT'S THE GIRL...
...WHO WAS CHOSEN IN SOME AUDI-TION!
GOSH, SHE HAS SUCH CLEAR SKIN!
WOW.
THE POSTER'S GONE AGAIN!!
WE PUT ONE UP, AND IT'S GONE IN 15 MINUTES!!
THIS ONE IS H-U-G-E! HOW DO THEY TAKE IT HOME?

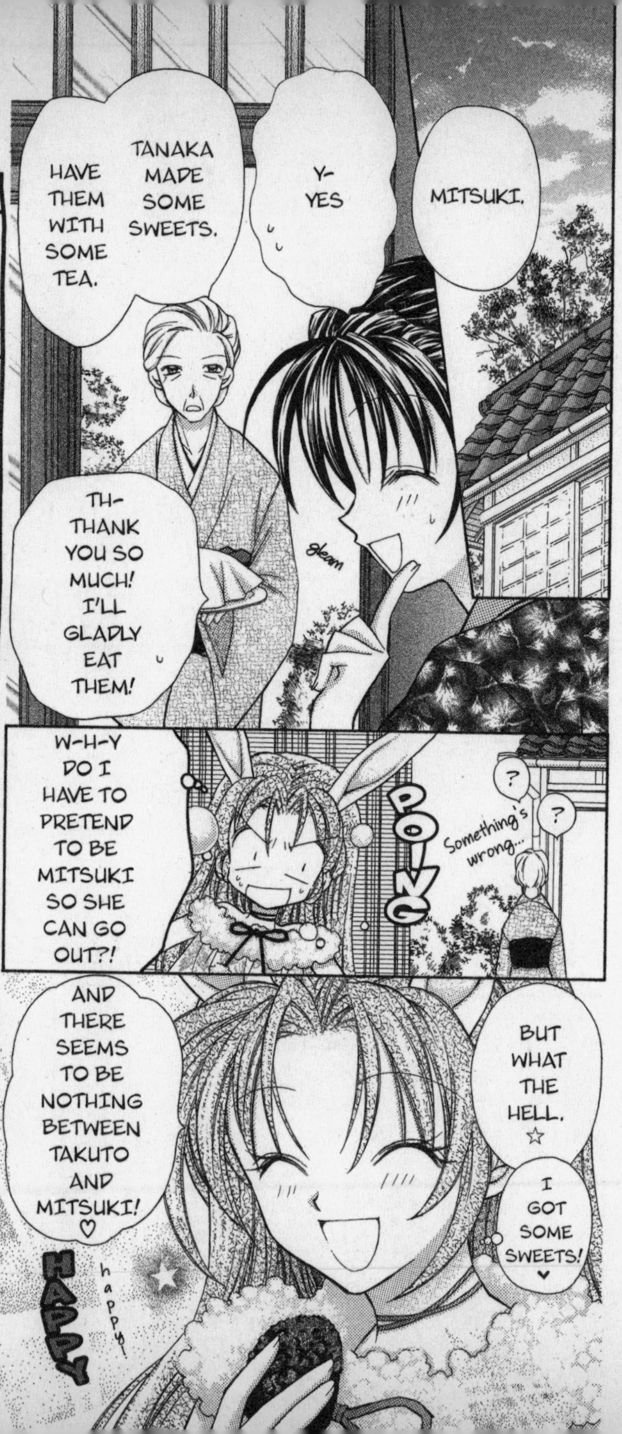
MITSUKI.
Y- YES
TANAKA MADE SOME SWEETS.
HAVE THEM WITH SOME TEA.
TH- THANK YOU SO MUCH! I'LL GLADLY EAT THEM!
gleam
?
?
Something's wrong...
POING
W-H-Y DO I HAVE TO PRETEND TO BE MITSUKI SO SHE CAN GO OUT?!
BUT WHAT THE HELL. ☆
I GOT SOME SWEETS! ♥
AND THERE SEEMS TO BE NOTHING BETWEEN TAKUTO AND MITSUKI! ♡
HAPPY
happy!

Arina Tanemura's Penchi de Shakin

Episode 47 ☆

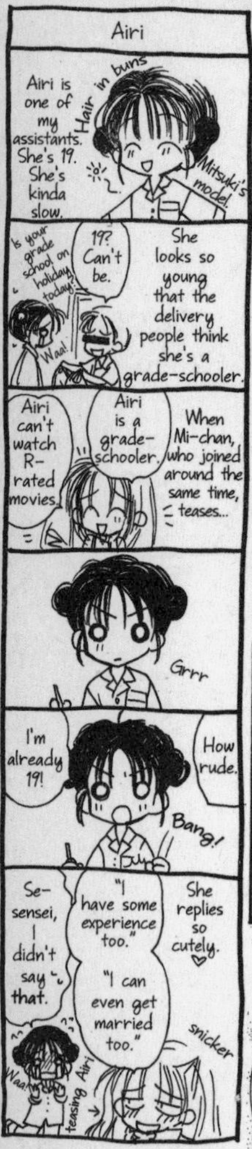
Airi
Airi is one of my assistants. She's 19. She's kinda slow.
Hair in buns
Mitsuki's model.
She looks so young that the delivery people think she's a grade-schooler.
19? Can't be.
Is your grade school on holiday today?
Waa!
When Mi-chan, who joined around the same time, teases...
Airi is a grade-schooler.
Airi can't watch R-rated movies.
Grrr
How rude.
I'm already 19!
Bang!
She replies so cutely. ♥
"I have some experience too."
"I can even get married too."
Se-sensei, I didn't say that.
snicker
teasing Airi
Waaa

Airi loves "Toro" from the Playstation game "Dokodemo Issho," so she always puts "nya" at the end of her sentences. I love Airi.♥ She's already 19, but only looks 13.♥

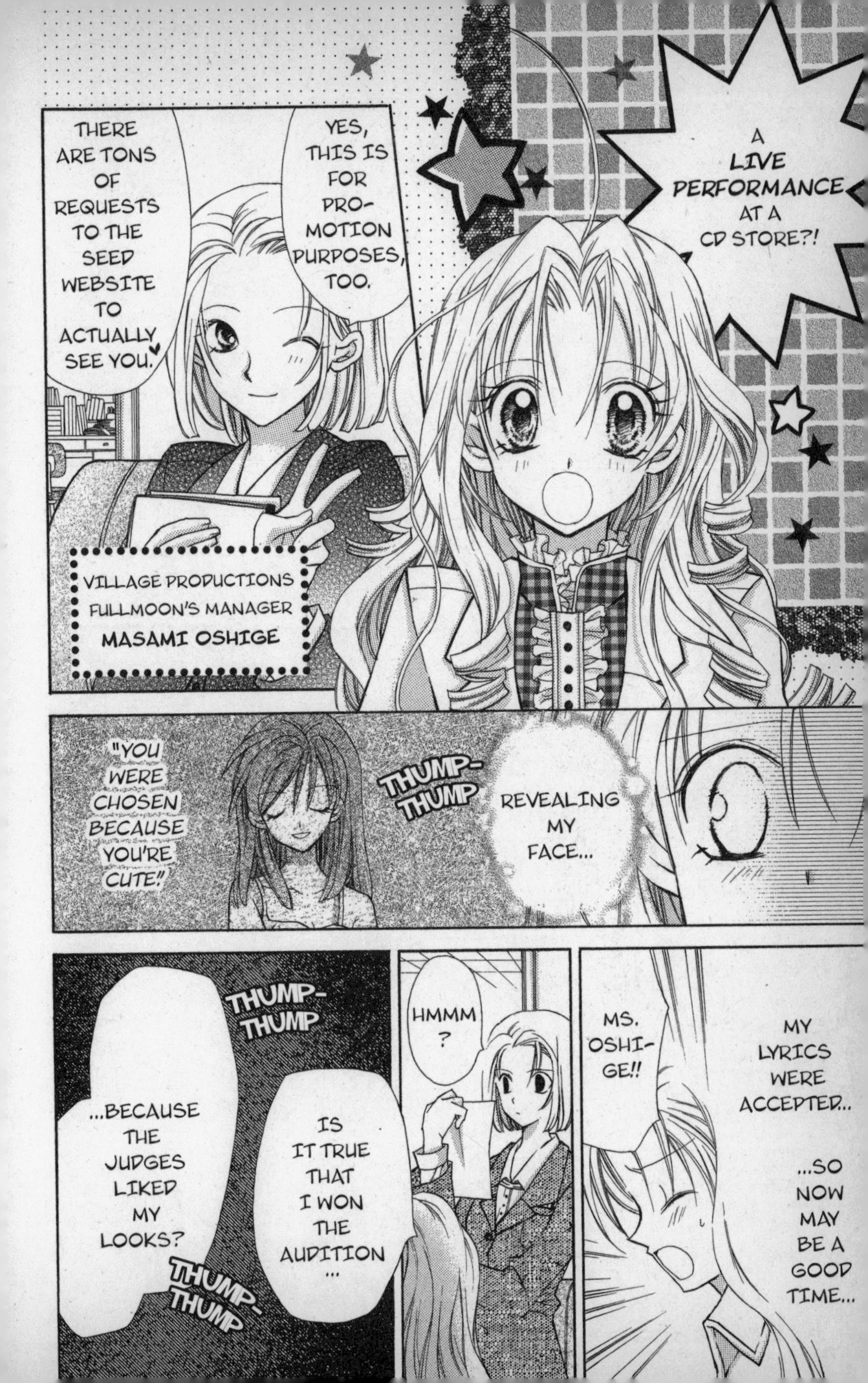
A **LIVE PERFORMANCE** AT A CD STORE?!
YES, THIS IS FOR PRO-MOTION PURPOSES, TOO.
THERE ARE TONS OF REQUESTS TO THE SEED WEBSITE TO ACTUALLY SEE YOU.♥
VILLAGE PRODUCTIONS FULLMOON'S MANAGER **MASAMI OSHIGE**
REVEALING MY FACE...
THUMP-THUMP
"YOU WERE CHOSEN BECAUSE YOU'RE CUTE!"
MY LYRICS WERE ACCEPTED...
MS. OSHI-GE!!
...SO NOW MAY BE A GOOD TIME...
HMMM?
THUMP-THUMP
IS IT TRUE THAT I WON THE AUDITION...
...BECAUSE THE JUDGES LIKED MY LOOKS?
THUMP-THUMP

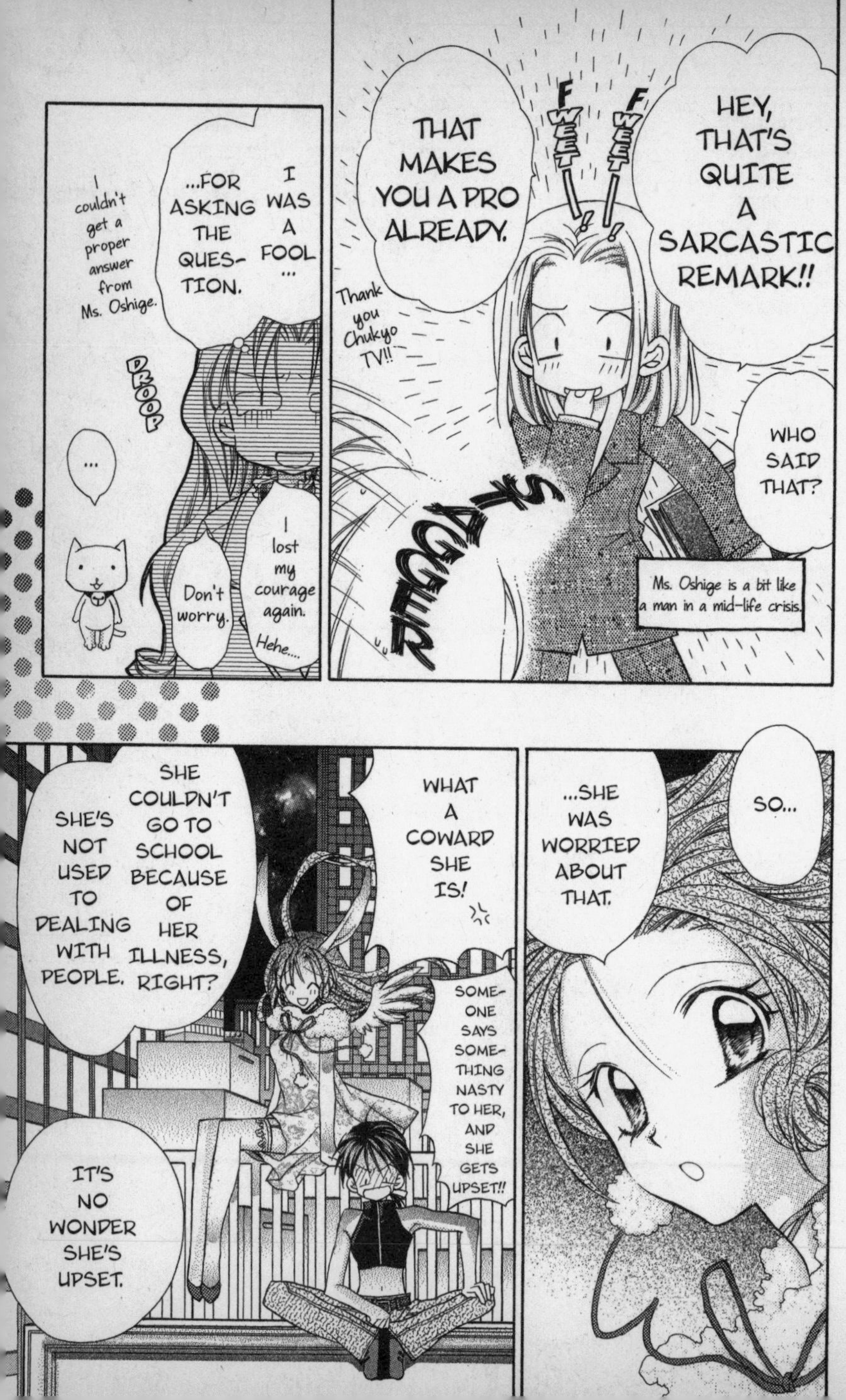
HEY, THAT'S QUITE A SARCASTIC REMARK!!
FWEET
FWEET
THAT MAKES YOU A PRO ALREADY.
Thank you Chukyo TV!!
WHO SAID THAT?
STAGGER
Ms. Oshige is a bit like a man in a mid-life crisis.
I WAS A FOOL ...
...FOR ASKING THE QUES-TION.
I couldn't get a proper answer from Ms. Oshige.
DROOP
...
I lost my courage again.
Hehe....
Don't worry.
SO...
...SHE WAS WORRIED ABOUT THAT.
WHAT A COWARD SHE IS!
SHE COULDN'T GO TO SCHOOL BECAUSE OF HER ILLNESS, RIGHT?
SHE'S NOT USED TO DEALING WITH PEOPLE.
SOME-ONE SAYS SOME-THING NASTY TO HER, AND SHE GETS UPSET!!
IT'S NO WONDER SHE'S UPSET.

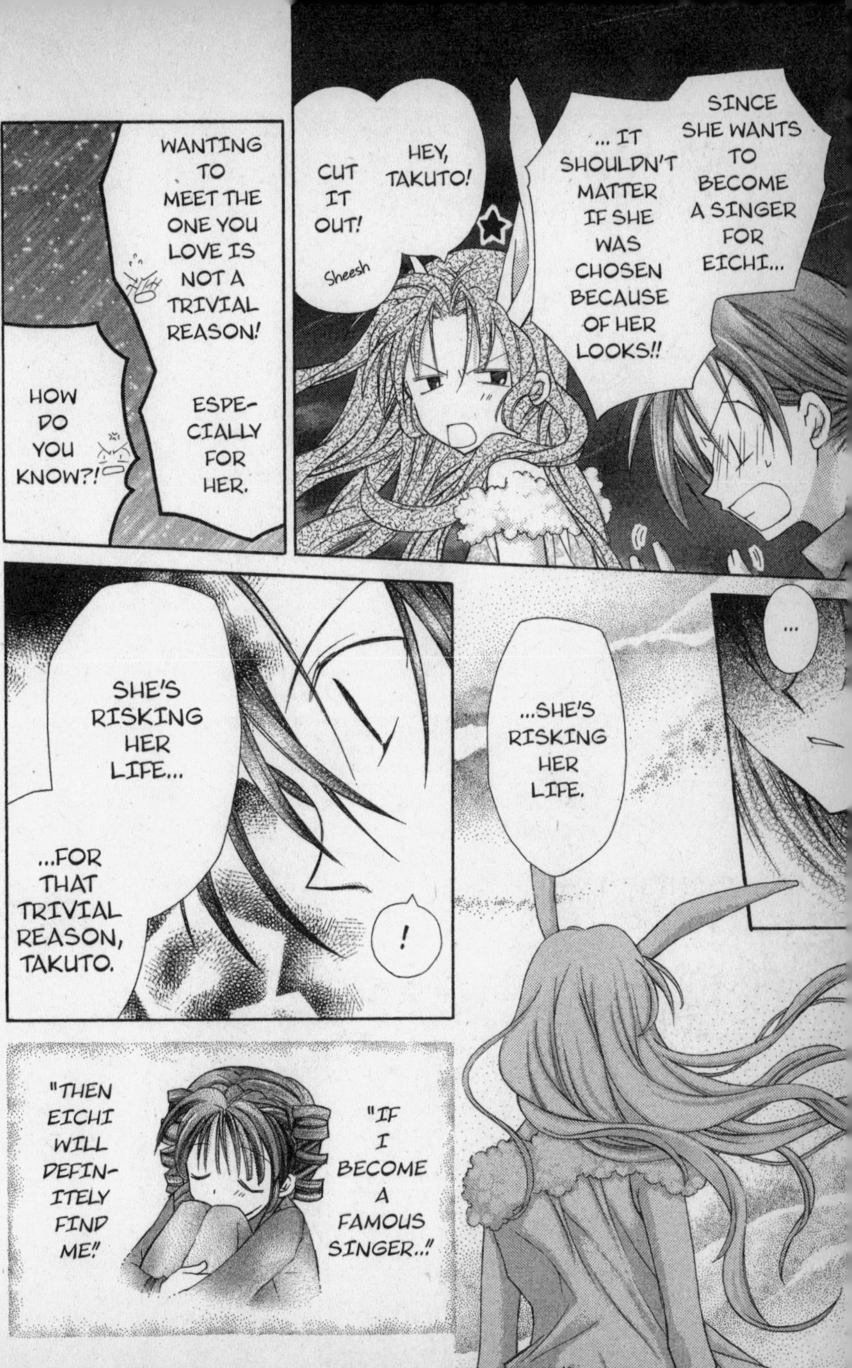
SINCE SHE WANTS TO BECOME A SINGER FOR EICHI...
...IT SHOULDN'T MATTER IF SHE WAS CHOSEN BECAUSE OF HER LOOKS!!
HEY, TAKUTO!
CUT IT OUT!
Sheesh
WANTING TO MEET THE ONE YOU LOVE IS NOT A TRIVIAL REASON!
ESPE-CIALLY FOR HER.
HOW DO YOU KNOW?!
...
...SHE'S RISKING HER LIFE.
SHE'S RISKING HER LIFE...
...FOR THAT TRIVIAL REASON, TAKUTO.
!
"IF I BECOME A FAMOUS SINGER..."
"THEN EICHI WILL DEFIN-ITELY FIND ME!"

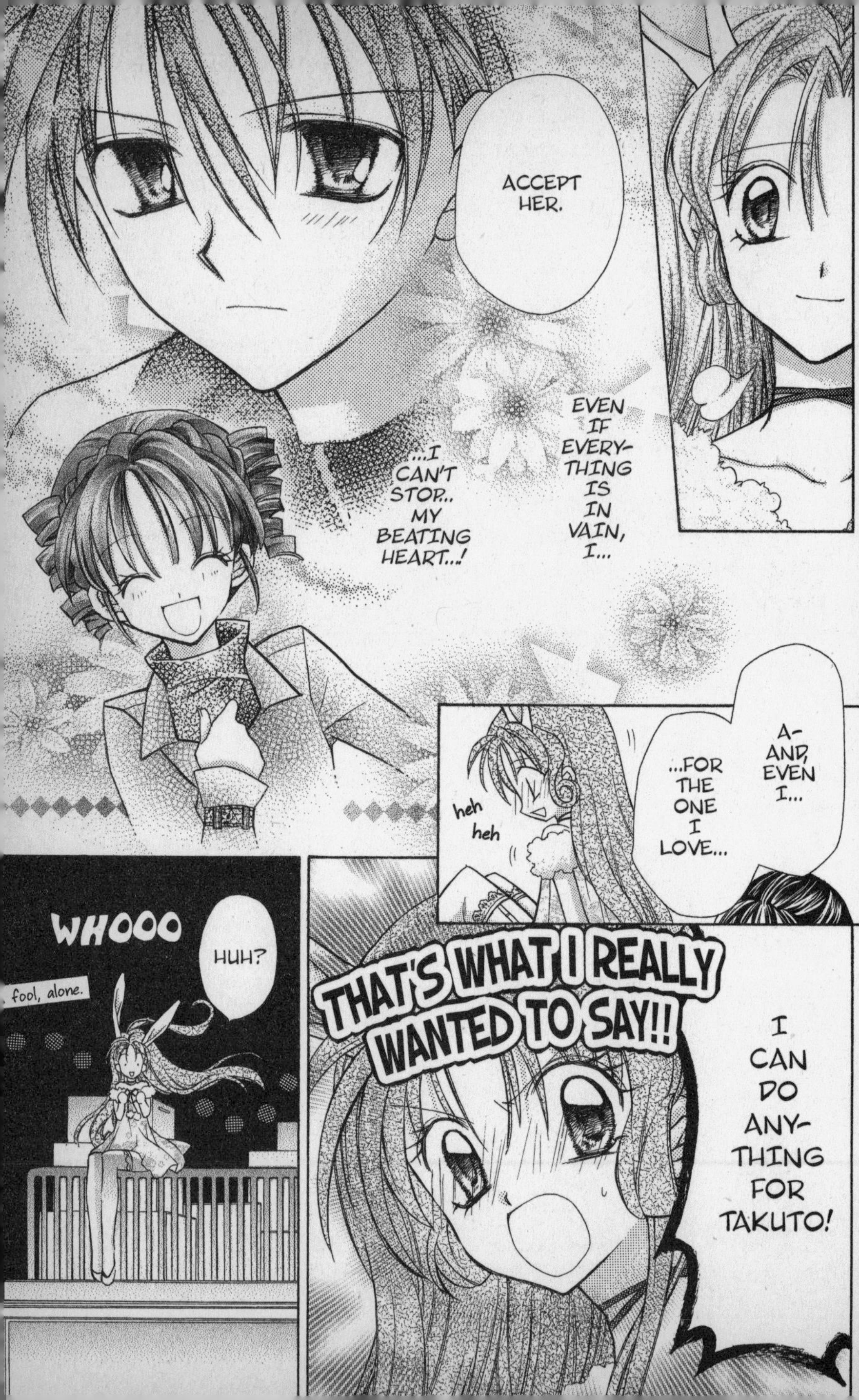
ACCEPT HER.
EVEN IF EVERYTHING IS IN VAIN, I...
...I CAN'T STOP.. MY BEATING HEART...!
A- AND, EVEN I...
...FOR THE ONE I LOVE...
heh heh
THAT'S WHAT I REALLY WANTED TO SAY!!
I CAN DO ANYTHING FOR TAKUTO!
WHOOO
HUH?
fool, alone.

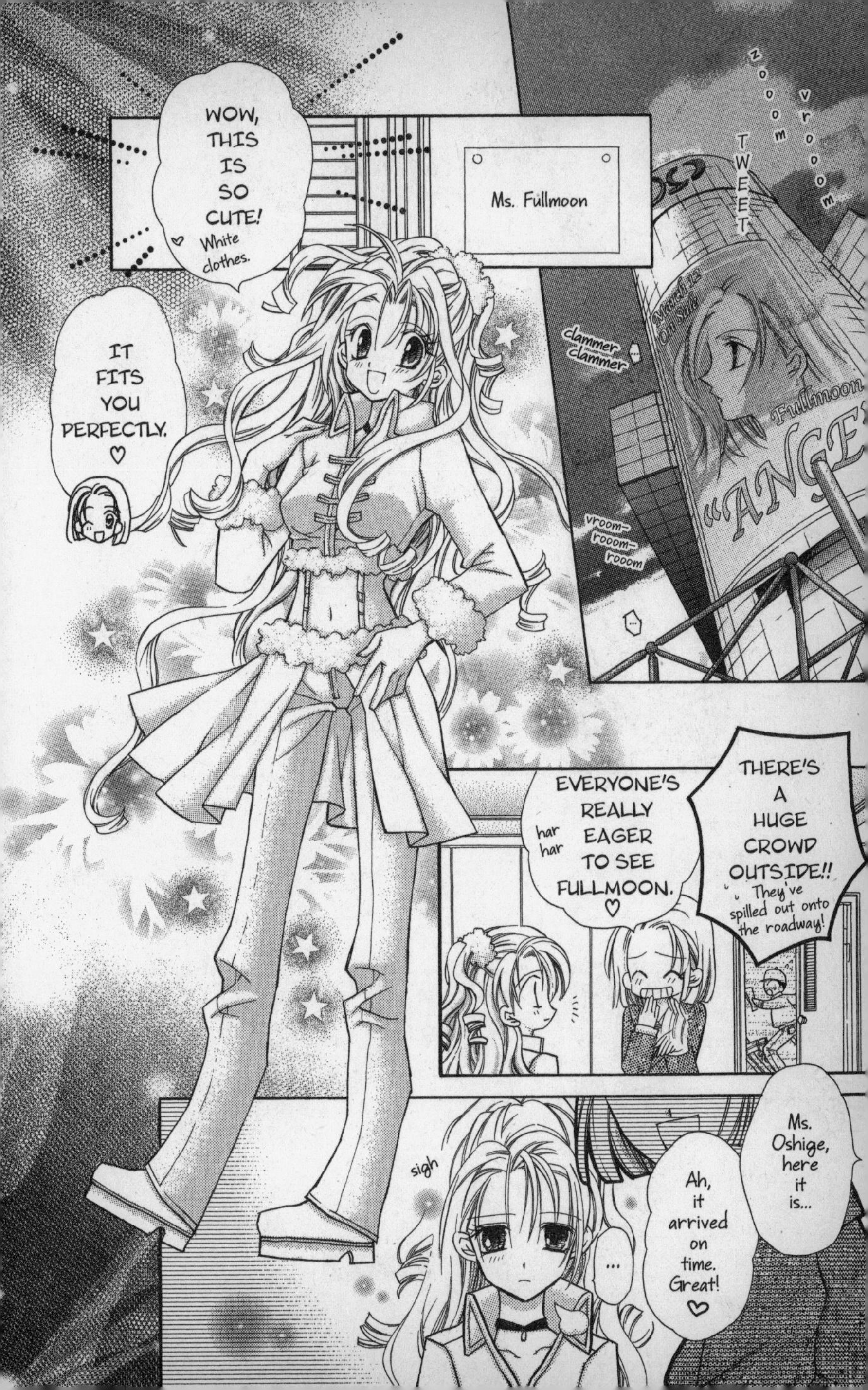
zoooom
vroooom
TWEET
March 12 On Sale
Fullmoon
clammer clammer
vroom-rooom-rooom
THERE'S A HUGE CROWD OUTSIDE!!
They've spilled out onto the roadway!
EVERYONE'S REALLY EAGER TO SEE FULLMOON. ♡
har har
Ms. Oshige, here it is...
Ah, it arrived on time. Great! ♡
...
sigh
Ms. Fullmoon
WOW, THIS IS SO CUTE! ♡ White clothes.
IT FITS YOU PERFECTLY. ♡

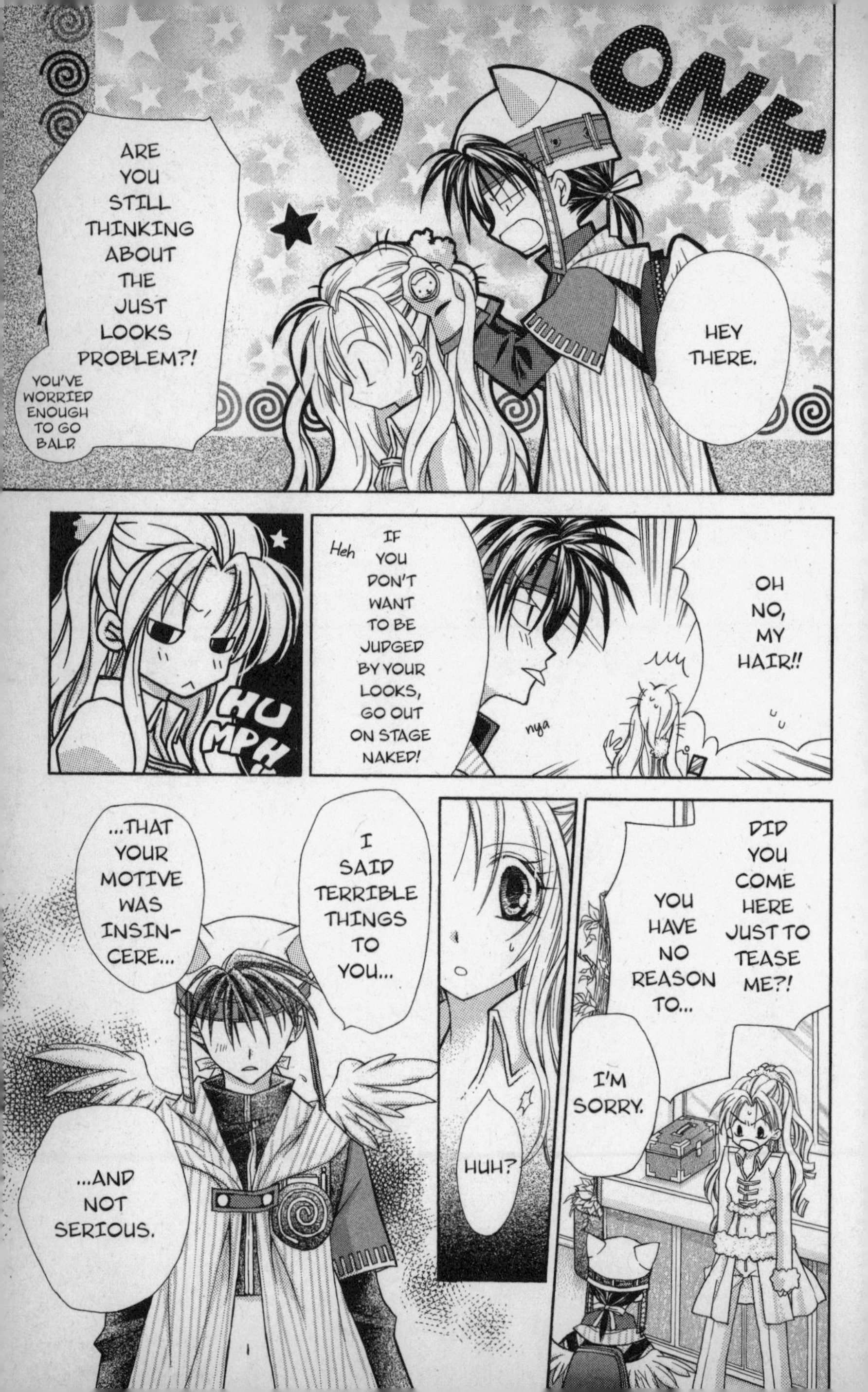
BONK
HEY THERE.
ARE YOU STILL THINKING ABOUT THE JUST LOOKS PROBLEM?!
YOU'VE WORRIED ENOUGH TO GO BALD.
OH NO, MY HAIR!!
nya
IF YOU DON'T WANT TO BE JUDGED BY YOUR LOOKS, GO OUT ON STAGE NAKED!
Heh
HUMPH
DID YOU COME HERE JUST TO TEASE ME?!
YOU HAVE NO REASON TO...
I'M SORRY.
HUH?
I SAID TERRIBLE THINGS TO YOU...
...THAT YOUR MOTIVE WAS INSINCERE...
...AND NOT SERIOUS.

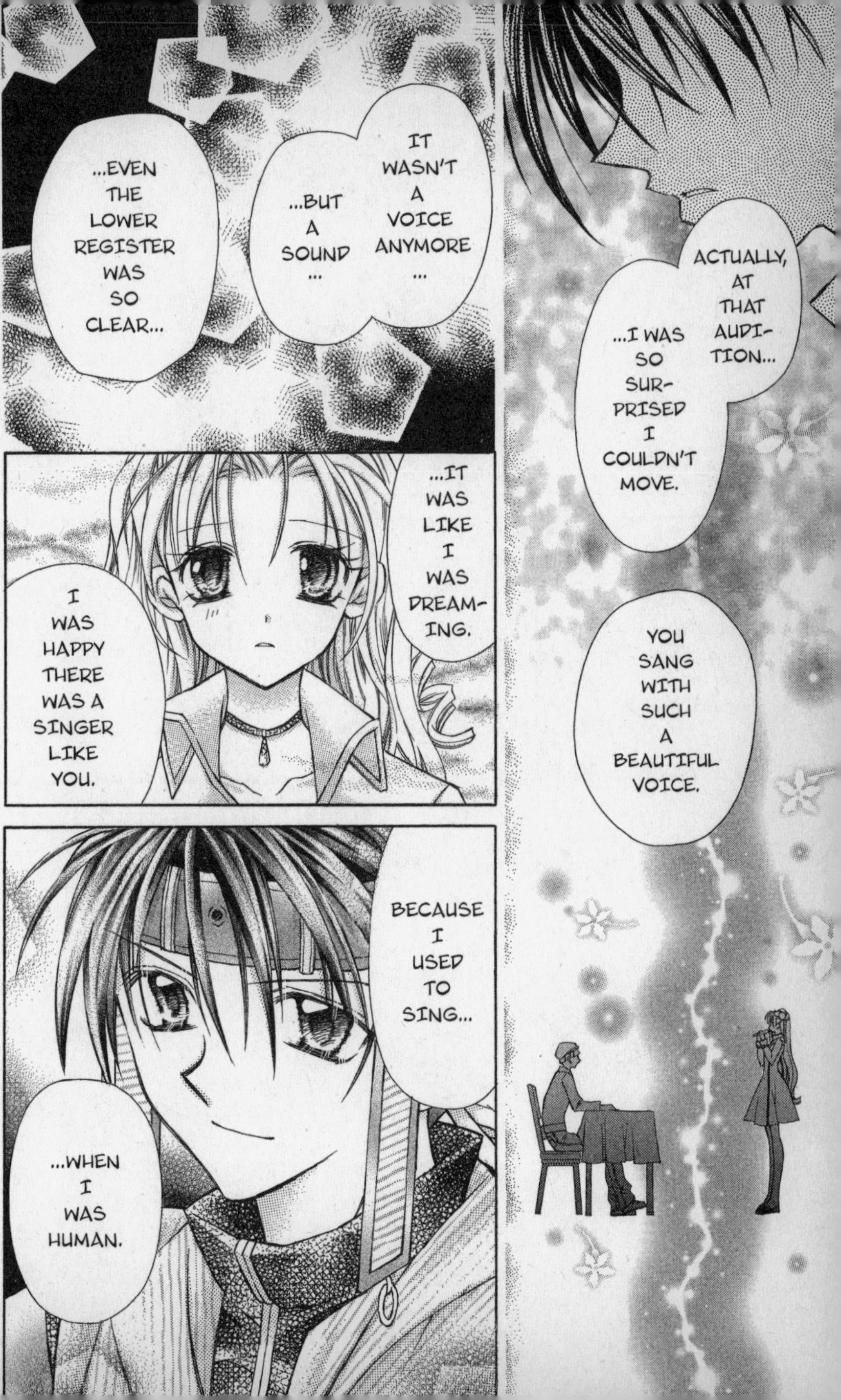
ACTUALLY, AT THAT AUDITION...
...I WAS SO SURPRISED I COULDN'T MOVE.
YOU SANG WITH SUCH A BEAUTIFUL VOICE.
IT WASN'T A VOICE ANYMORE...
...BUT A SOUND...
...EVEN THE LOWER REGISTER WAS SO CLEAR...
...IT WAS LIKE I WAS DREAMING.
I WAS HAPPY THERE WAS A SINGER LIKE YOU.
BECAUSE I USED TO SING...
...WHEN I WAS HUMAN.

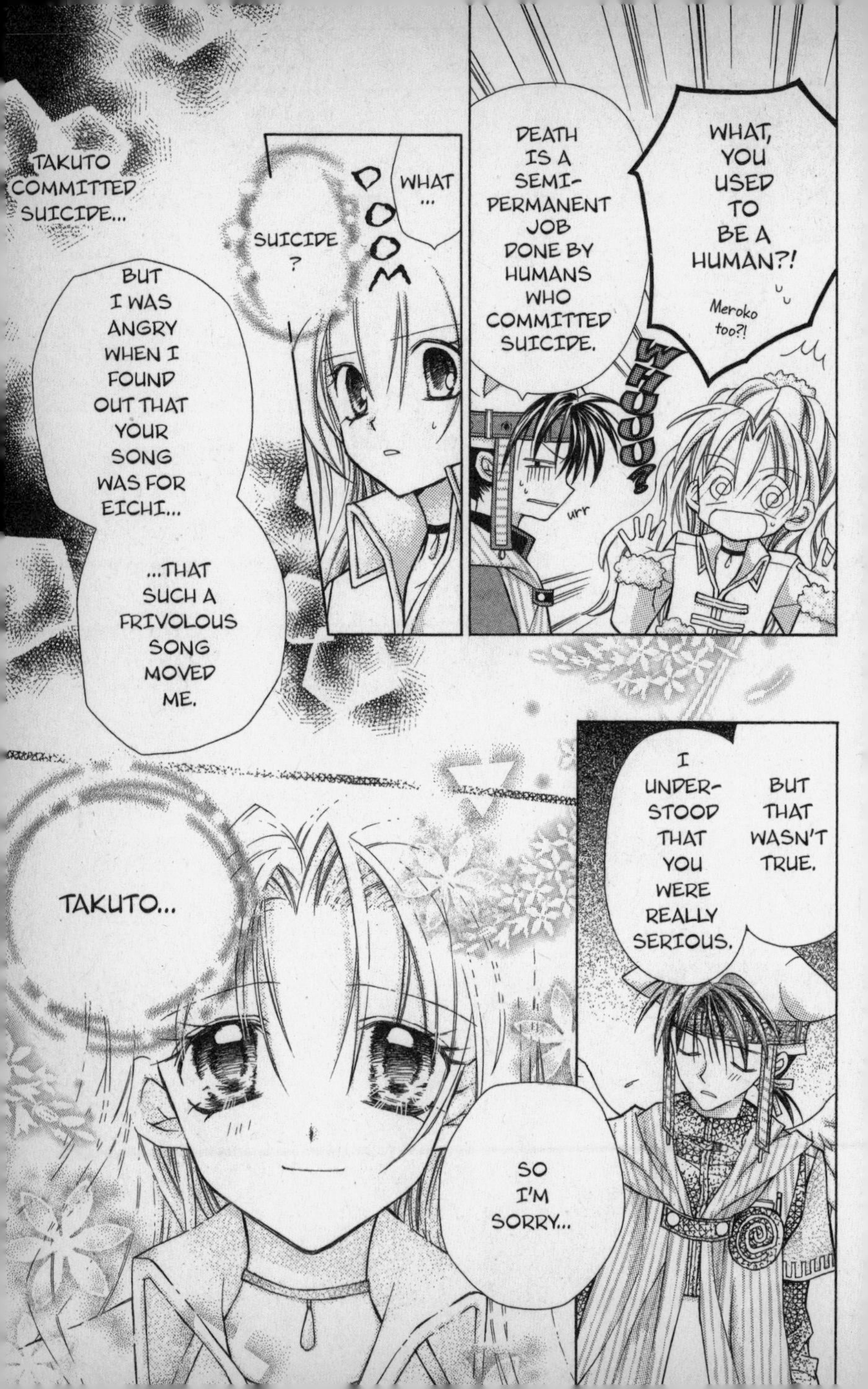
WHAT, YOU USED TO BE A HUMAN?!
Meroko too?!
DEATH IS A SEMI-PERMANENT JOB DONE BY HUMANS WHO COMMITTED SUICIDE.
urr
WHAT ...
DOOOM
SUICIDE ?
TAKUTO COMMITTED SUICIDE...
BUT I WAS ANGRY WHEN I FOUND OUT THAT YOUR SONG WAS FOR EICHI...
...THAT SUCH A FRIVOLOUS SONG MOVED ME.
BUT THAT WASN'T TRUE.
I UNDER-STOOD THAT YOU WERE REALLY SERIOUS.
SO I'M SORRY...
TAKUTO...

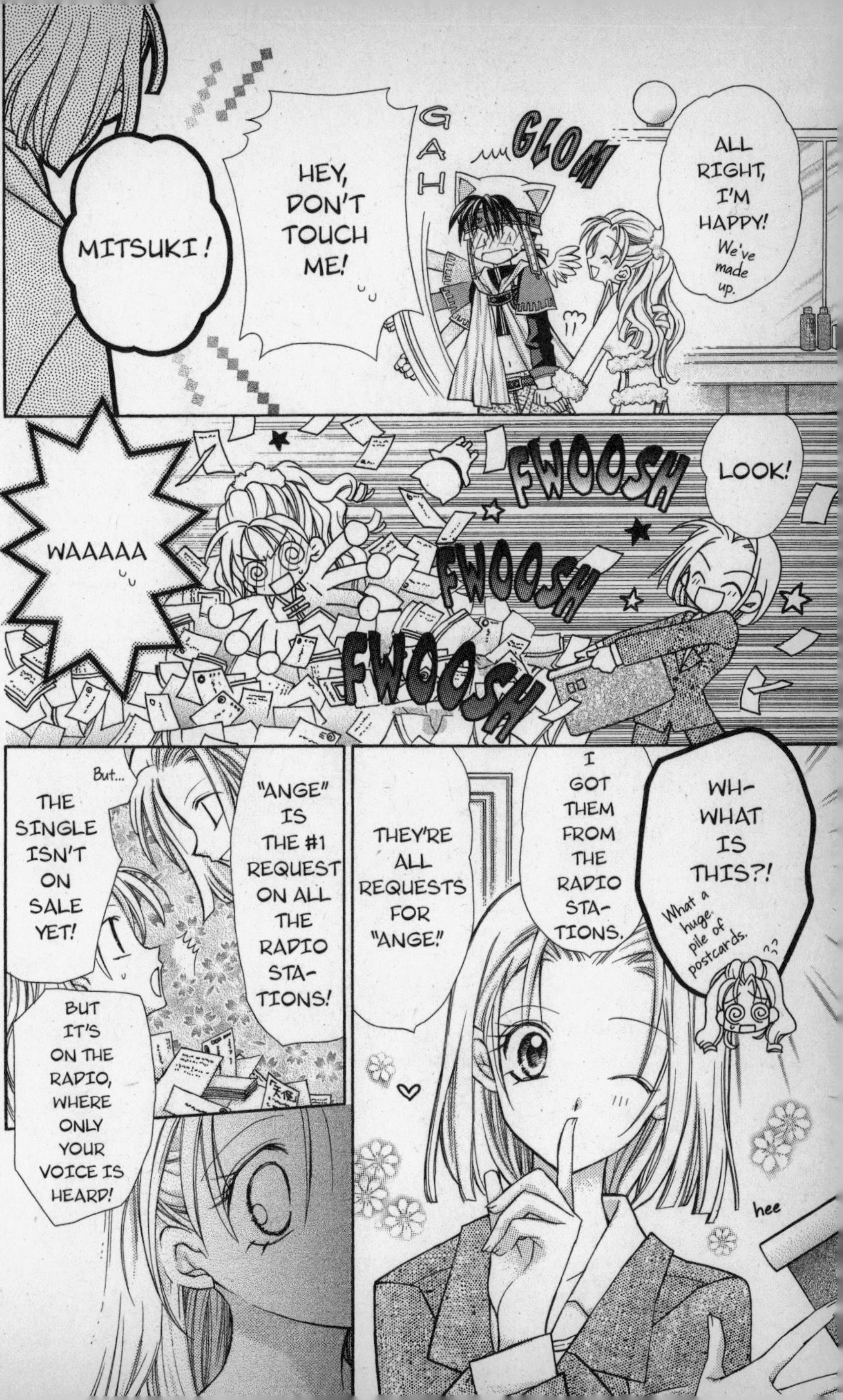
ALL RIGHT, I'M HAPPY!
We've made up.
GLOM
GAH
HEY, DON'T TOUCH ME!
MITSUKI!
LOOK!
FWOOSH
FWOOSH
FWOOSH
WAAAAA
WH-WHAT IS THIS?!
What a huge pile of postcards.
I GOT THEM FROM THE RADIO STATIONS.
THEY'RE ALL REQUESTS FOR "ANGE."
hee
"ANGE" IS THE #1 REQUEST ON ALL THE RADIO STATIONS!
But...
THE SINGLE ISN'T ON SALE YET!
BUT IT'S ON THE RADIO, WHERE ONLY YOUR VOICE IS HEARD!

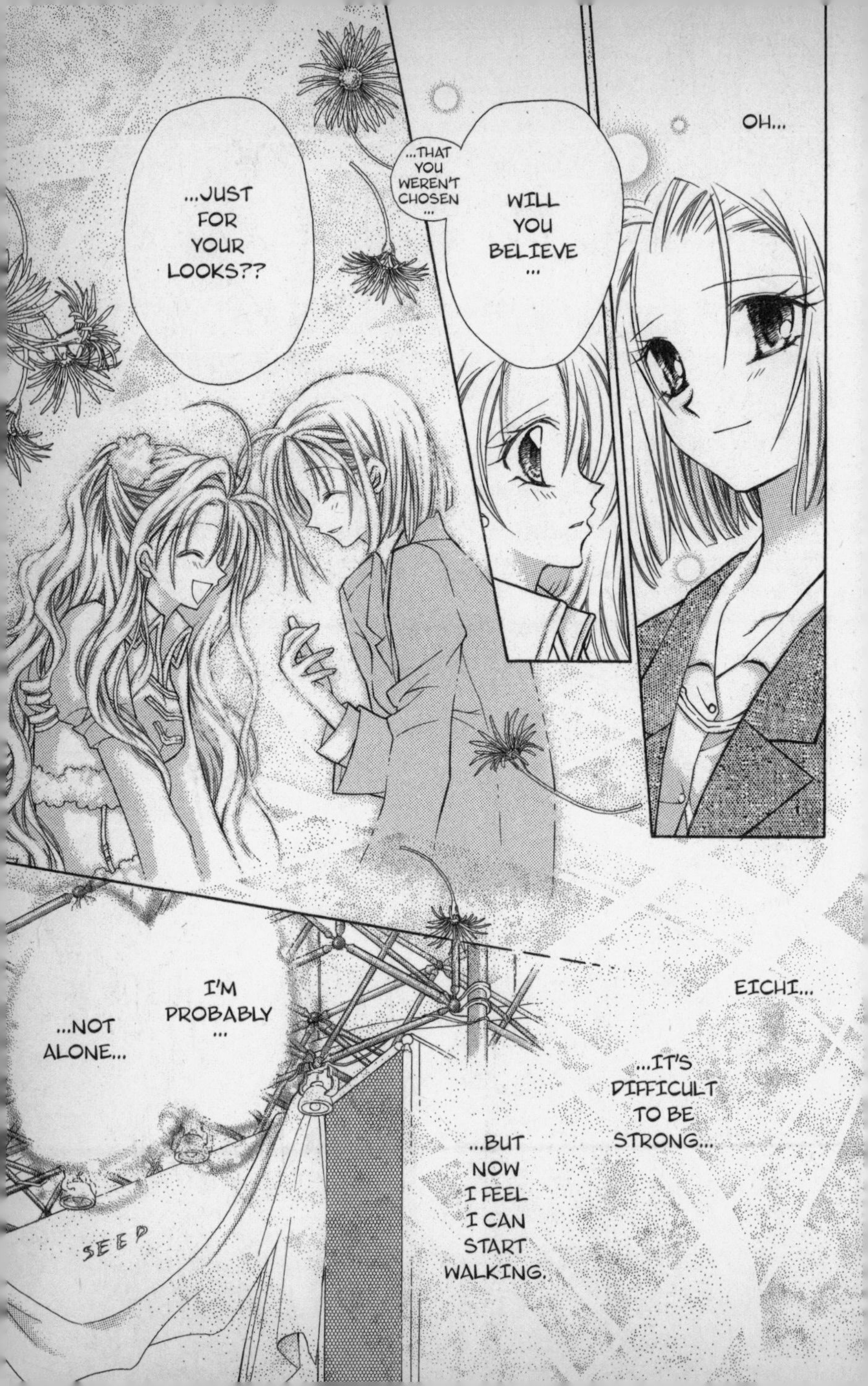
OH...
WILL YOU BELIEVE ...
...THAT YOU WEREN'T CHOSEN ...
...JUST FOR YOUR LOOKS??
EICHI...
...IT'S DIFFICULT TO BE STRONG...
...BUT NOW I FEEL I CAN START WALKING.
I'M PROBABLY ...
...NOT ALONE...
SEED

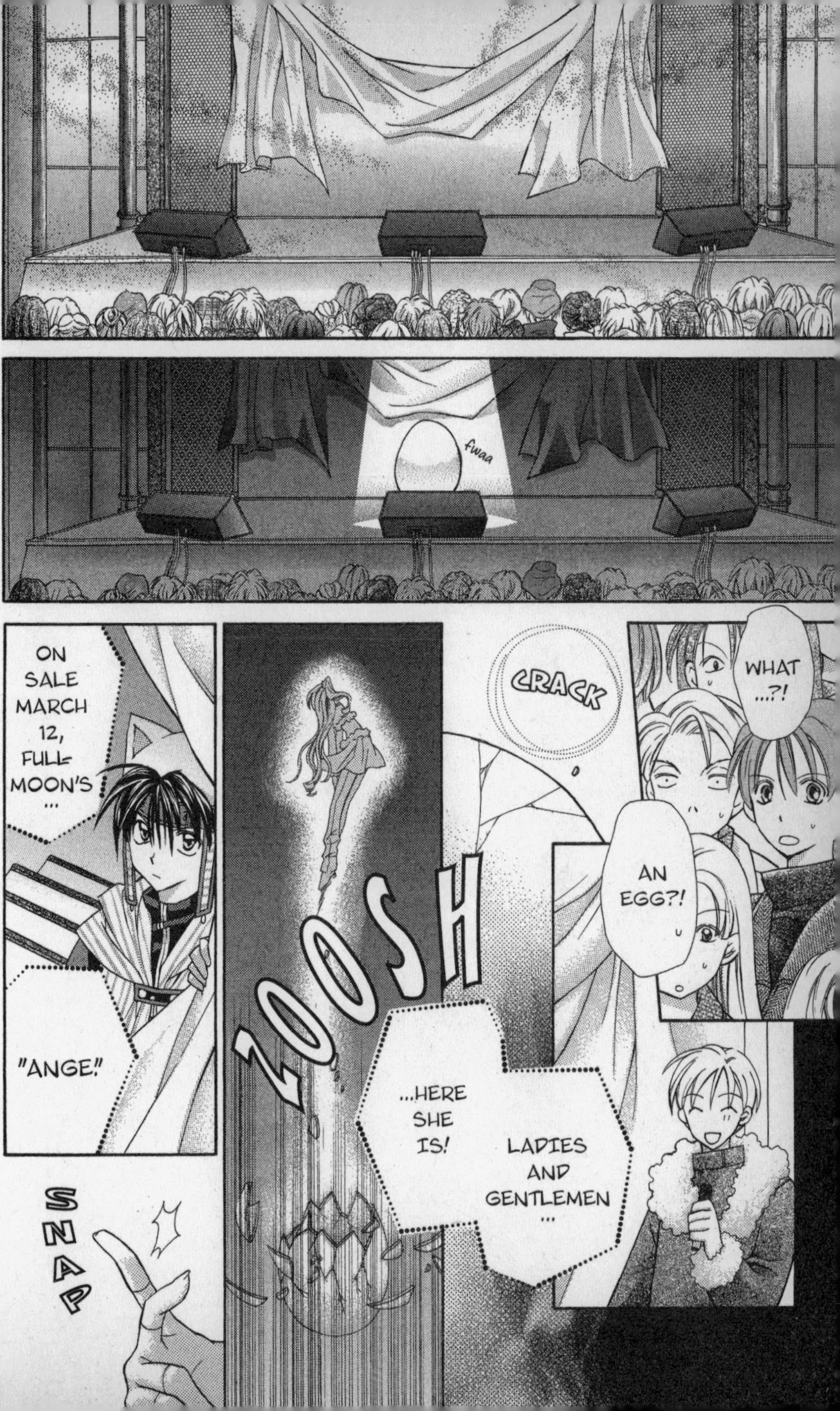
fwaa
WHAT ...?!
AN EGG?!
LADIES AND GENTLEMEN ...
...HERE SHE IS!
CRACK
ZOOSH
ON SALE MARCH 12, FULL-MOON'S ...
"ANGE!"
SNAP

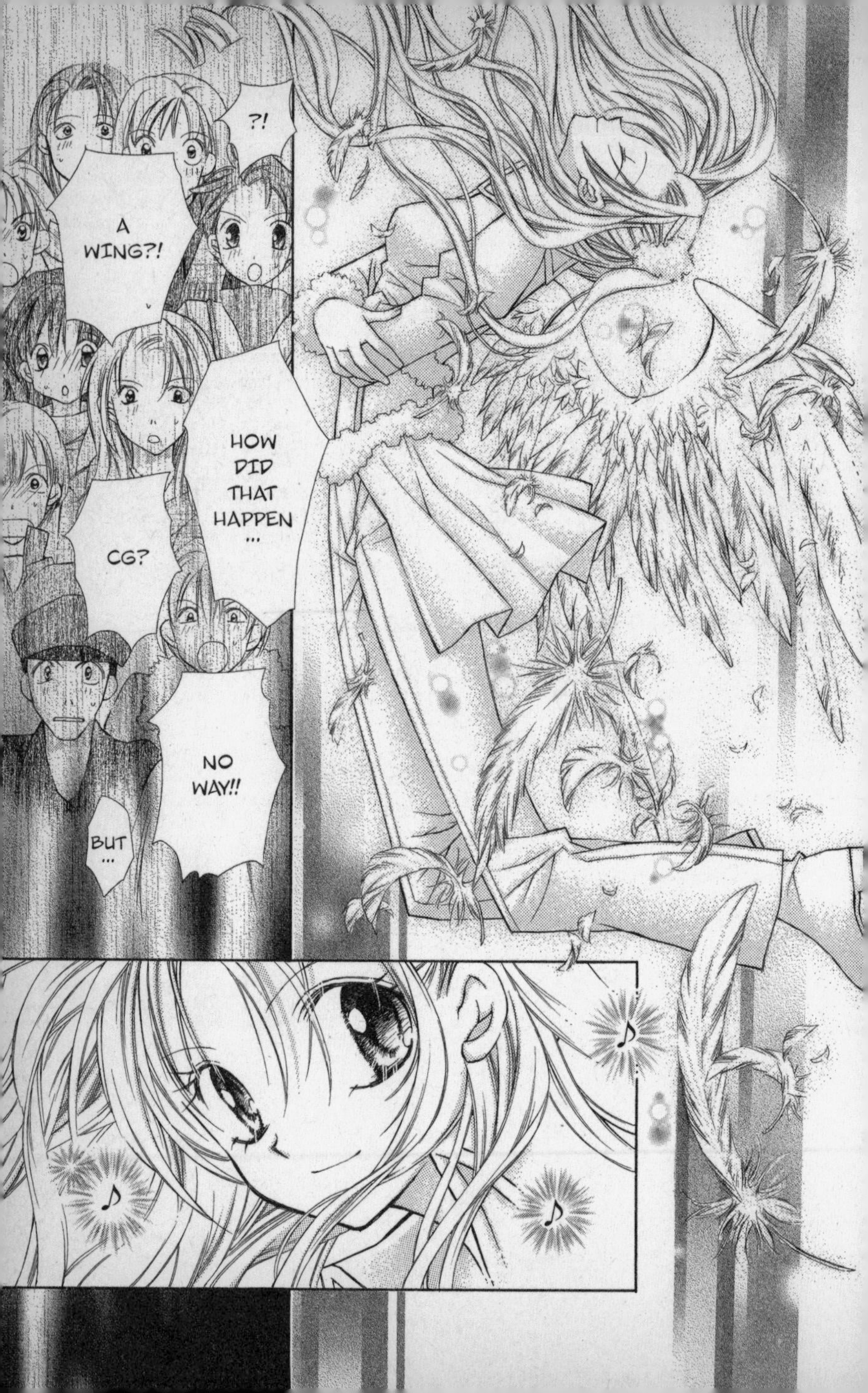
?!
A WING?!
HOW DID THAT HAPPEN ...
CG?
NO WAY!!
BUT ...
♪
♪
♪

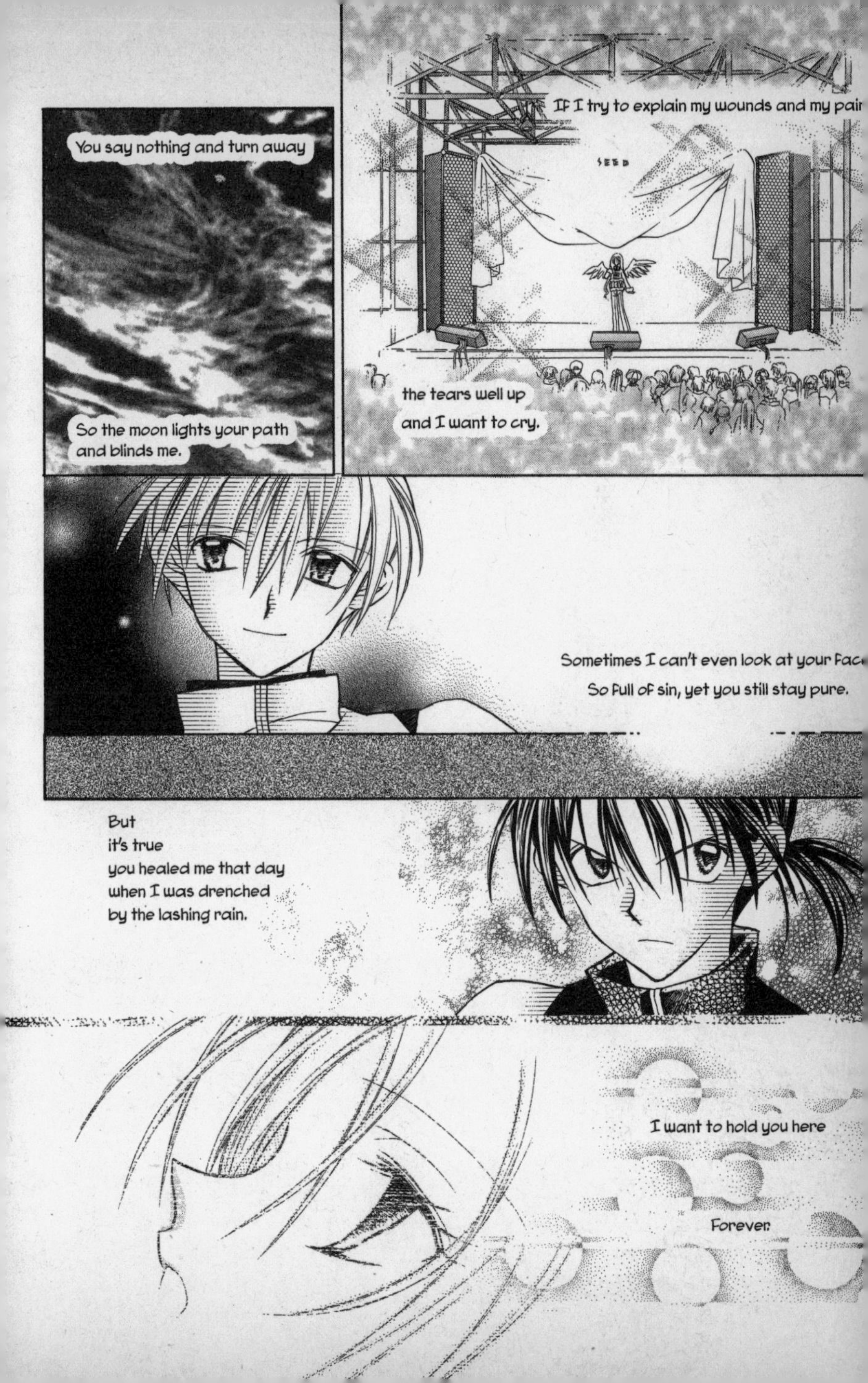
If I try to explain my wounds and my pai
SEED
the tears well up and I want to cry.
You say nothing and turn away
So the moon lights your path and blinds me.
Sometimes I can't even look at your fac
So full of sin, yet you still stay pure.
But it's true you healed me that day when I was drenched by the lashing rain.
I want to hold you here
Forever.

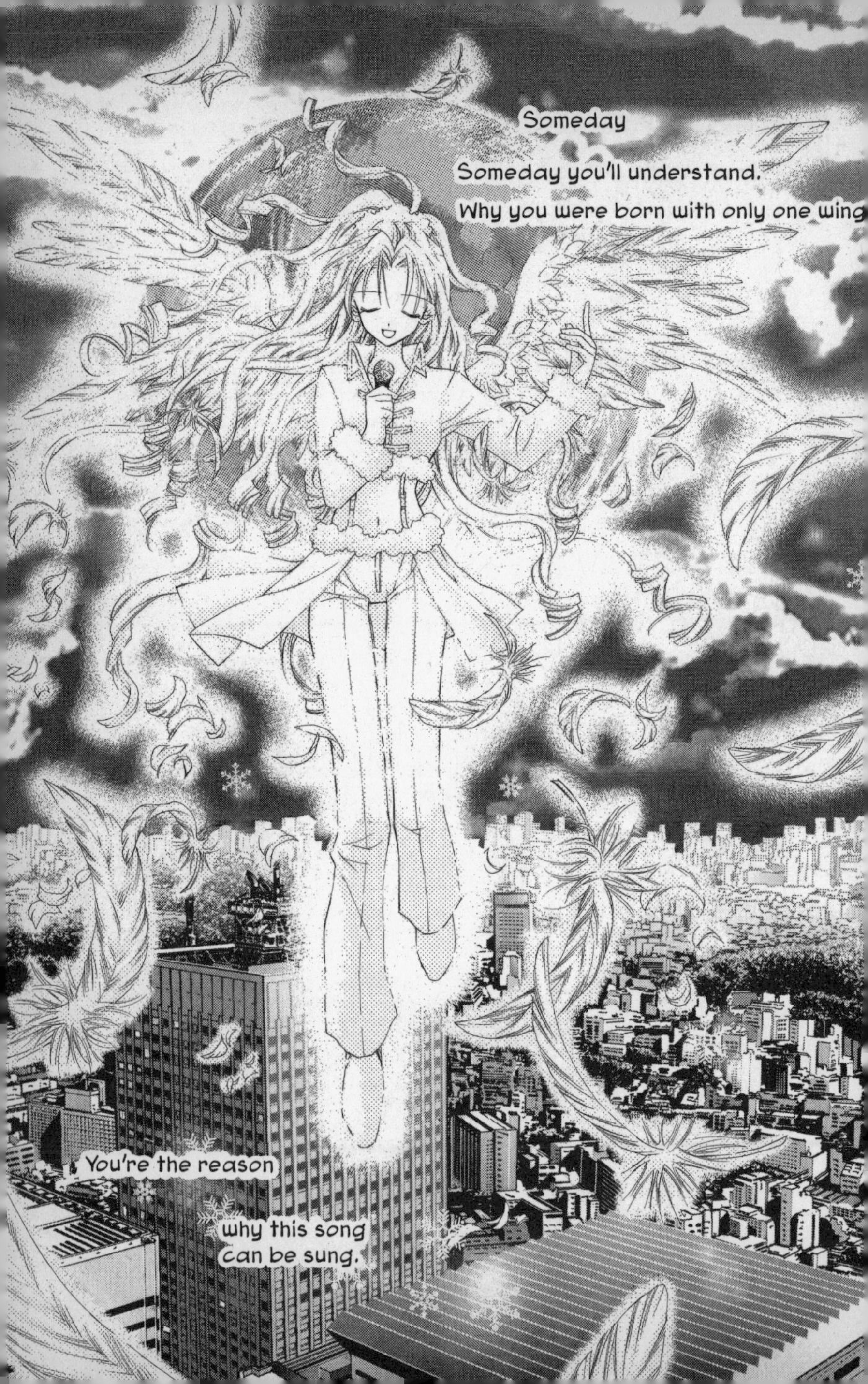
Someday
Someday you'll understand.
Why you were born with only one wing
You're the reason
why this song
can be sung.

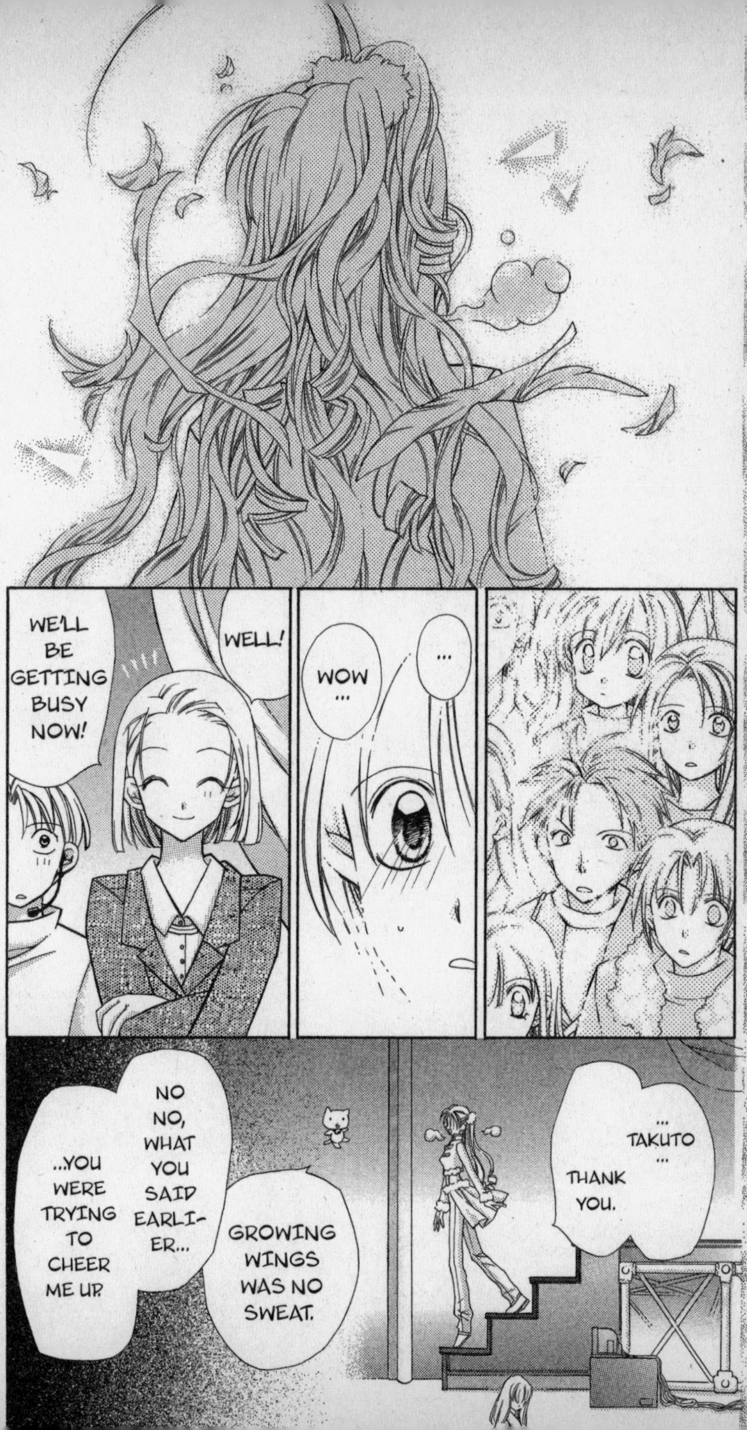
...
WOW ...
WELL!
WE'LL BE GETTING BUSY NOW!
... TAKUTO ...
THANK YOU.
GROWING WINGS WAS NO SWEAT.
NO NO, WHAT YOU SAID EARLI-ER...
...YOU WERE TRYING TO CHEER ME UP.

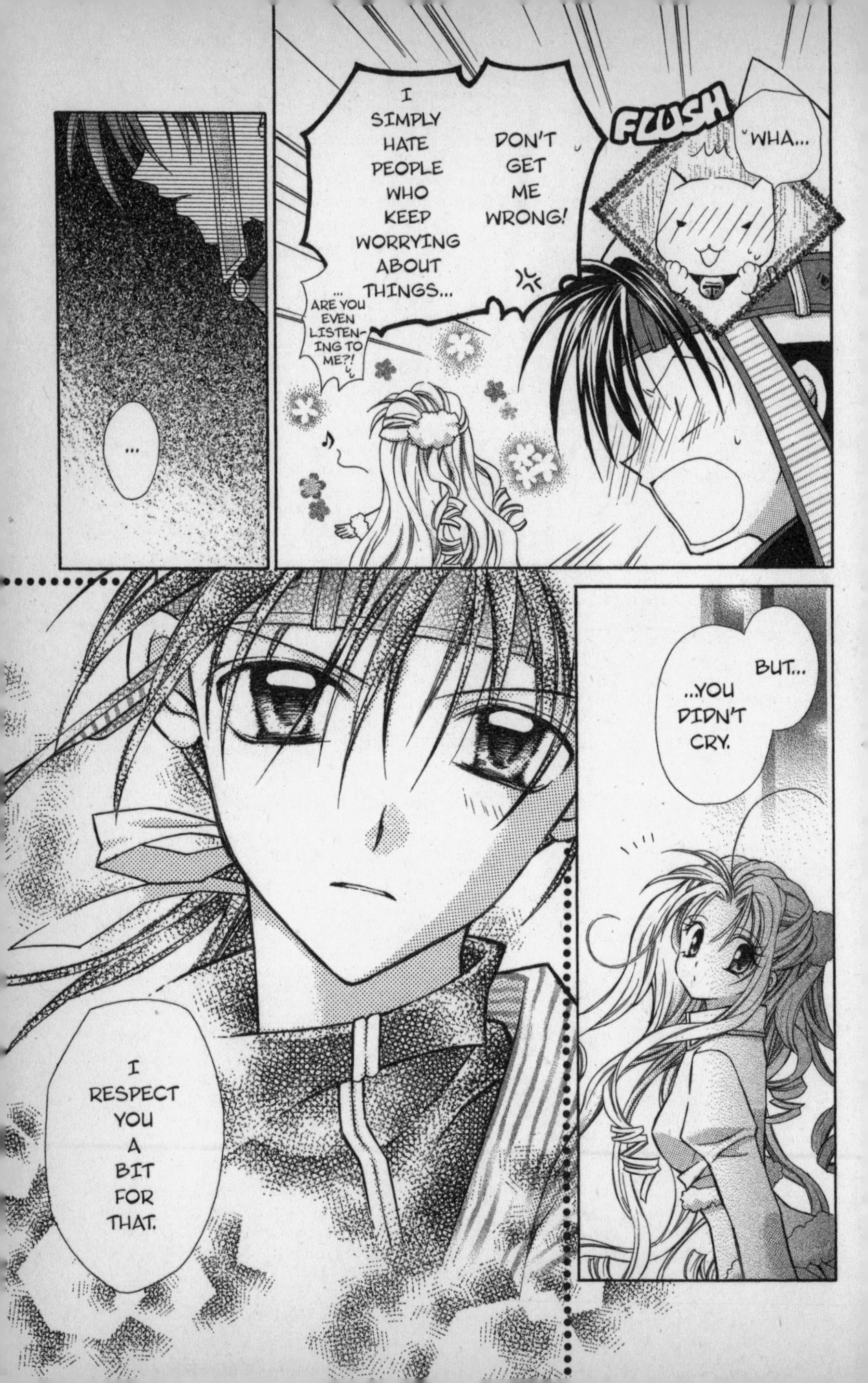
FLUSH
WHA...
DON'T GET ME WRONG!
I SIMPLY HATE PEOPLE WHO KEEP WORRYING ABOUT THINGS...
...ARE YOU EVEN LISTENING TO ME?!
...
BUT...
...YOU DIDN'T CRY.
I RESPECT YOU A BIT FOR THAT.

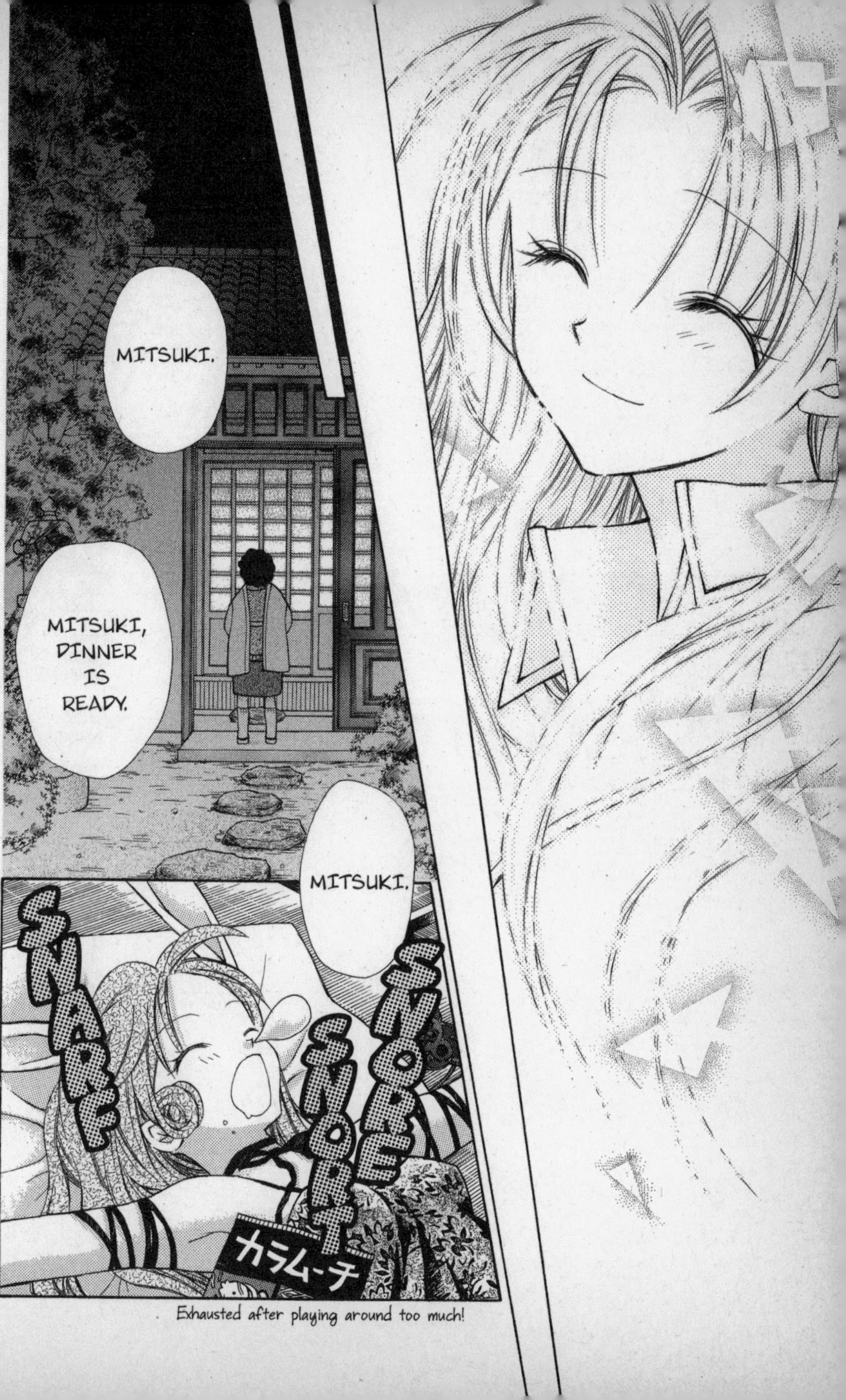
MITSUKI.
MITSUKI, DINNER IS READY.
MITSUKI.
SNORE
SNORT
SNARF
カラムーチ

Exhausted after playing around too much!

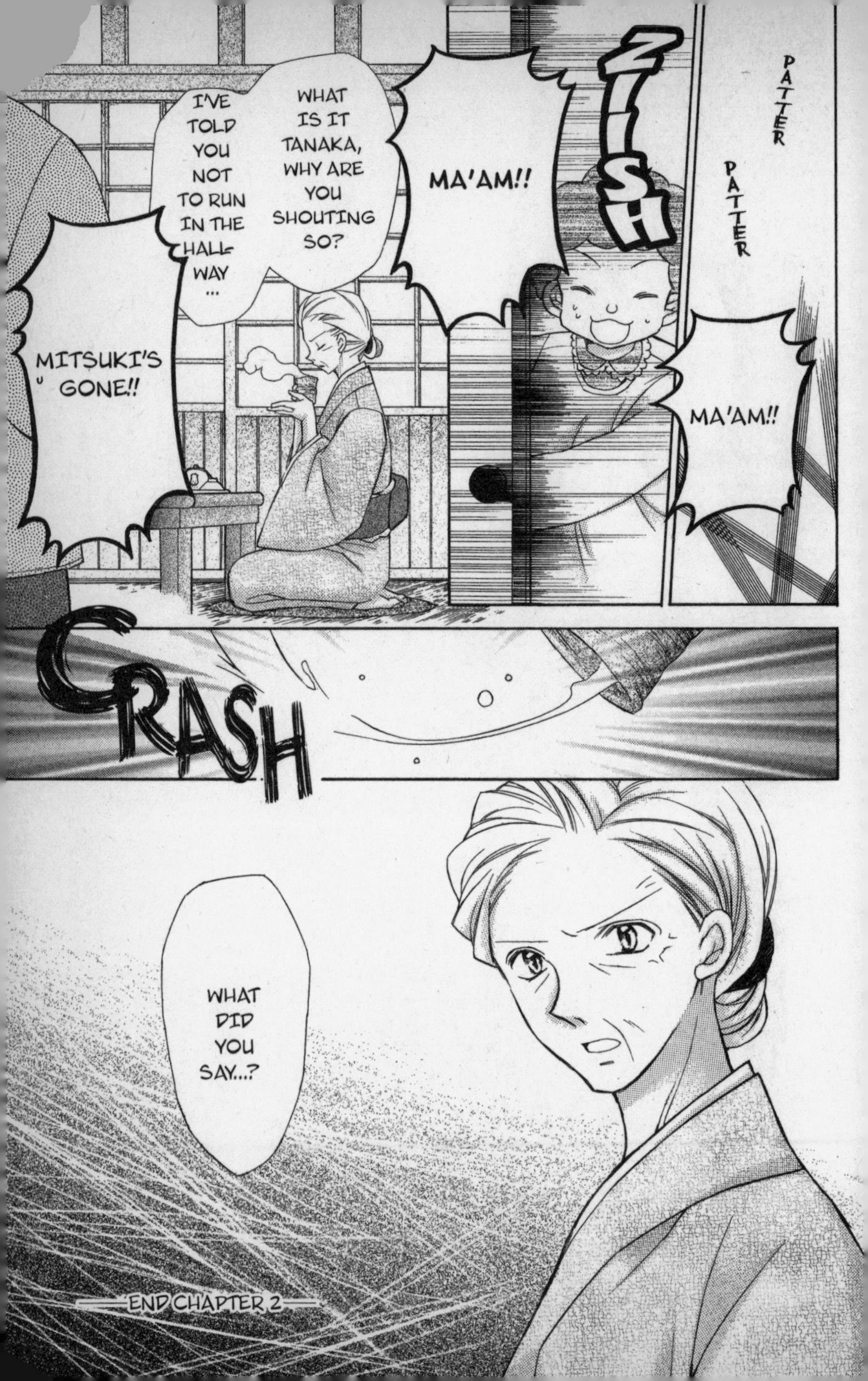
PATTER
PATTER
MA'AM!!
ZIISH
MA'AM!!
WHAT IS IT TANAKA, WHY ARE YOU SHOUTING SO?
I'VE TOLD YOU NOT TO RUN IN THE HALLWAY...
MITSUKI'S GONE!!
CRASH
WHAT DID YOU SAY...?
END CHAPTER 2

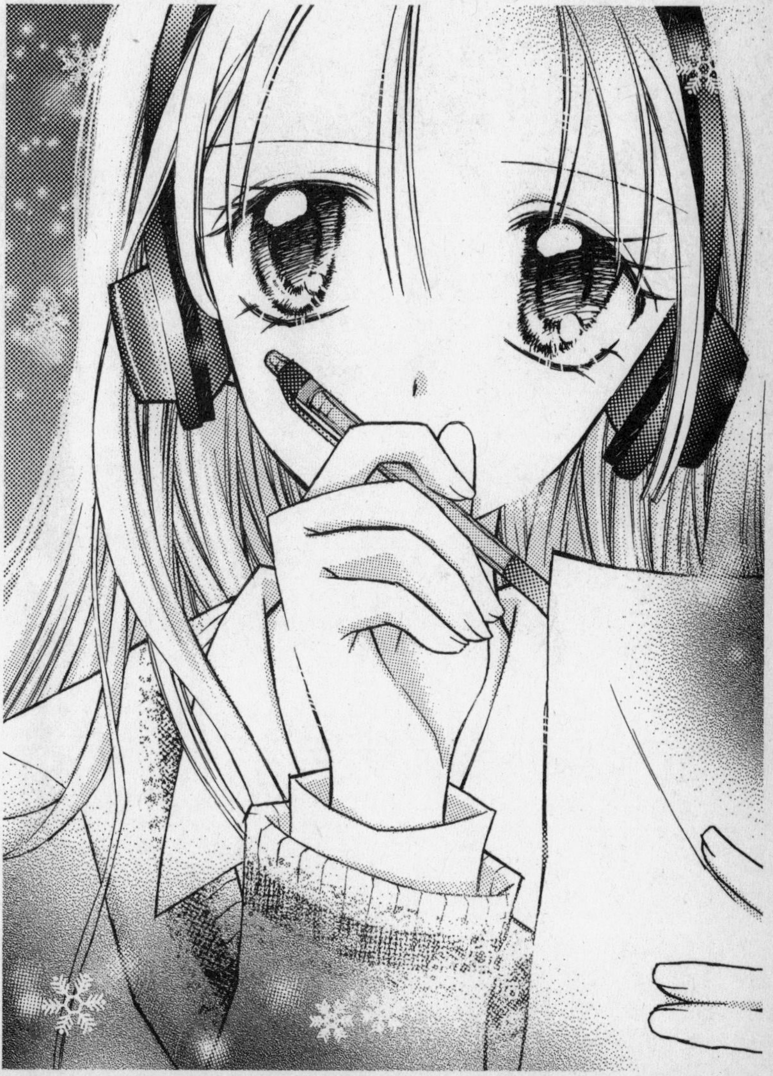

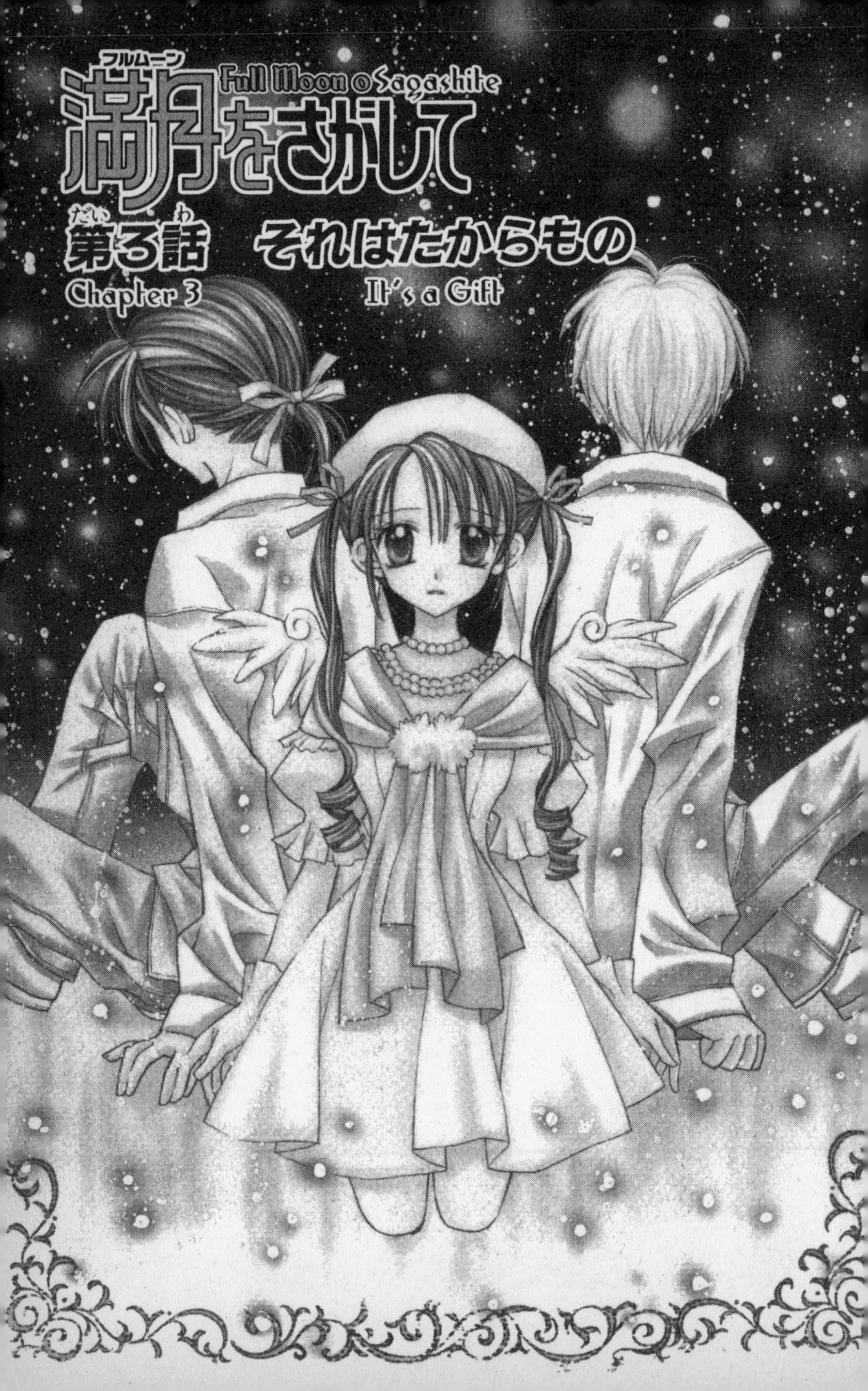
フルムーン
満月をさがして
Full Moon o Sagashite
だい わ
第3話
それはたからもの
Chapter 3
It's a Gift

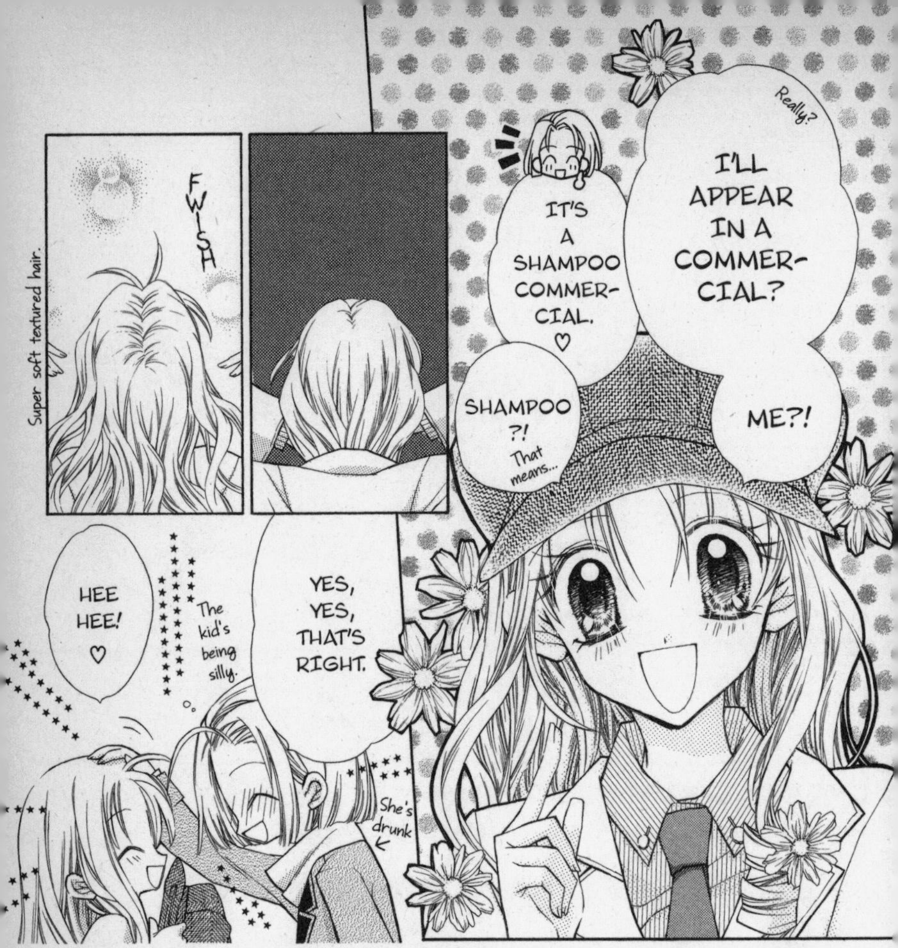
Really?
I'LL APPEAR IN A COMMERCIAL?
IT'S A SHAMPOO COMMERCIAL. ♡
ME?!
SHAMPOO?!
That means...
FWISH
Super soft textured hair.
YES, YES, THAT'S RIGHT.
HEE HEE! ♡
The kid's being silly.
She's drunk

Chapter 3 It's a Gift

Cover Copy → I'll sing my love for you...

I like this illustration a lot. The two guys showing their backs is what I like. I drew this with Matsuura Aya's "Hyakkai no Kiss" in mind. I'm a great fan of her. I received some fan letters asking whether Takuto and Eichi are the same person, but that's not true. Sorry. Did people think so when they saw this picture? Especially since the two are wearing the same clothes. If I don't write about the manga, there's not much to fill this space. So I'll draw a manga. But it's not too good.

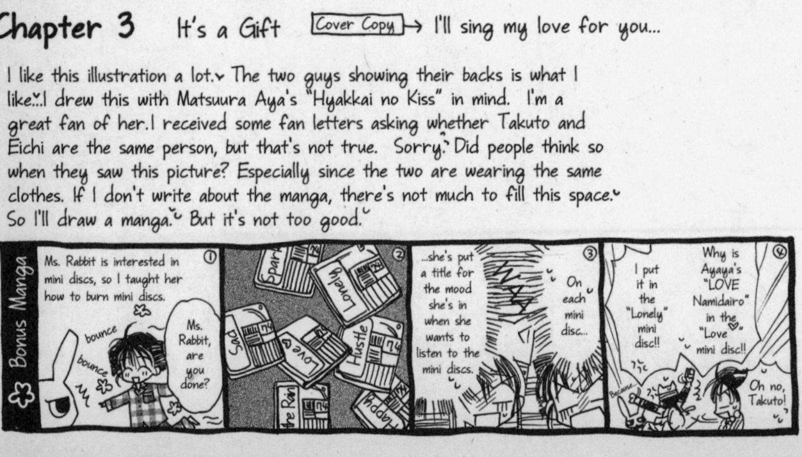
Bonus Manga
Ms. Rabbit is interested in mini discs, so I taught her how to burn mini discs.
bounce
bounce
Ms. Rabbit, are you done?
Lonely
Sad
Love
Hustle
...she's put a title for the mood she's in when she wants to listen to the mini discs.
On each mini disc...
I put it in the "Lonely" mini disc!!
Why is Ayaya's "LOVE Namidairo" in the "Love" mini disc!!
Oh no, Takuto!

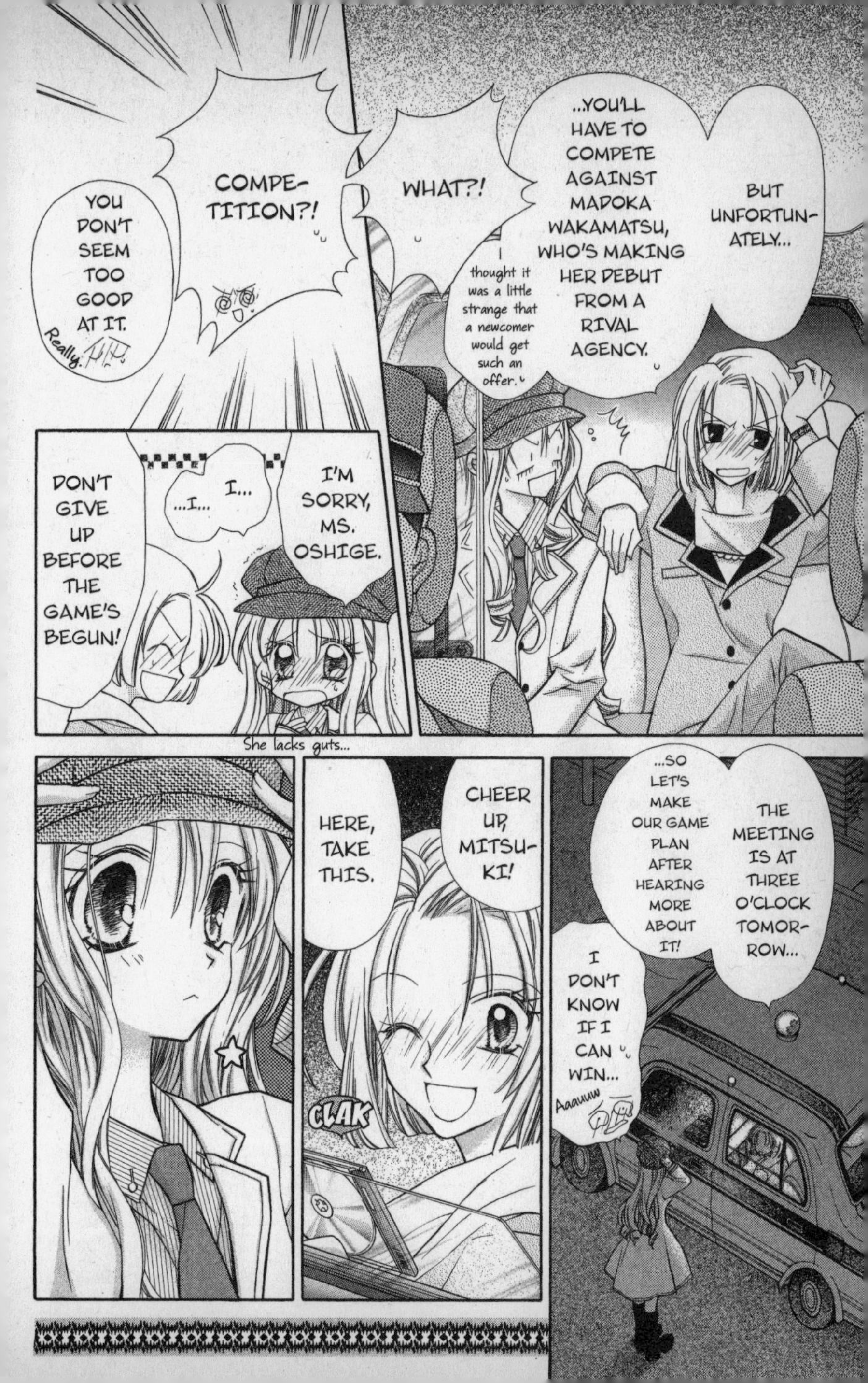

BUT UNFORTUNATELY...
...YOU'LL HAVE TO COMPETE AGAINST MADOKA WAKAMATSU, WHO'S MAKING HER DEBUT FROM A RIVAL AGENCY.
I thought it was a little strange that a newcomer would get such an offer.
WHAT?!
COMPETITION?!
YOU DON'T SEEM TOO GOOD AT IT.
Really
I'M SORRY, MS. OSHIGE.
I...
...I...
DON'T GIVE UP BEFORE THE GAME'S BEGUN!
She lacks guts...
THE MEETING IS AT THREE O'CLOCK TOMORROW...
...SO LET'S MAKE OUR GAME PLAN AFTER HEARING MORE ABOUT IT!
I DON'T KNOW IF I CAN WIN...
Aaauuw
CHEER UP, MITSUKI!
HERE, TAKE THIS.
CLAK

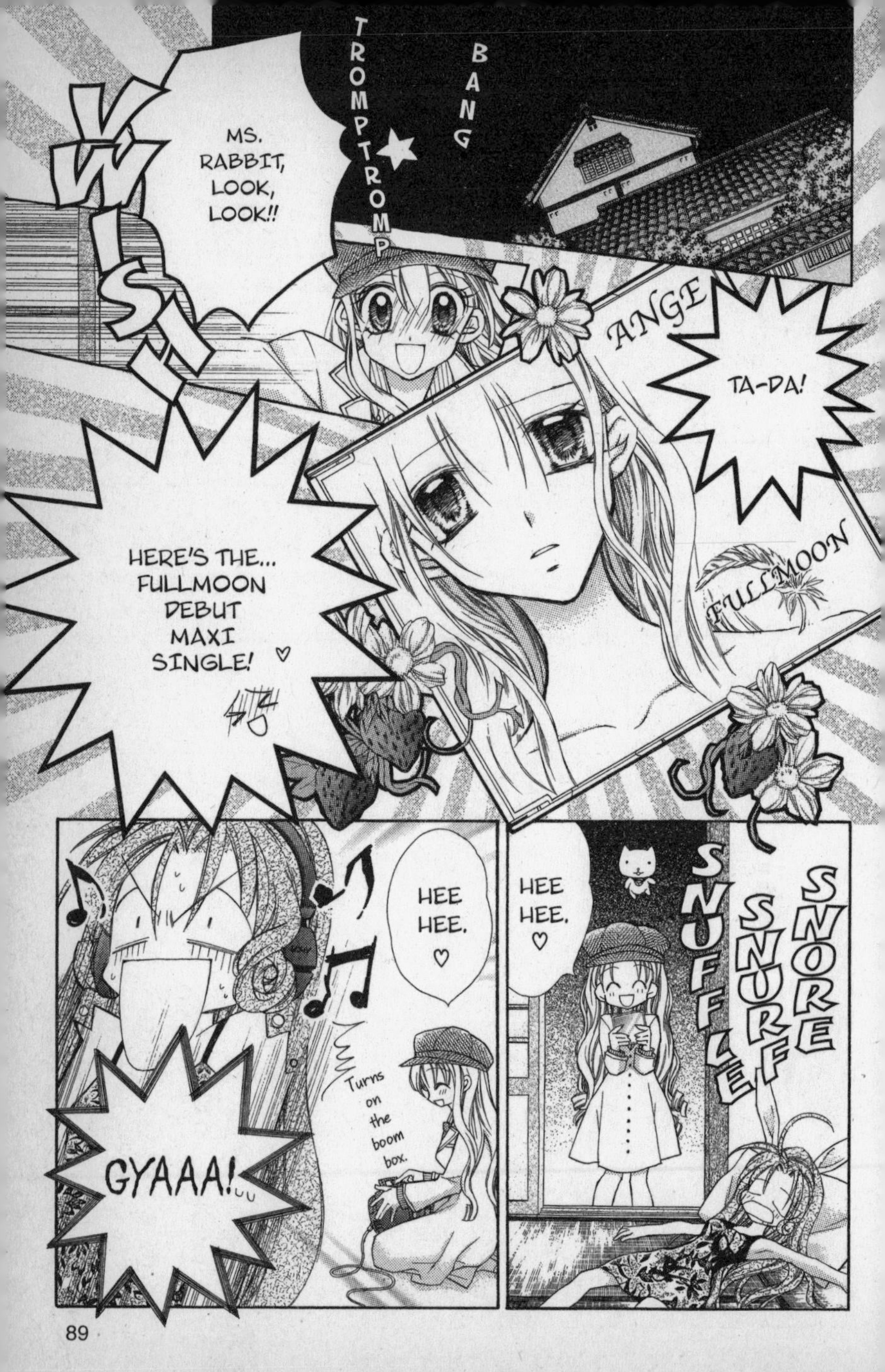
BANG
TROMPTROMP
MS. RABBIT, LOOK, LOOK!!
VWISH
ANGE
TA-DA!
FULLMOON
HERE'S THE... FULLMOON DEBUT MAXI SINGLE! ♡
SNORE
SNURF
SNUFFLE
HEE HEE. ♡
HEE HEE. ♡
Turns on the boom box.
GYAAA!

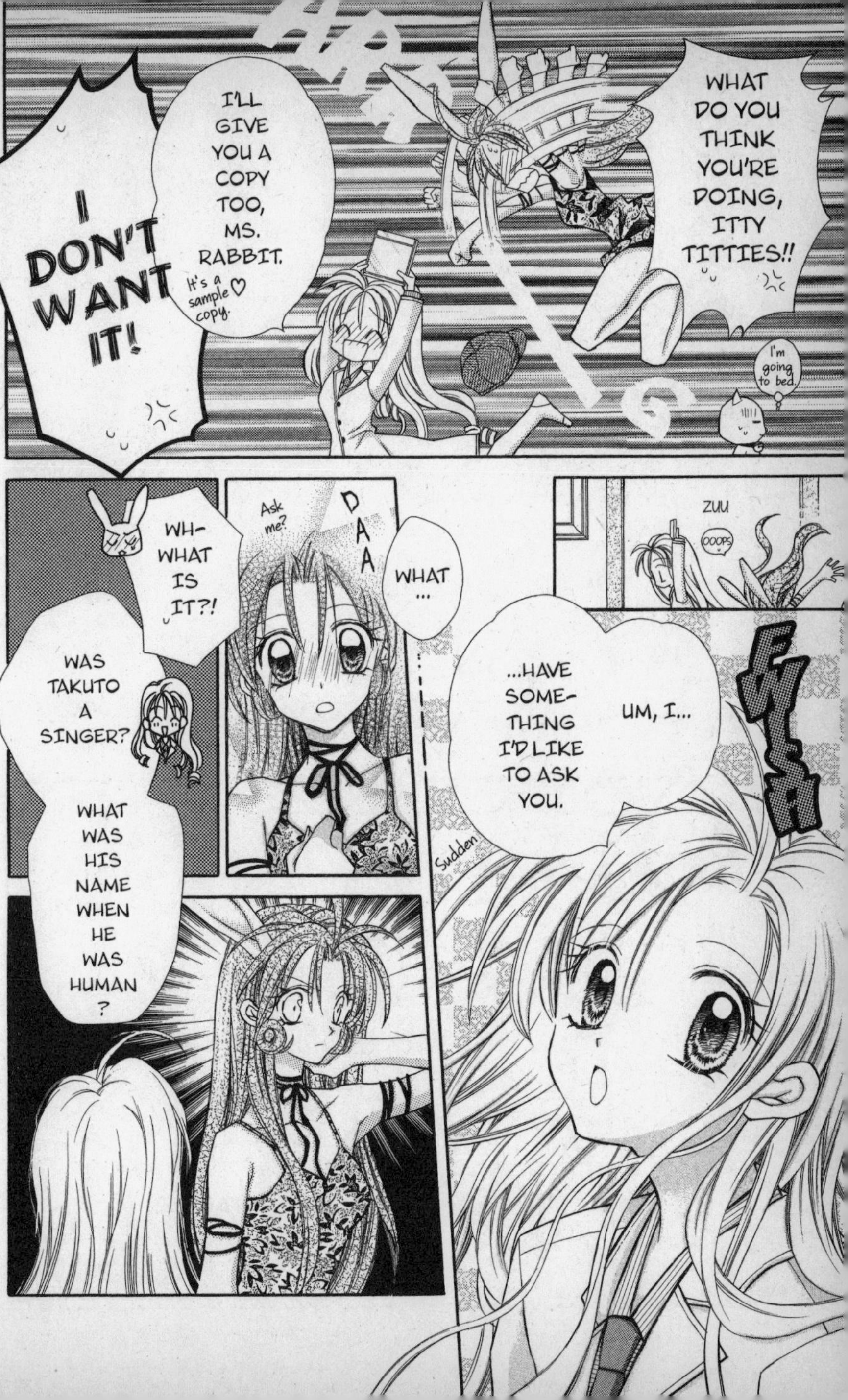

WHAT DO YOU THINK YOU'RE DOING, ITTY TITTIES!!
I'm going to bed.
I'LL GIVE YOU A COPY TOO, MS. RABBIT.
It's a sample ♡ copy.
I DON'T WANT IT!
ZUU
OOOPS
UM, I...
...HAVE SOMETHING I'D LIKE TO ASK YOU.
Sudden
WHAT ...
Ask me?
DAA
WH-WHAT IS IT?!
WAS TAKUTO A SINGER?
WHAT WAS HIS NAME WHEN HE WAS HUMAN?

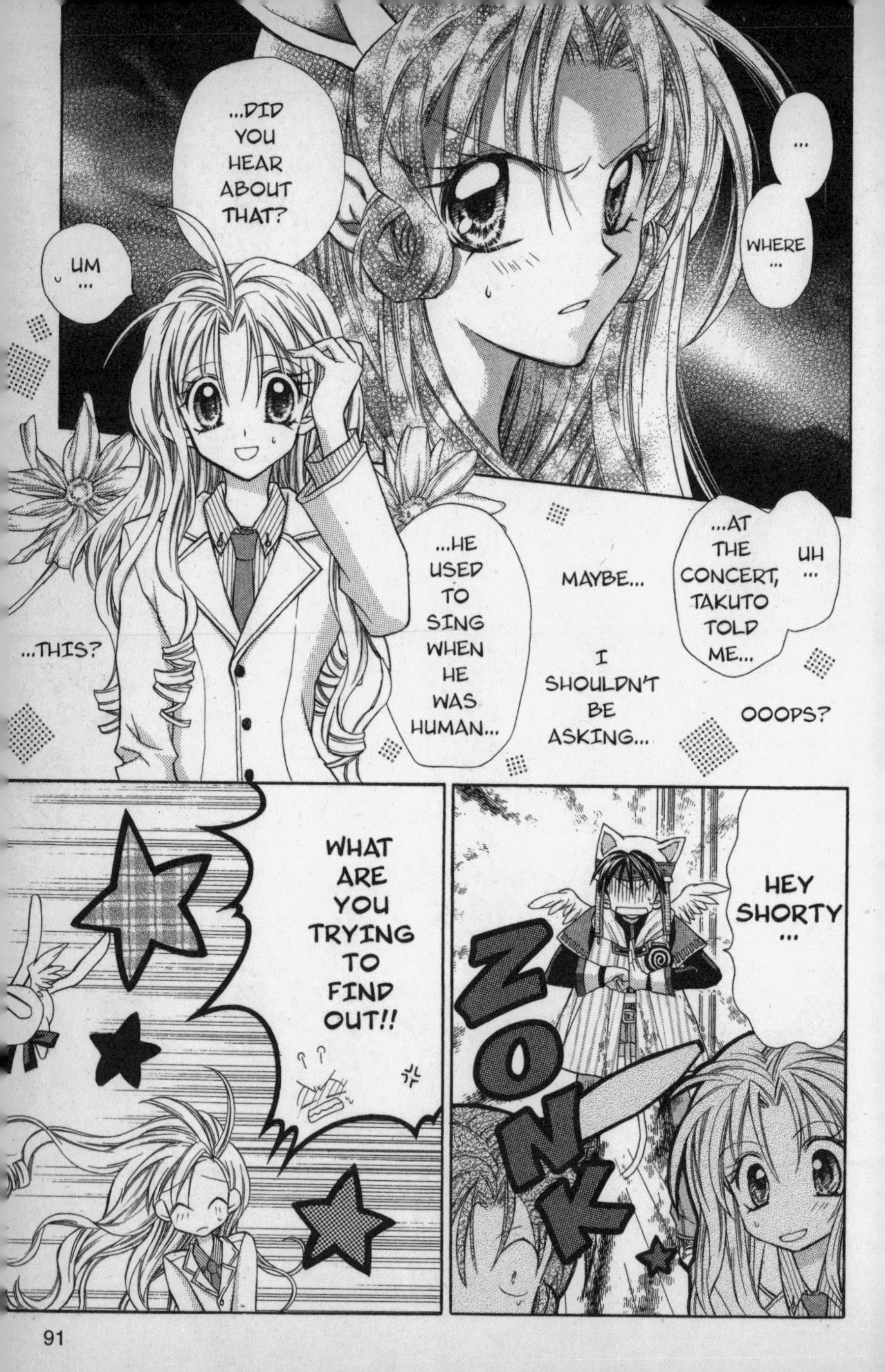
...
WHERE ...
...DID YOU HEAR ABOUT THAT?
UM ...
UH ...
...AT THE CONCERT, TAKUTO TOLD ME...
OOOPS?
MAYBE... I SHOULDN'T BE ASKING...
...HE USED TO SING WHEN HE WAS HUMAN...
...THIS?
HEY SHORTY ...
ZONK
WHAT ARE YOU TRYING TO FIND OUT!!

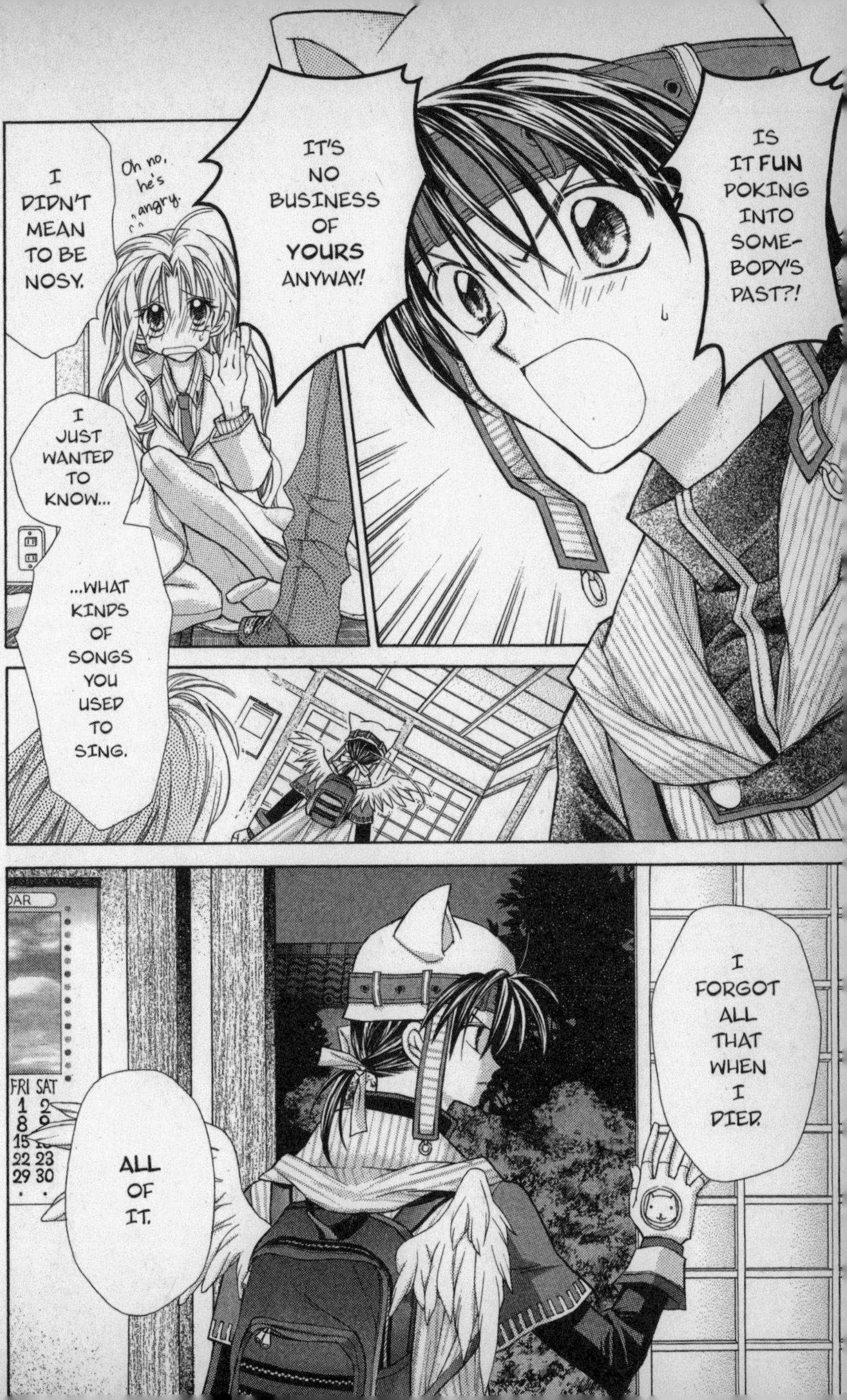
IS IT FUN POKING INTO SOMEBODY'S PAST?!
IT'S NO BUSINESS OF YOURS ANYWAY!
Oh no, he's angry.
I DIDN'T MEAN TO BE NOSY.
I JUST WANTED TO KNOW...
...WHAT KINDS OF SONGS YOU USED TO SING.
I FORGOT ALL THAT WHEN I DIED.
ALL OF IT.

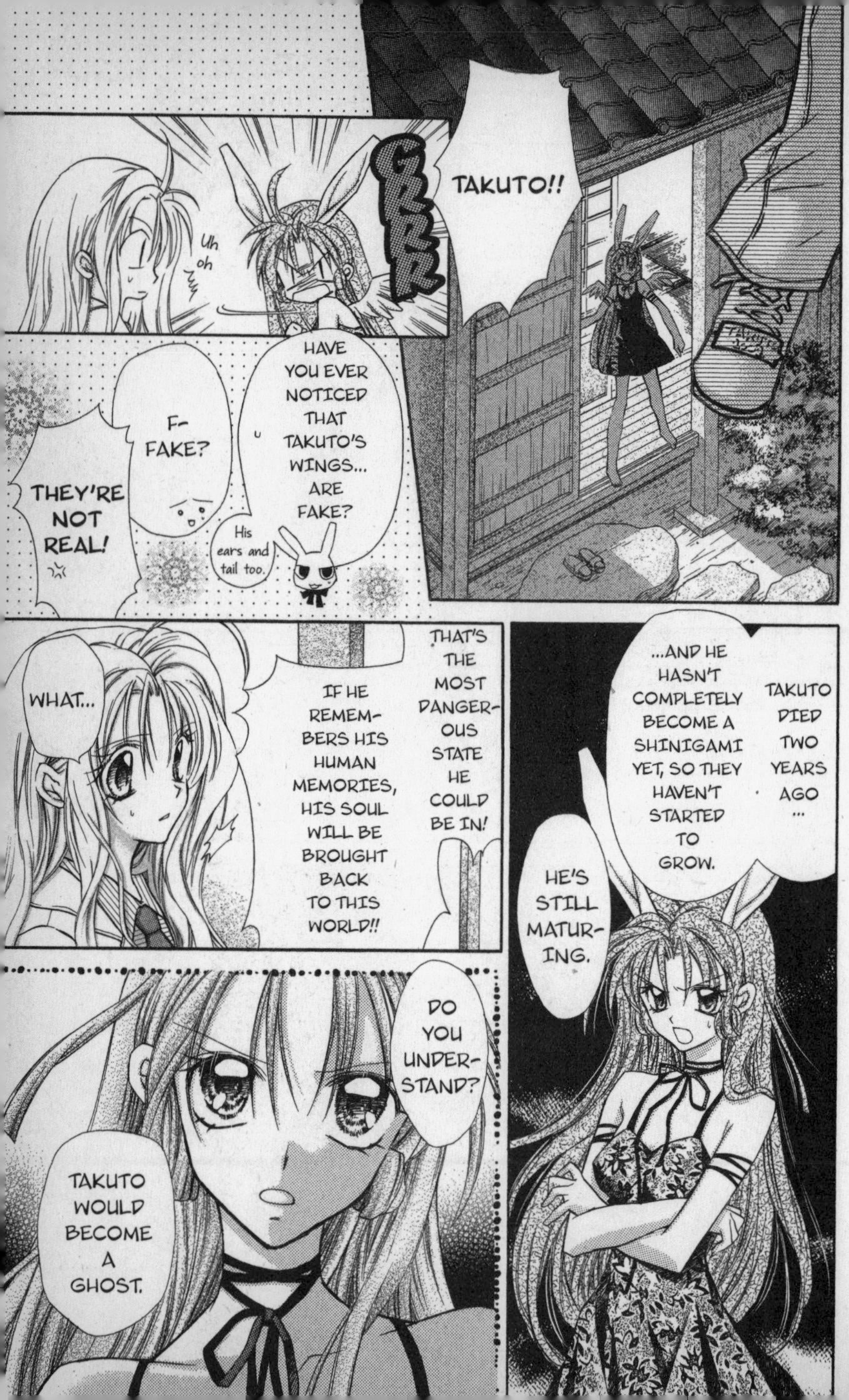
TAKUTO!!
GRRR
Uh oh
HAVE YOU EVER NOTICED THAT TAKUTO'S WINGS... ARE FAKE?
F- FAKE?
His ears and tail too.
THEY'RE NOT REAL!
TAKUTO DIED TWO YEARS AGO...
...AND HE HASN'T COMPLETELY BECOME A SHINIGAMI YET, SO THEY HAVEN'T STARTED TO GROW.
HE'S STILL MATURING.
THAT'S THE MOST DANGEROUS STATE HE COULD BE IN!
IF HE REMEMBERS HIS HUMAN MEMORIES, HIS SOUL WILL BE BROUGHT BACK TO THIS WORLD!!
WHAT...
DO YOU UNDERSTAND?
TAKUTO WOULD BECOME A GHOST.

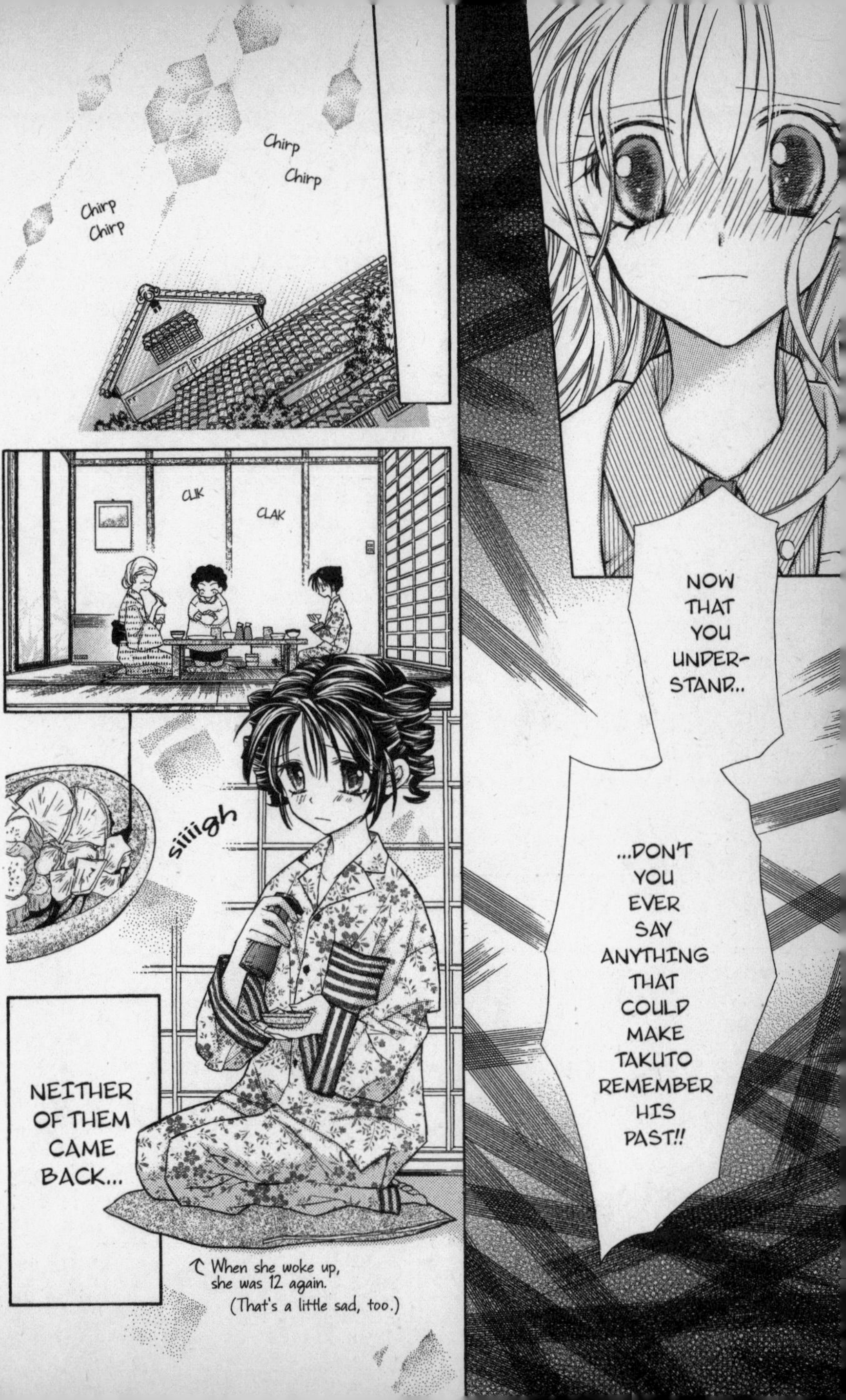
NOW THAT YOU UNDER-STAND...
...DON'T YOU EVER SAY ANYTHING THAT COULD MAKE TAKUTO REMEMBER HIS PAST!!
Chirp
Chirp
Chirp
Chirp
CLIK
CLAK
siiiigh
NEITHER OF THEM CAME BACK...
When she woke up, she was 12 again.
(That's a little sad, too.)

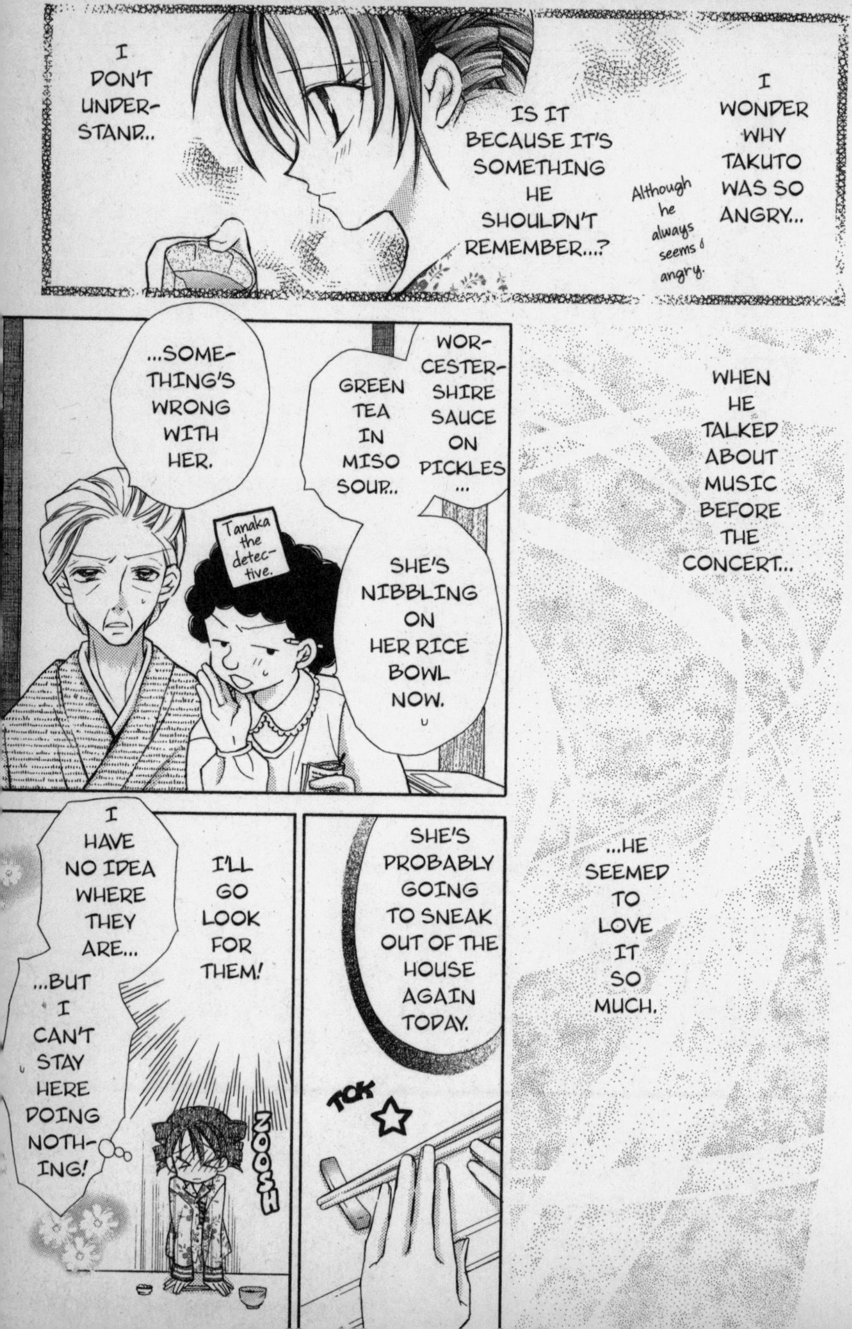
I WONDER WHY TAKUTO WAS SO ANGRY...
Although he always seems angry.
IS IT BECAUSE IT'S SOMETHING HE SHOULDN'T REMEMBER...?
I DON'T UNDER-STAND...
WHEN HE TALKED ABOUT MUSIC BEFORE THE CONCERT...
...HE SEEMED TO LOVE IT SO MUCH.
WOR-CESTER-SHIRE SAUCE ON PICKLES...
GREEN TEA IN MISO SOUP...
...SOME-THING'S WRONG WITH HER.
Tanaka the detec-tive.
SHE'S NIBBLING ON HER RICE BOWL NOW.
SHE'S PROBABLY GOING TO SNEAK OUT OF THE HOUSE AGAIN TODAY.
TOK
I'LL GO LOOK FOR THEM!
I HAVE NO IDEA WHERE THEY ARE...
...BUT I CAN'T STAY HERE DOING NOTH-ING!
WHOOSH

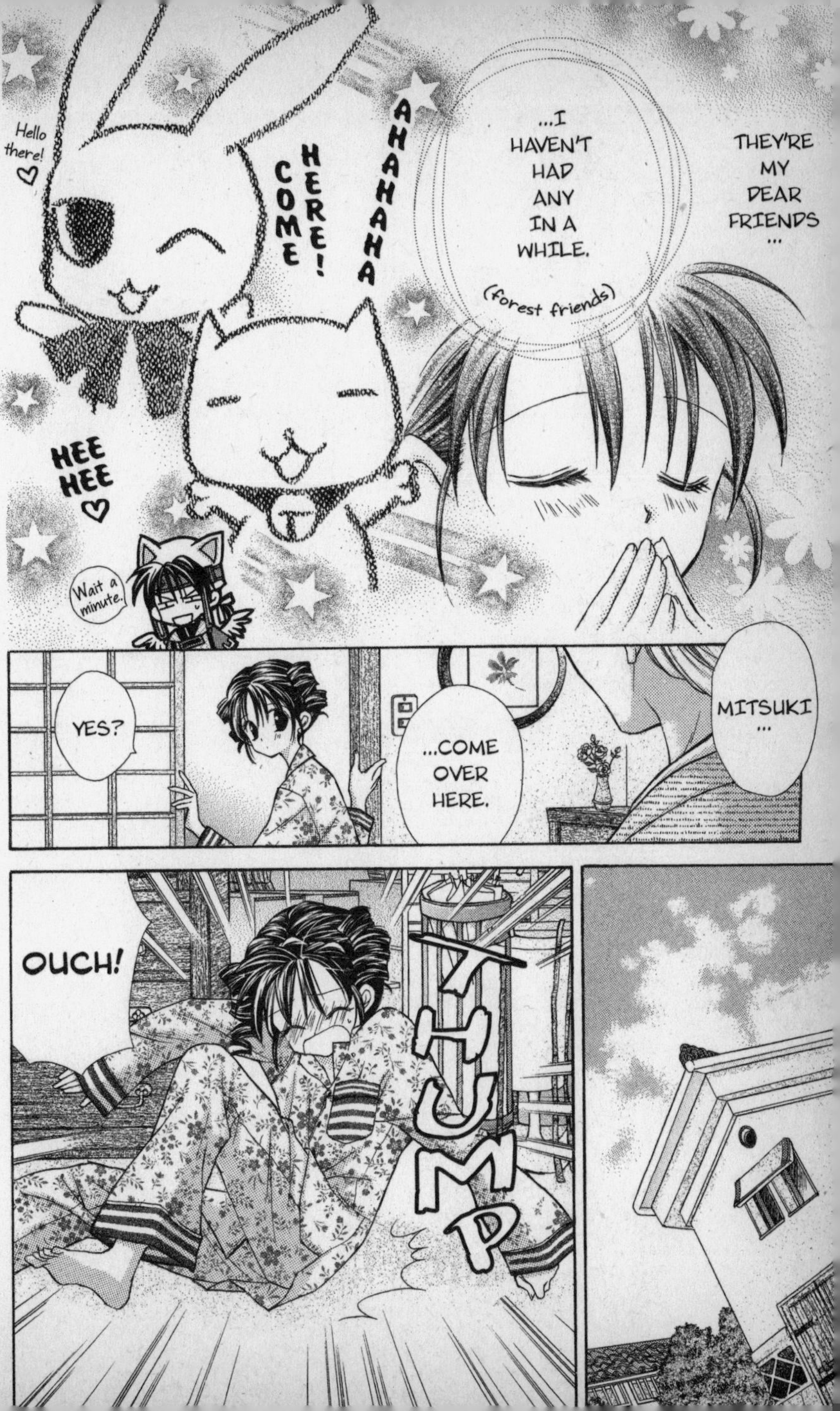

THEY'RE MY DEAR FRIENDS ...
...I HAVEN'T HAD ANY IN A WHILE.
(forest friends)
AHAHAHA
COME HERE!
Hello there! ♡
HEE HEE ♡
Wait a minute.
MITSUKI ...
...COME OVER HERE.
YES?
THUMP
OUCH!

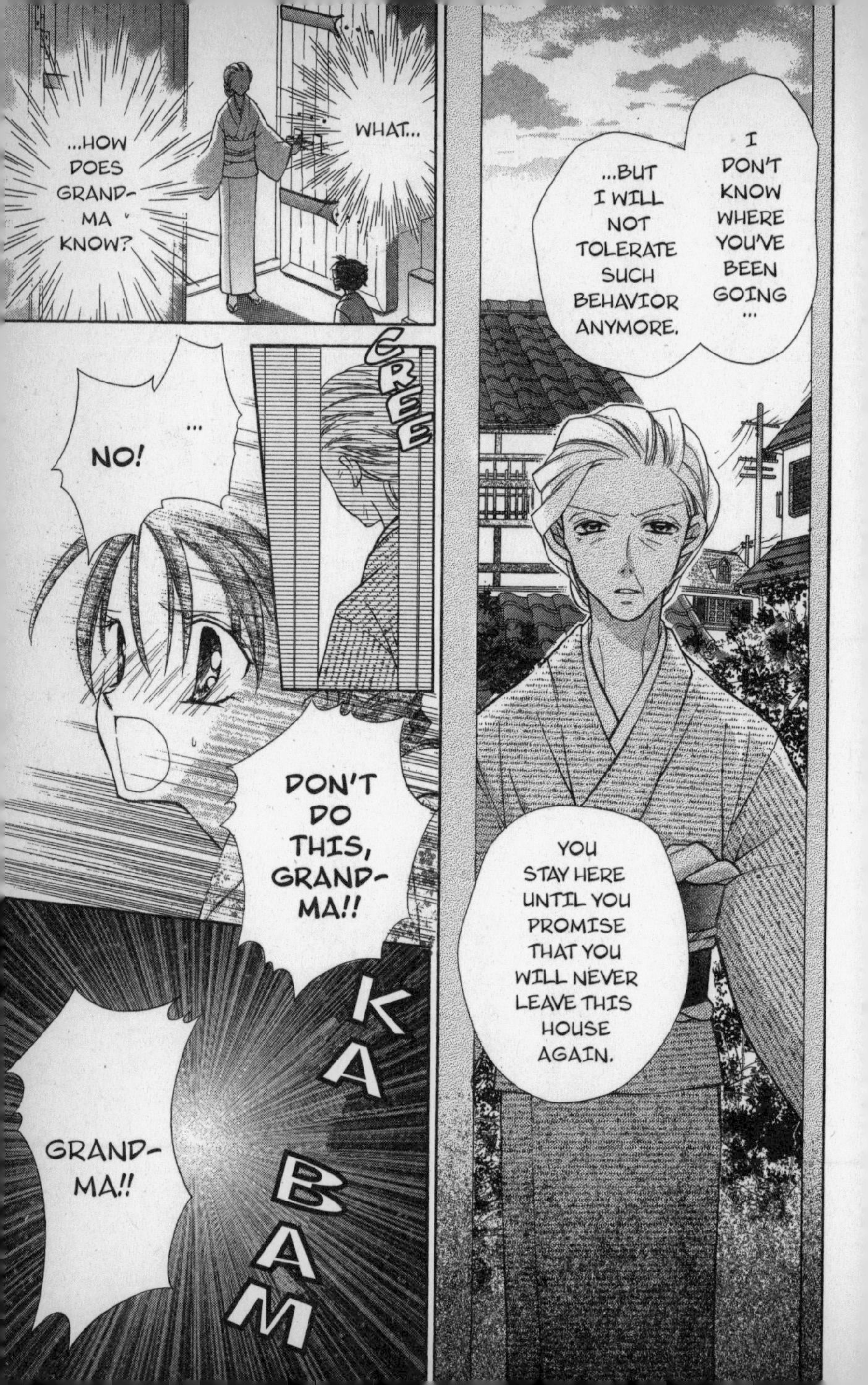
I DON'T KNOW WHERE YOU'VE BEEN GOING...
...BUT I WILL NOT TOLERATE SUCH BEHAVIOR ANYMORE.
YOU STAY HERE UNTIL YOU PROMISE THAT YOU WILL NEVER LEAVE THIS HOUSE AGAIN.
WHAT...
...HOW DOES GRAND-MA KNOW?
CREE
...
NO!
DON'T DO THIS, GRAND-MA!!
KA BAM
GRAND-MA!!

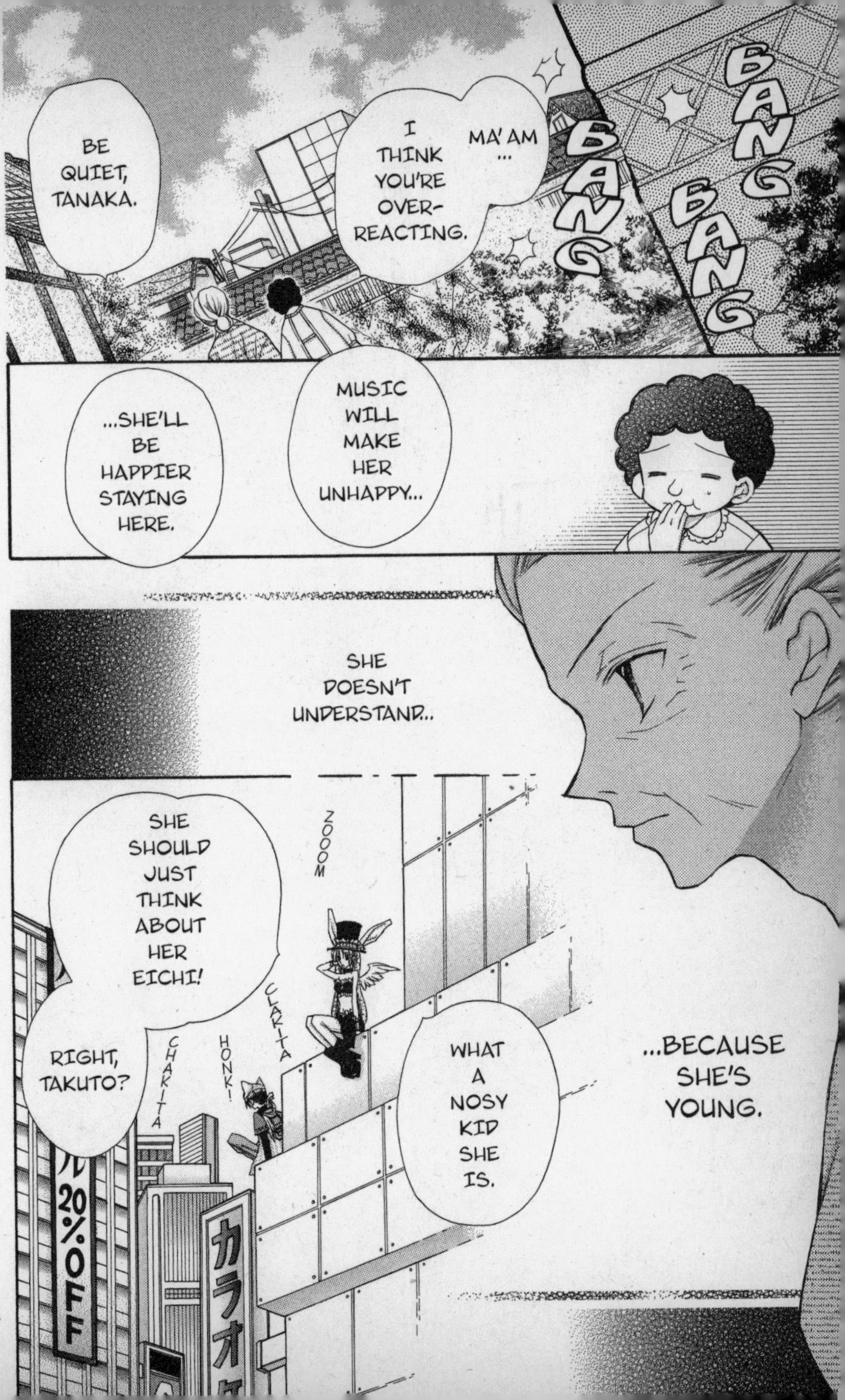
BANG BANG
BANG
MA'AM ...
I THINK YOU'RE OVER-REACTING.
BE QUIET, TANAKA.
MUSIC WILL MAKE HER UNHAPPY...
...SHE'LL BE HAPPIER STAYING HERE.
SHE DOESN'T UNDERSTAND...
...BECAUSE SHE'S YOUNG.
WHAT A NOSY KID SHE IS.
ZOOOM
CLAKITA
SHE SHOULD JUST THINK ABOUT HER EICHI!
HONK!
CHAKITA
RIGHT, TAKUTO?
20%OFF
カラオ

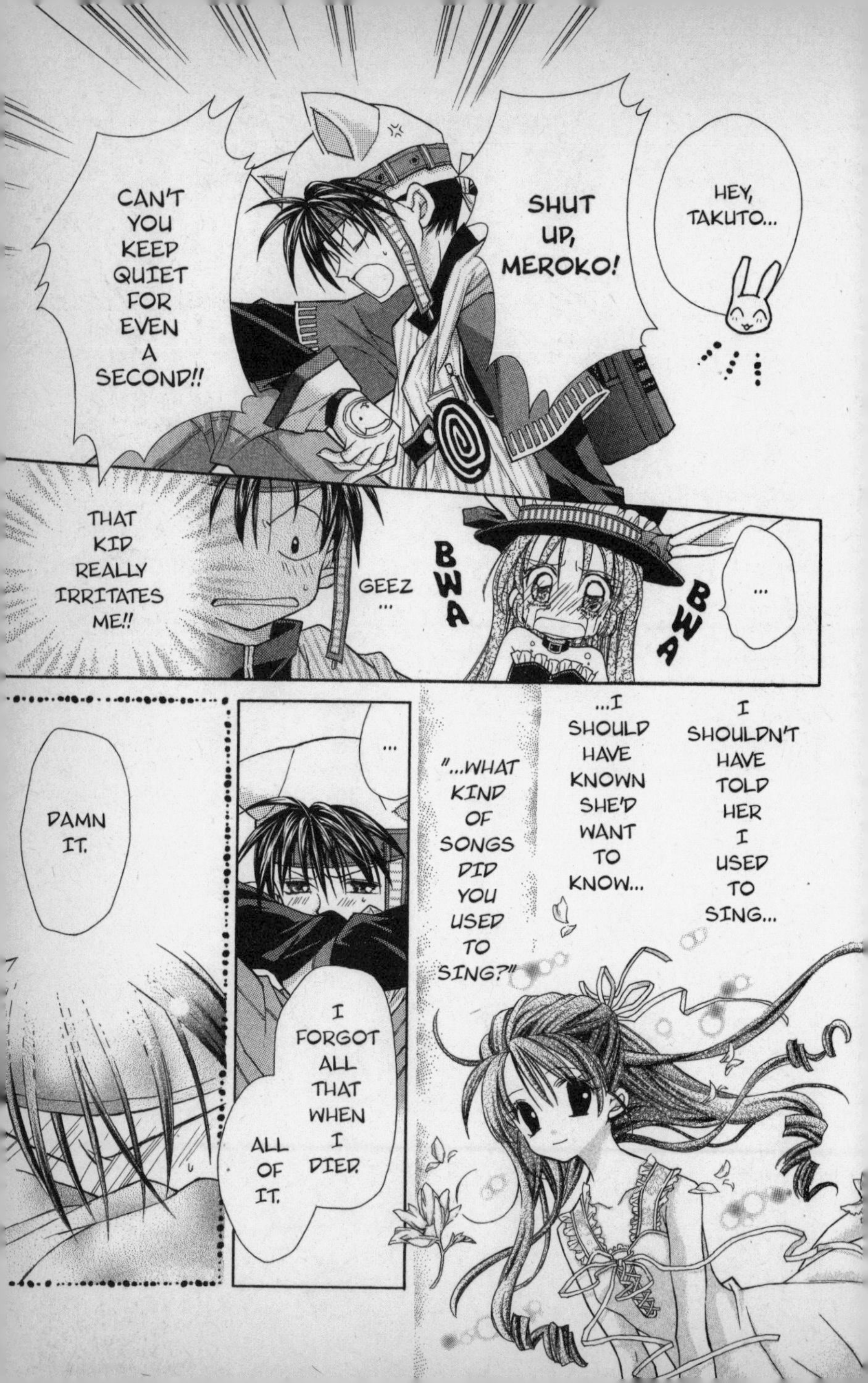
HEY, TAKUTO...
SHUT UP, MEROKO!
CAN'T YOU KEEP QUIET FOR EVEN A SECOND!!
...
BWA
BWA
GEEZ...
THAT KID REALLY IRRITATES ME!!
I SHOULDN'T HAVE TOLD HER I USED TO SING...
...I SHOULD HAVE KNOWN SHE'D WANT TO KNOW...
"...WHAT KIND OF SONGS DID YOU USED TO SING?"
...
I FORGOT ALL THAT WHEN I DIED.
ALL OF IT.
DAMN IT.

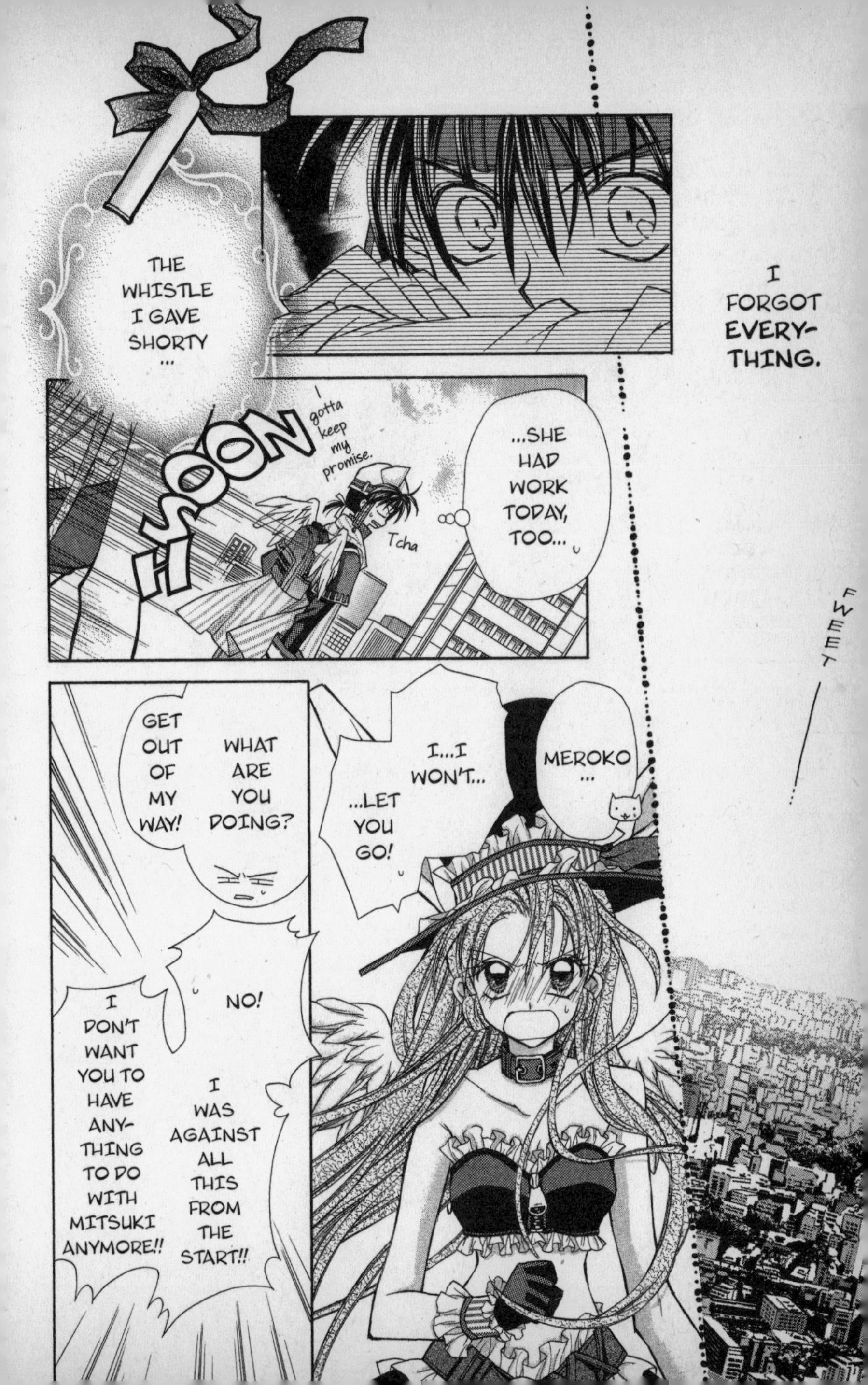
I FORGOT EVERYTHING.
THE WHISTLE I GAVE SHORTY...
...SHE HAD WORK TODAY, TOO...
I gotta keep my promise.
Tcha
ZOOSH!
FWEET
MEROKO...
I...I WON'T...
...LET YOU GO!
WHAT ARE YOU DOING?
GET OUT OF MY WAY!
NO!
I DON'T WANT YOU TO HAVE ANYTHING TO DO WITH MITSUKI ANYMORE!!
I WAS AGAINST ALL THIS FROM THE START!!

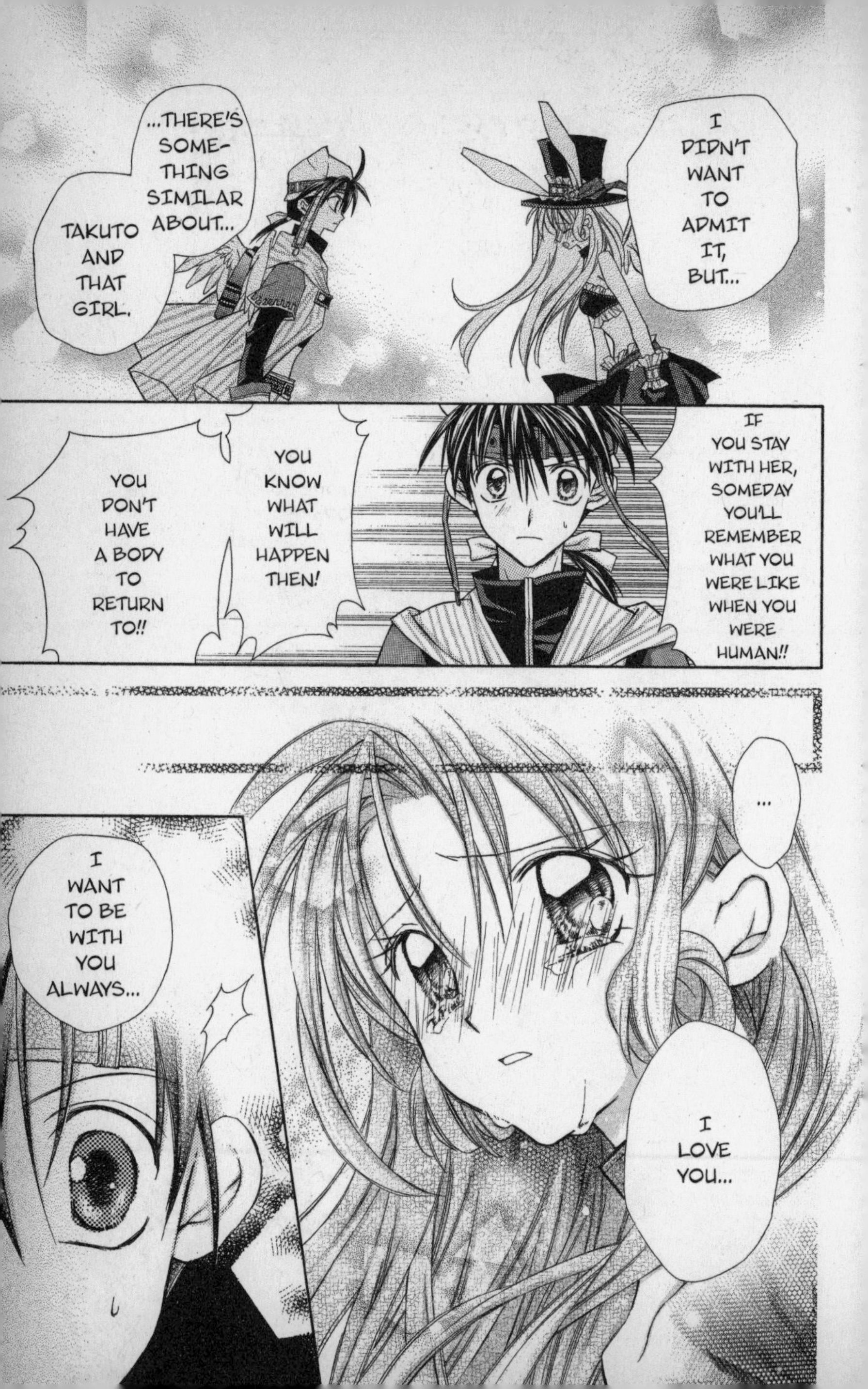
I DIDN'T WANT TO ADMIT IT, BUT...
...THERE'S SOME-THING SIMILAR ABOUT...
TAKUTO AND THAT GIRL.
IF YOU STAY WITH HER, SOMEDAY YOU'LL REMEMBER WHAT YOU WERE LIKE WHEN YOU WERE HUMAN!!
YOU KNOW WHAT WILL HAPPEN THEN!
YOU DON'T HAVE A BODY TO RETURN TO!!
...
I LOVE YOU...
I WANT TO BE WITH YOU ALWAYS...

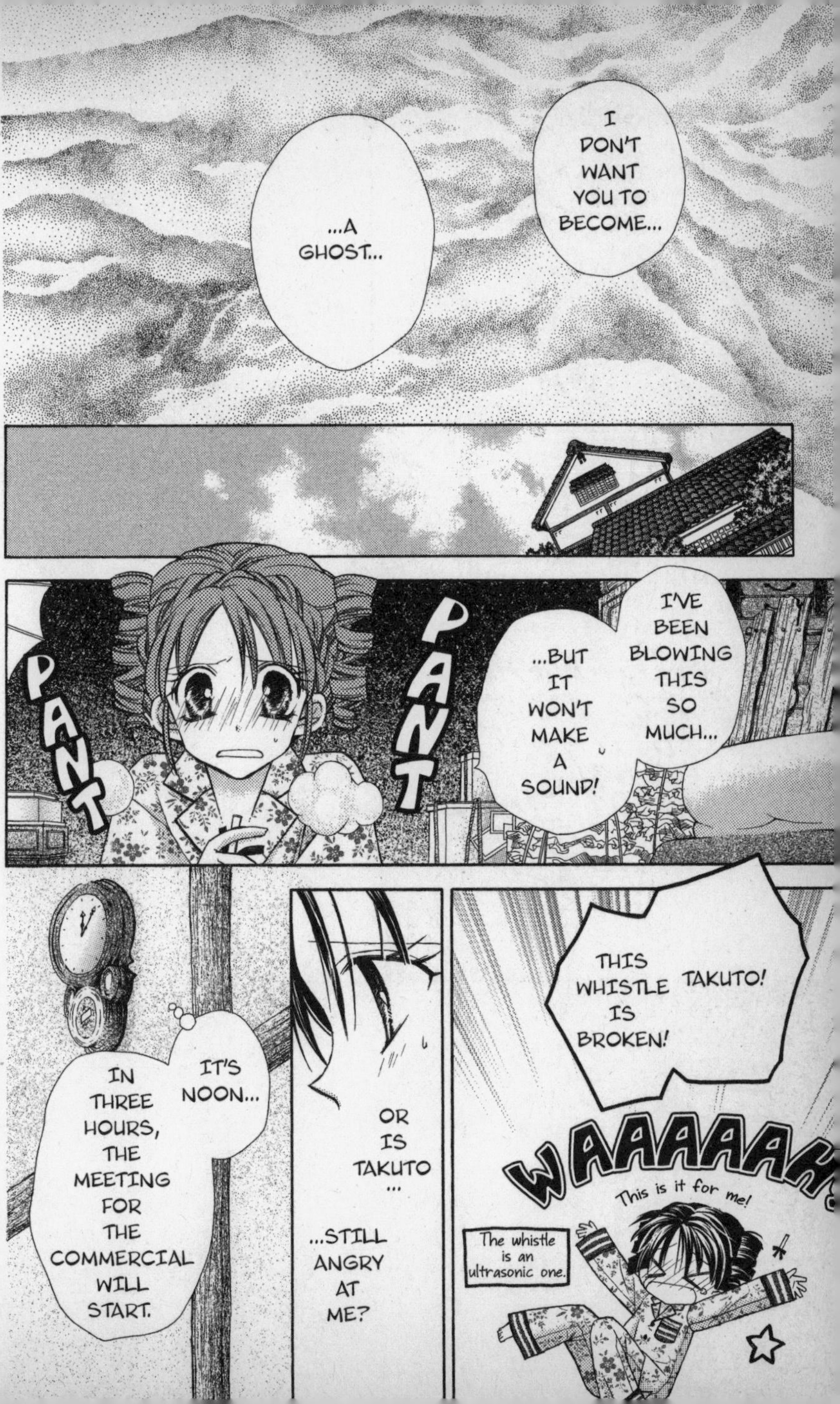
I DON'T WANT YOU TO BECOME...
...A GHOST...
I'VE BEEN BLOWING THIS SO MUCH...
...BUT IT WON'T MAKE A SOUND!
PANT
PANT
TAKUTO!
THIS WHISTLE IS BROKEN!
WAAAAAAH!
This is it for me!
The whistle is an ultrasonic one.
OR IS TAKUTO ...
...STILL ANGRY AT ME?
IT'S NOON...
IN THREE HOURS, THE MEETING FOR THE COMMERCIAL WILL START.

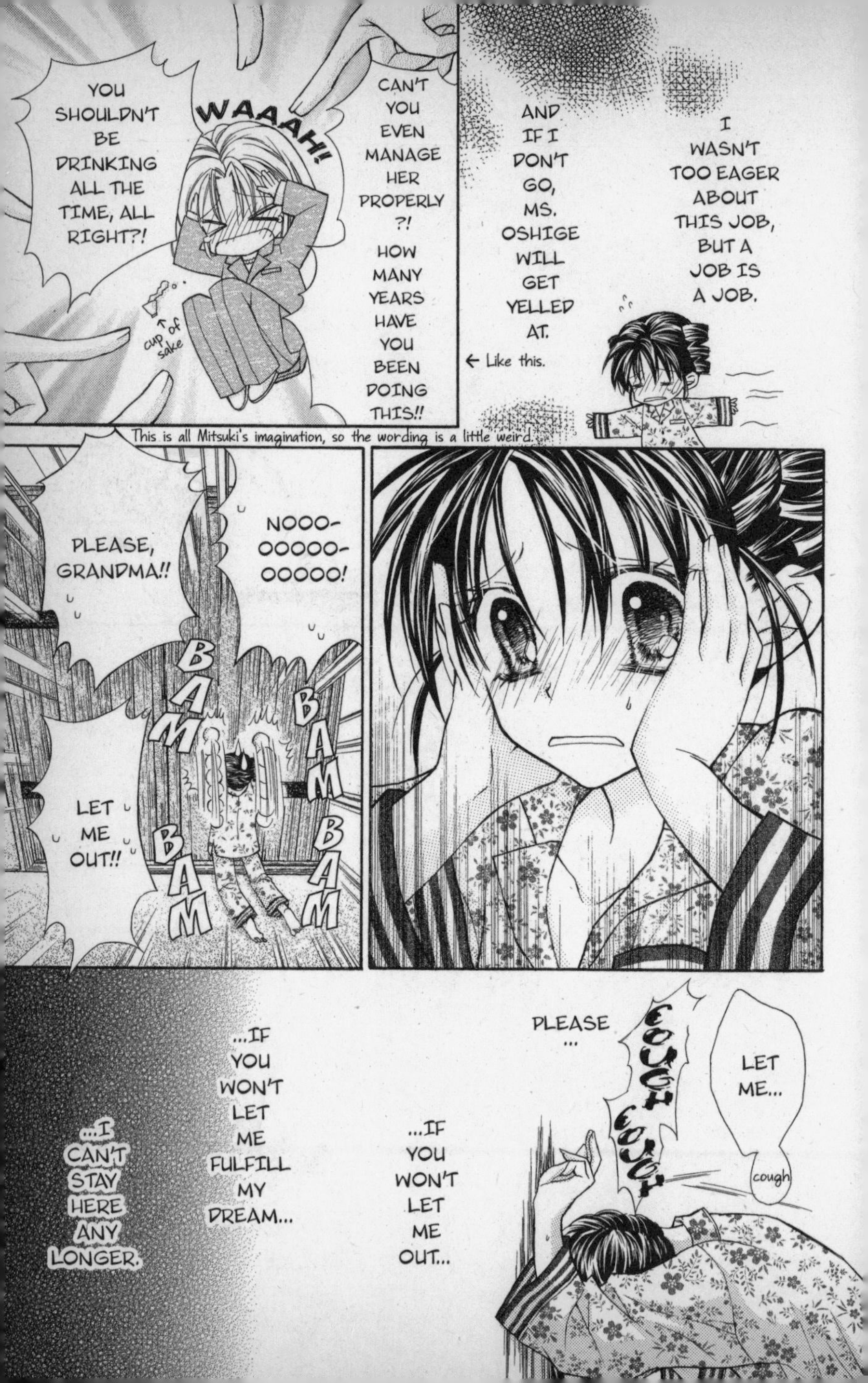
I WASN'T TOO EAGER ABOUT THIS JOB, BUT A JOB IS A JOB.
AND IF I DON'T GO, MS. OSHIGE WILL GET YELLED AT.
← Like this.
CAN'T YOU EVEN MANAGE HER PROPERLY?!
HOW MANY YEARS HAVE YOU BEEN DOING THIS!!
WAAAH!!
YOU SHOULDN'T BE DRINKING ALL THE TIME, ALL RIGHT?!
↑ cup of sake
This is all Mitsuki's imagination, so the wording is a little weird.
NOOO-OOOOO-OOOOO!
PLEASE, GRANDMA!!
BAM BAM
BAM BAM
LET ME OUT!!
LET ME...
cough
COUGH COUGH
PLEASE...
...IF YOU WON'T LET ME OUT...
...IF YOU WON'T LET ME FULFILL MY DREAM...
...I CAN'T STAY HERE ANY LONGER.

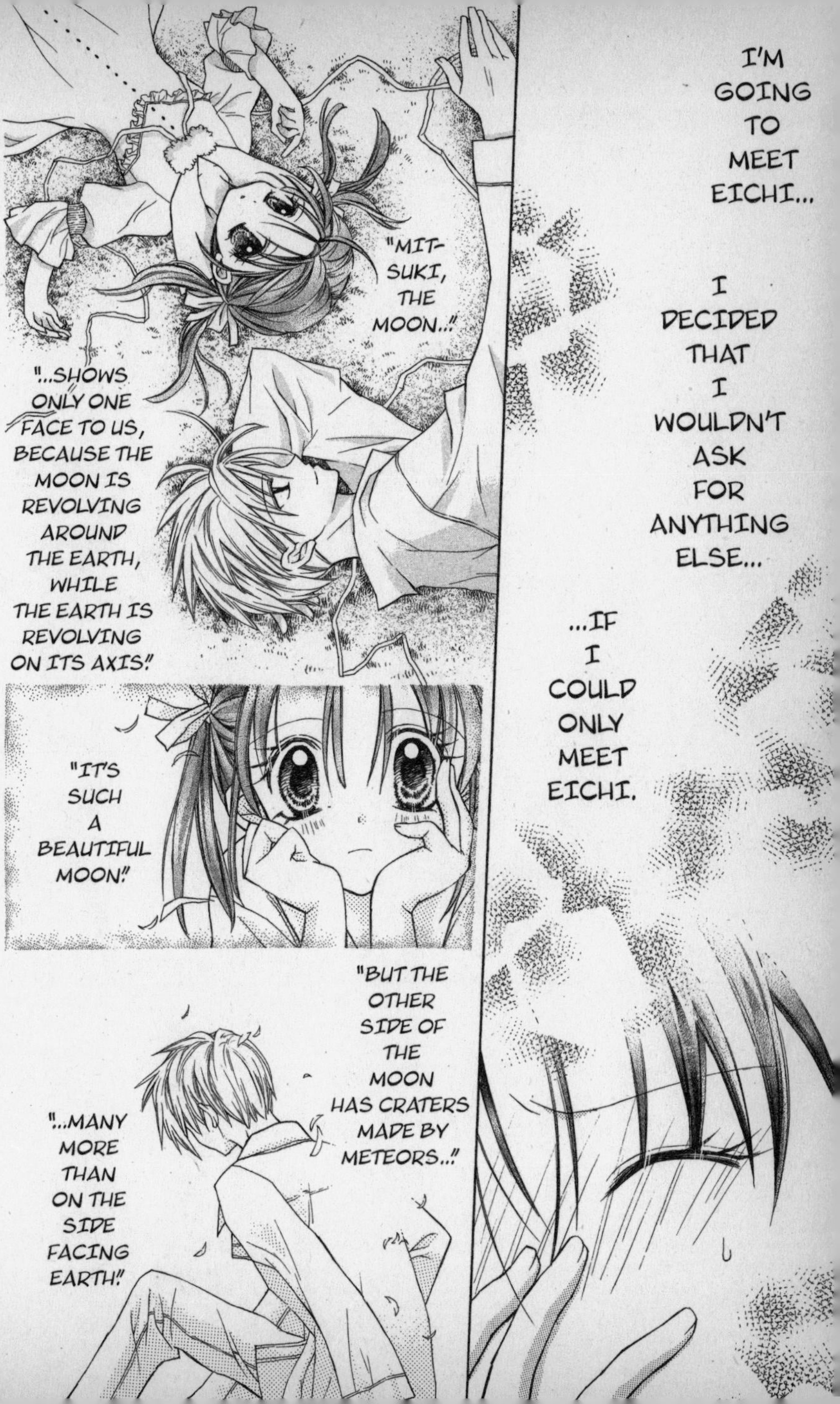
I'M GOING TO MEET EICHI...
I DECIDED THAT I WOULDN'T ASK FOR ANYTHING ELSE...
...IF I COULD ONLY MEET EICHI.
"MIT-SUKI, THE MOON..."
"...SHOWS ONLY ONE FACE TO US, BECAUSE THE MOON IS REVOLVING AROUND THE EARTH, WHILE THE EARTH IS REVOLVING ON ITS AXIS!"
"IT'S SUCH A BEAUTIFUL MOON!"
"BUT THE OTHER SIDE OF THE MOON HAS CRATERS MADE BY METEORS..."
"...MANY MORE THAN ON THE SIDE FACING EARTH!"

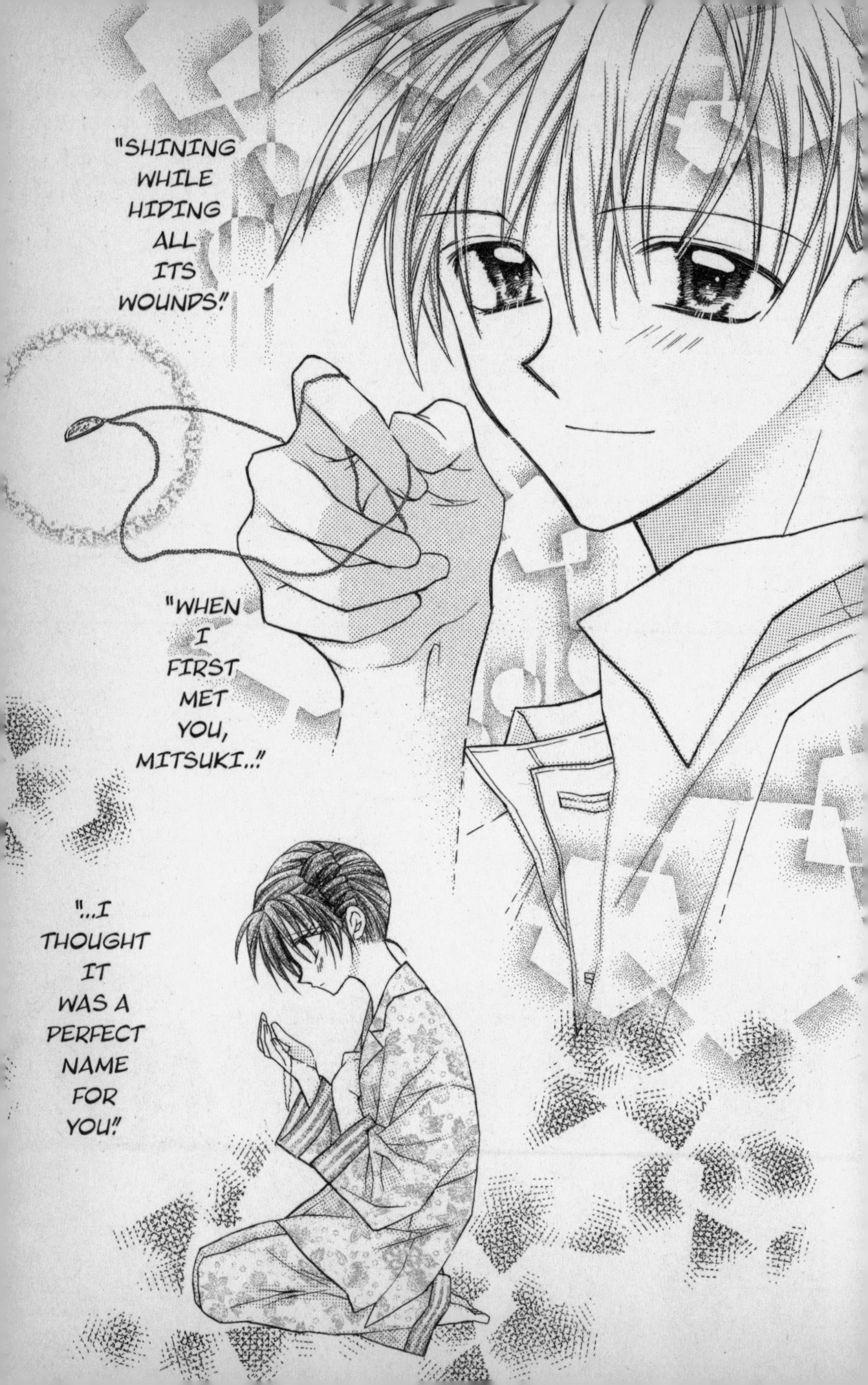
"SHINING WHILE HIDING ALL ITS WOUNDS."
"WHEN I FIRST MET YOU, MITSUKI..."
"...I THOUGHT IT WAS A PERFECT NAME FOR YOU."

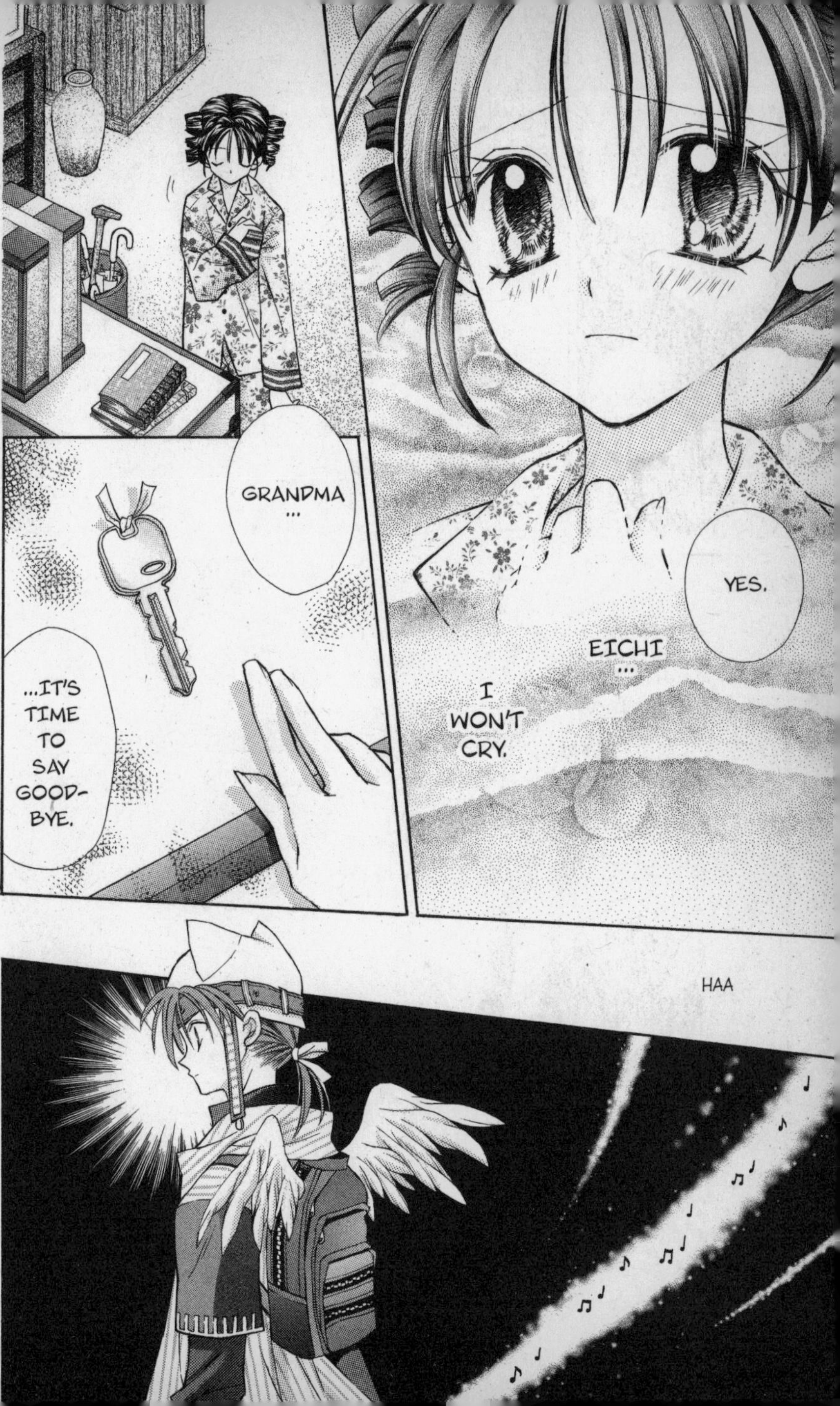
YES.
EICHI...
I WON'T CRY.
GRANDMA...
...IT'S TIME TO SAY GOOD-BYE.
HAA

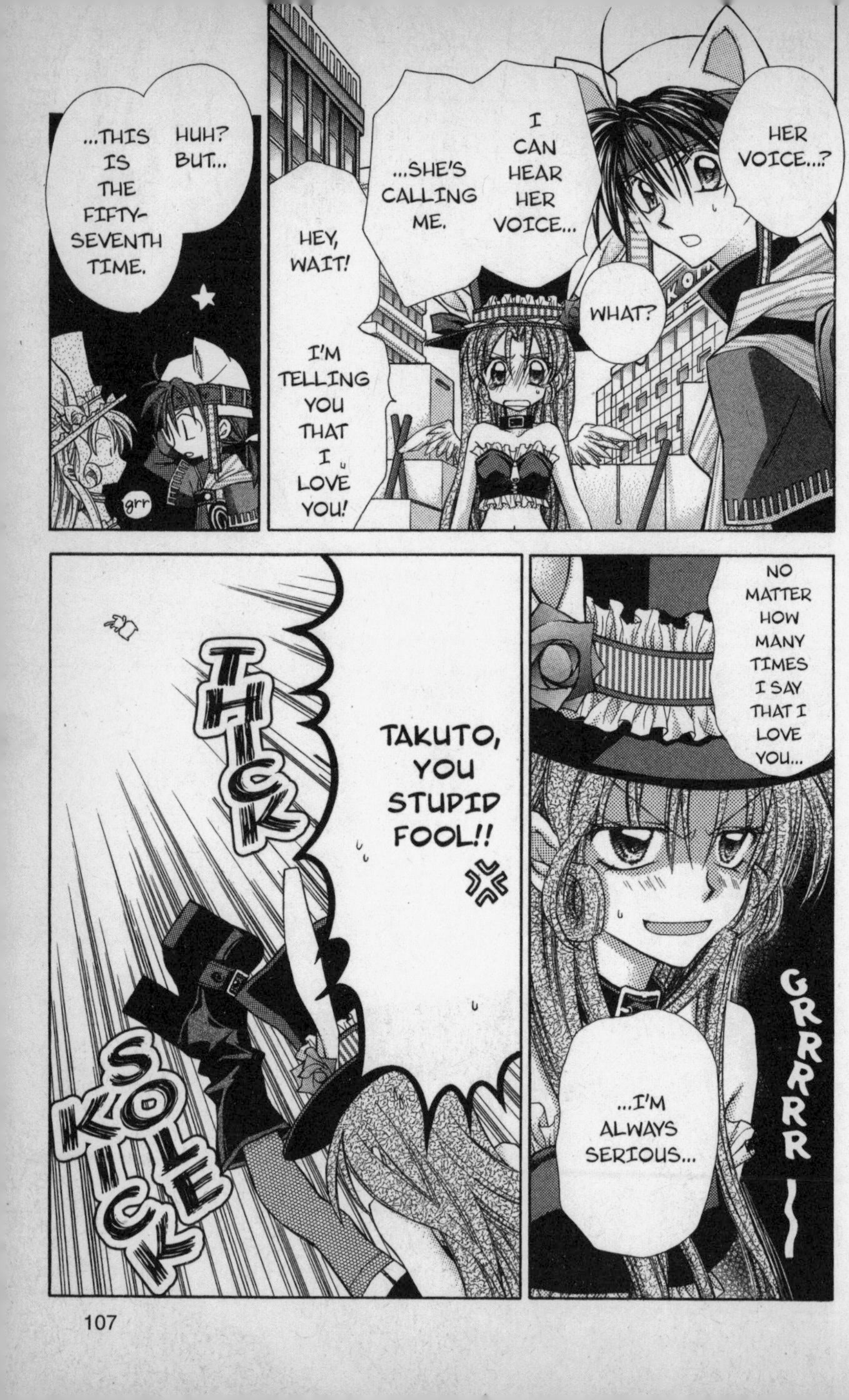
HER VOICE...?
I CAN HEAR HER VOICE...
...SHE'S CALLING ME.
WHAT?
HEY, WAIT!
I'M TELLING YOU THAT I LOVE YOU!
HUH? BUT...
...THIS IS THE FIFTY-SEVENTH TIME.
grr
NO MATTER HOW MANY TIMES I SAY THAT I LOVE YOU...
GRRRR~
...I'M ALWAYS SERIOUS...
TAKUTO, YOU STUPID FOOL!!
THICK
SOLE KICK

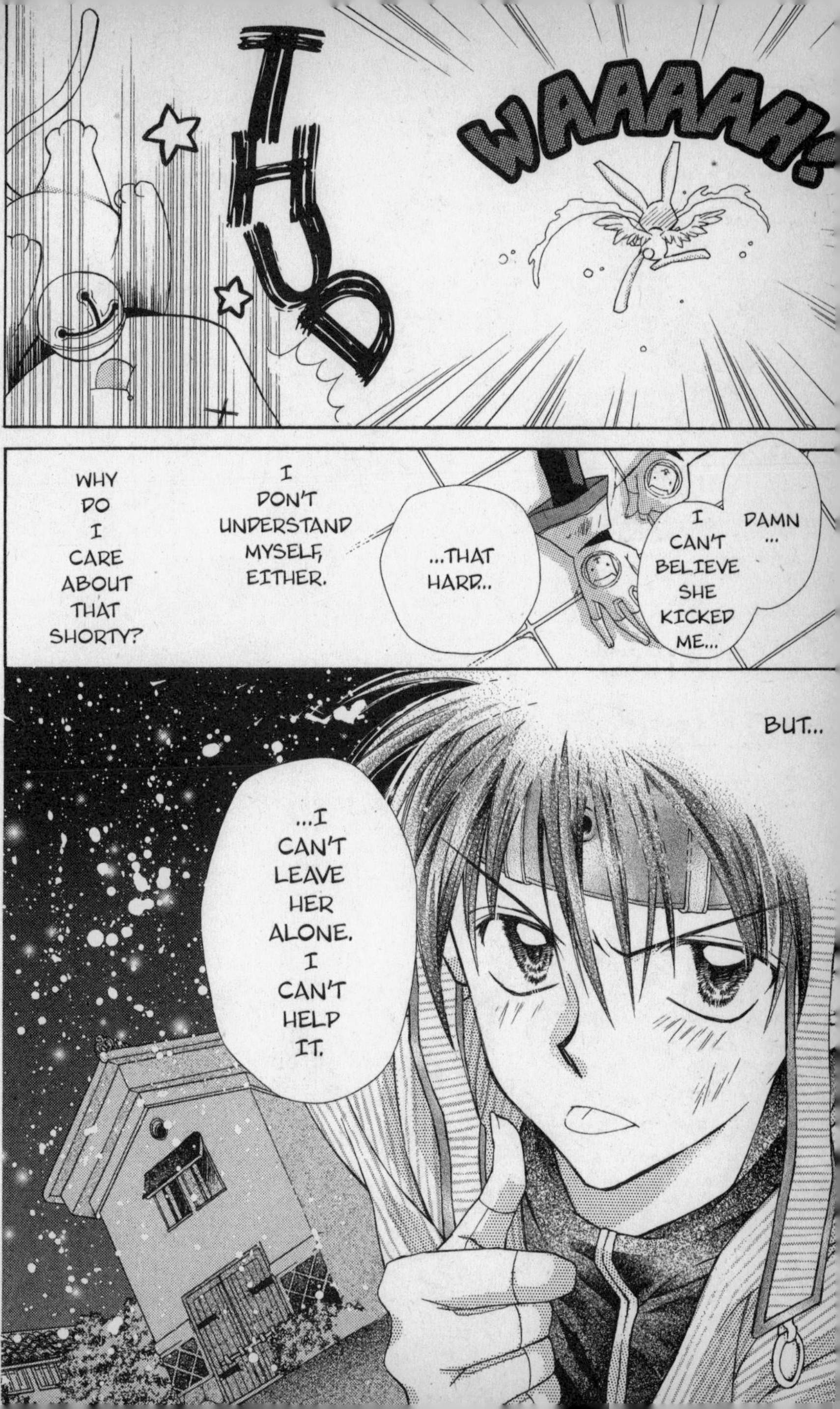
WAAAAAH!
THUD
DAMN...
I CAN'T BELIEVE SHE KICKED ME...
...THAT HARD...
I DON'T UNDERSTAND MYSELF, EITHER.
WHY DO I CARE ABOUT THAT SHORTY?
BUT...
...I CAN'T LEAVE HER ALONE. I CAN'T HELP IT.

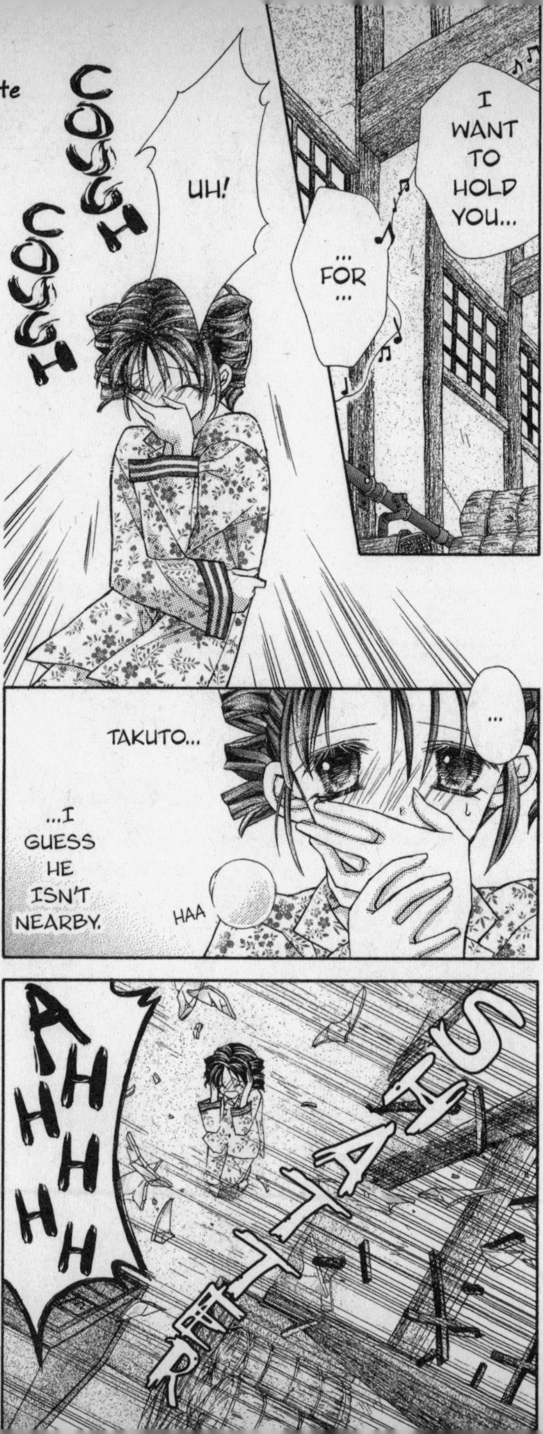
I WANT TO HOLD YOU...
...FOR...
UH!
COUGH COUGH
...
TAKUTO...
...I GUESS HE ISN'T NEARBY.
HAA
SHATTER
AHHHHHH

About Full Moon o Sagashite

I received a fan letter asking "Is this the 'last work' you've always wanted to draw?!" Not quite.

The Difference:
↓

① I've always wanted to use that title someday.

② But it's not the title for that "last work."
≡ Slight difference!!

That last work will never be drawn!!

The Reason:

① There's lots of murder in it, so I can't draw it for Ribon. Maybe if I insist, they may let me draw it, but I don't have the confidence.
It's a long story.

② I only intend to draw for Ribon!! Forever!! So let's forget about that (the last work), and talk about Full Moon.

I started working on "Full Moon o Sagashite" as I was near finishing "KYOKO." In the beginning, I wanted to draw about "ordinary" idols, but it turned out this way.
(I don't intend to draw fantasies all the time.)

My stories and characters aren't realistic. But since the time I was drawing "I-O-N," I've always wanted to draw an ordinary story!!
To be continued.

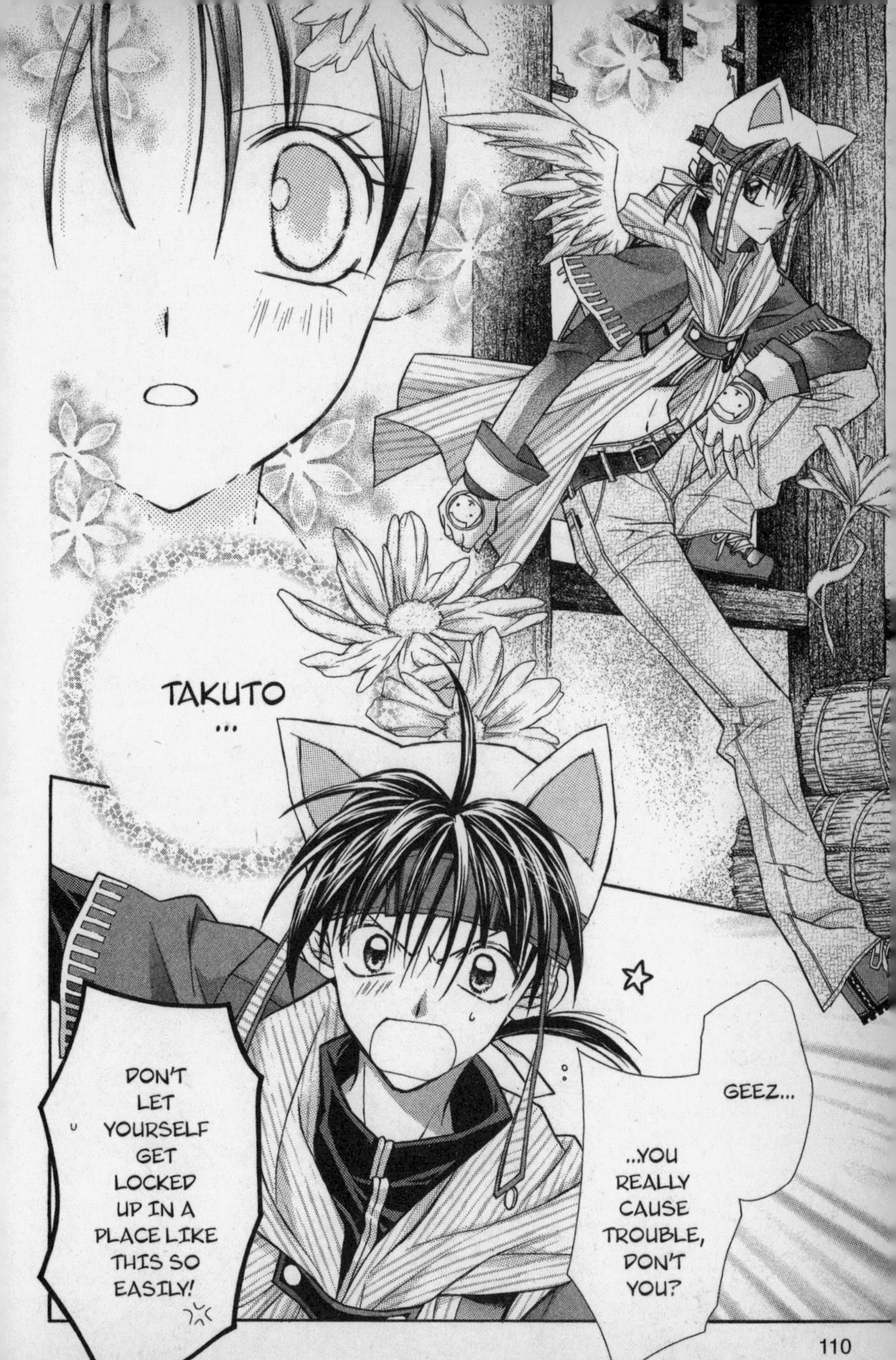
TAKUTO ...
GEEZ...
...YOU REALLY CAUSE TROUBLE, DON'T YOU?
DON'T LET YOURSELF GET LOCKED UP IN A PLACE LIKE THIS SO EASILY!

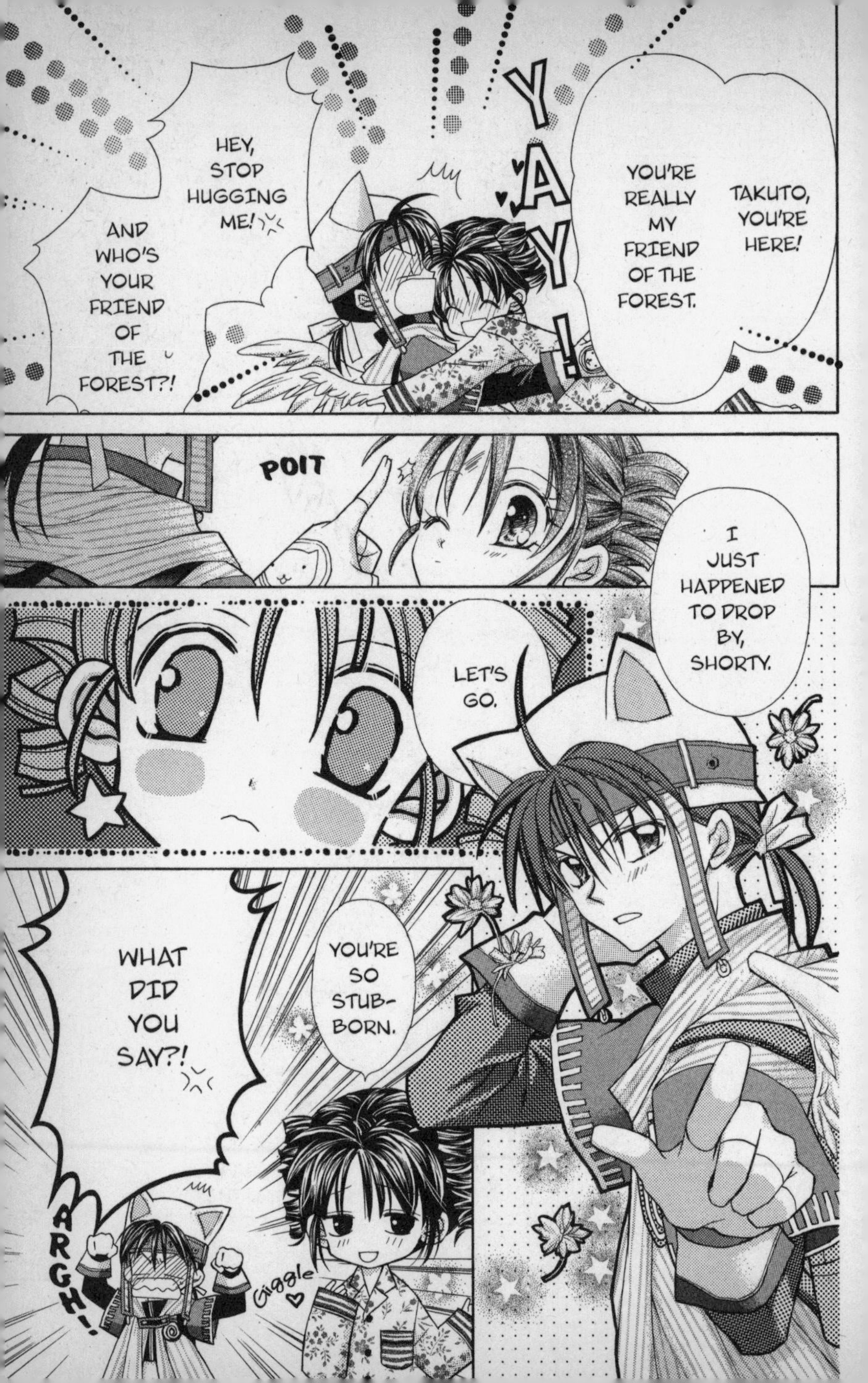
TAKUTO, YOU'RE HERE!
YOU'RE REALLY MY FRIEND OF THE FOREST.
YAY!
HEY, STOP HUGGING ME!
AND WHO'S YOUR FRIEND OF THE FOREST?!
I JUST HAPPENED TO DROP BY, SHORTY.
POIT
LET'S GO.
YOU'RE SO STUBBORN.
WHAT DID YOU SAY?!
ARGH!
Giggle

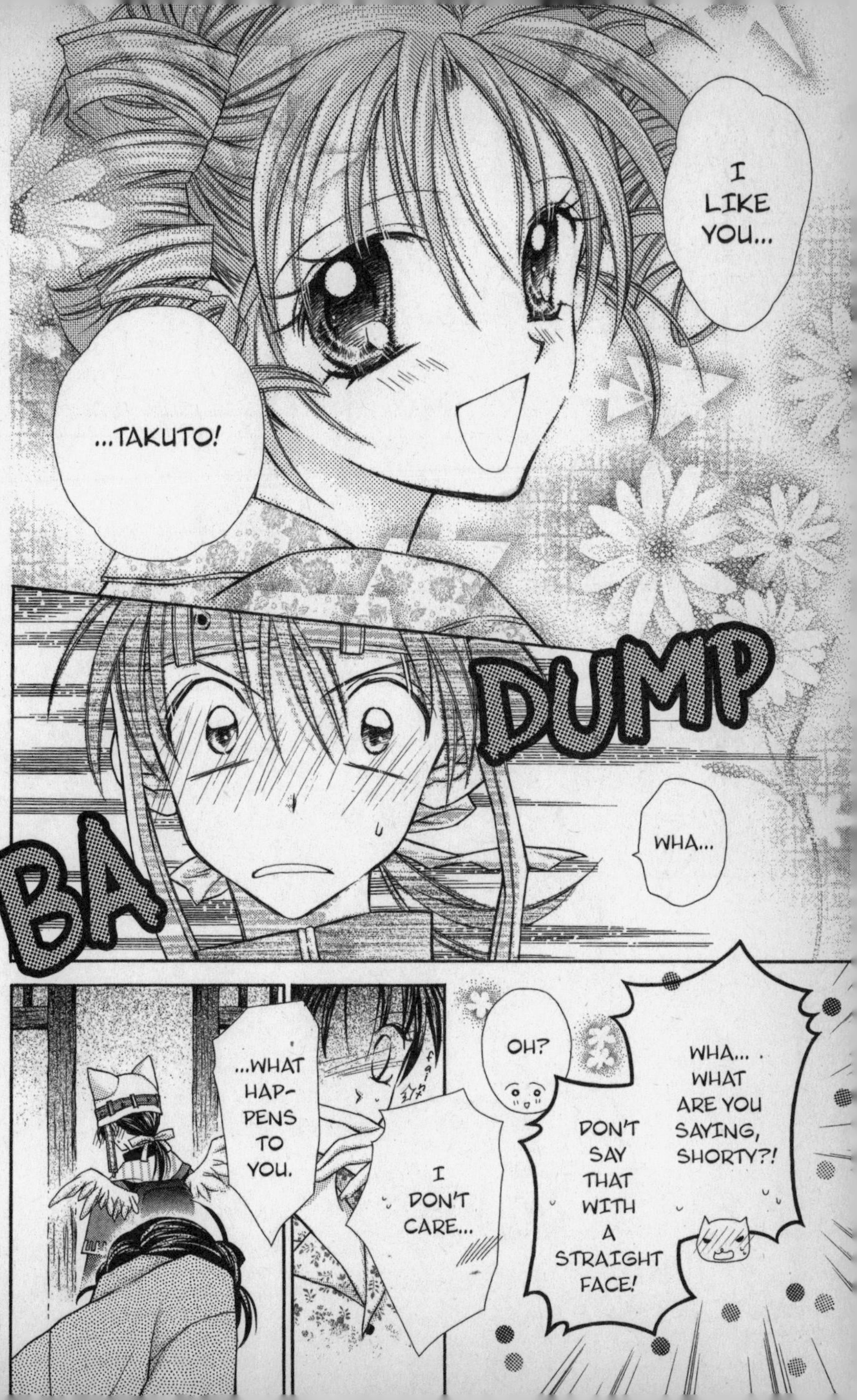
I LIKE YOU...
...TAKUTO!
BA DUMP
WHA...
WHA... WHAT ARE YOU SAYING, SHORTY?!
DON'T SAY THAT WITH A STRAIGHT FACE!
OH?
I DON'T CARE...
...WHAT HAPPENS TO YOU.

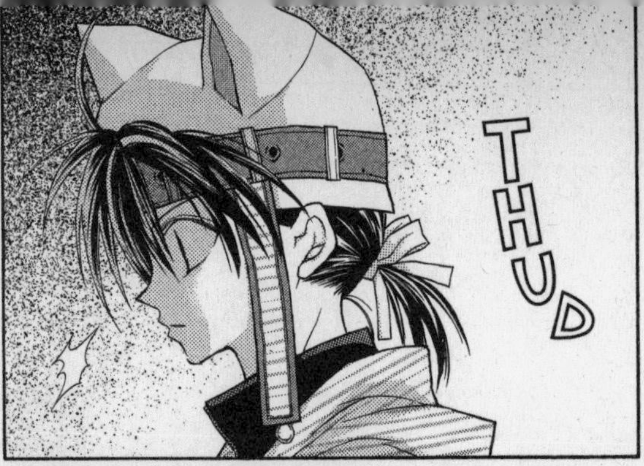
THUD

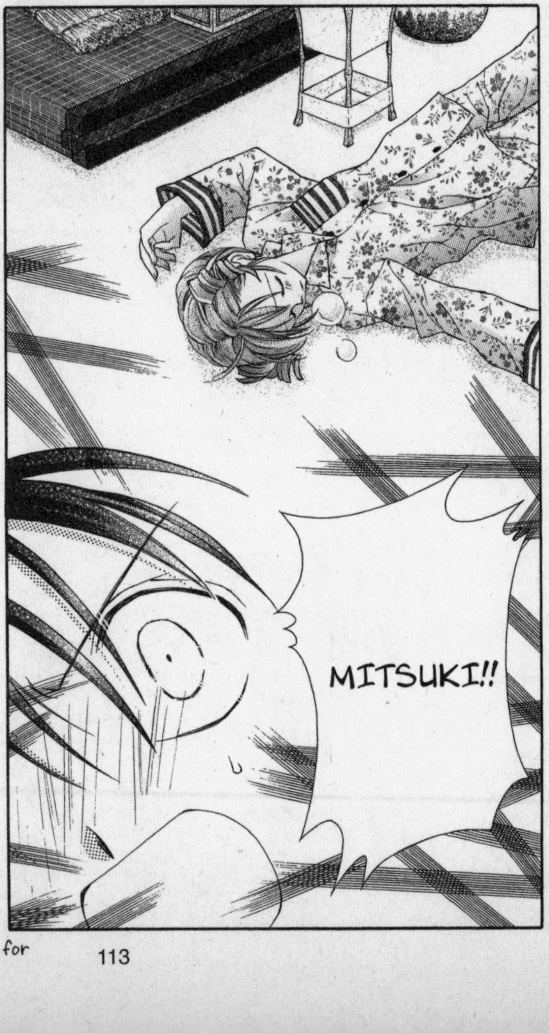
MITSUKI!!

Full Moon o Sagashite (cont.)

To continue what I started writing... When I made my debut, I didn't intend to draw fantasies at all. (If you thought "no way!" please believe me.) =_=

I was so bad at creating characters that my first editor constantly told me to "think of some defining characteristic for the main characters."(Well, maybe he tells everyone this, not just me.) A defining characteristic is something like "mermaid" or "princess." Until that is the done, the editor wouldn't okay my plot.

Actually, there was one time I hated doing it.

It was because I felt I was being "forced to draw." And since I didn't intend to draw fantasies, I didn't want to take the easy route by using fantasies as a defining characteristic. So one time I chose "a young lady" to escape from fantasies. (My sentence is getting weird.)

If you want to know which work I'm talking about, please buy the Ribon Mascot Comics "Kanshakudama no Yuu-utsu!"

What a long preface. (Sorry!)

So anyway, as time went by, this became a habit. That's my excuse. It's editor O's fault.

I'll send some liquor if editor O gets upset about this.

To be continued. →

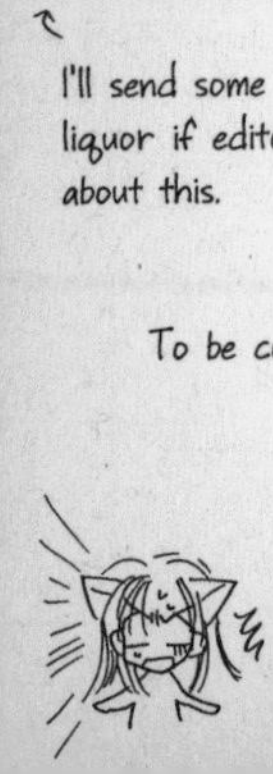

Using one sidebar just for preliminary remarks! What a woman!!

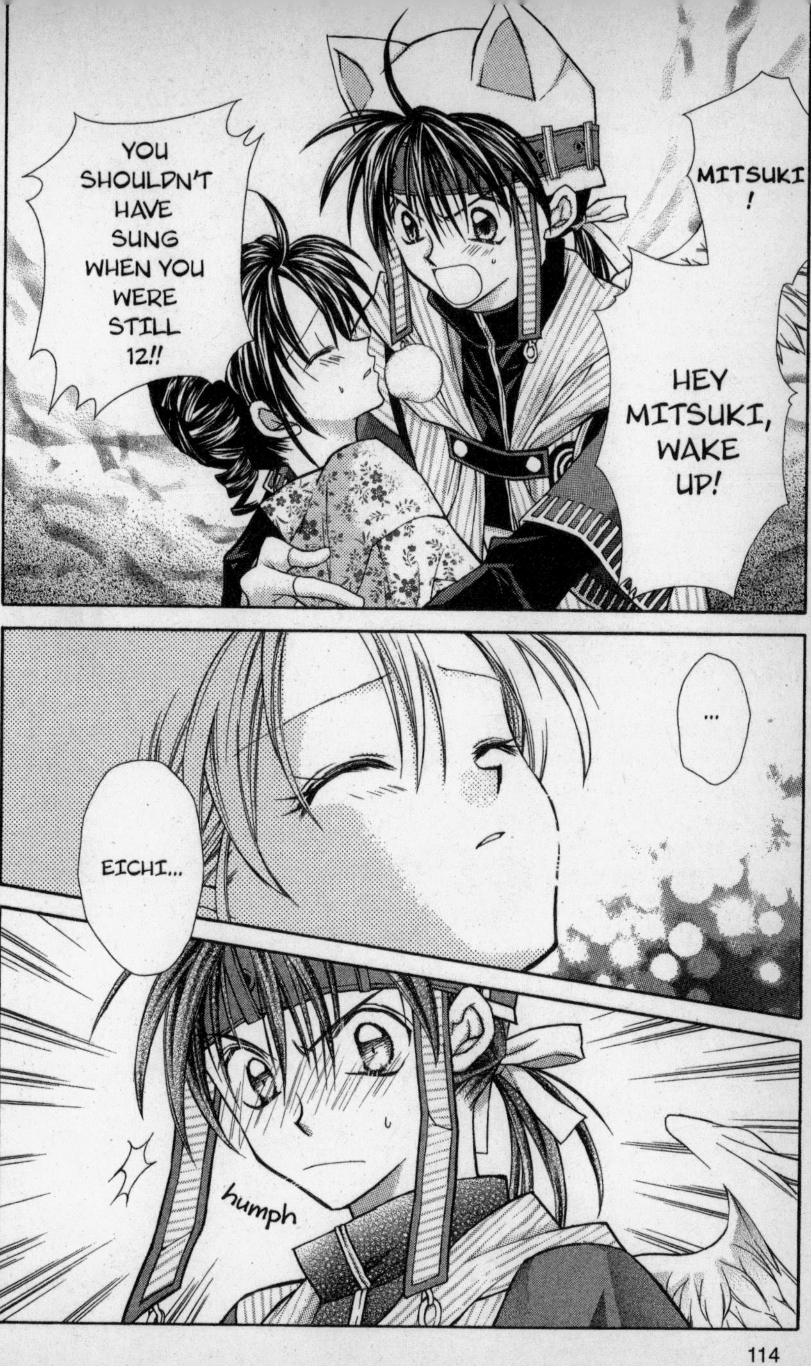
MITSUKI!
HEY MITSUKI, WAKE UP!
YOU SHOULDN'T HAVE SUNG WHEN YOU WERE STILL 12!!
...
EICHI...
humph

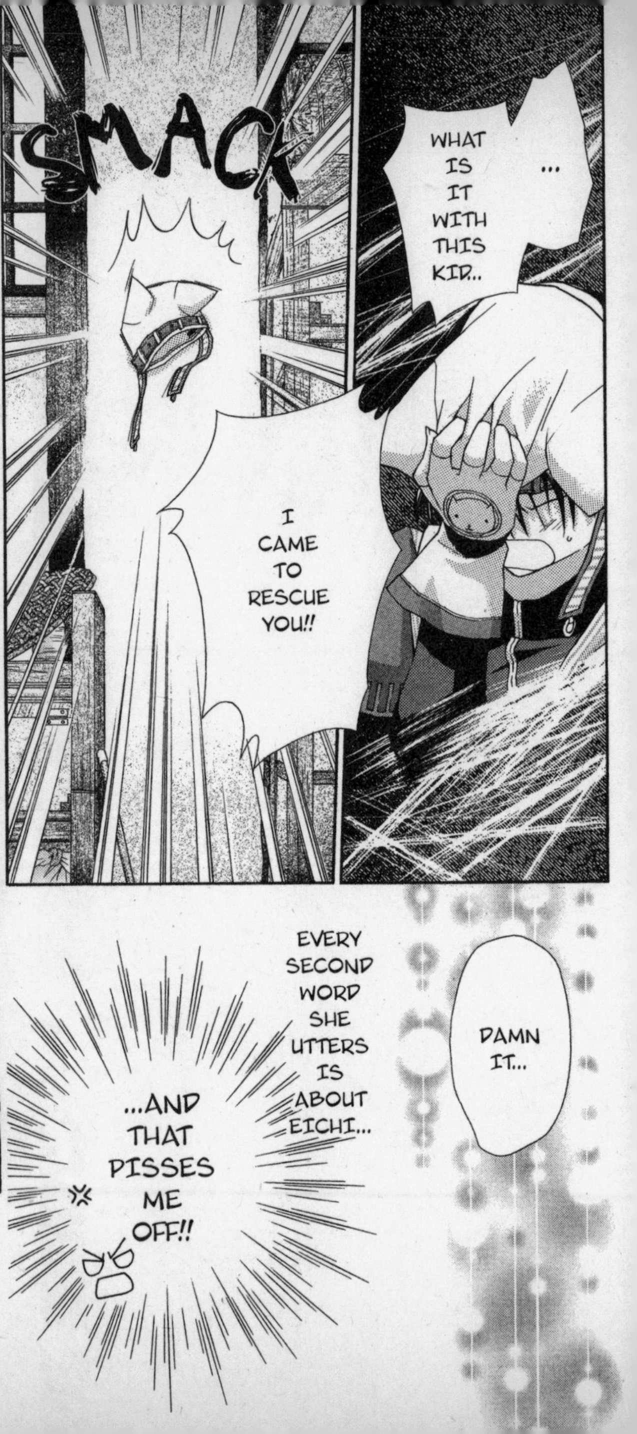
...
WHAT IS IT WITH THIS KID...
SMACK
I CAME TO RESCUE YOU!!
DAMN IT...
EVERY SECOND WORD SHE UTTERS IS ABOUT EICHI...
...AND THAT PISSES ME OFF!!

Arina Tanemura's "Penchi de Shakin"

episode 48

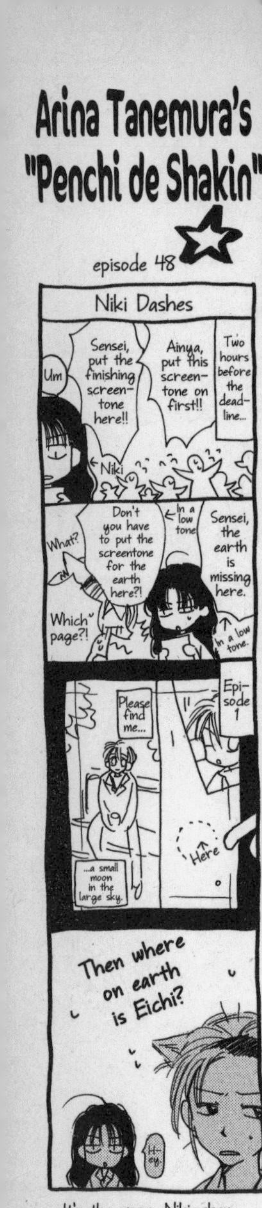
Niki Dashes
Two hours before the deadline...
Ainya, put this screentone on first!!
Sensei, put the finishing screentone here!!
Um
Niki
Sensei, the earth is missing here.
In a low tone
Don't you have to put the screentone for the earth here?!
What?
Which page?!
In a low tone.
Episode 1
Please find me...
...a small moon in the large sky.
Here
Then where on earth is Eichi?
H-Hey.

It's the moon, Niki-chan. (smile)

We're always working right up to the deadline. I'm sorry.

Mr. Koike...

And to all my assistants...

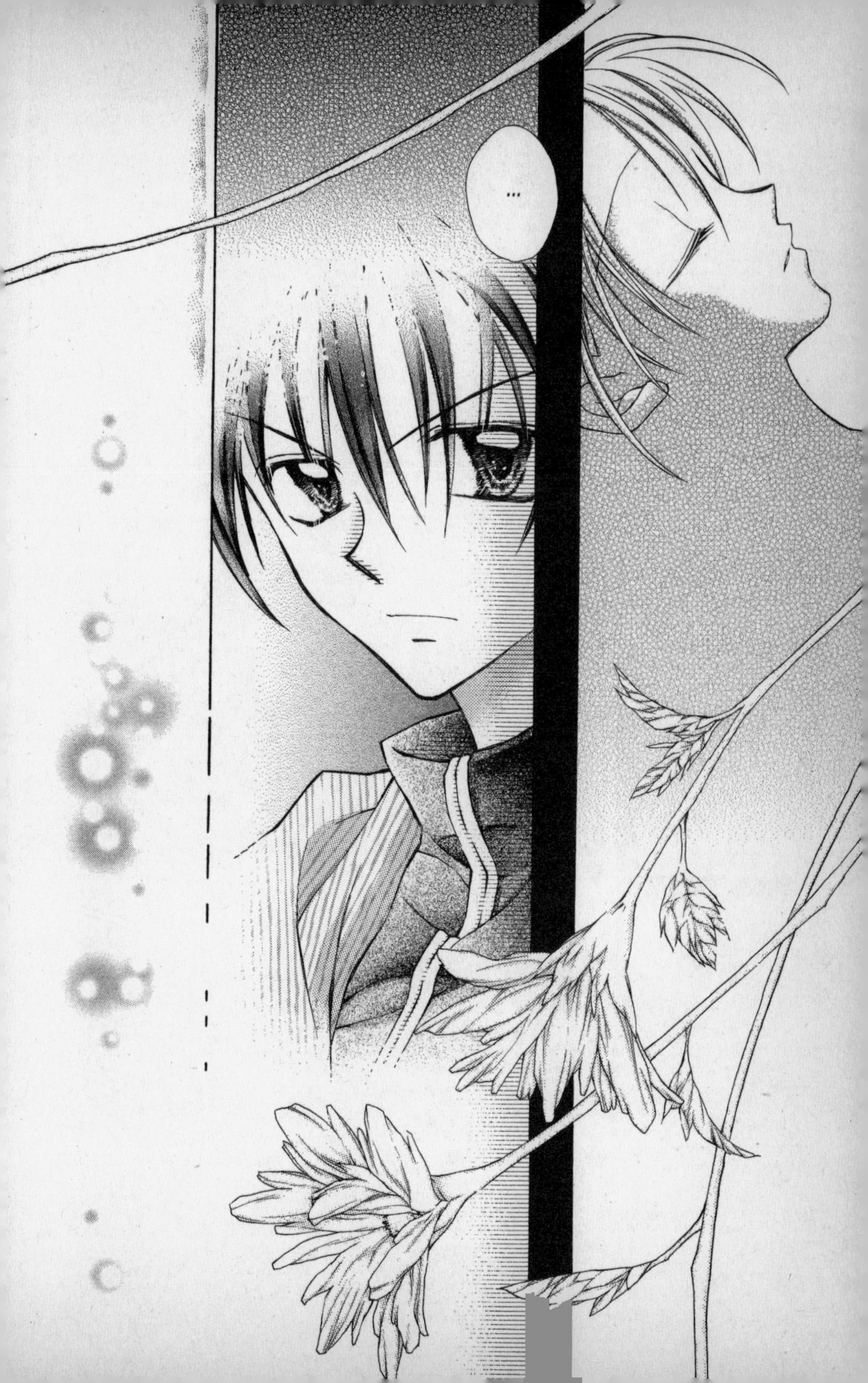
...

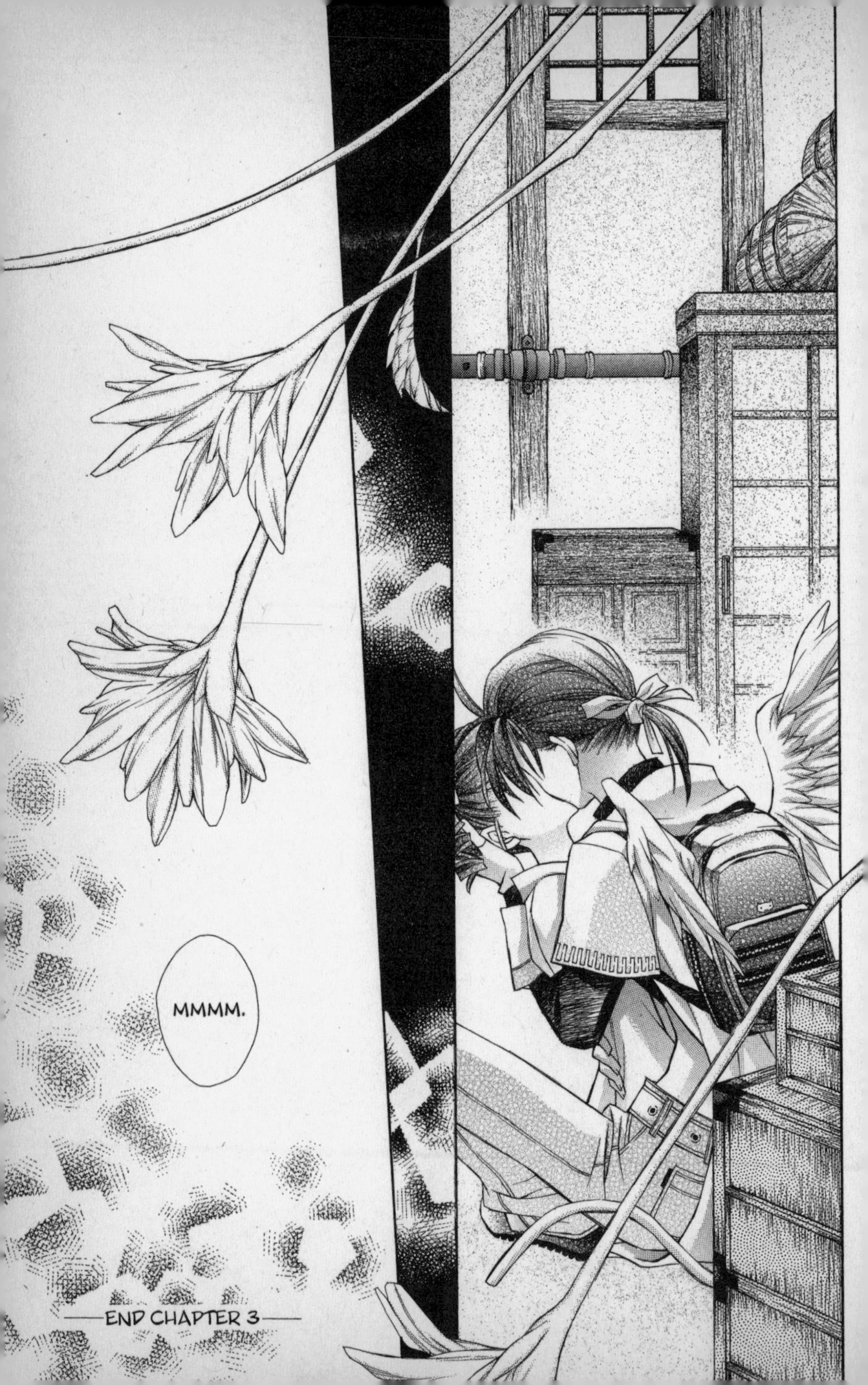
MMMM.
—END CHAPTER 3—

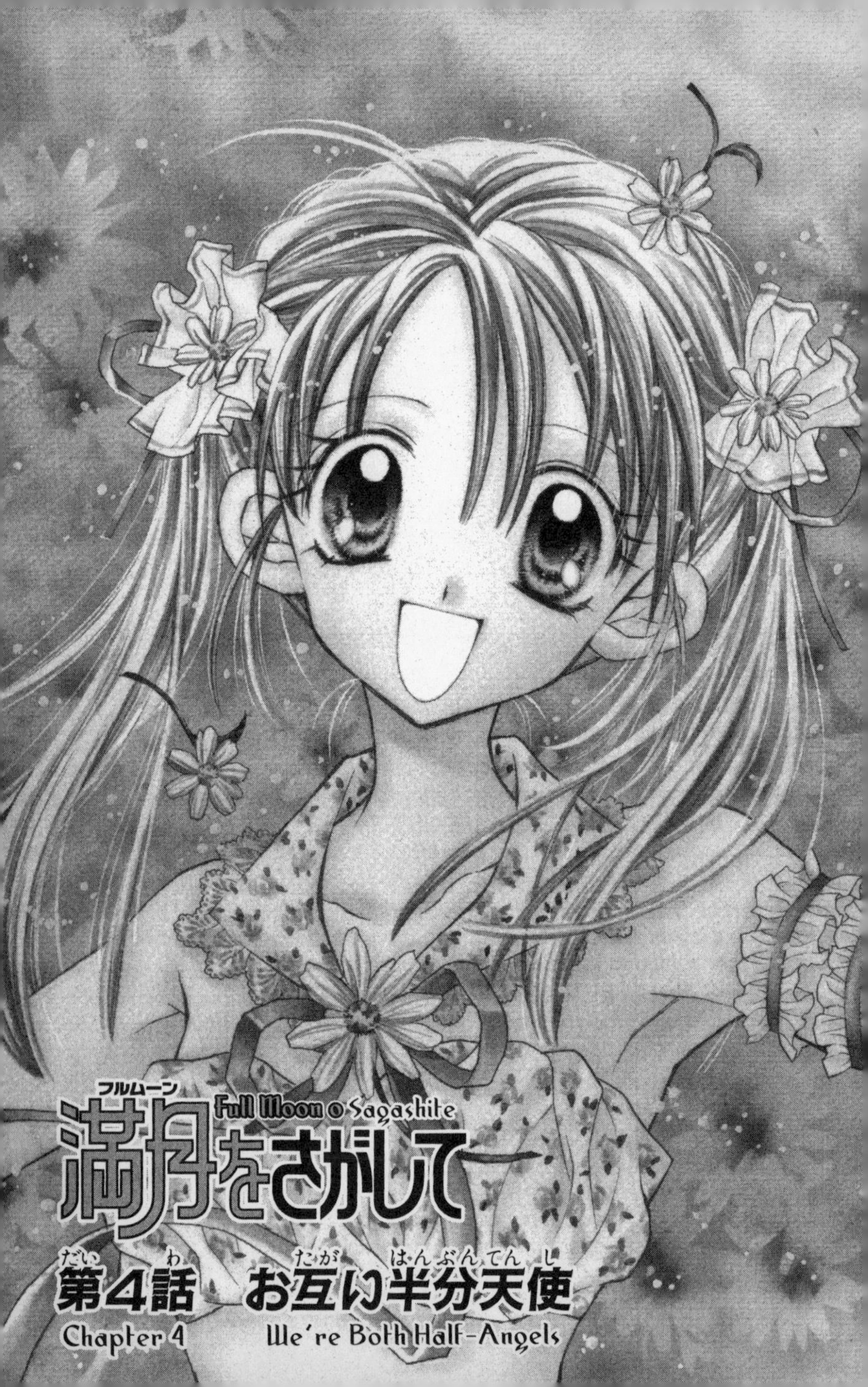
フルムーン
満月をさがして
Full Moon o Sagashite
第4話 お互い半分天使
Chapter 4 We're Both Half-Angels

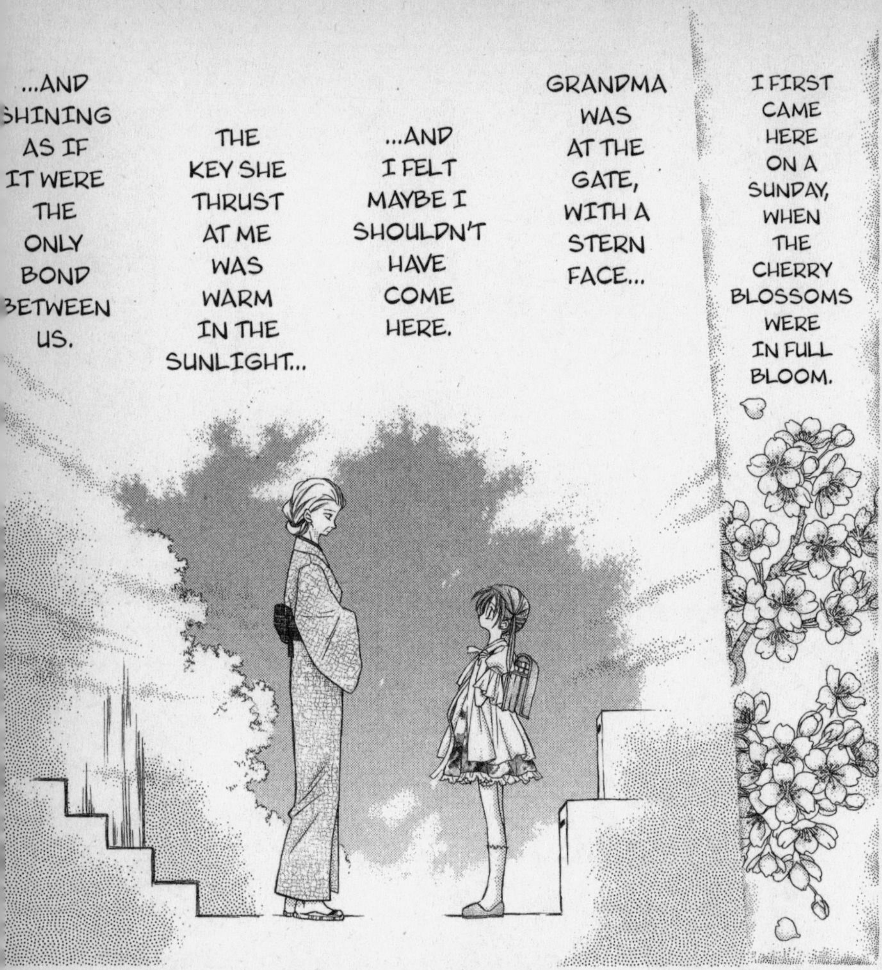
I FIRST CAME HERE ON A SUNDAY, WHEN THE CHERRY BLOSSOMS WERE IN FULL BLOOM.
GRANDMA WAS AT THE GATE, WITH A STERN FACE...
...AND I FELT MAYBE I SHOULDN'T HAVE COME HERE.
THE KEY SHE THRUST AT ME WAS WARM IN THE SUNLIGHT...
...AND SHINING AS IF IT WERE THE ONLY BOND BETWEEN US.

Chapter 4 We're Both Half-Angels → Cover Text → She has a dream. She has friends. That's why Mitsuki is okay.

The fans really liked this cover text. (my editor writes them each time). I like this illustration quite a bit. (It's what Ribon covers should be like.) What sort of cover is that? I like the subtitle too. (There aren't many subtitles that I like in Full Moon...) The subtitle refers to Mitsuki and Takuto. I'm not sure which of the two said this.

Chapter 5 In the Middle of a Hollow Sea → Cover Text → What lies beyond their gaze? It is each other's dream...

This is that. (What?) I drew this with Yui Horie's "Kosai Ippai no Yuuki" in mind. The song is the last song on her second CD. The image is that of an RPG game or the Wizard of Oz. Let's go on an adventure to find oranges! The dog beside Takuto is the boy that appears in this episode. (Oh a spoiler!) ← But it's so obvious..

Then who is the red and white striped dragon that Eichi is holding? ← It has nothing to do with the story. (If you've listened to "Kosaji Ippai no Yuuki," you'd get it, right?) If you do, please say that line.

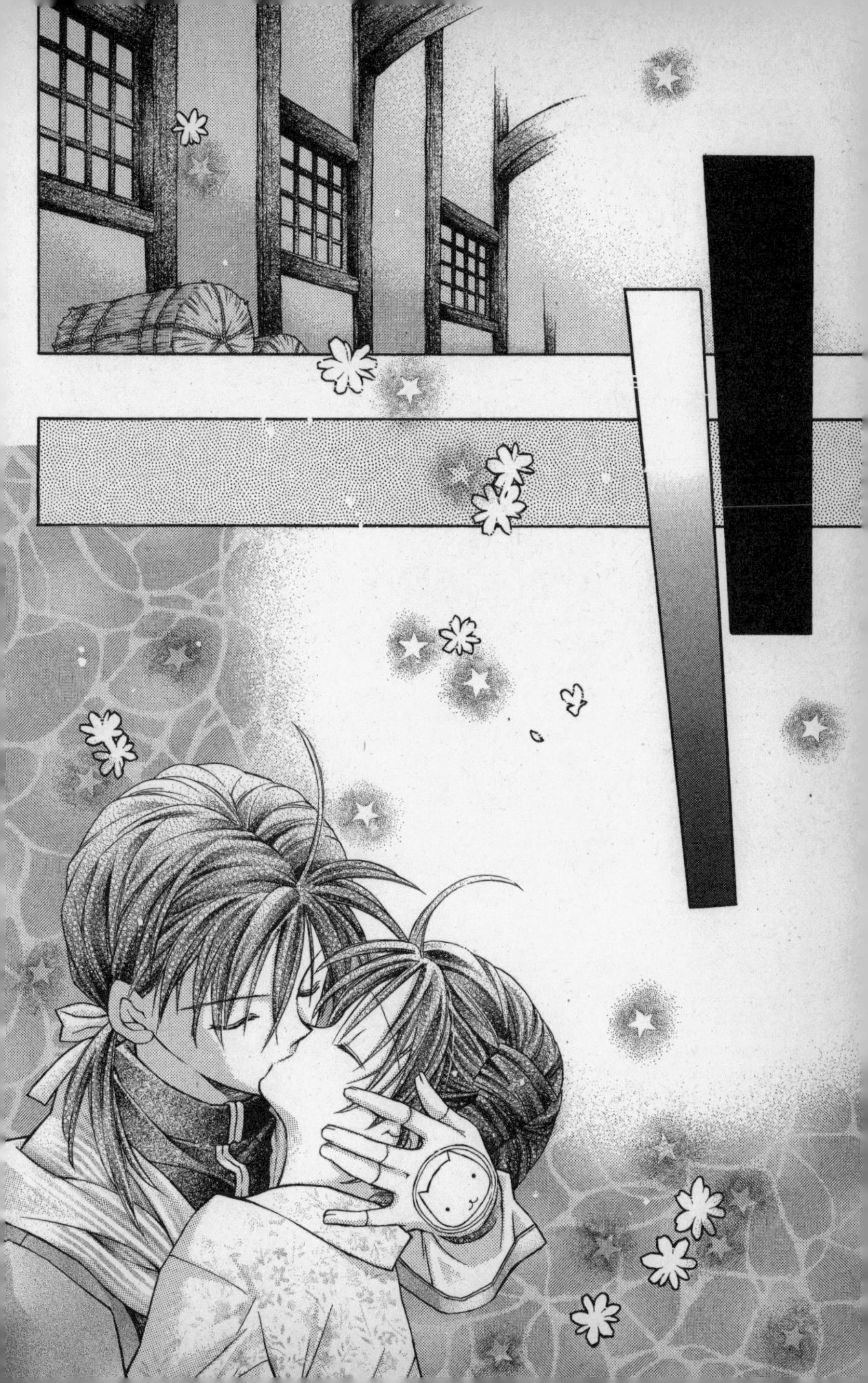

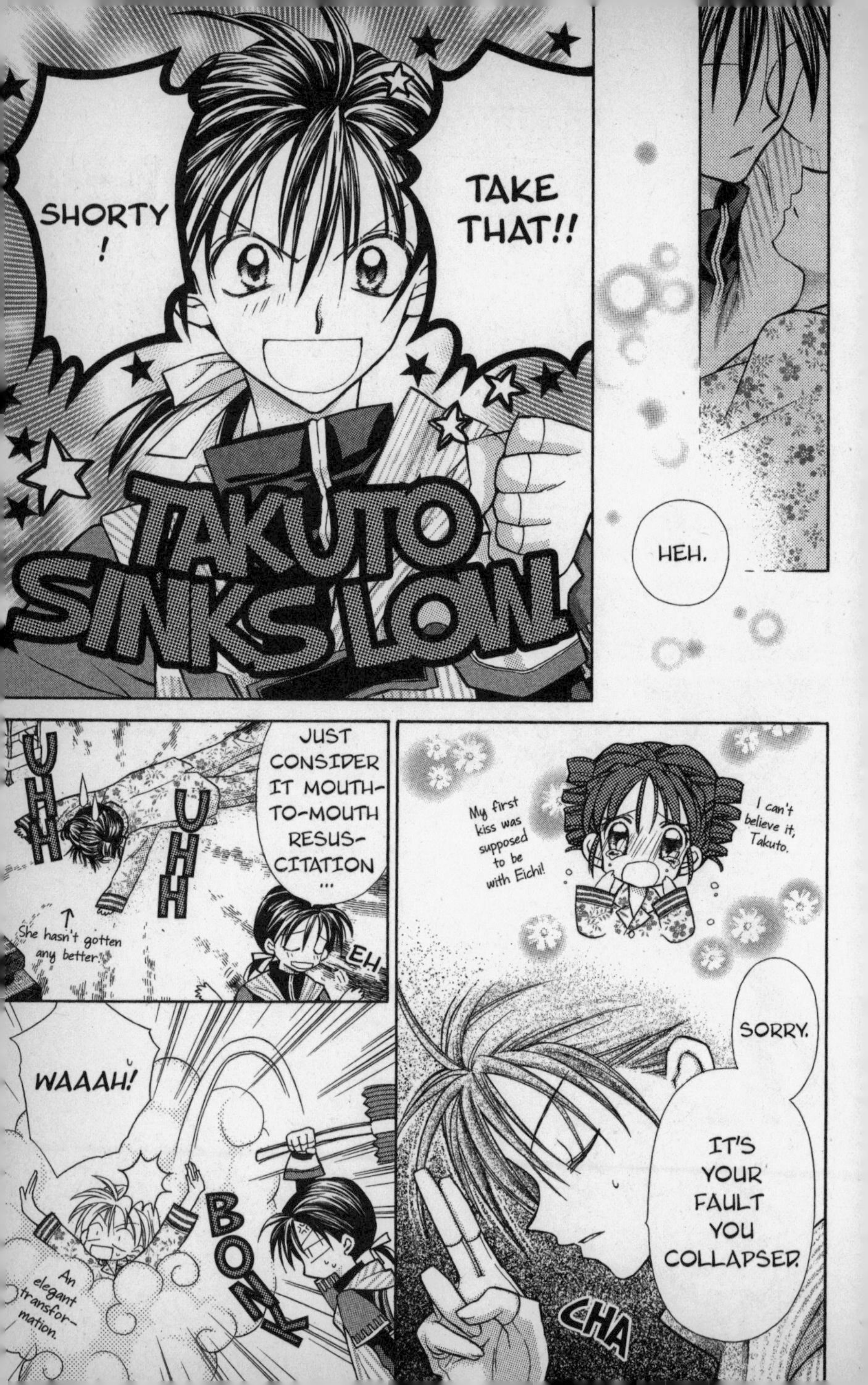

HEH.
TAKE THAT!!
SHORTY!
TAKUTO SINKS LOW!
I can't believe it, Takuto.
My first kiss was supposed to be with Eichi!
SORRY.
IT'S YOUR FAULT YOU COLLAPSED.
CHA
JUST CONSIDER IT MOUTH-TO-MOUTH RESUSCITATION...
UHHH
UHHH
She hasn't gotten any better.
EH
WAAAH!
BONK
An elegant transformation.

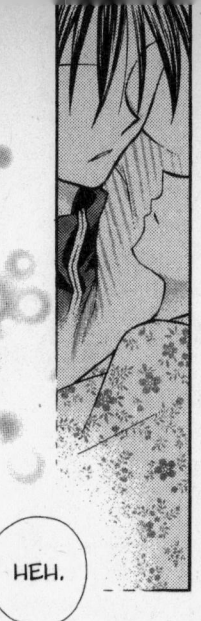

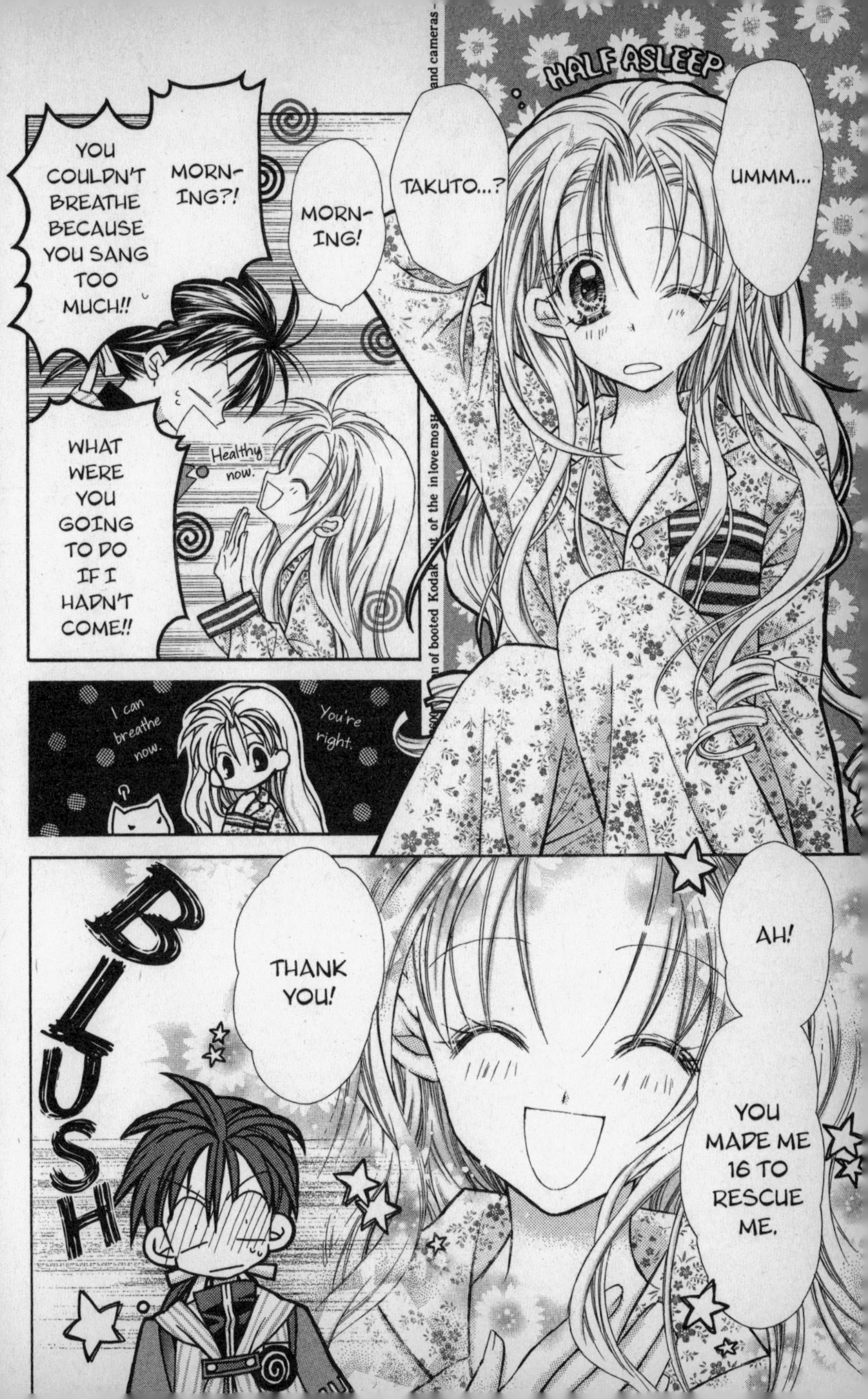
HALF ASLEEP
UMMM...
TAKUTO...?
MORN-ING!
MORN-ING?!
YOU COULDN'T BREATHE BECAUSE YOU SANG TOO MUCH!!
Healthy now.
WHAT WERE YOU GOING TO DO IF I HADN'T COME!!
You're right.
I can breathe now.
AH!
YOU MADE ME 16 TO RESCUE ME.
THANK YOU!
BLUSH

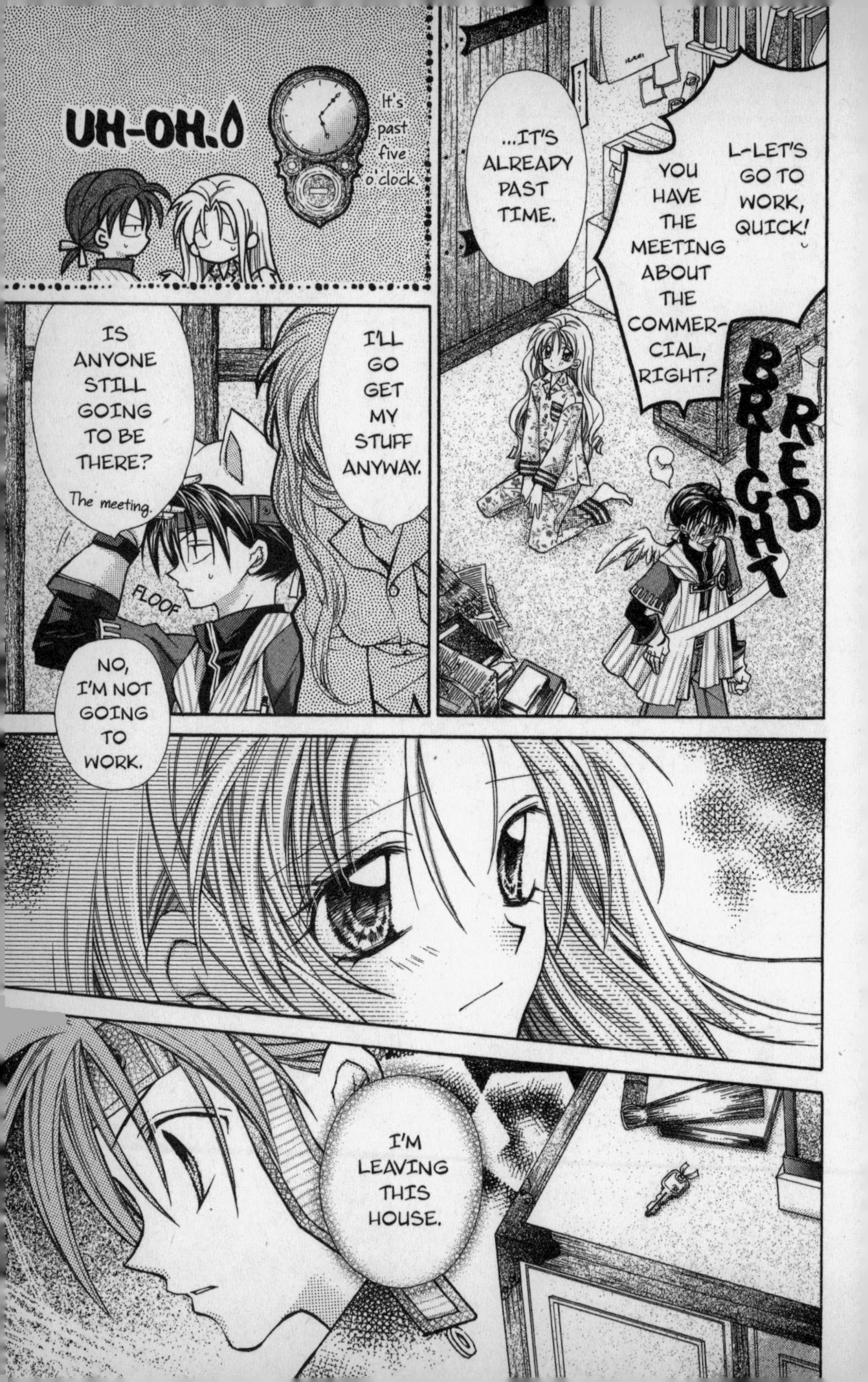

YOU HAVE THE MEETING ABOUT THE COMMERCIAL, RIGHT?
L-LET'S GO TO WORK, QUICK!
...IT'S ALREADY PAST TIME.
BRIGHT RED
It's past five o'clock.
UH-OH.
I'LL GO GET MY STUFF ANYWAY.
IS ANYONE STILL GOING TO BE THERE?
The meeting.
FLOOF
NO, I'M NOT GOING TO WORK.
I'M LEAVING THIS HOUSE.

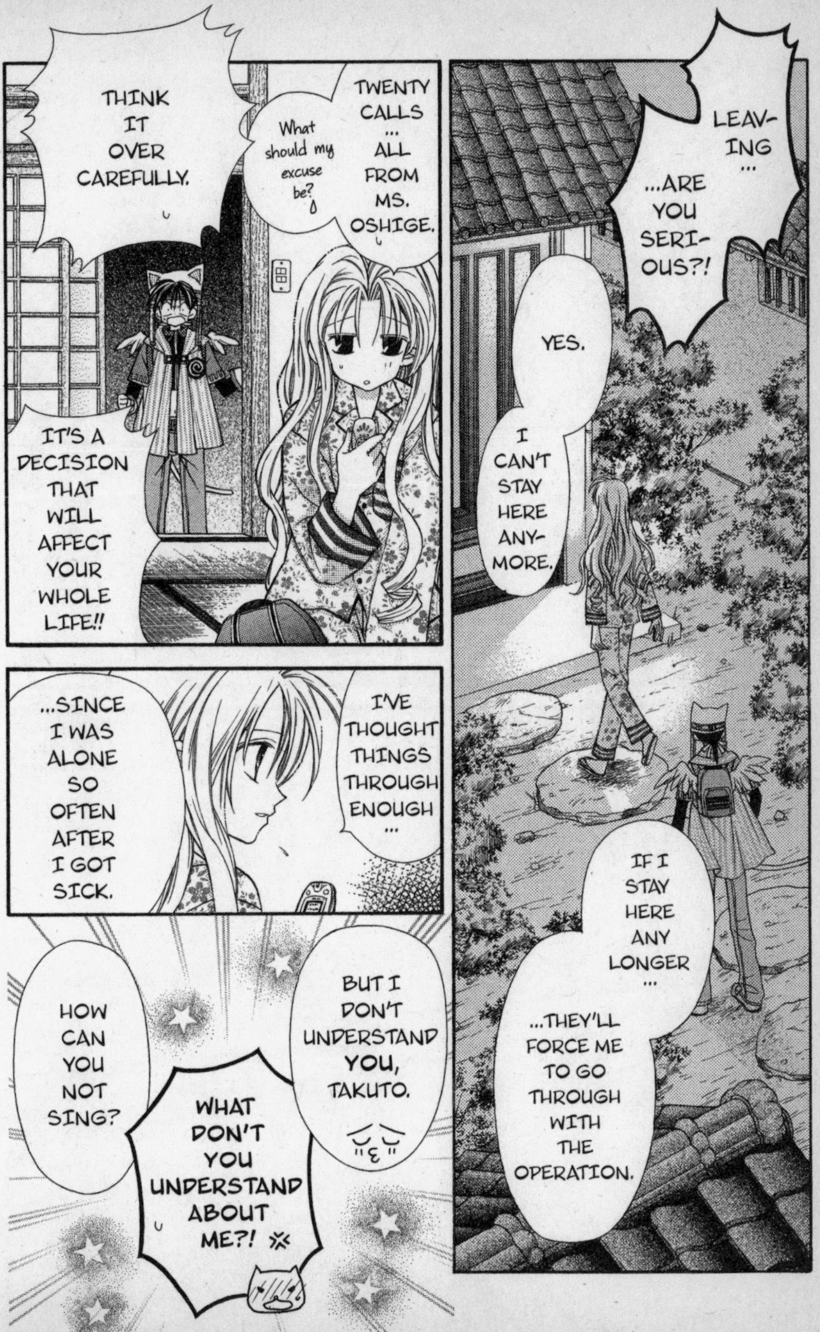
LEAVING... ...ARE YOU SERIOUS?!
YES.
I CAN'T STAY HERE ANYMORE.
IF I STAY HERE ANY LONGER...
...THEY'LL FORCE ME TO GO THROUGH WITH THE OPERATION.
TWENTY CALLS... ALL FROM MS. OSHIGE.
What should my excuse be?
THINK IT OVER CAREFULLY.
IT'S A DECISION THAT WILL AFFECT YOUR WHOLE LIFE!!
I'VE THOUGHT THINGS THROUGH ENOUGH...
...SINCE I WAS ALONE SO OFTEN AFTER I GOT SICK.
BUT I DON'T UNDERSTAND YOU, TAKUTO.
HOW CAN YOU NOT SING?
WHAT DON'T YOU UNDERSTAND ABOUT ME?!

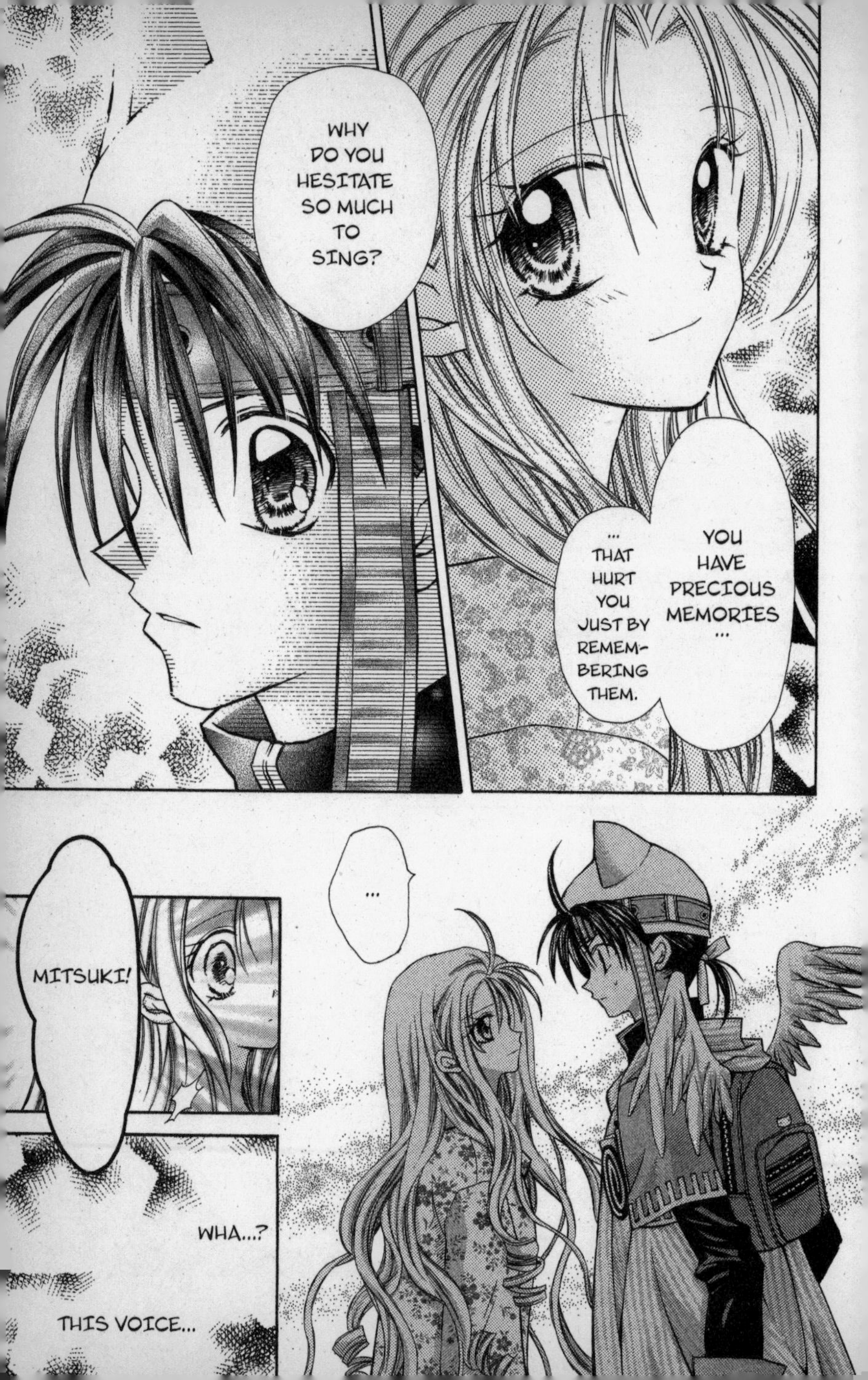
WHY DO YOU HESITATE SO MUCH TO SING?
YOU HAVE PRECIOUS MEMORIES...
...THAT HURT YOU JUST BY REMEM-BERING THEM.
...
MITSUKI!
WHA...?
THIS VOICE...

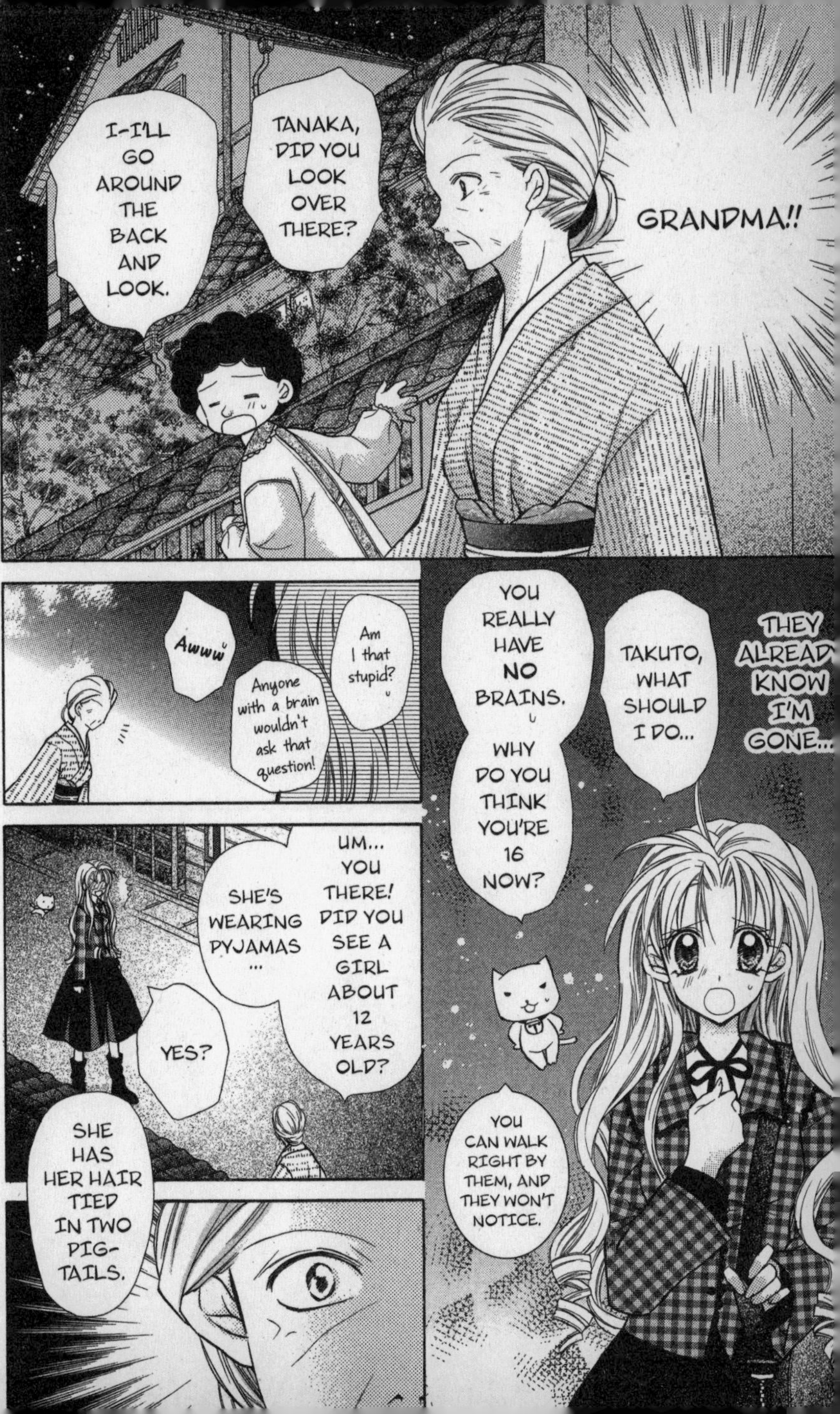
GRANDMA!!
TANAKA, DID YOU LOOK OVER THERE?
I-I'LL GO AROUND THE BACK AND LOOK.
THEY ALREADY KNOW I'M GONE...
TAKUTO, WHAT SHOULD I DO...
YOU REALLY HAVE NO BRAINS.
WHY DO YOU THINK YOU'RE 16 NOW?
YOU CAN WALK RIGHT BY THEM, AND THEY WON'T NOTICE.
Am I that stupid?
Anyone with a brain wouldn't ask that question!
Awww
UM... YOU THERE! DID YOU SEE A GIRL ABOUT 12 YEARS OLD?
SHE'S WEARING PYJAMAS...
YES?
SHE HAS HER HAIR TIED IN TWO PIG-TAILS.

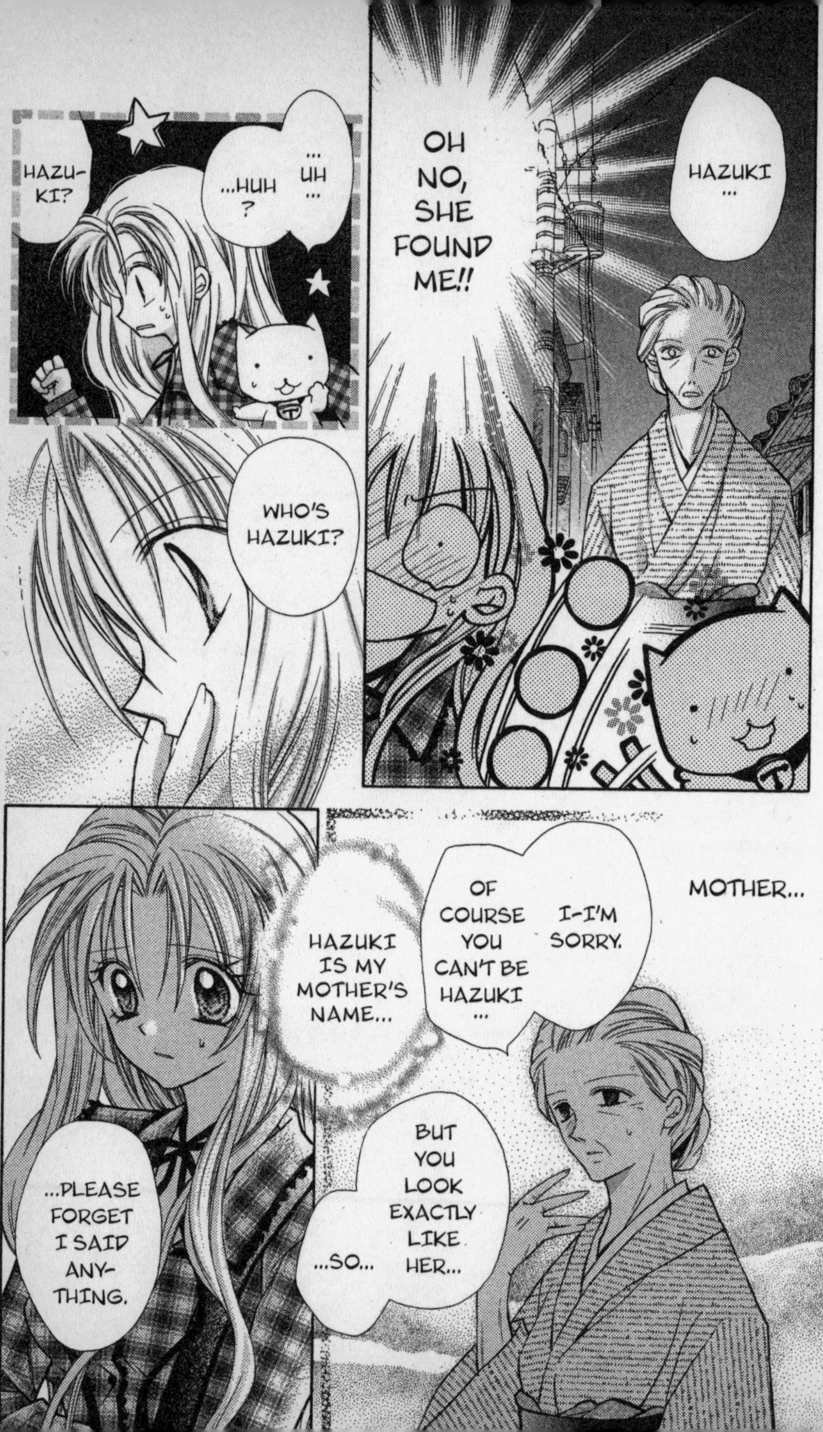
HAZUKI ...
OH NO, SHE FOUND ME!!
... UH ...
...HUH ?
HAZU-KI?
WHO'S HAZUKI?
MOTHER...
I-I'M SORRY.
OF COURSE YOU CAN'T BE HAZUKI ...
HAZUKI IS MY MOTHER'S NAME...
BUT YOU LOOK EXACTLY LIKE HER...
...SO...
...PLEASE FORGET I SAID ANYTHING.

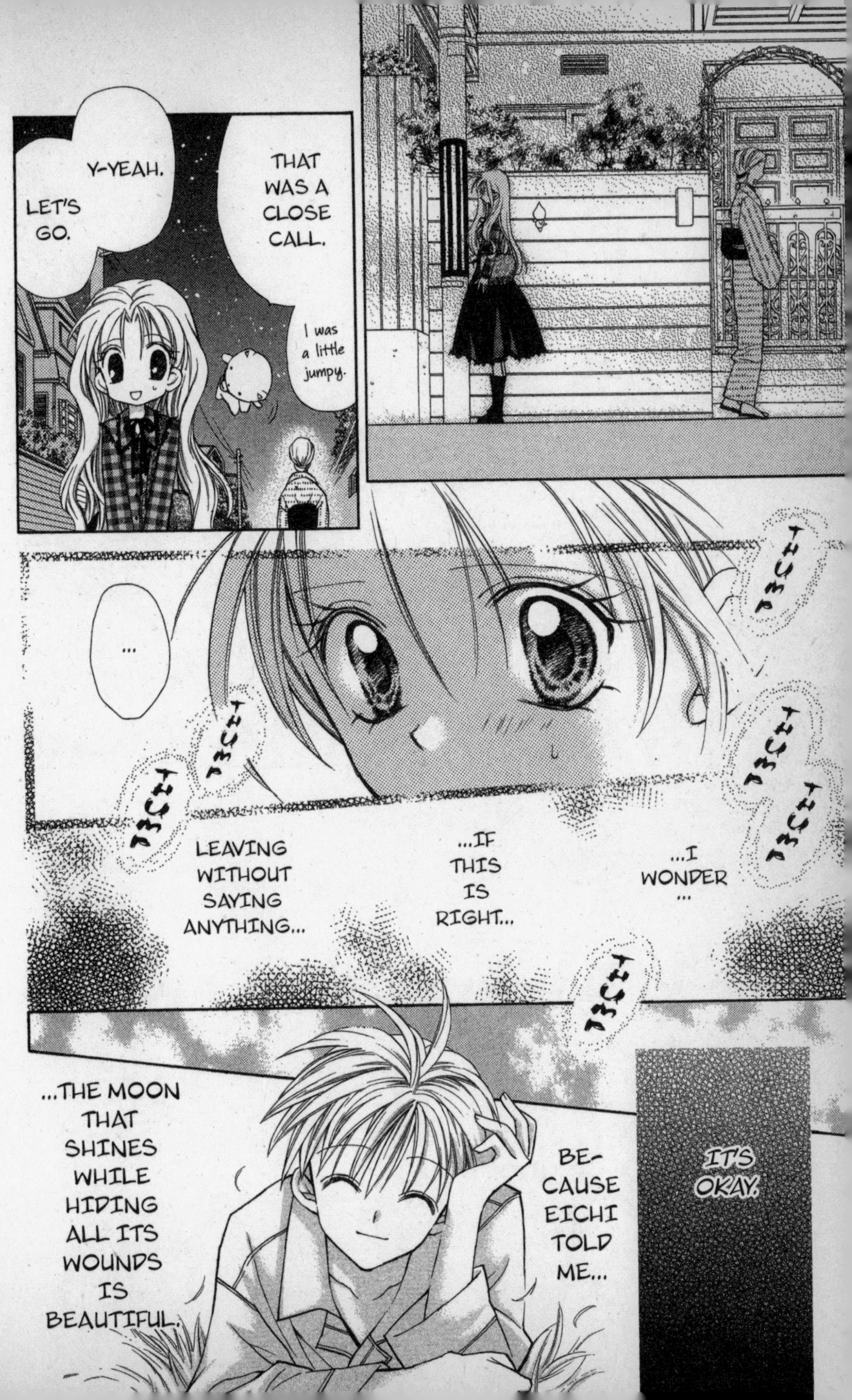
THAT WAS A CLOSE CALL.
Y-YEAH. LET'S GO.
I was a little jumpy.
THUMP
THUMP
THUMP
...
THUMP
THUMP
...I WONDER...
...IF THIS IS RIGHT...
LEAVING WITHOUT SAYING ANYTHING...
THUMP
IT'S OKAY.
BE-CAUSE EICHI TOLD ME...
...THE MOON THAT SHINES WHILE HIDING ALL ITS WOUNDS IS BEAUTIFUL.

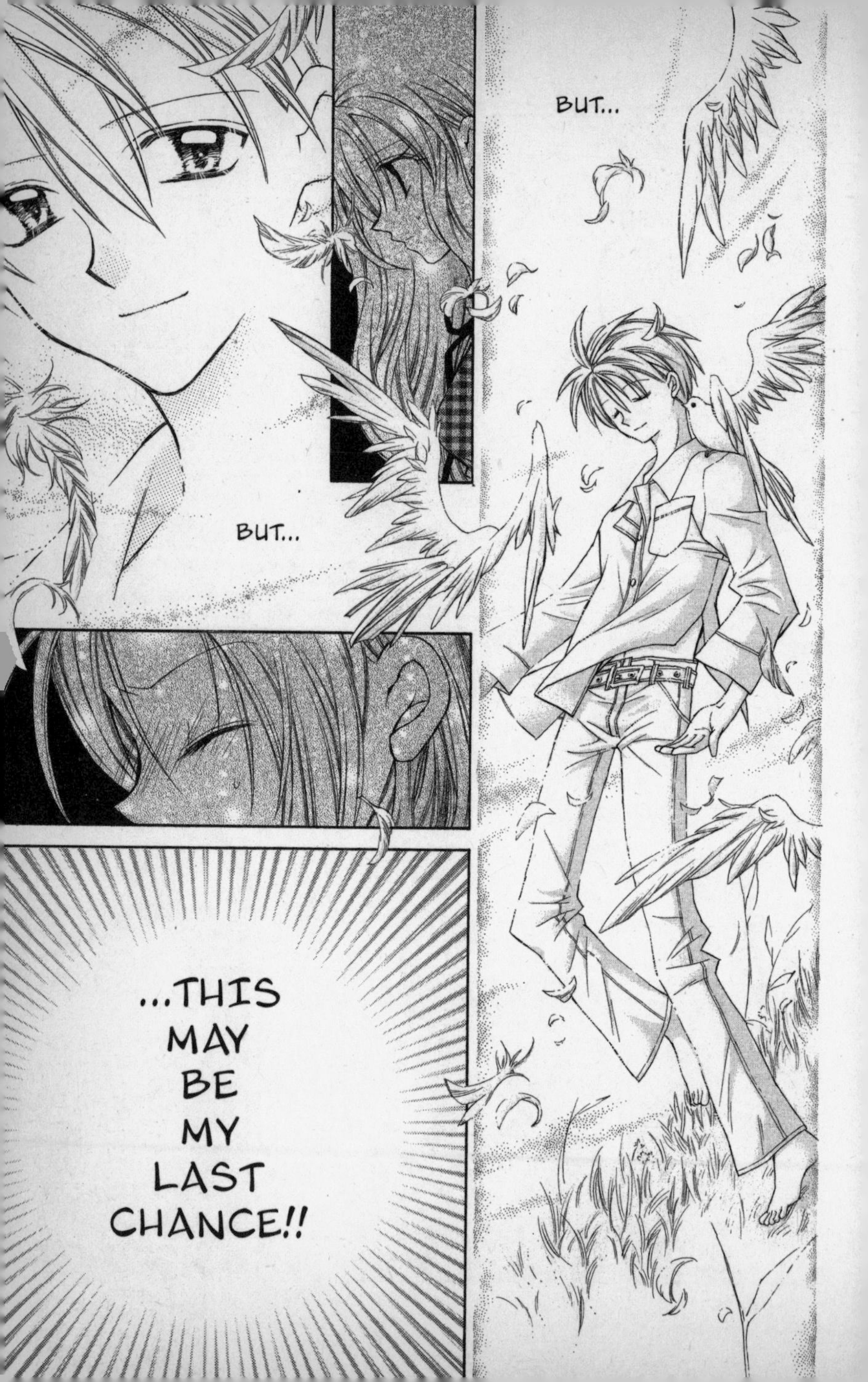
BUT...
BUT...
...THIS MAY BE MY LAST CHANCE!!

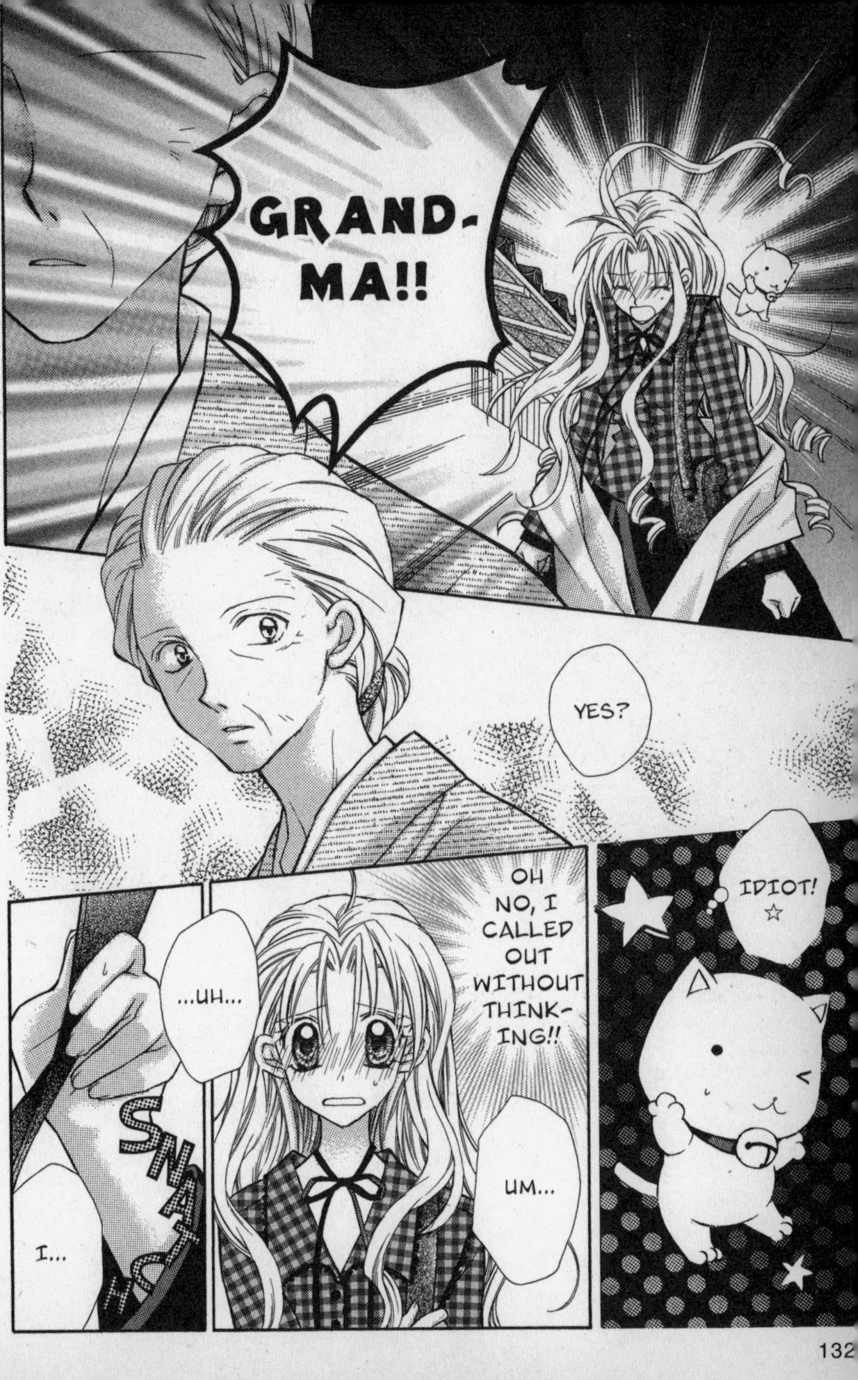
GRAND-MA!!
YES?
IDIOT! ☆
OH NO, I CALLED OUT WITHOUT THINKING!!
...UH...
UM...
SNATCH
I...

More about Full Moon o Sagashite

Although I thought up this story in six months...I have strong feelings for the manga...so I won't talk too much about the background of the story. (That's why the character introductions are so shallow.) Sorry to all my fans, but I don't want to talk about it too much. For all the people who wanted to hear about that, I'm sorry. I don't intend to talk about it.

But in the final volume, I may write a lot about it. (But this promise may not be kept, so don't believe it yet!) I don't want to say it. (?!) (I'm a pretty stubborn person...and I'm afraid I'll say something that will be taken the wrong way.)
It's that important to me!

WAA!

embarrassed

That's why I don't like doing this (doing what?)

Since I'm stubborn, I don't make a very good impression on people. (People find me hard to understand.) I'm a warped, shy person. But I can't be stubborn or lie in my manga, so my manga is my truth!

The end.

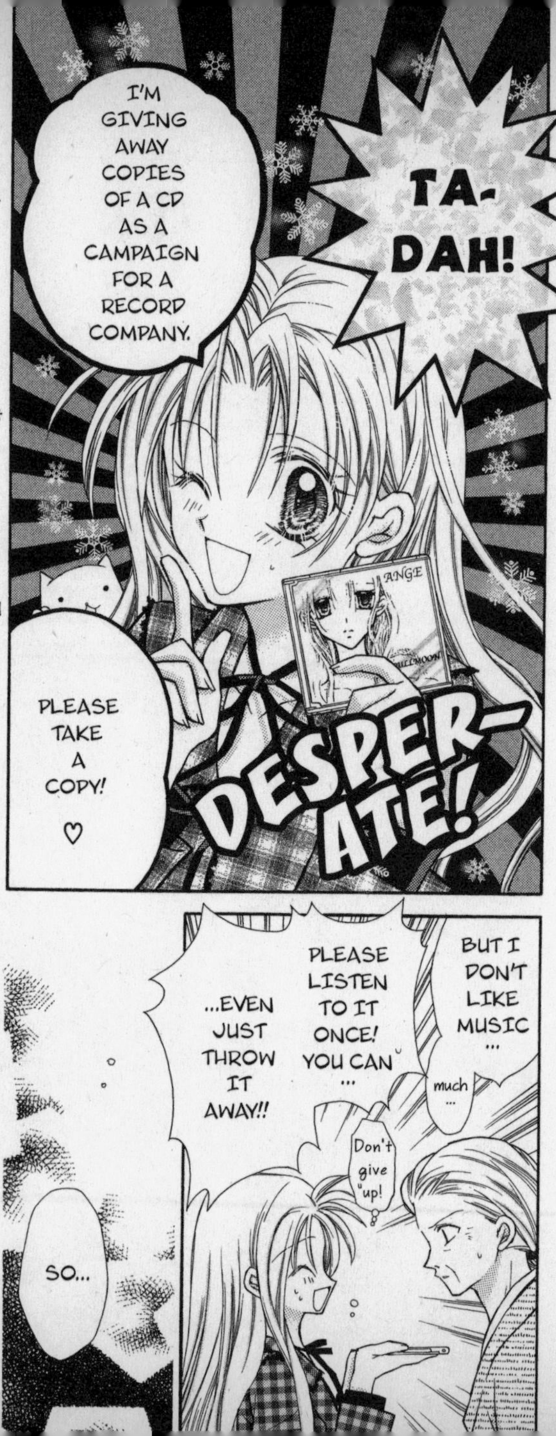
TA-DAH!
I'M GIVING AWAY COPIES OF A CD AS A CAMPAIGN FOR A RECORD COMPANY.
ANGE
DESPER-ATE!
PLEASE TAKE A COPY! ♡
BUT I DON'T LIKE MUSIC...
much...
PLEASE LISTEN TO IT ONCE! YOU CAN...
...EVEN JUST THROW IT AWAY!!
Don't give up!
SO...

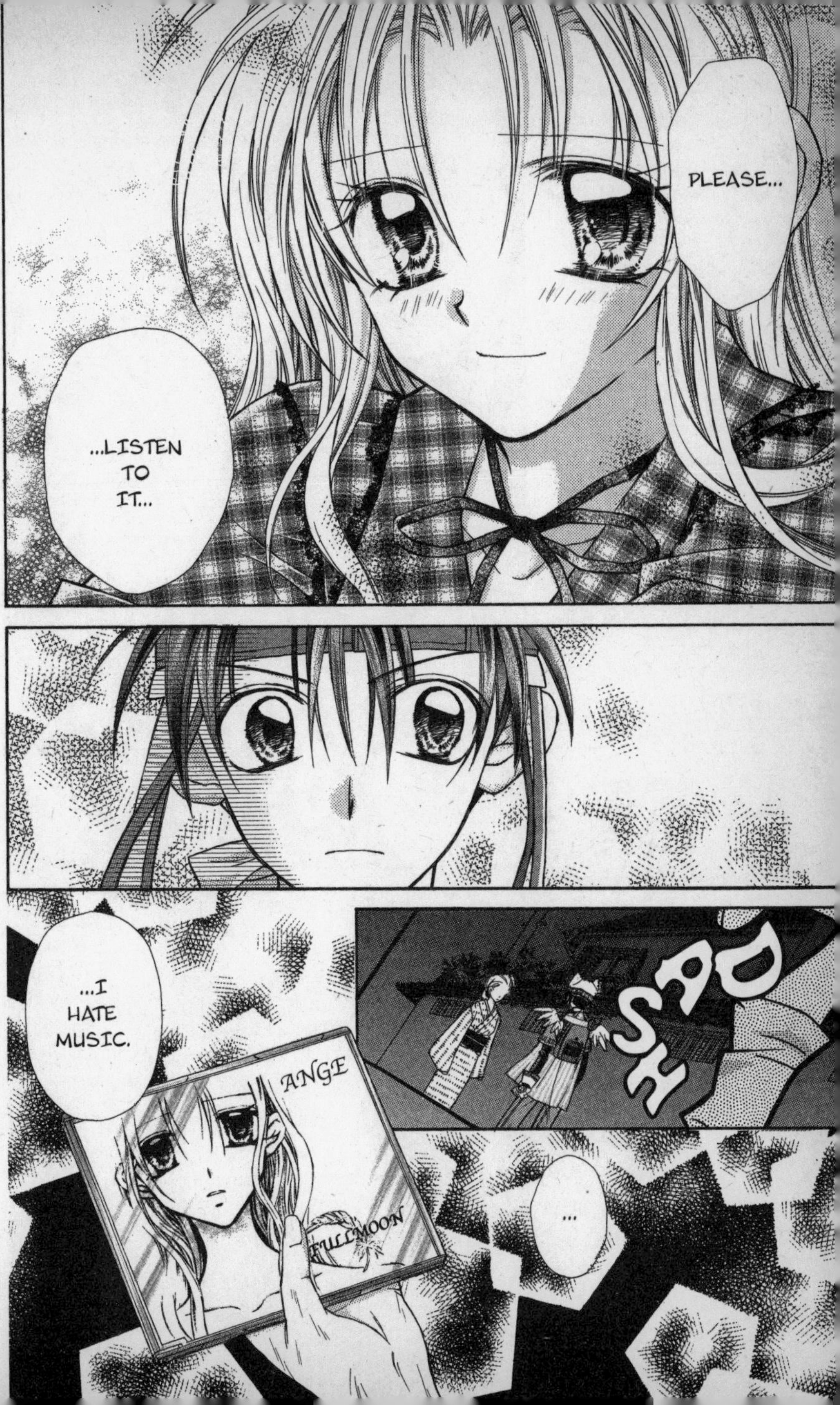
PLEASE...
...LISTEN TO IT...
DASH
...I HATE MUSIC.
ANGE
FULLMOON
...

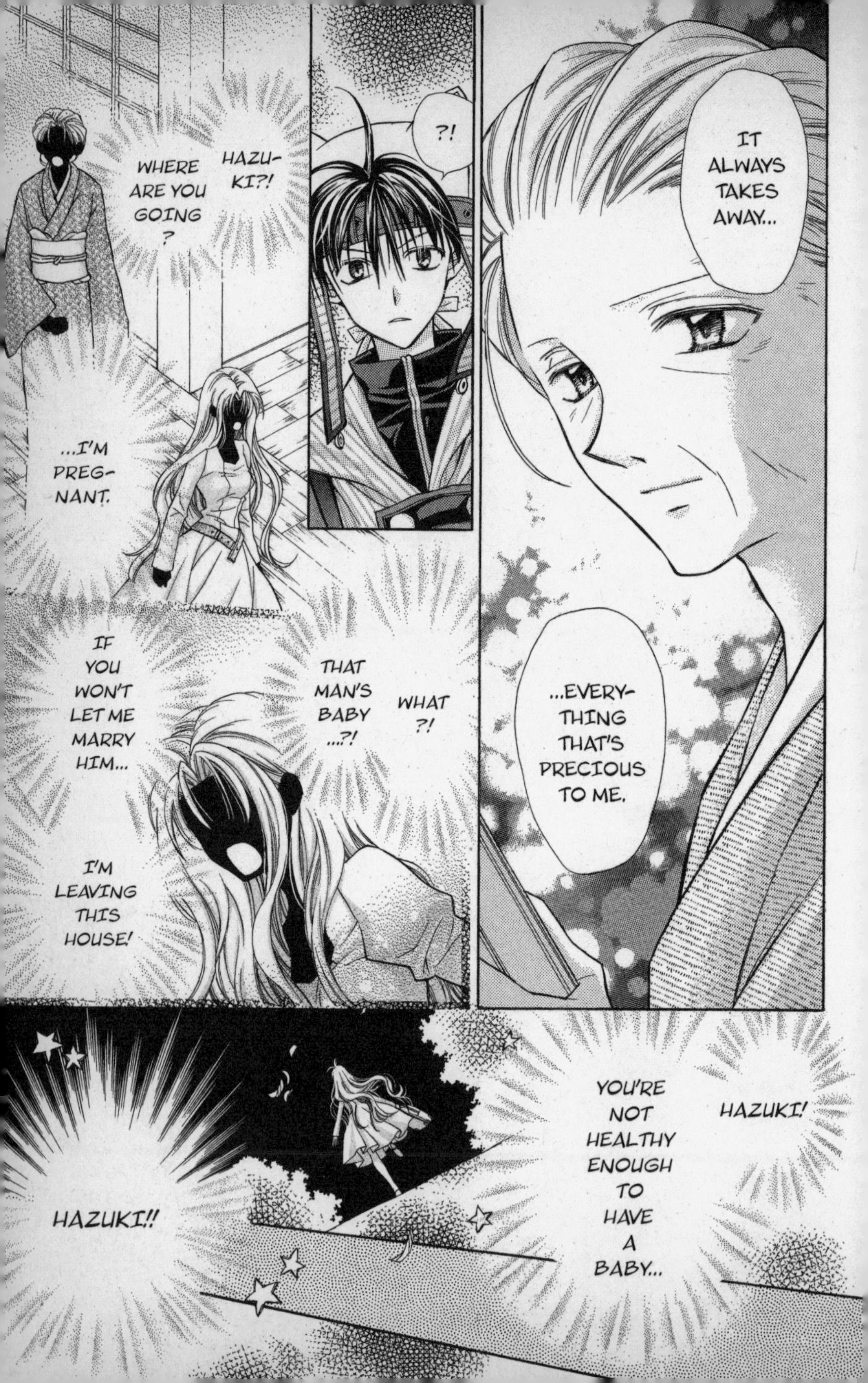
IT ALWAYS TAKES AWAY...
...EVERYTHING THAT'S PRECIOUS TO ME.
?!
HAZUKI?!
WHERE ARE YOU GOING?
...I'M PREGNANT.
WHAT?!
THAT MAN'S BABY...?!
IF YOU WON'T LET ME MARRY HIM...
I'M LEAVING THIS HOUSE!
HAZUKI!
YOU'RE NOT HEALTHY ENOUGH TO HAVE A BABY...
HAZUKI!!

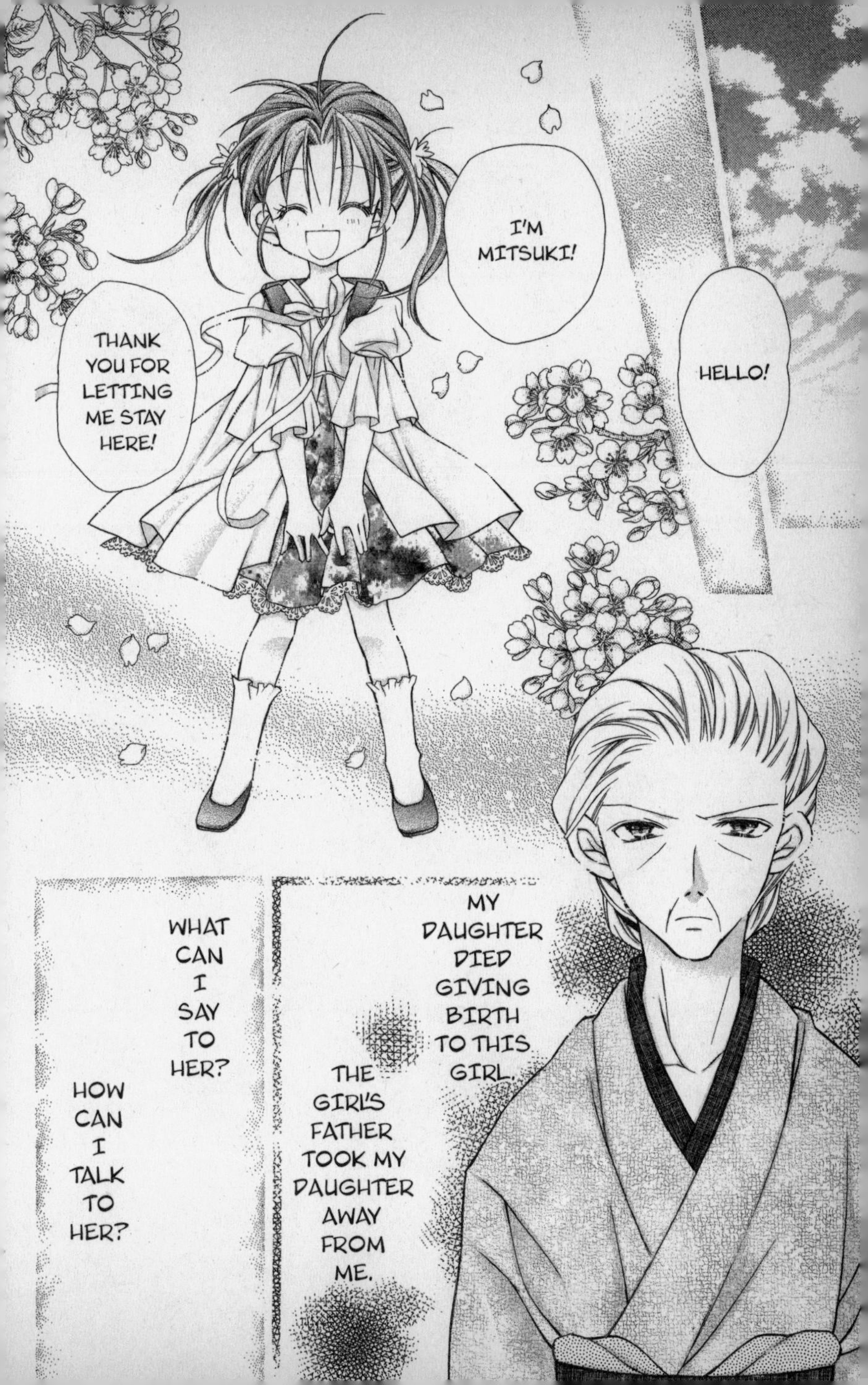
HELLO!
I'M MITSUKI!
THANK YOU FOR LETTING ME STAY HERE!
MY DAUGHTER DIED GIVING BIRTH TO THIS GIRL.
THE GIRL'S FATHER TOOK MY DAUGHTER AWAY FROM ME.
WHAT CAN I SAY TO HER?
HOW CAN I TALK TO HER?

I can't sleep, so I'll write something.

(What a reason.)

FF10

● ← I put this in the wrong place! Sorry...I'm really sorry.

FF10 is great!! It might be better than FF9! So please continue the story! (Don't think that customers are satisfied with that side story!!)

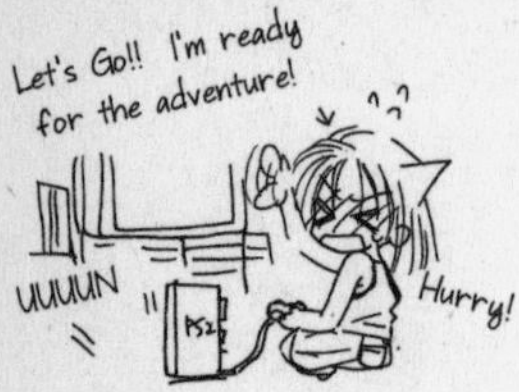

Let's Go!! I'm ready for the adventure!
UUUUN
PS2
Hurry!

● Kingdom Hearts (game)

This is good...I love Disney and FF, so I bought it right away!

Winnie the Pooh's voice was different from what I'd imagined (this is since I rode the Honey Hunt ride at Tokyo Disneyland). ← Was that on TV? But I grew to like it with this game. (Square is great!!)

Aeryth! Aeryth! A-e-r-y-t-h!

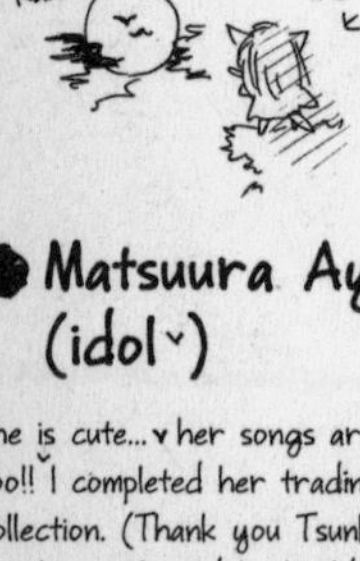

kaa
Kaa
Shouting at the sunset.

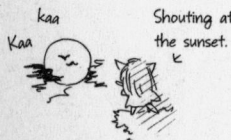

● Matsuura Aya (idol)

She is cute... her songs are good too!! I completed her trading card collection. (Thank you Tsunku♂ You know what idols should be like!! So I put the ♂ after your name, although I wonder about it being there.) I love the songs "Egao ni Namida" and "Oshare!"

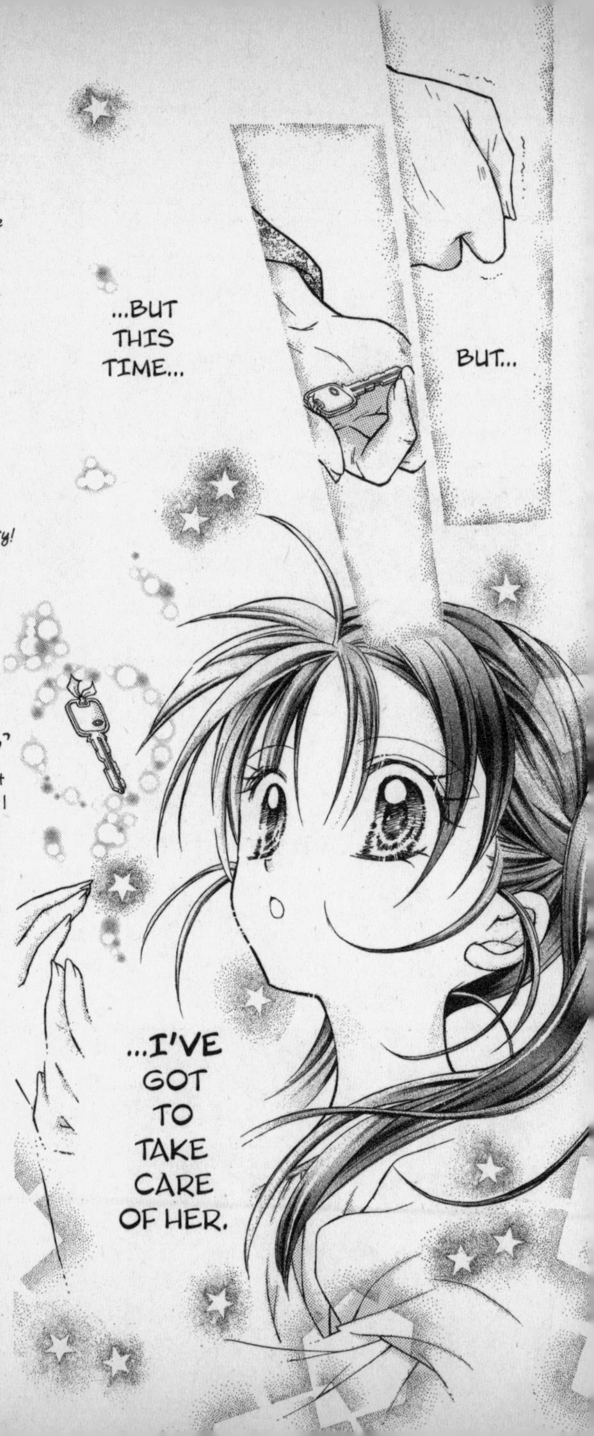

BUT...
...BUT THIS TIME...
...I'VE GOT TO TAKE CARE OF HER.

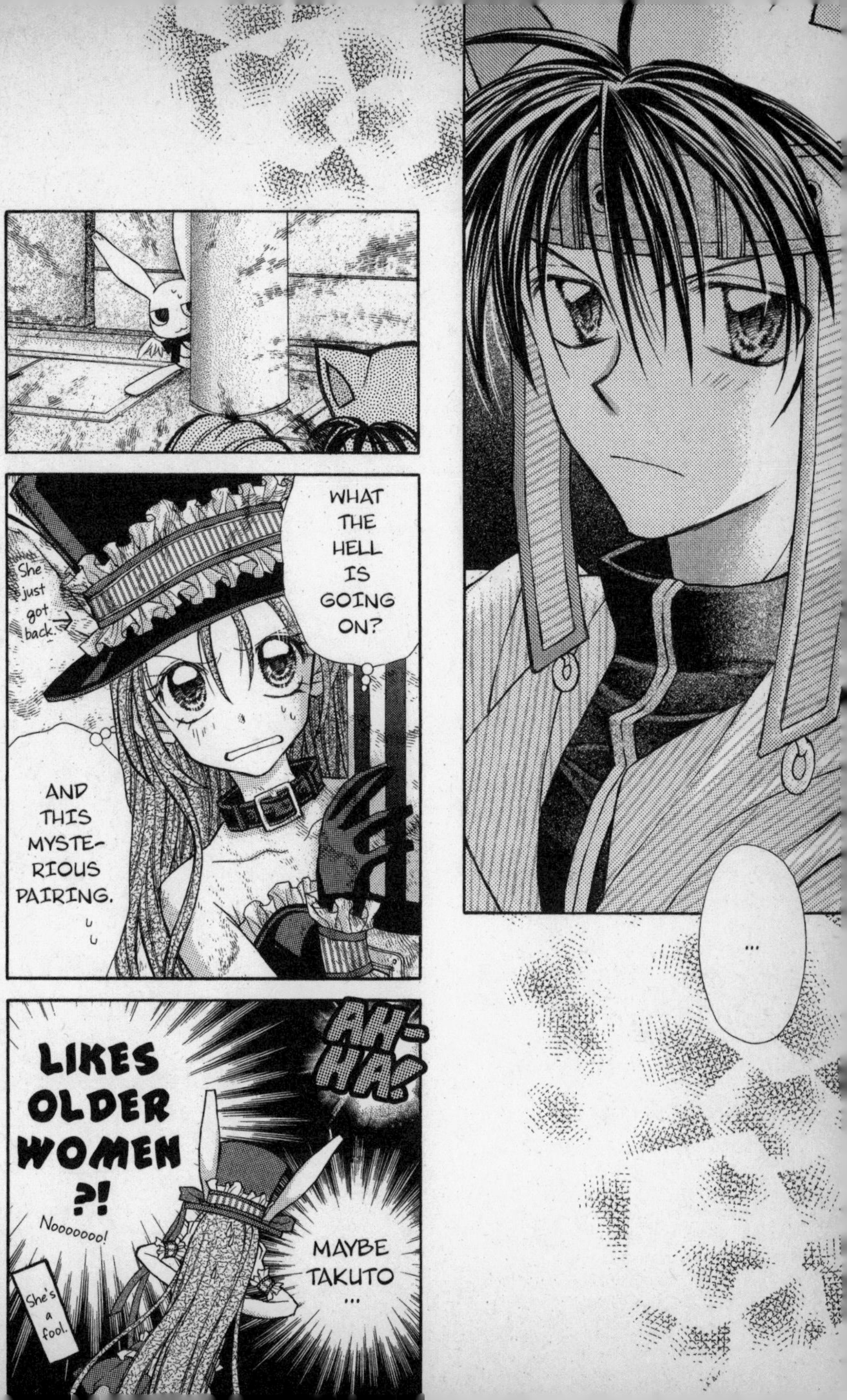
...
WHAT THE HELL IS GOING ON?
She just got back.
AND THIS MYSTERIOUS PAIRING.
AH-HA!
MAYBE TAKUTO...
LIKES OLDER WOMEN?!
Nooooooo!
She's a fool.

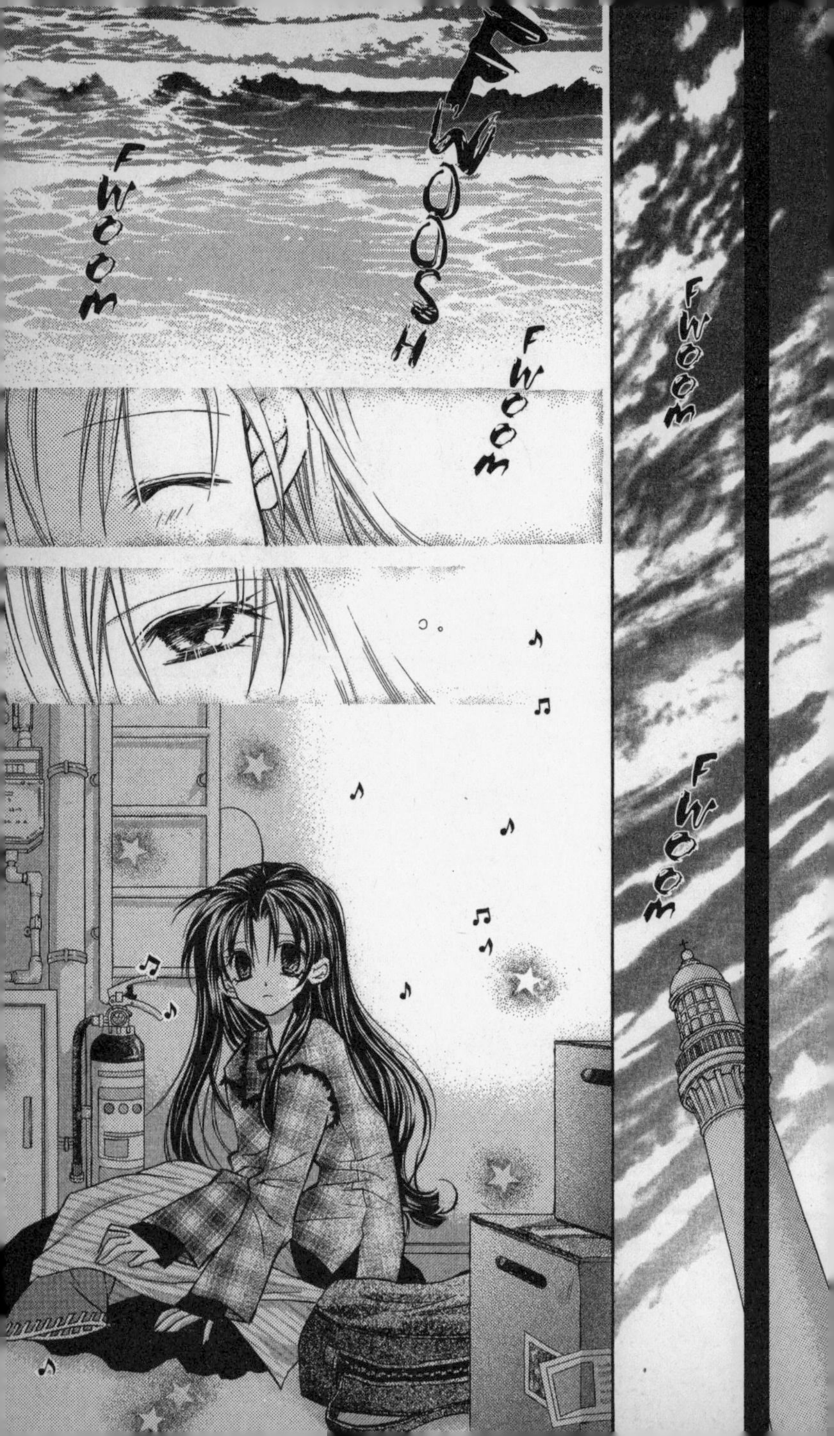
FWOOM
FWOOM
FWOOSH
FWOOM
FWOOM

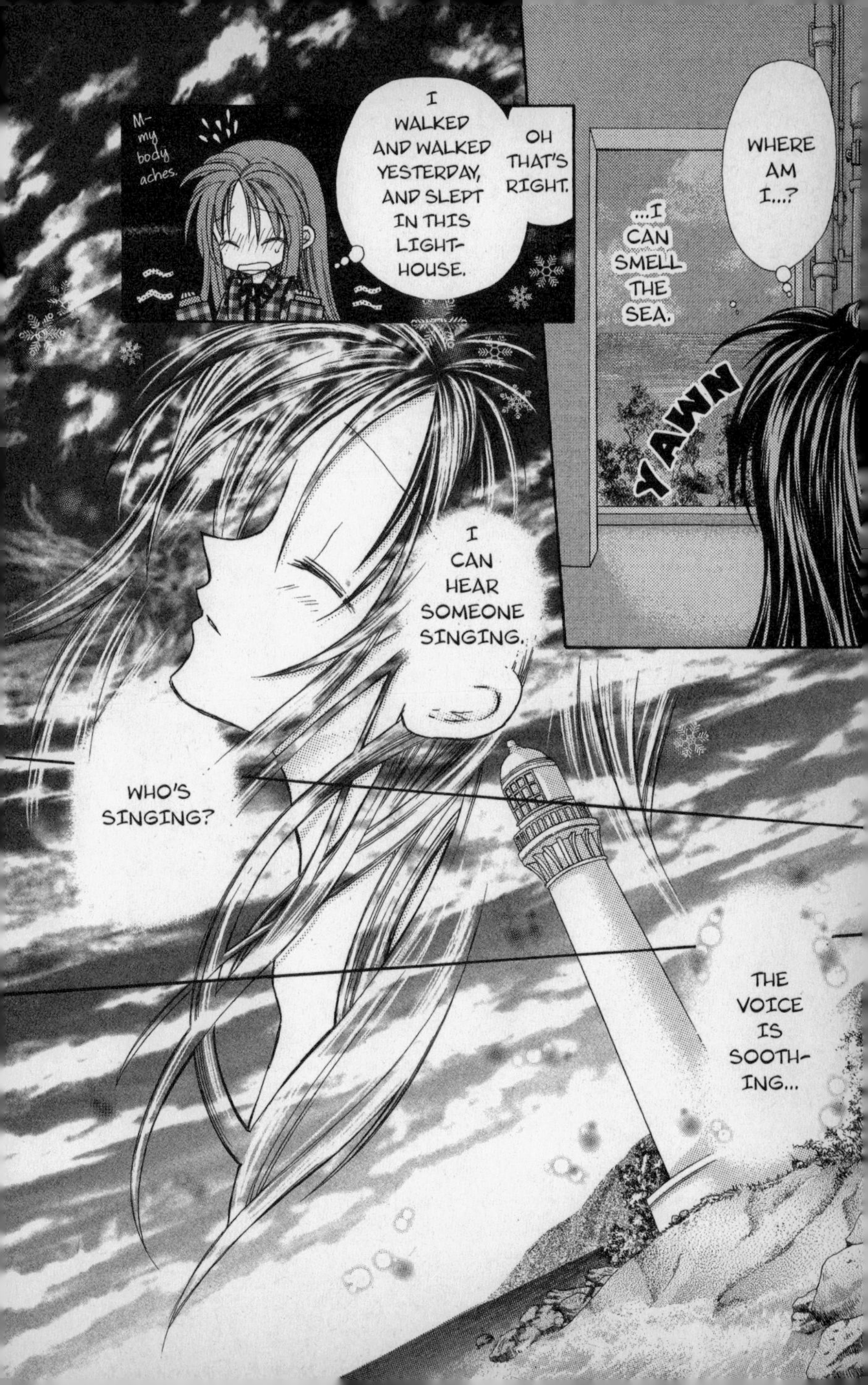
WHERE AM I...?
...I CAN SMELL THE SEA.
YAWN
OH THAT'S RIGHT.
I WALKED AND WALKED YESTERDAY, AND SLEPT IN THIS LIGHT-HOUSE.
M-my body aches.
I CAN HEAR SOMEONE SINGING.
WHO'S SINGING?
THE VOICE IS SOOTH-ING...

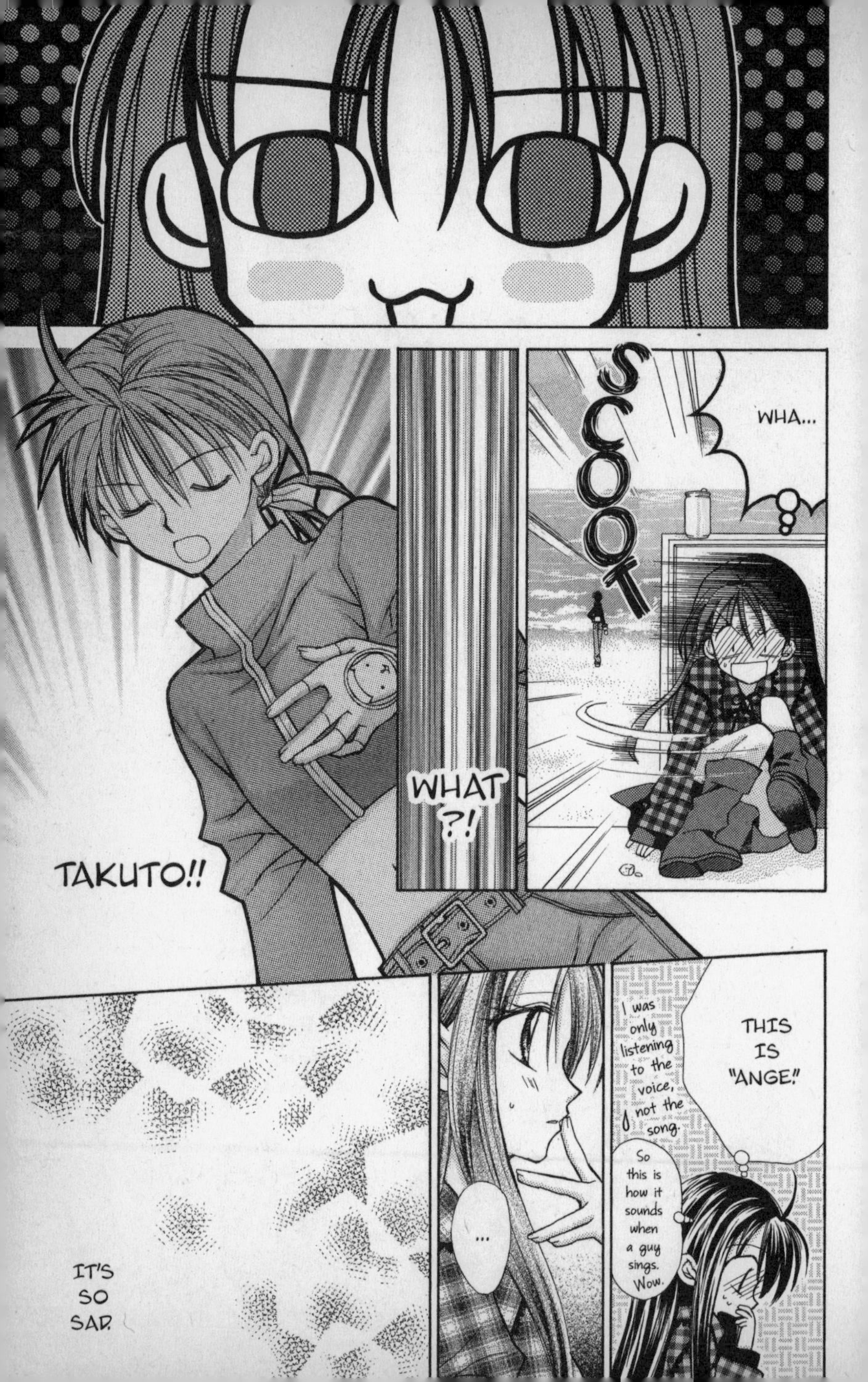

WHA...
SCOOT
WHAT?!
TAKUTO!!
THIS IS "ANGE."
I was only listening to the voice, not the song.
So this is how it sounds when a guy sings. Wow.
...
IT'S SO SAD.

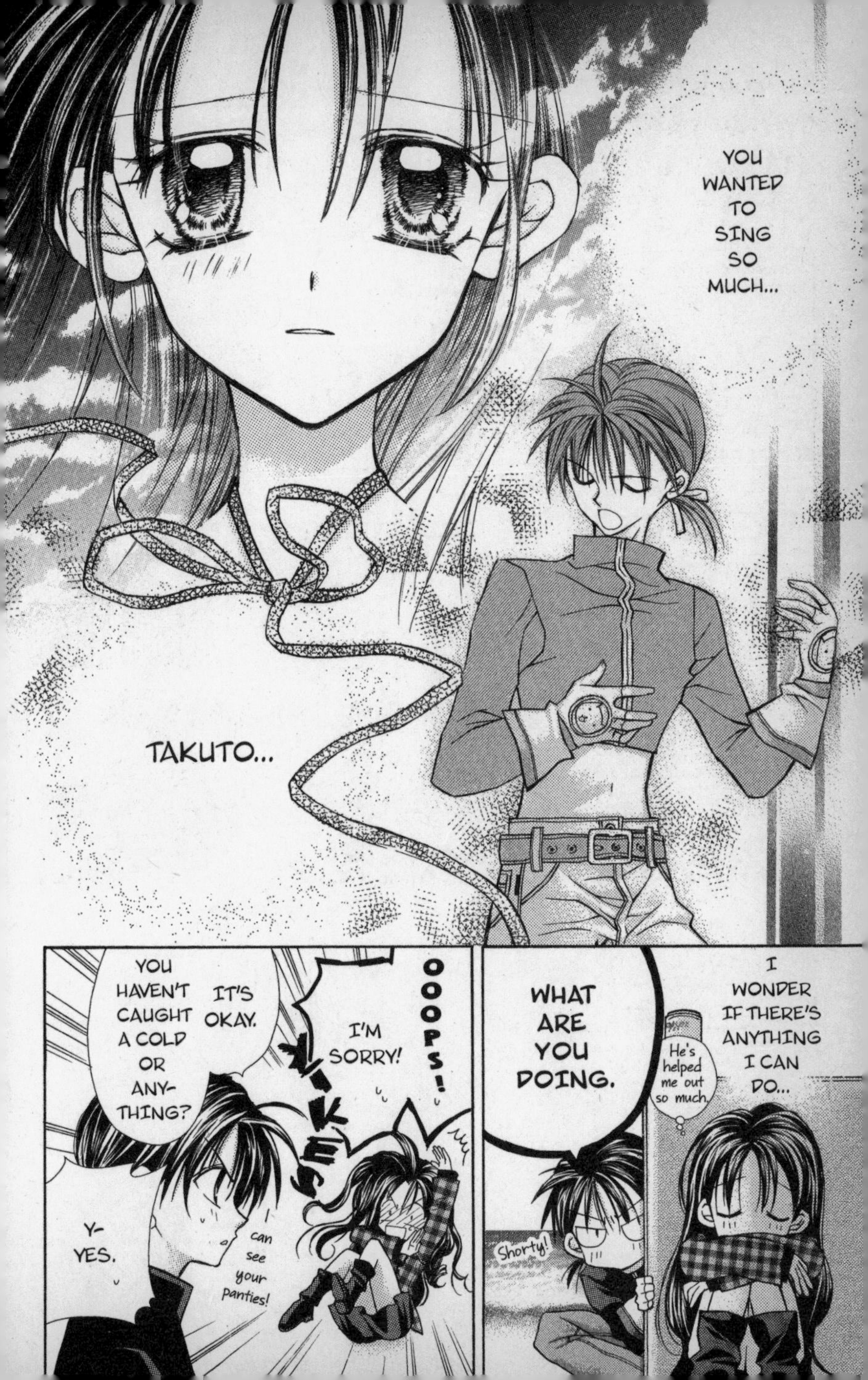
YOU WANTED TO SING SO MUCH...
TAKUTO...
I WONDER IF THERE'S ANYTHING I CAN DO...
He's helped me out so much.
WHAT ARE YOU DOING.
Shorty!
OOOPS!
I'M SORRY!
YIKES!
IT'S OKAY.
YOU HAVEN'T CAUGHT A COLD OR ANY-THING?
I can see your panties!
Y-YES.

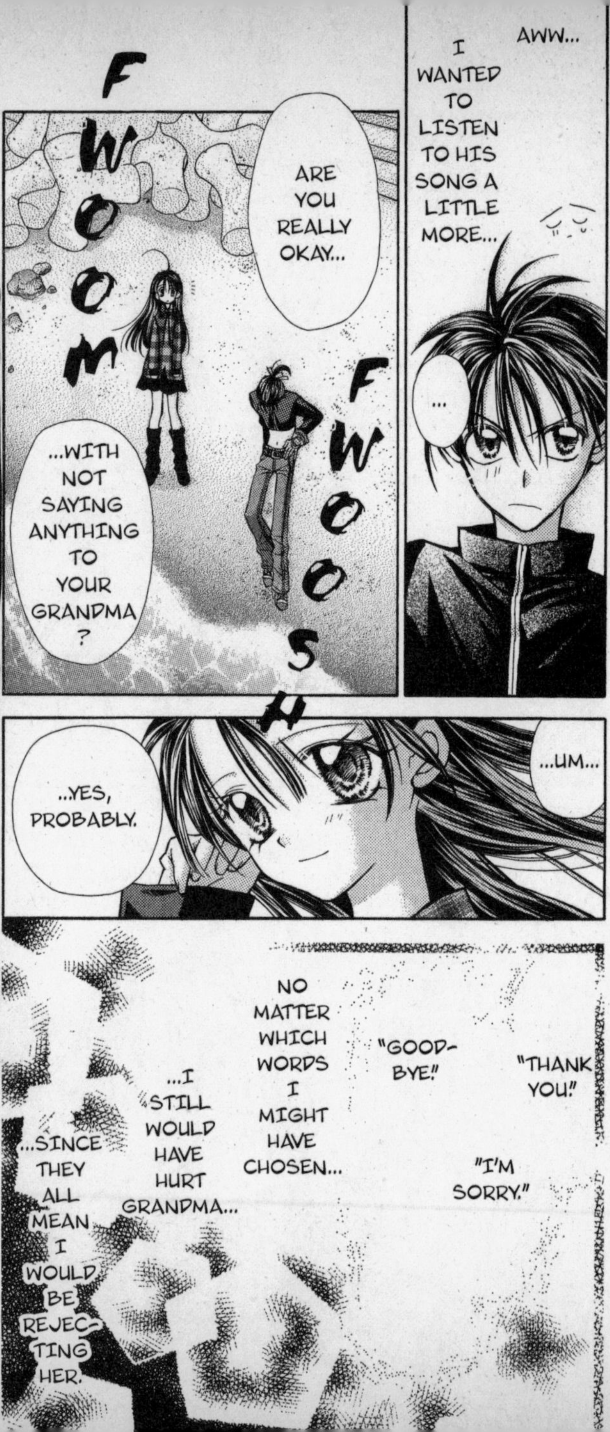
FWOOM
AWW...
I WANTED TO LISTEN TO HIS SONG A LITTLE MORE...
...
ARE YOU REALLY OKAY...
...WITH NOT SAYING ANYTHING TO YOUR GRANDMA?
FWOOSH
...UM...
...YES, PROBABLY.
"THANK YOU!"
"I'M SORRY."
"GOOD-BYE."
NO MATTER WHICH WORDS I MIGHT HAVE CHOSEN...
...I STILL WOULD HAVE HURT GRANDMA...
...SINCE THEY ALL MEAN I WOULD BE REJECTING HER.

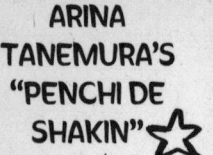

ARINA TANEMURA'S "PENCHI DE SHAKIN"☆

episode 49

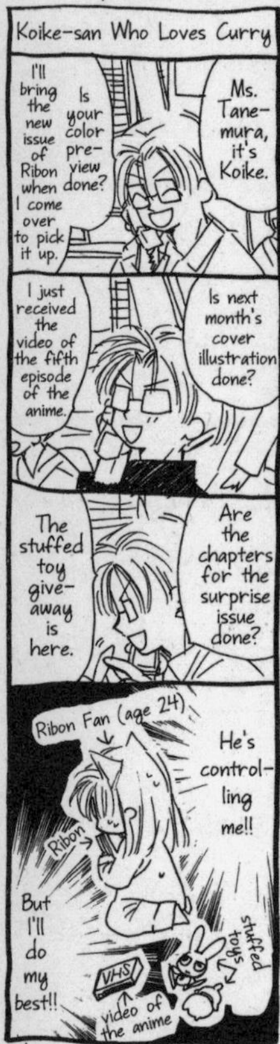
Koike-san Who Loves Curry
Ms. Tanemura, it's Koike.
Is your color preview done?
I'll bring the new issue of Ribon when I come over to pick it up.
Is next month's cover illustration done?
I just received the video of the fifth episode of the anime.
Are the chapters for the surprise issue done?
The stuffed toy give-away is here.
Ribon Fan (age 24)
He's controlling me!!
Ribon
But I'll do my best!!
stuffed toys
VHS
video of the anime

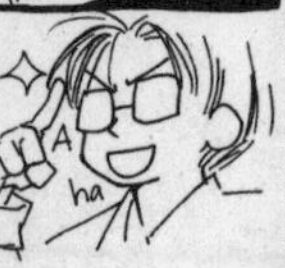
A
ha

In Jimbocho (where Shueisha is located), there's a curry dish called "Koike special."

Mr. Koike gives me Yuzuyu-tan wristbands, Ribon trading cards, and trading card folders. Today I turned my chapters in. I'm speeding up my work.

...Yes, I've been tamed by Mr. Koike.

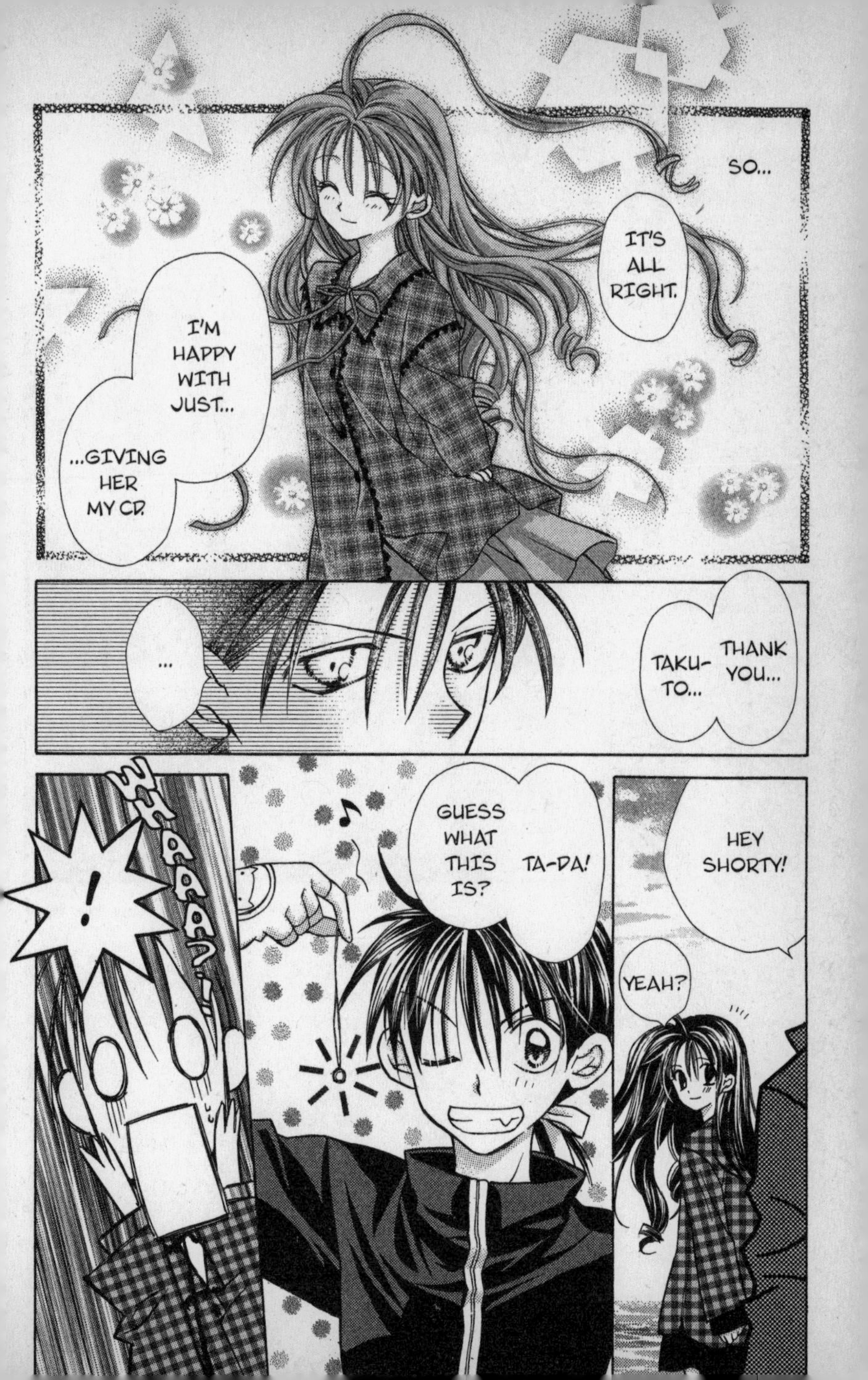
SO...
IT'S ALL RIGHT.
I'M HAPPY WITH JUST...
...GIVING HER MY CD.
THANK YOU...
TAKU-TO...
...
HEY SHORTY!
YEAH?
TA-DA!
GUESS WHAT THIS IS?
!
WHAAAA?!

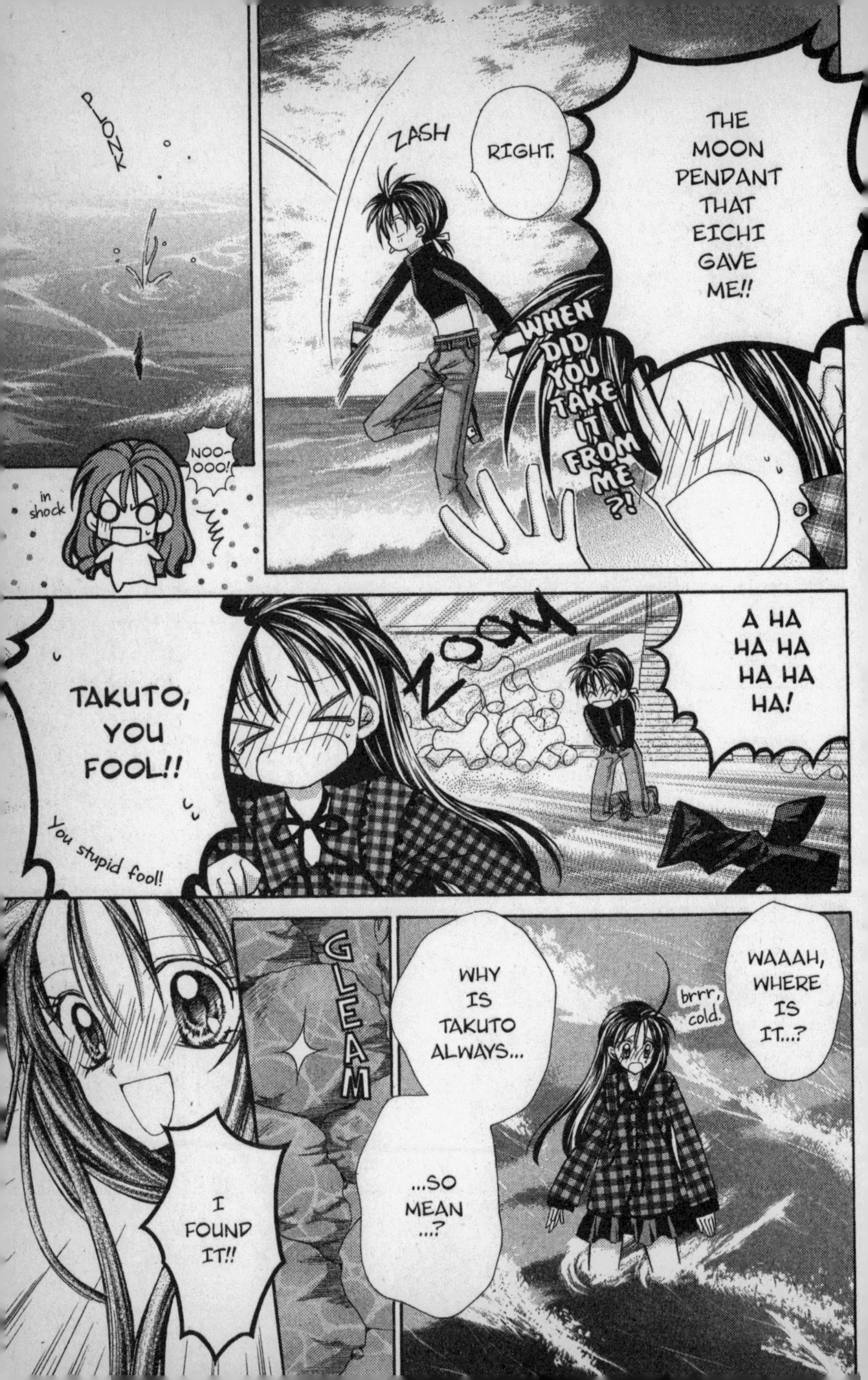
THE MOON PENDANT THAT EICHI GAVE ME!!
WHEN DID YOU TAKE IT FROM ME?!
RIGHT.
ZASH
PLONK
NOO-OOO!
in shock
A HA HA HA HA HA HA!
ZOOM
TAKUTO, YOU FOOL!!
You stupid fool!
WAAAH, WHERE IS IT...?
brrr, cold.
WHY IS TAKUTO ALWAYS...
...SO MEAN ...?
GLEAM
I FOUND IT!!

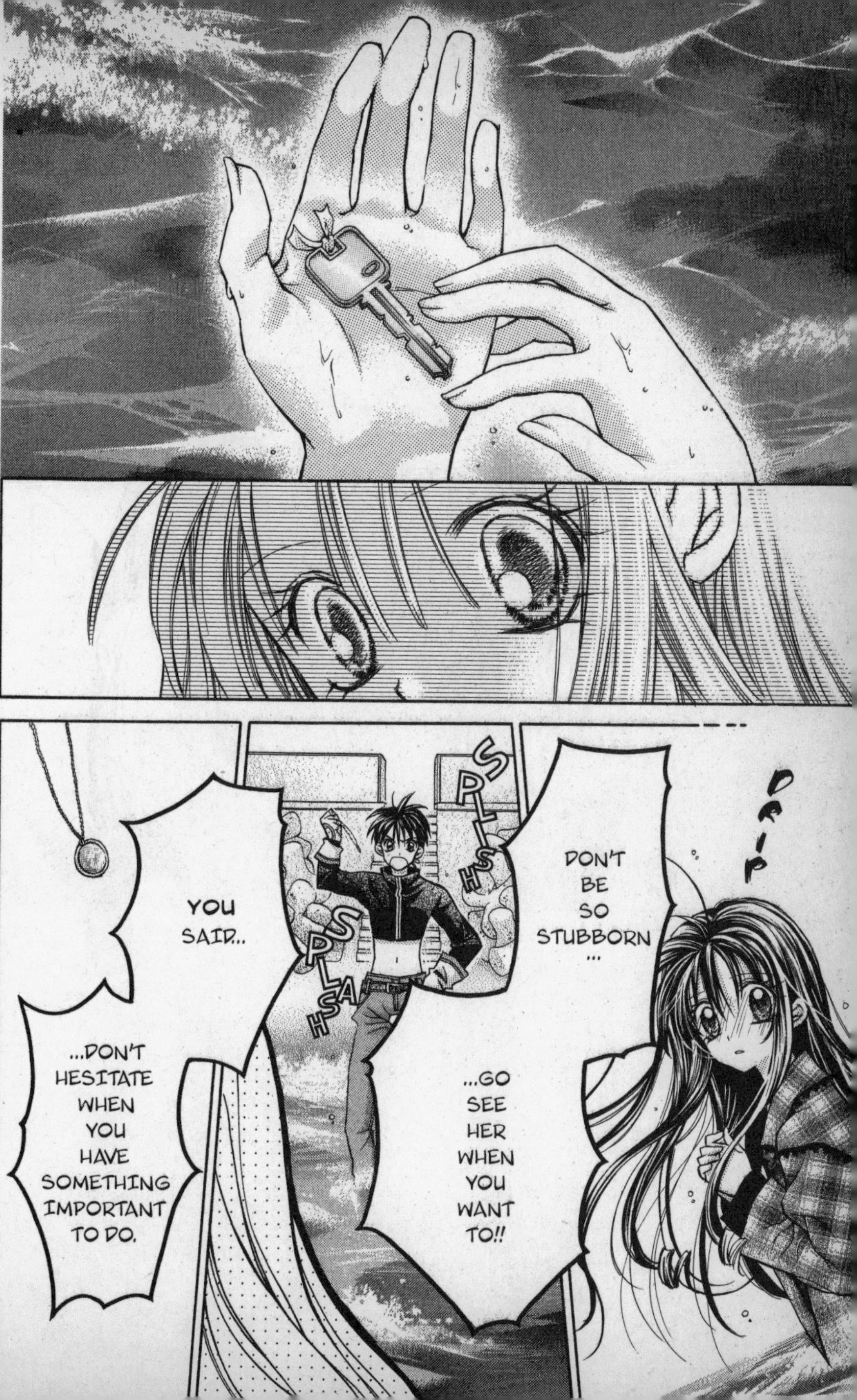
DRIP
DON'T BE SO STUBBORN ...
SPLSH
SPLASH
...GO SEE HER WHEN YOU WANT TO!!
YOU SAID...
...DON'T HESITATE WHEN YOU HAVE SOMETHING IMPORTANT TO DO.

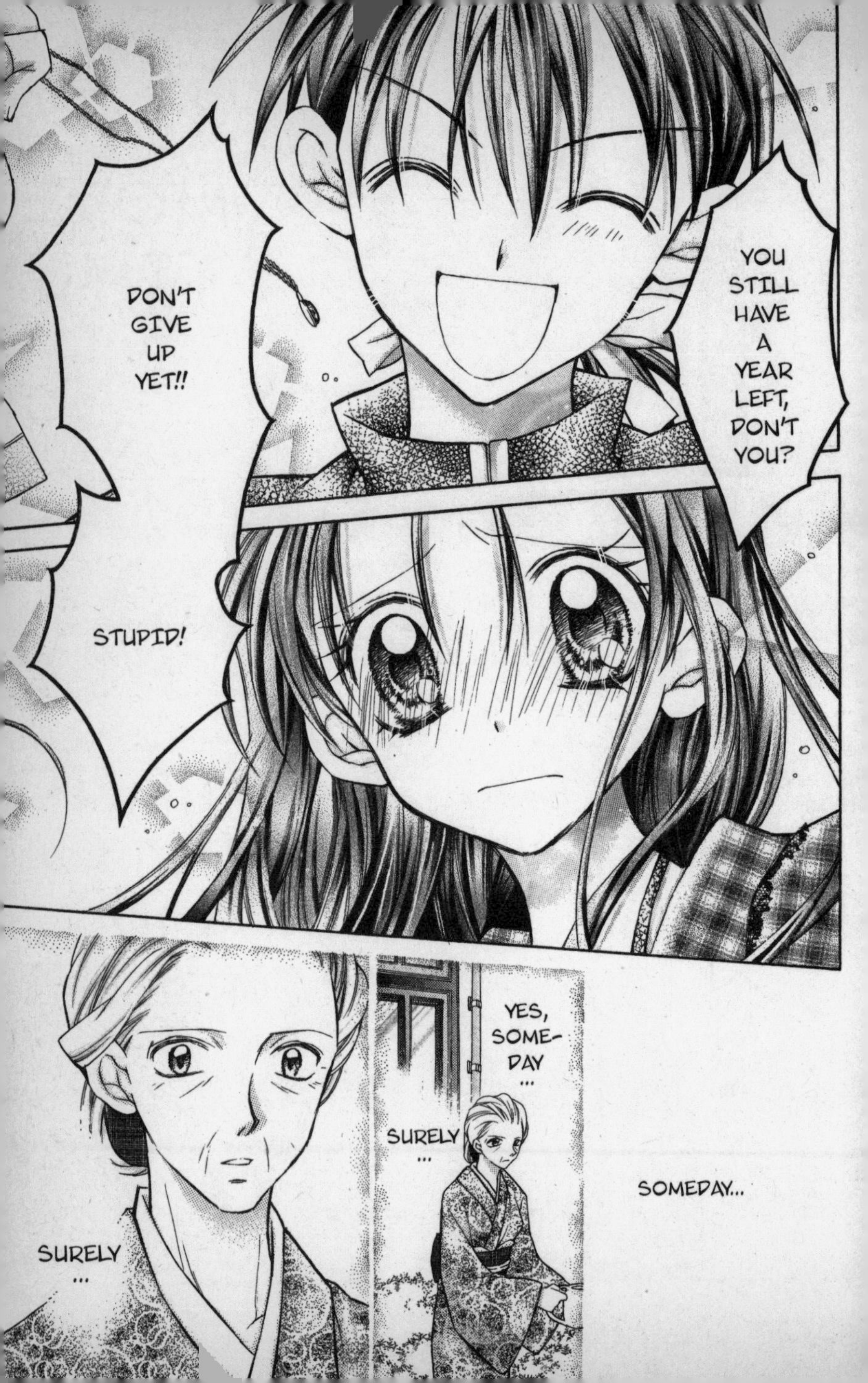
YOU STILL HAVE A YEAR LEFT, DON'T YOU?
DON'T GIVE UP YET!!
STUPID!
SOMEDAY...
YES, SOME-DAY ...
SURELY ...
SURELY ...

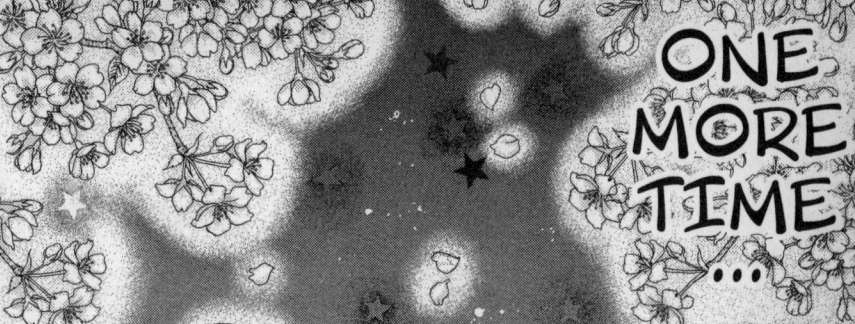

ONE MORE TIME...

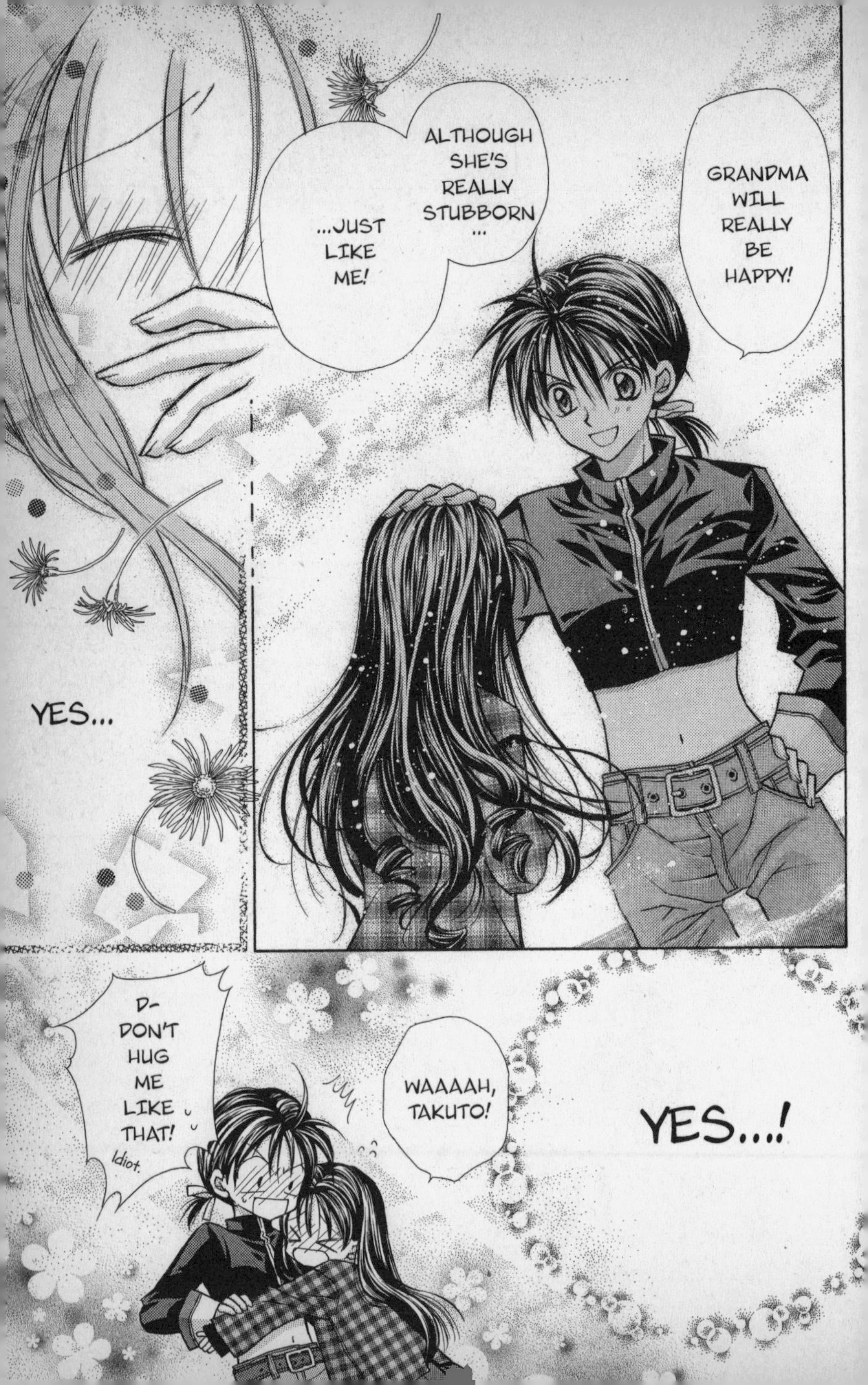
GRANDMA WILL REALLY BE HAPPY!
ALTHOUGH SHE'S REALLY STUBBORN...
...JUST LIKE ME!
YES...
YES...!
WAAAAH, TAKUTO!
D-DON'T HUG ME LIKE THAT!
Idiot.

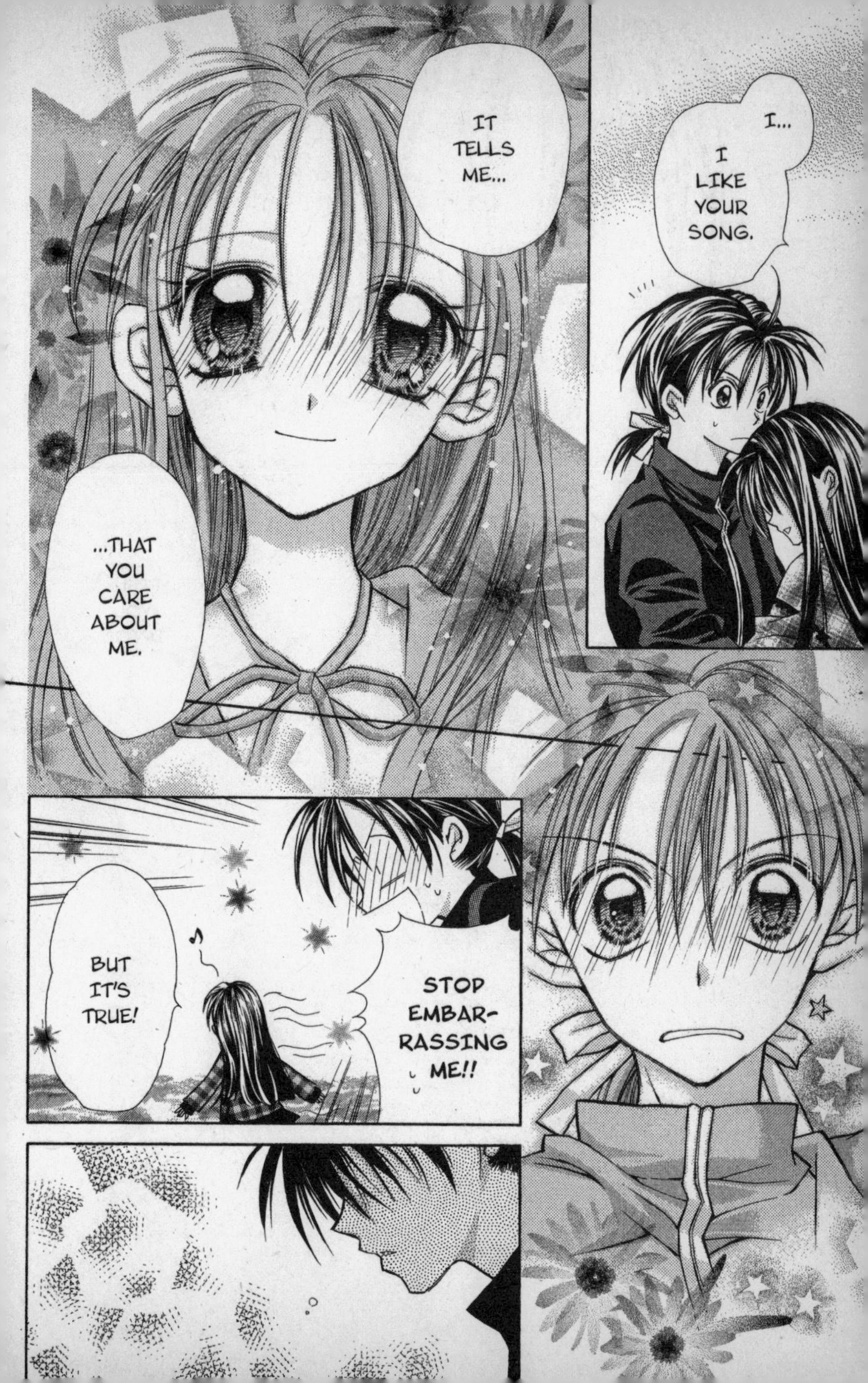
I...
I LIKE YOUR SONG.
IT TELLS ME...
...THAT YOU CARE ABOUT ME.
STOP EMBAR-RASSING ME!!
BUT IT'S TRUE!

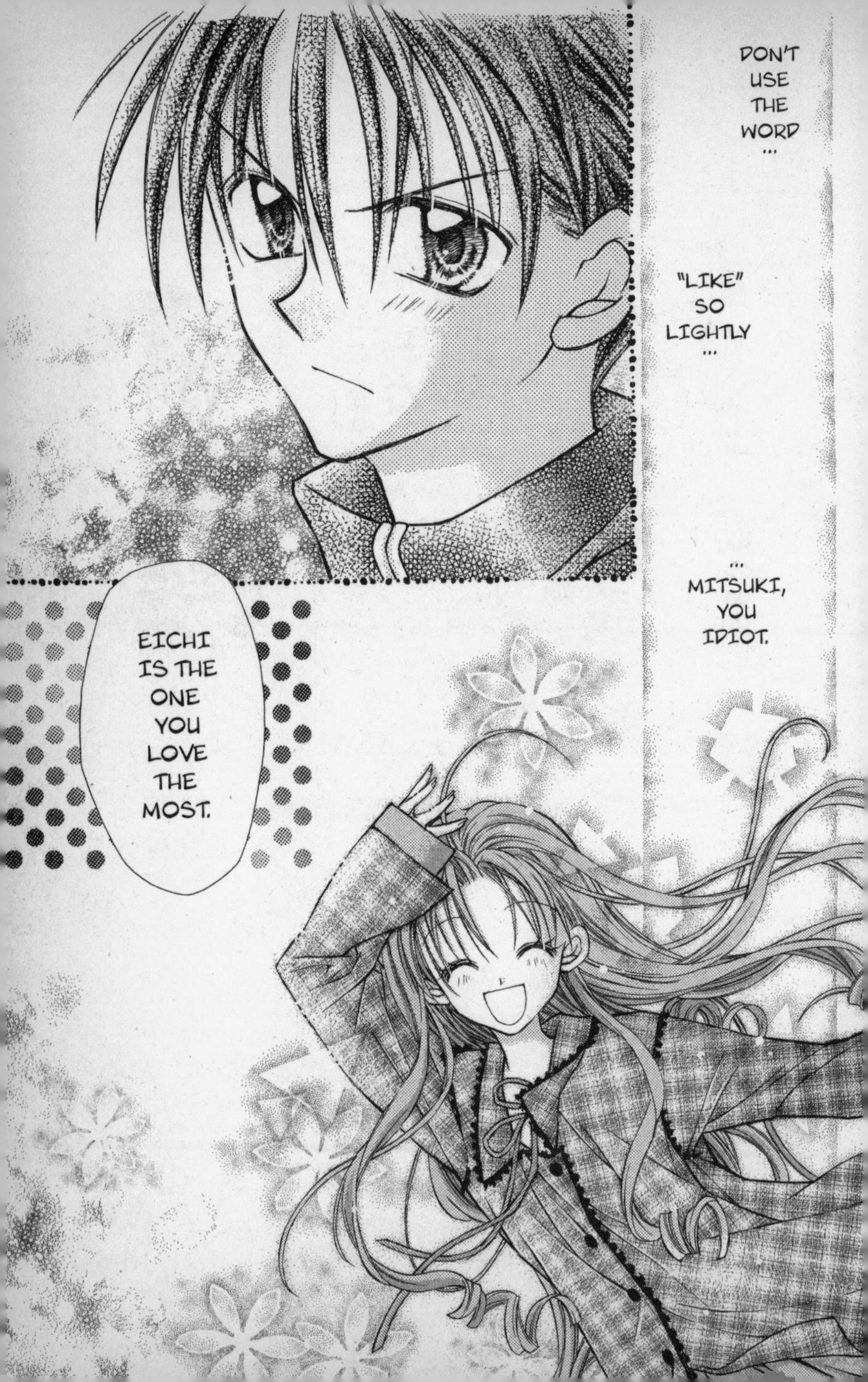
DON'T USE THE WORD ...
"LIKE" SO LIGHTLY ...
... MITSUKI, YOU IDIOT.
EICHI IS THE ONE YOU LOVE THE MOST.

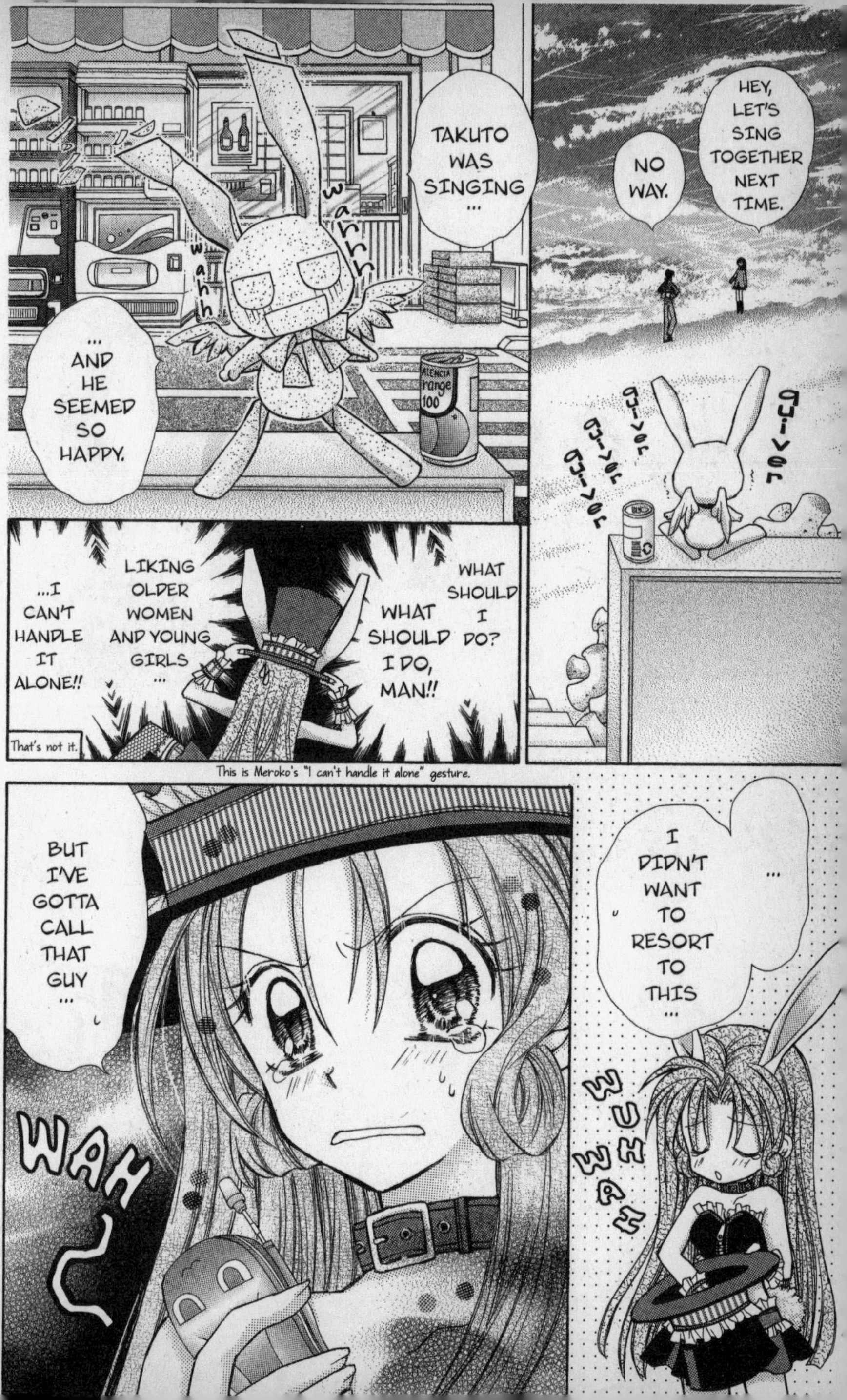
HEY, LET'S SING TOGETHER NEXT TIME.
NO WAY.
quiver quiver quiver quiver
TAKUTO WAS SINGING ...
wahhh wahh
... AND HE SEEMED SO HAPPY.
WHAT SHOULD I DO?
WHAT SHOULD I DO, MAN!!
LIKING OLDER WOMEN AND YOUNG GIRLS ...
...I CAN'T HANDLE IT ALONE!!
That's not it.
This is Meroko's "I can't handle it alone" gesture.
I DIDN'T WANT TO RESORT TO THIS ...
...
WUHWAH
BUT I'VE GOTTA CALL THAT GUY ...
WAH

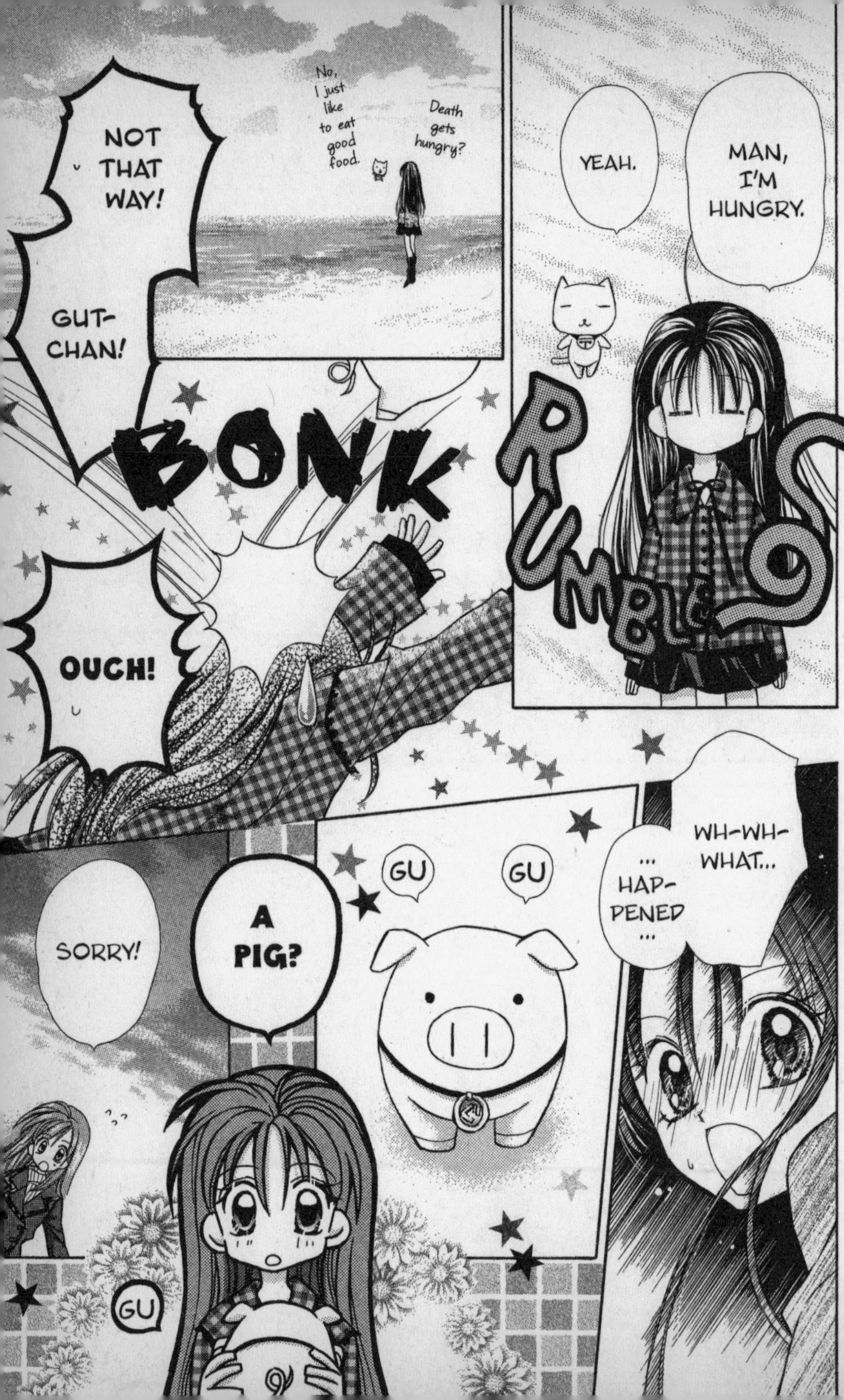
MAN, I'M HUNGRY.
YEAH.
RUMBLE
Death gets hungry?
No, I just like to eat good food.
NOT THAT WAY!
GUT-CHAN!
BONK
OUCH!
WH-WH-WHAT...
... HAP-PENED ...
GU
GU
A PIG?
SORRY!
GU

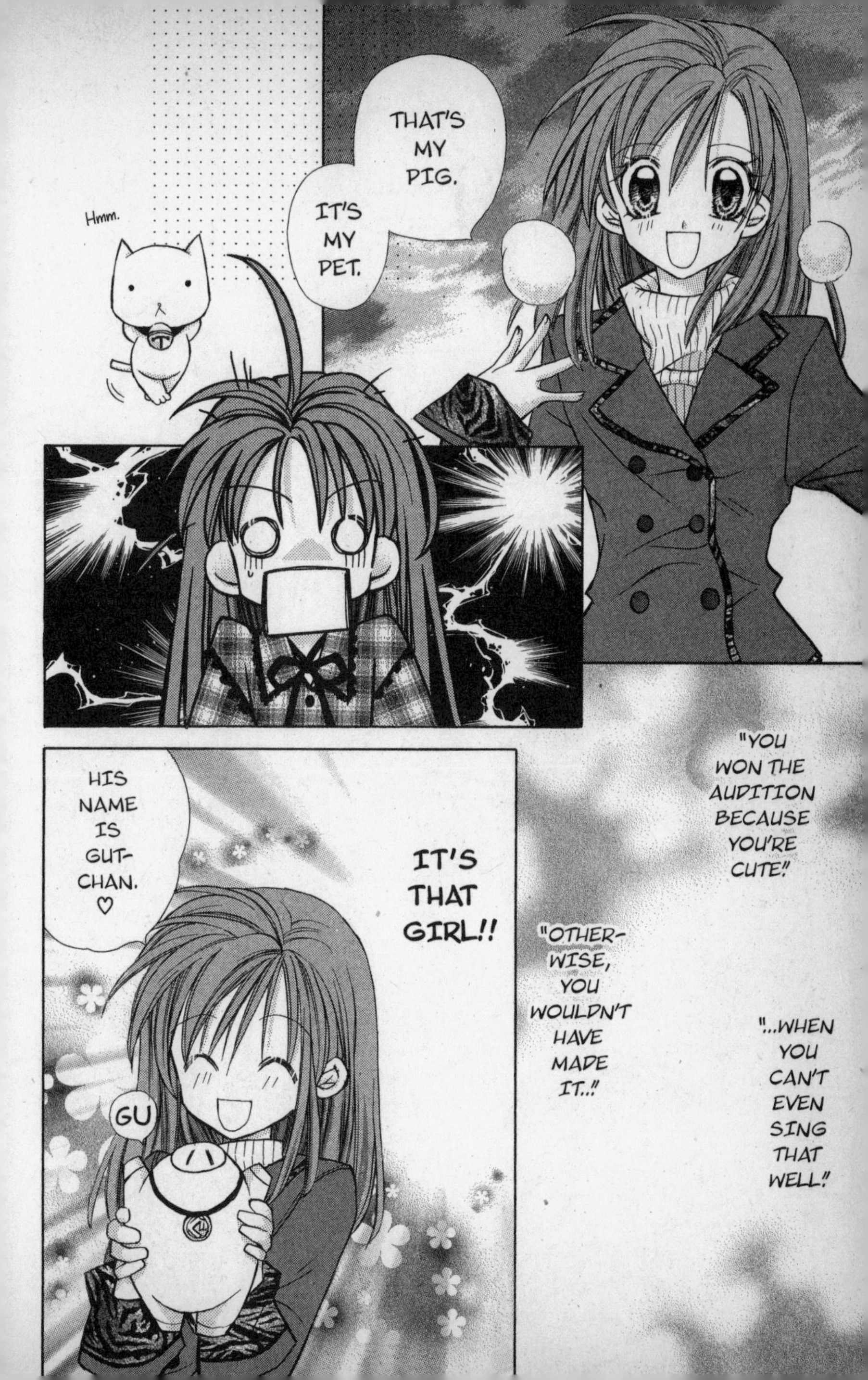
THAT'S MY PIG.
IT'S MY PET.
Hmm.
"YOU WON THE AUDITION BECAUSE YOU'RE CUTE!"
"...WHEN YOU CAN'T EVEN SING THAT WELL."
"OTHER-WISE, YOU WOULDN'T HAVE MADE IT..."
IT'S THAT GIRL!!
HIS NAME IS GUT-CHAN. ♡
GU

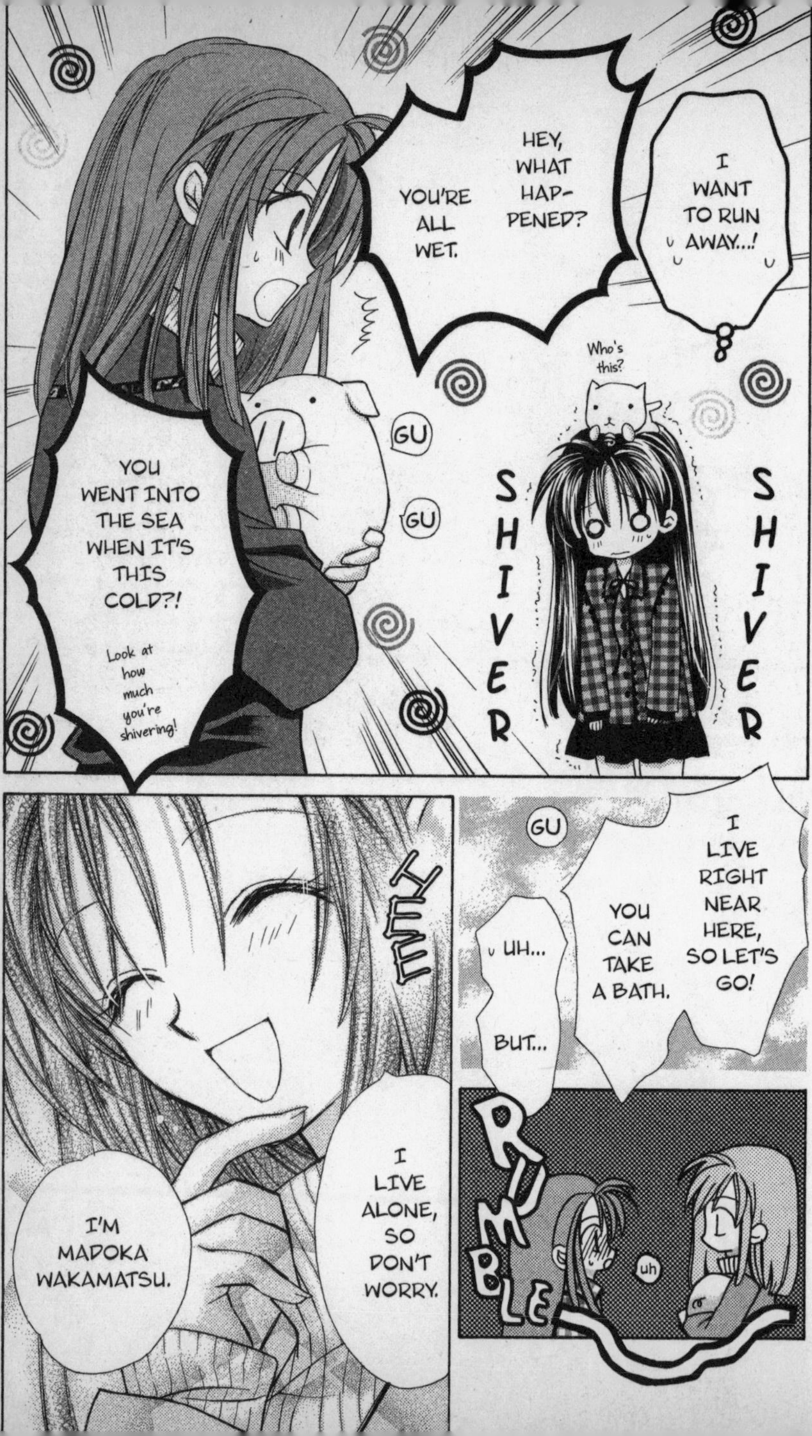
I WANT TO RUN AWAY...!
HEY, WHAT HAPPENED?
YOU'RE ALL WET.
Who's this?
GU
GU
SHIVER
SHIVER
YOU WENT INTO THE SEA WHEN IT'S THIS COLD?!
Look at how much you're shivering!
GU
I LIVE RIGHT NEAR HERE, SO LET'S GO!
YOU CAN TAKE A BATH.
UH...
BUT...
RUMBLE
uh
HEH
I LIVE ALONE, SO DON'T WORRY.
I'M MADOKA WAKAMATSU.

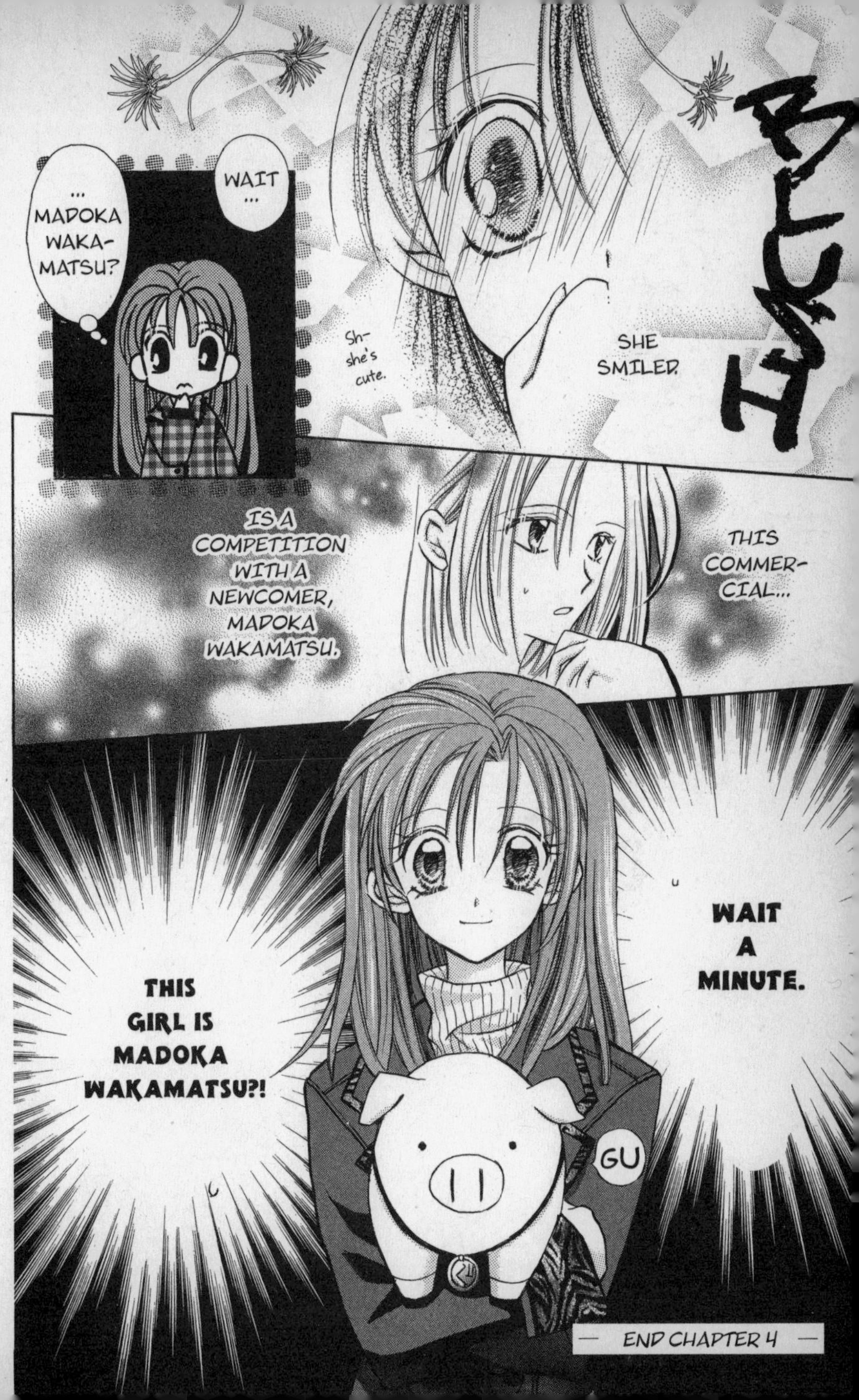
SHE SMILED.
Sh- she's cute.
WAIT ...
... MADOKA WAKA-MATSU?
THIS COMMERCIAL...
IS A COMPETITION WITH A NEWCOMER, MADOKA WAKAMATSU.
WAIT A MINUTE.
THIS GIRL IS MADOKA WAKAMATSU?!
GU
END CHAPTER 4

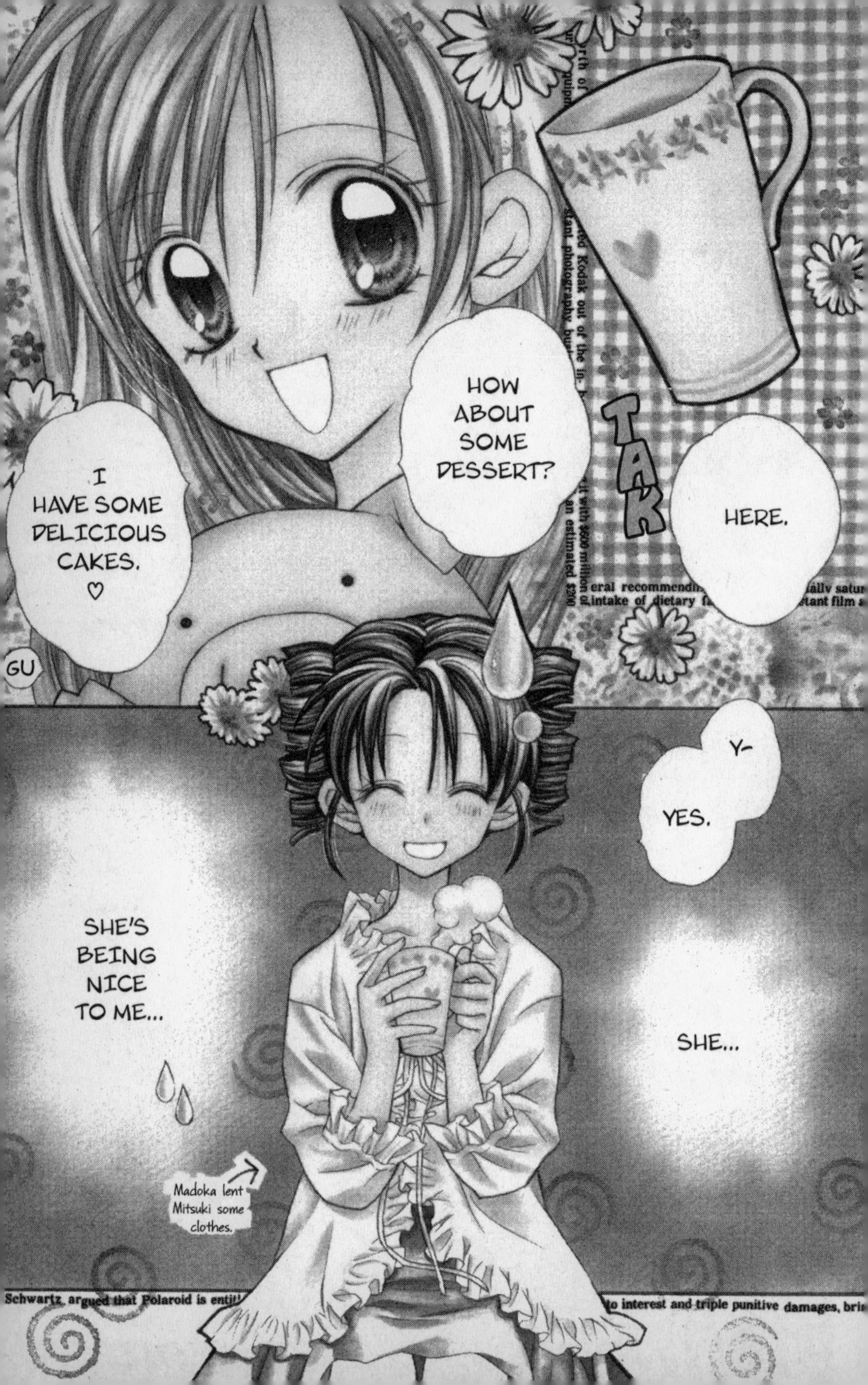
TAK
HERE.
HOW ABOUT SOME DESSERT?
I HAVE SOME DELICIOUS CAKES. ♡
GU
Y- YES.
SHE...
SHE'S BEING NICE TO ME...
Madoka lent Mitsuki some clothes.

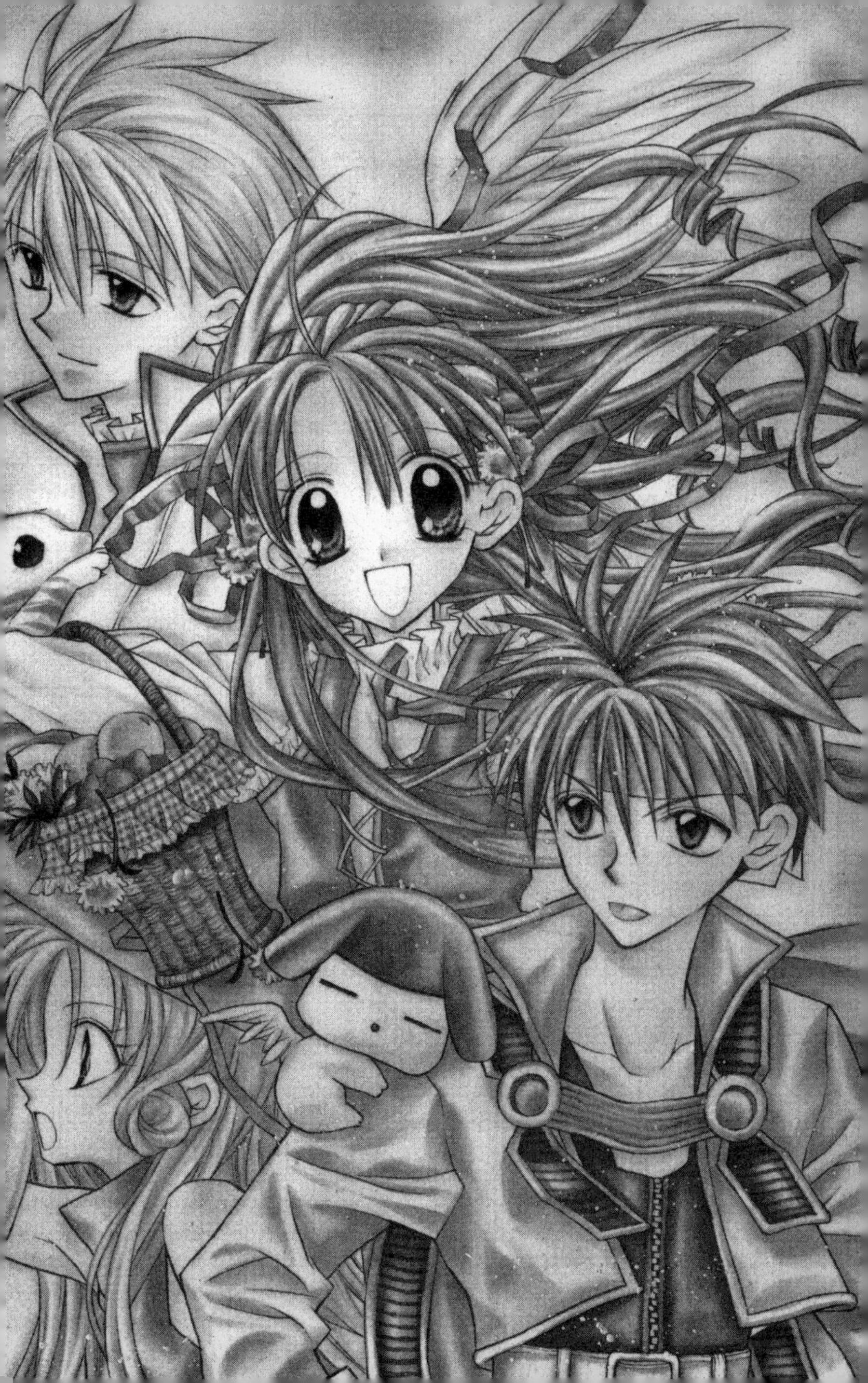

満月をさがして
Full Moon o Sagashite

第5話　虚ろな海のまんなかで

Chapter 5　In the Middle of a Hollow Sea

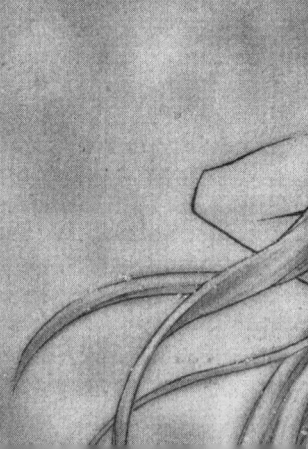

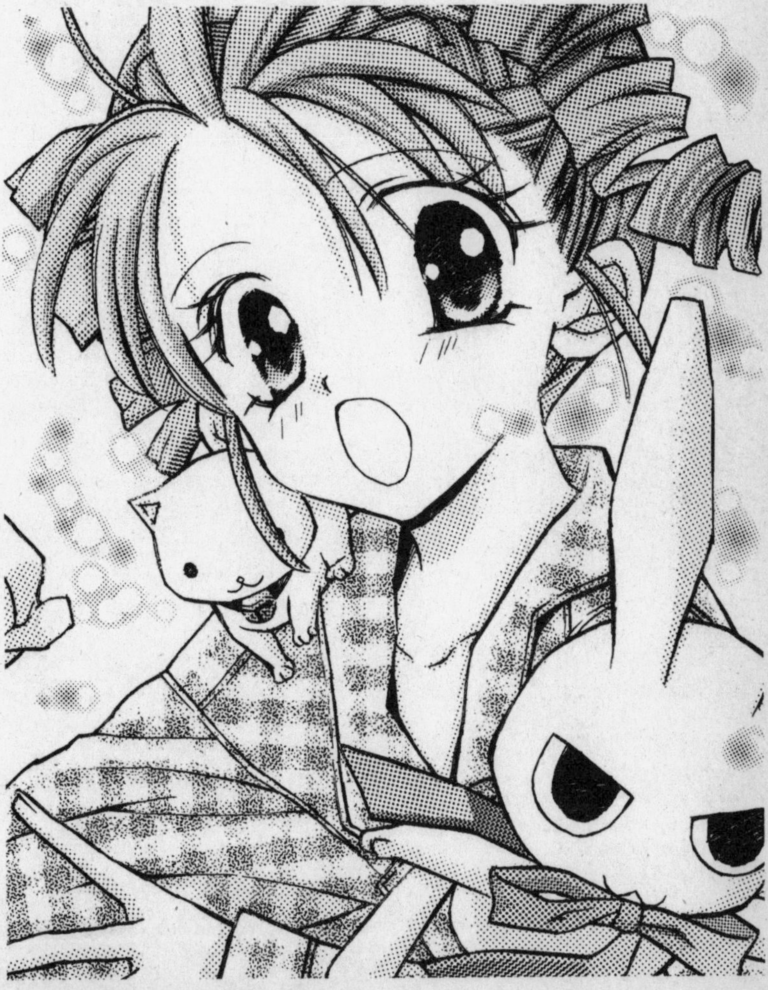

GU

GU

GU

I can't process all this information.

BUT WHEN SHE'S THIS DIFFERENT...

I KNOW, I KNOW.

...SO OF COURSE SHE'S ACTING NICE TO YOU.

THERE'S NO WAY SHE KNOWS THAT FULLMOON IS MITSUKI...

THIS IS...

ESCAPE FROM REALITY, HUH?

WOW, LOOK TAKUTO, GUT-CHAN IS WATCHING TV. ♡

GU GU

MADOKA?

HUH?

❀ Special Thanks ❀

Ms. Sumiko Miura, Chiyoda Clinic
Toshiharu Jitsukawa, Voice Trainer

I interviewed them before starting this series.
I had voice training lessons too.
I will do my best to create a good series.
Thank so much.
Sorry for this illustration.

Is it you?!

Ms. Oshige convinced me to do this...

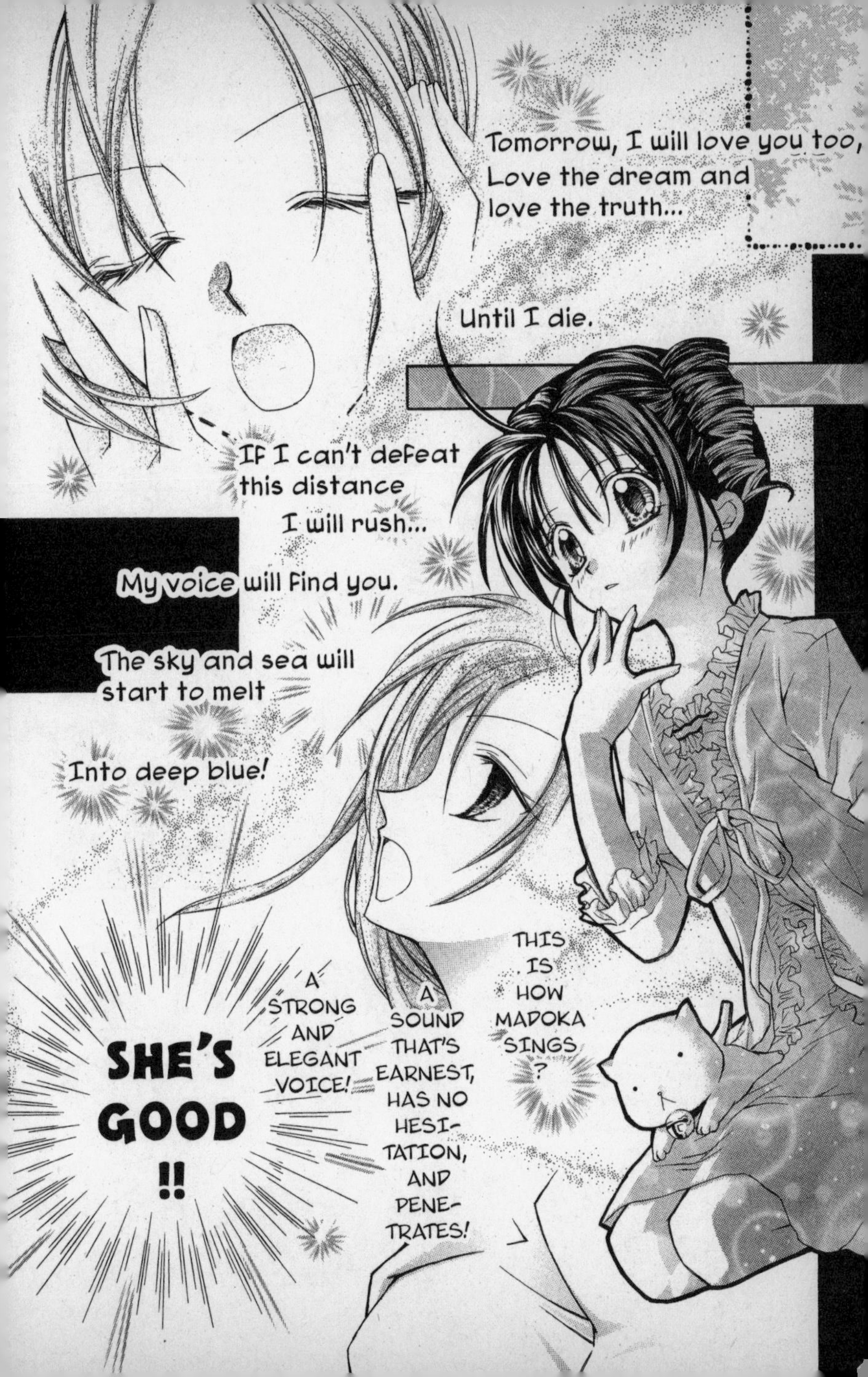

Tomorrow, I will love you too, Love the dream and love the truth...
Until I die.
If I can't defeat this distance I will rush...
My voice will find you.
The sky and sea will start to melt
Into deep blue!
THIS IS HOW MADOKA SINGS?
A SOUND THAT'S EARNEST, HAS NO HESITATION, AND PENETRATES!
A STRONG AND ELEGANT VOICE!
SHE'S GOOD!!

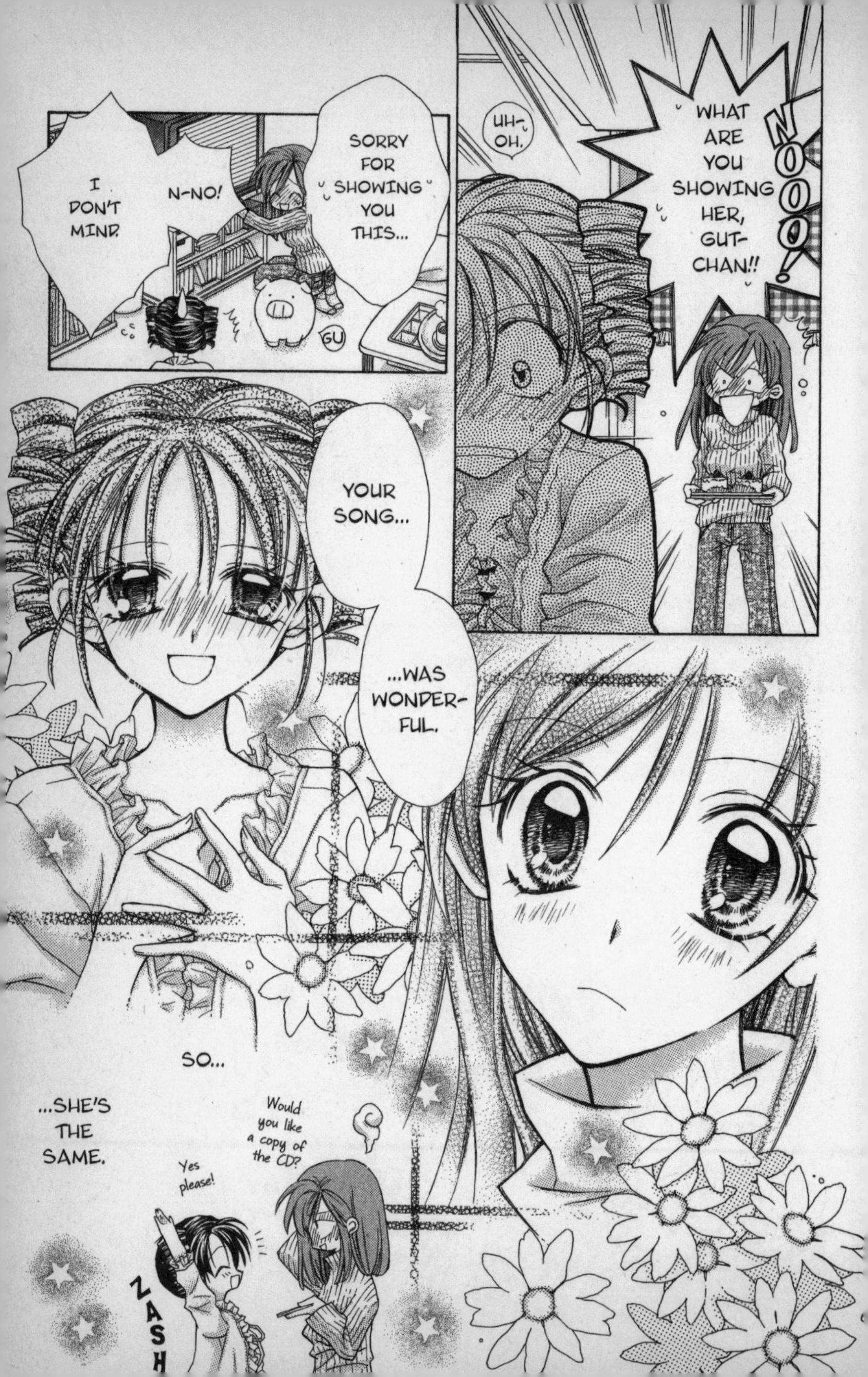
NOOOO!
WHAT ARE YOU SHOWING HER, GUT-CHAN!!
UH-OH.
SORRY FOR SHOWING YOU THIS...
N-NO!
I DON'T MIND.
GU
YOUR SONG...
...WAS WONDERFUL.
SO...
...SHE'S THE SAME.
Would you like a copy of the CD?
Yes please!
ZASH

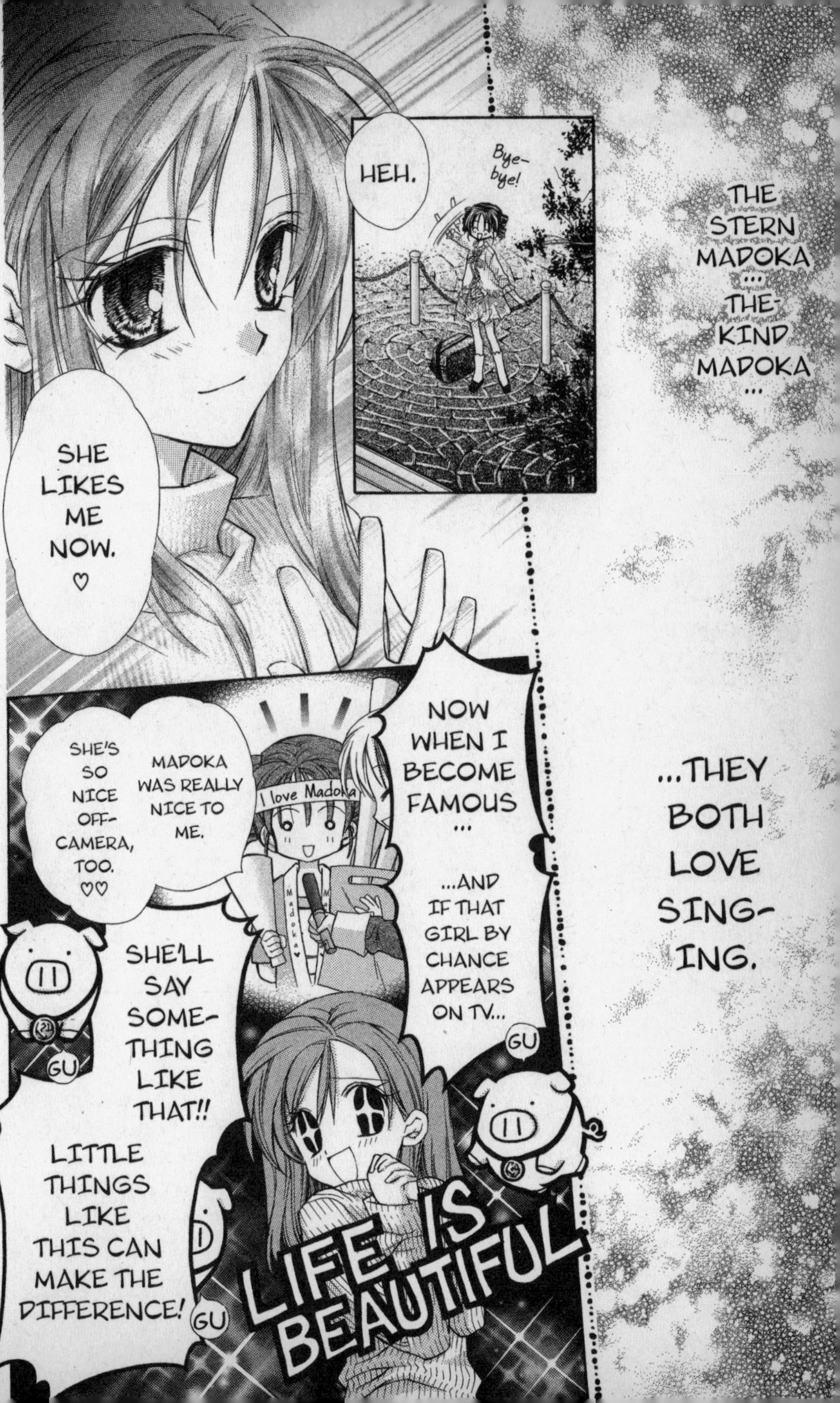

THE STERN MADOKA... THE-KIND MADOKA...
...THEY BOTH LOVE SING-ING.
HEH.
Bye-bye!
SHE LIKES ME NOW. ♡
NOW WHEN I BECOME FAMOUS...
...AND IF THAT GIRL BY CHANCE APPEARS ON TV...
MADOKA WAS REALLY NICE TO ME.
SHE'S SO NICE OFF-CAMERA, TOO. ♡♡
I love Madoka
SHE'LL SAY SOME-THING LIKE THAT!!
GU
GU
LITTLE THINGS LIKE THIS CAN MAKE THE DIFFERENCE!
GU
LIFE IS BEAUTIFUL

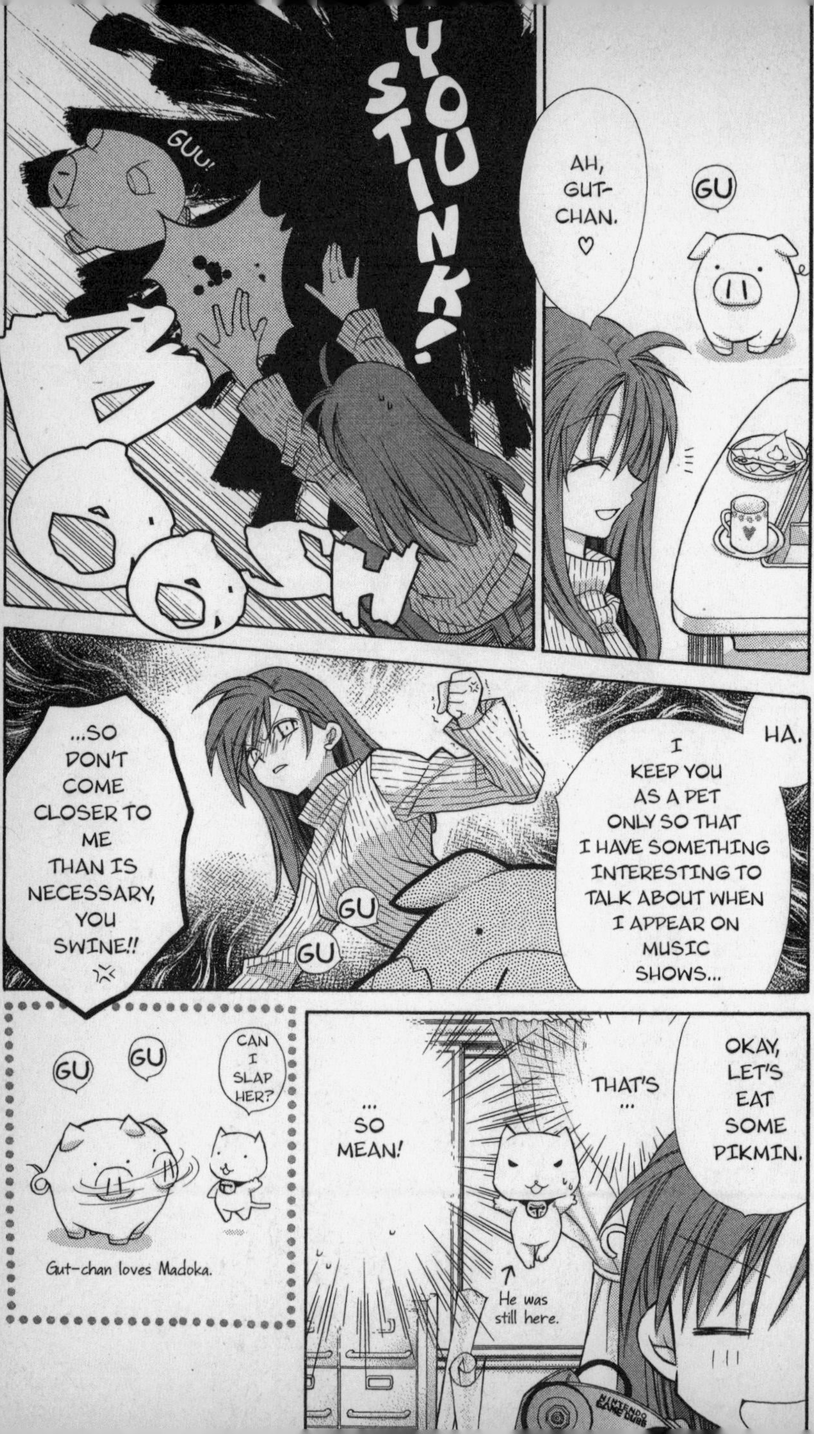
GU
AH, GUT-CHAN. ♡
YOU STINK!
GUU!
HA.
I KEEP YOU AS A PET ONLY SO THAT I HAVE SOMETHING INTERESTING TO TALK ABOUT WHEN I APPEAR ON MUSIC SHOWS...
GU
GU
...SO DON'T COME CLOSER TO ME THAN IS NECESSARY, YOU SWINE!!
OKAY, LET'S EAT SOME PIKMIN.
THAT'S ...
... SO MEAN!
He was still here.
NINTENDO GAME CUBE
CAN I SLAP HER?
GU
GU
Gut-chan loves Madoka.

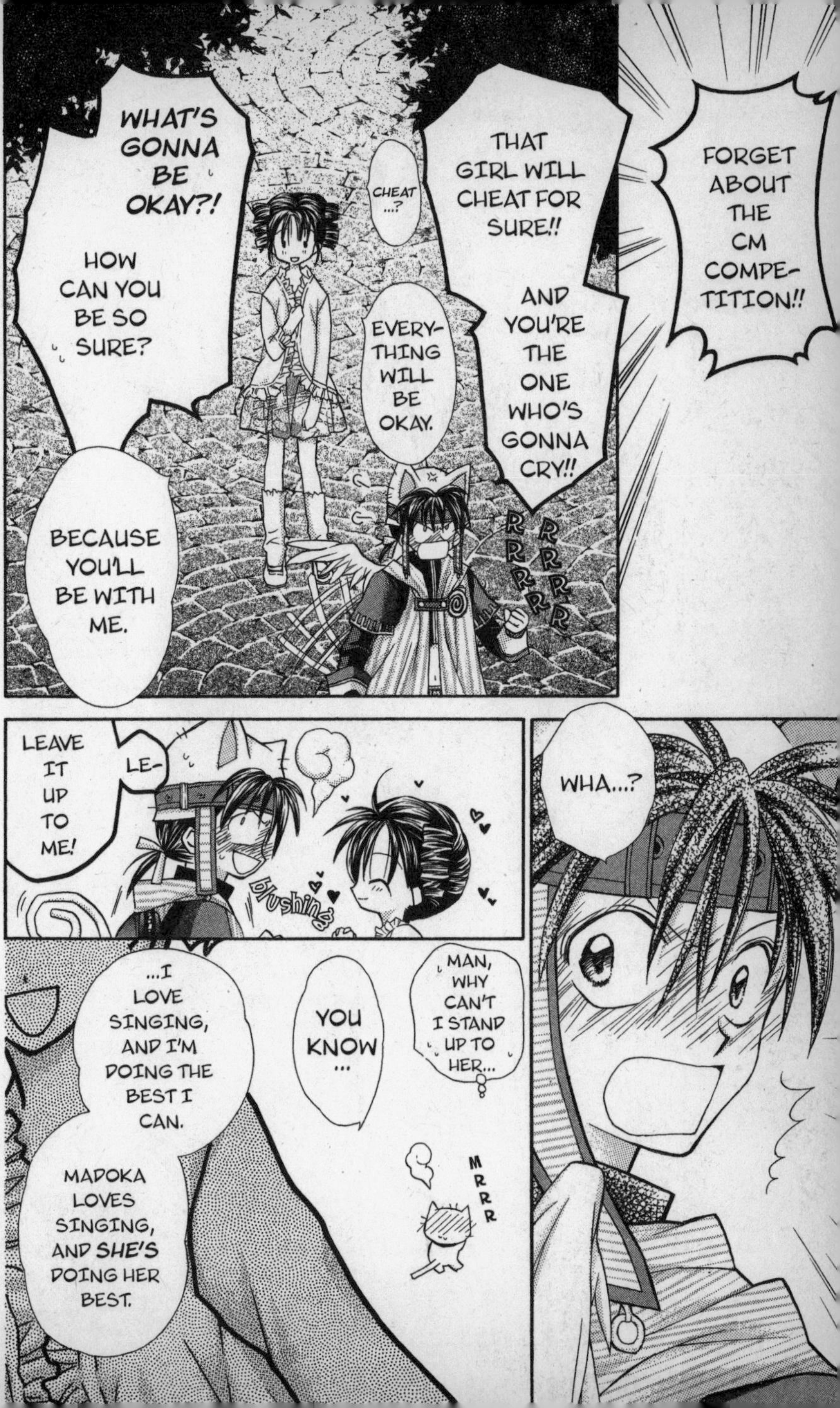

FORGET ABOUT THE CM COMPETITION!!
THAT GIRL WILL CHEAT FOR SURE!!
AND YOU'RE THE ONE WHO'S GONNA CRY!!
CHEAT ...?
EVERYTHING WILL BE OKAY.
RRRRRRR
WHAT'S GONNA BE OKAY?!
HOW CAN YOU BE SO SURE?
BECAUSE YOU'LL BE WITH ME.
WHA...?
LE-
LEAVE IT UP TO ME!
blushing
MAN, WHY CAN'T I STAND UP TO HER...
YOU KNOW ...
...I LOVE SINGING, AND I'M DOING THE BEST I CAN.
MADOKA LOVES SINGING, AND SHE'S DOING HER BEST.
MRRR

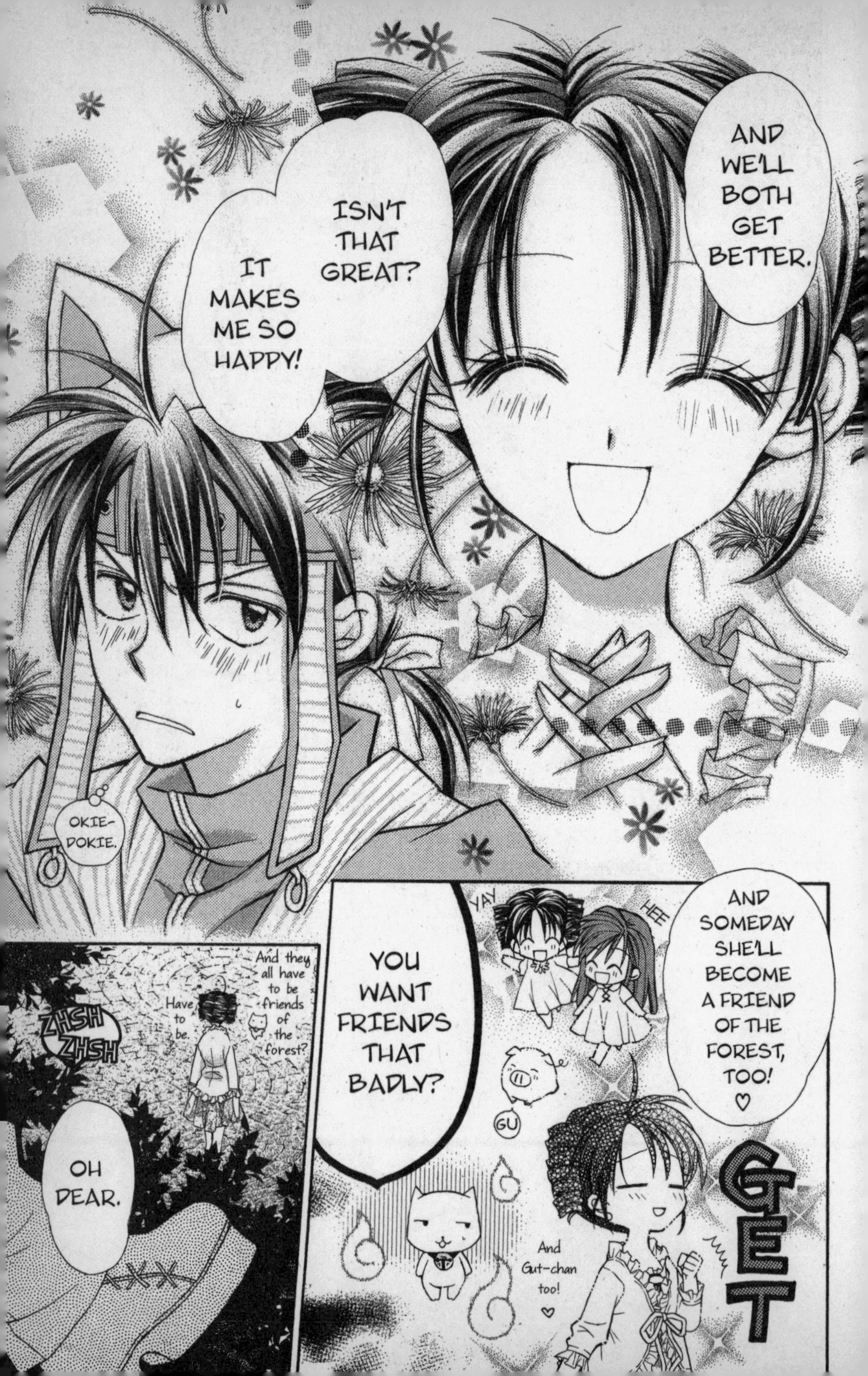
AND WE'LL BOTH GET BETTER.
ISN'T THAT GREAT?
IT MAKES ME SO HAPPY!
OKIE-DOKIE.
AND SOMEDAY SHE'LL BECOME A FRIEND OF THE FOREST, TOO! ♡
HEE
YAY
YOU WANT FRIENDS THAT BADLY?
GU
GET
And Gut-chan too! ♡
And they all have to be friends of the forest?
Have to be.
ZHSH ZHSH
OH DEAR.

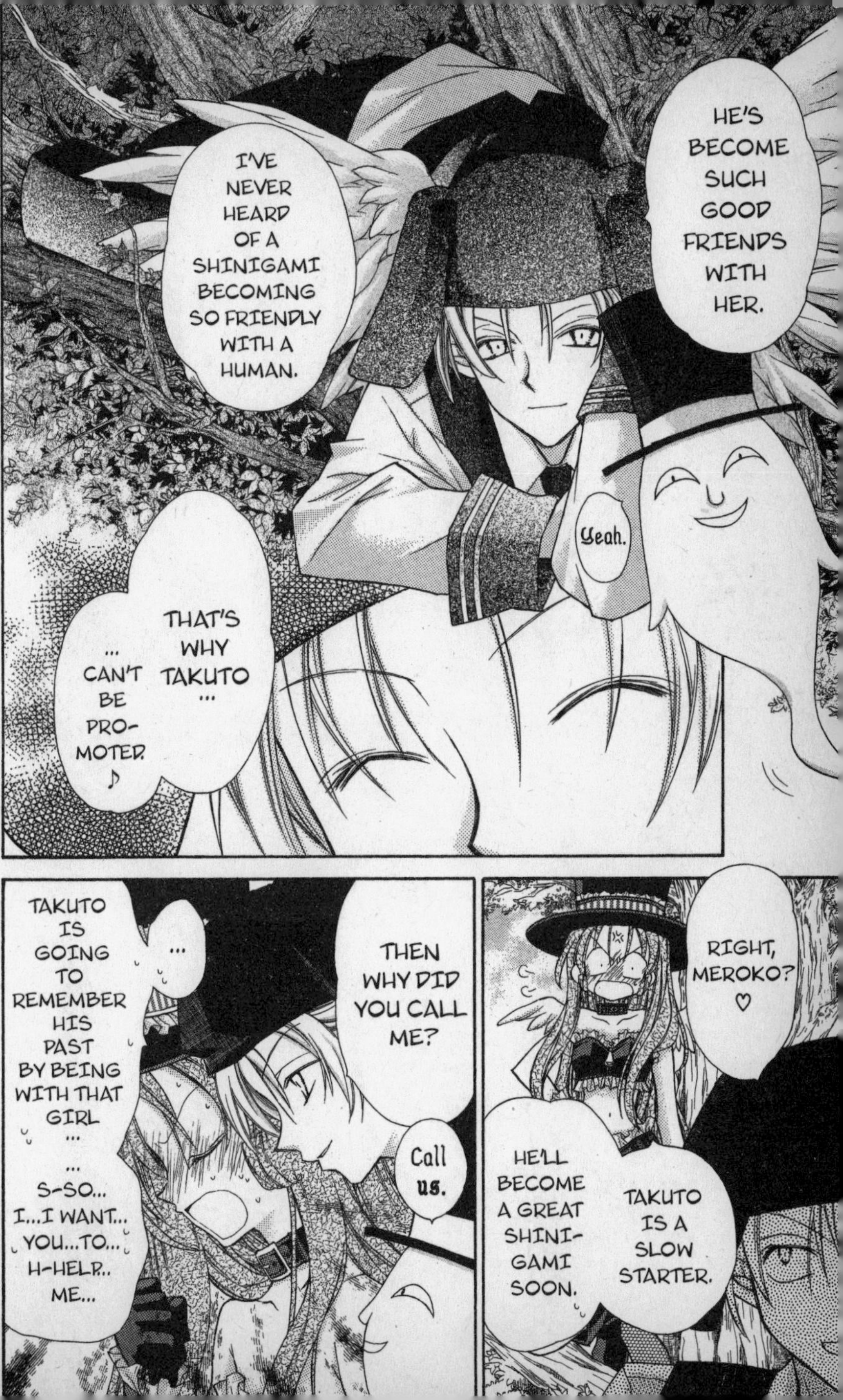
HE'S BECOME SUCH GOOD FRIENDS WITH HER.
I'VE NEVER HEARD OF A SHINIGAMI BECOMING SO FRIENDLY WITH A HUMAN.
Yeah.
THAT'S WHY TAKUTO ...
... CAN'T BE PRO-MOTED. ♪
RIGHT, MEROKO? ♡
TAKUTO IS A SLOW STARTER.
HE'LL BECOME A GREAT SHINI-GAMI SOON.
THEN WHY DID YOU CALL ME?
Call us.
...
TAKUTO IS GOING TO REMEMBER HIS PAST BY BEING WITH THAT GIRL ...
... S-SO... I...I WANT... YOU...TO... H-HELP.. ME...

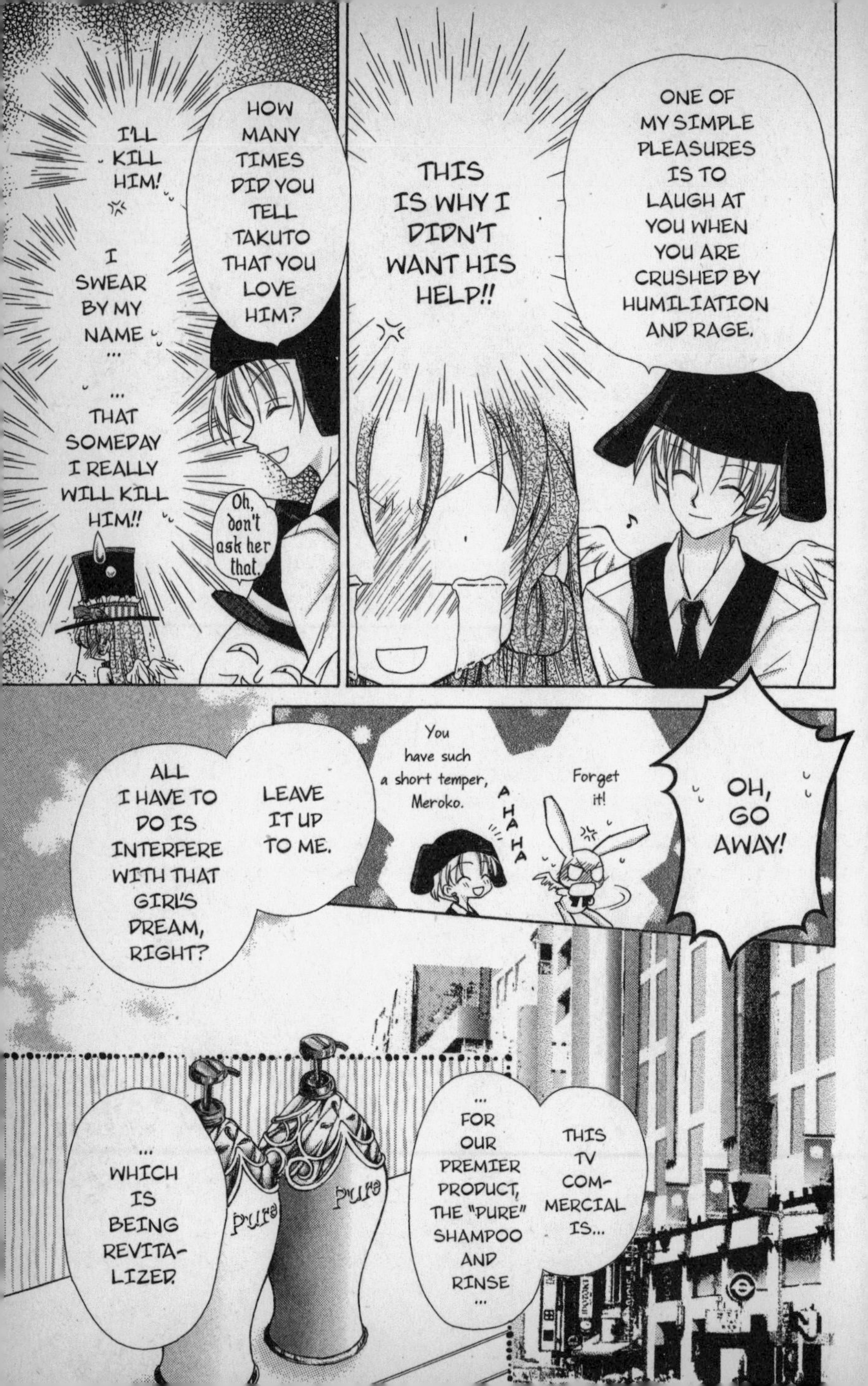
ONE OF MY SIMPLE PLEASURES IS TO LAUGH AT YOU WHEN YOU ARE CRUSHED BY HUMILIATION AND RAGE.
THIS IS WHY I DIDN'T WANT HIS HELP!!
HOW MANY TIMES DID YOU TELL TAKUTO THAT YOU LOVE HIM?
I'LL KILL HIM!
I SWEAR BY MY NAME ...
... THAT SOMEDAY I REALLY WILL KILL HIM!!
Oh, don't ask her that.
OH, GO AWAY!
Forget it!
AHAHA
You have such a short temper, Meroko.
LEAVE IT UP TO ME.
ALL I HAVE TO DO IS INTERFERE WITH THAT GIRL'S DREAM, RIGHT?
THIS TV COMMERCIAL IS...
... FOR OUR PREMIER PRODUCT, THE "PURE" SHAMPOO AND RINSE ...
... WHICH IS BEING REVITALIZED.
pure
pure

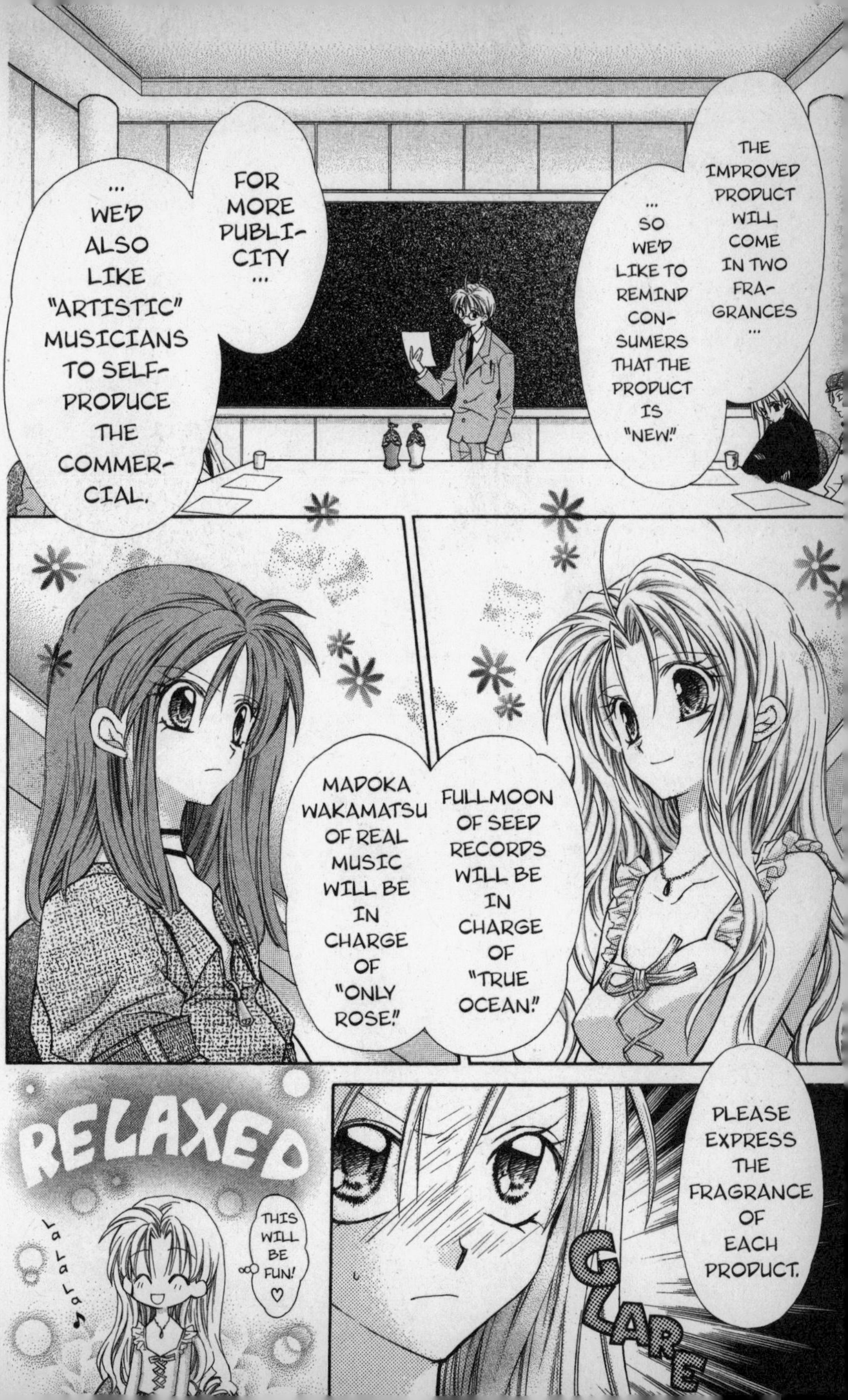
THE IMPROVED PRODUCT WILL COME IN TWO FRAGRANCES ...
... SO WE'D LIKE TO REMIND CONSUMERS THAT THE PRODUCT IS "NEW."
FOR MORE PUBLICITY ...
... WE'D ALSO LIKE "ARTISTIC" MUSICIANS TO SELF-PRODUCE THE COMMERCIAL.
FULLMOON OF SEED RECORDS WILL BE IN CHARGE OF "TRUE OCEAN."
MADOKA WAKAMATSU OF REAL MUSIC WILL BE IN CHARGE OF "ONLY ROSE."
PLEASE EXPRESS THE FRAGRANCE OF EACH PRODUCT.
GLARE
RELAXED
THIS WILL BE FUN! ♡
La La La ♪

Harry Potter (the book)

I'm a Potterian.♪ I bought the 30000 yen robe.

(I'm a bit embarrassed)

I love Hermione.
(I love strong-willed women.)
But I don't like meddlers.

Volume One was okay...and I've been re-reading Volume Two and Three many times (although I like Volume One too).

I saw the movie twice and ordered a copy of the DVD, but I didn't like it too much. The cast and the artwork were great, but I wouldn't have enjoyed it if I hadn't read the book first. However, the movie was great material for my imagination while reading the book.

Let's stop abbreviating Harry Potter as "Haripota." It sounds like crackers a grandma would eat. If you are an otaku, let's call it "Haripo!"

Animal Yokocho (manga)

I love this manga!! It's not because the author Ryo-kun is my friend! I simply love Ani-Yoko!! ♥♥

If you don't know what I'm talking about, this is a comedy manga in Ribon, which features animals, but is not heartwarming at all!! ✧

Two volumes are in print (about 400 yen each). I definitely recommend buying them. I love Iyo. ♥♥♥

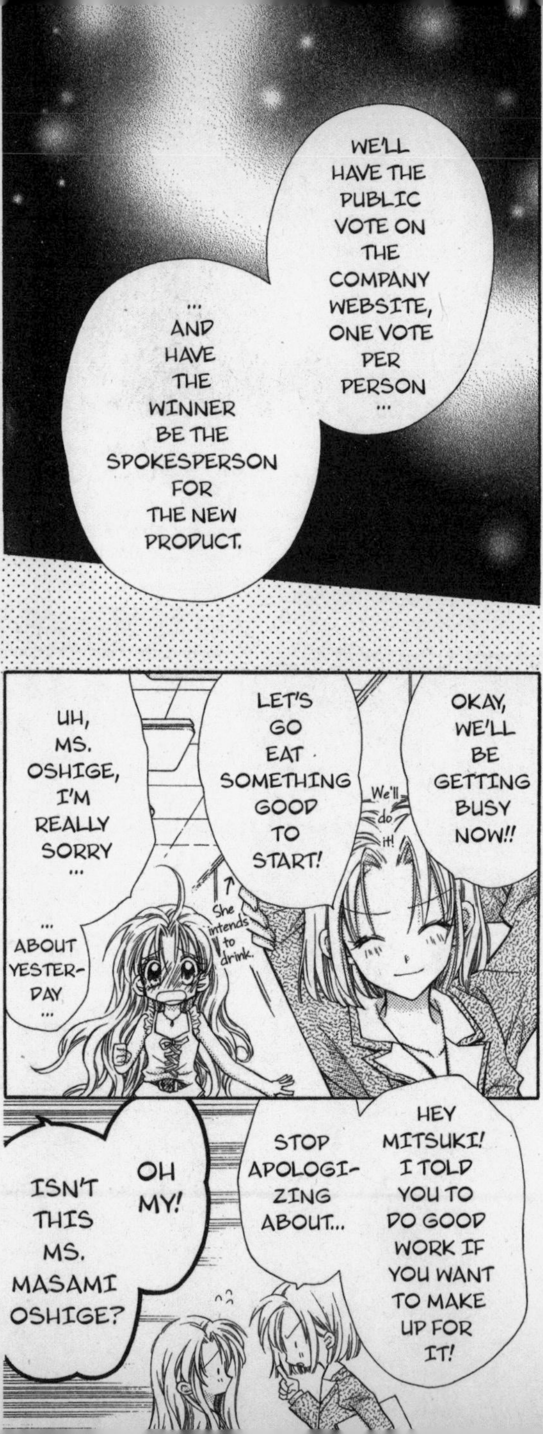
WE'LL HAVE THE PUBLIC VOTE ON THE COMPANY WEBSITE, ONE VOTE PER PERSON ...
... AND HAVE THE WINNER BE THE SPOKESPERSON FOR THE NEW PRODUCT.
OKAY, WE'LL BE GETTING BUSY NOW!!
We'll do it!
LET'S GO EAT SOMETHING GOOD TO START!
She intends to drink.
UH, MS. OSHIGE, I'M REALLY SORRY ...
... ABOUT YESTER-DAY ...
HEY MITSUKI! I TOLD YOU TO DO GOOD WORK IF YOU WANT TO MAKE UP FOR IT!
STOP APOLOGI-ZING ABOUT...
OH MY!
ISN'T THIS MS. MASAMI OSHIGE?

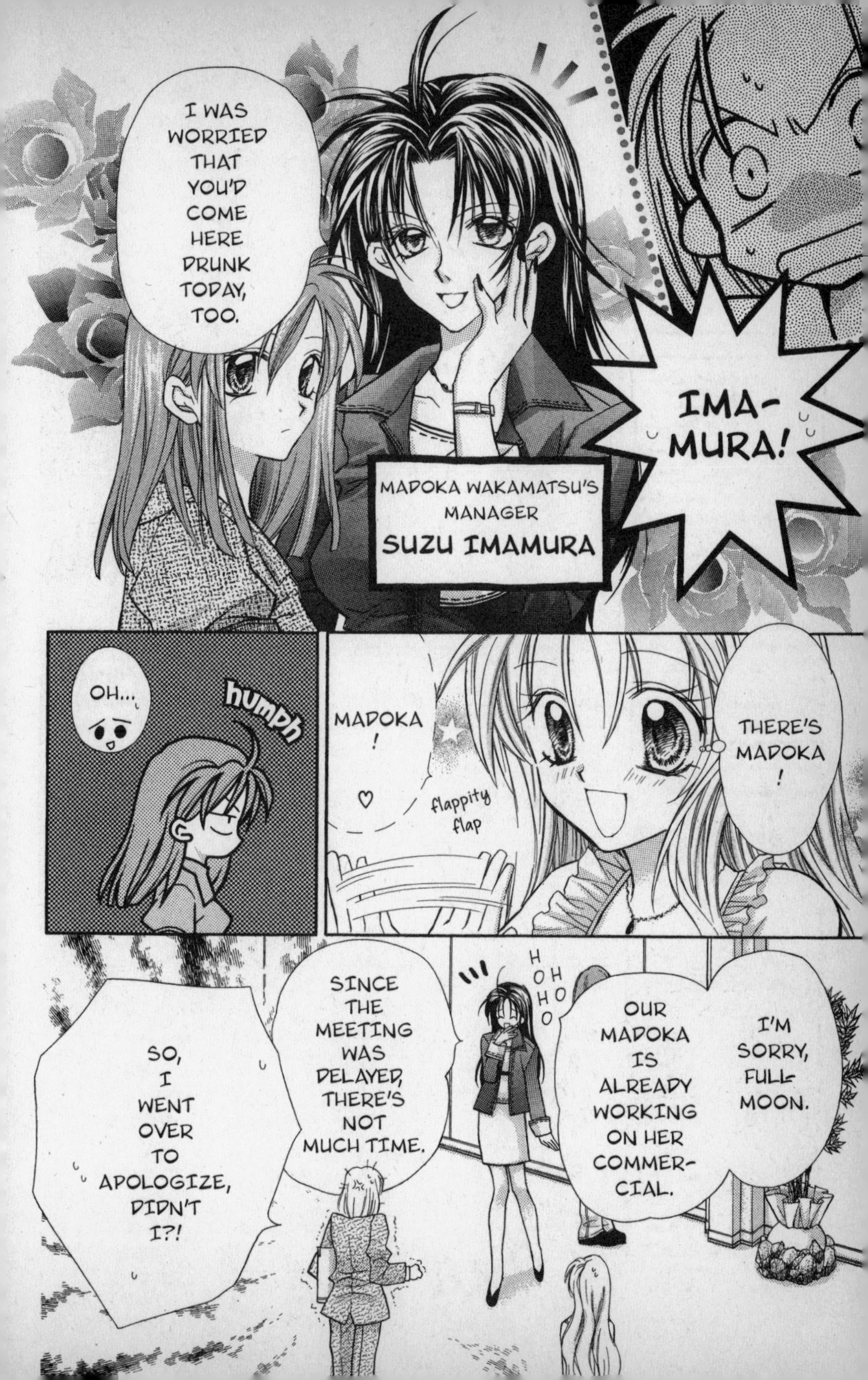
I WAS WORRIED THAT YOU'D COME HERE DRUNK TODAY, TOO.
MADOKA WAKAMATSU'S MANAGER SUZU IMAMURA
IMA-MURA!
THERE'S MADOKA!
MADOKA!
flappity flap
OH...
humph
I'M SORRY, FULL-MOON.
OUR MADOKA IS ALREADY WORKING ON HER COMMERCIAL.
HOHOHO
SINCE THE MEETING WAS DELAYED, THERE'S NOT MUCH TIME.
SO, I WENT OVER TO APOLOGIZE, DIDN'T I?!

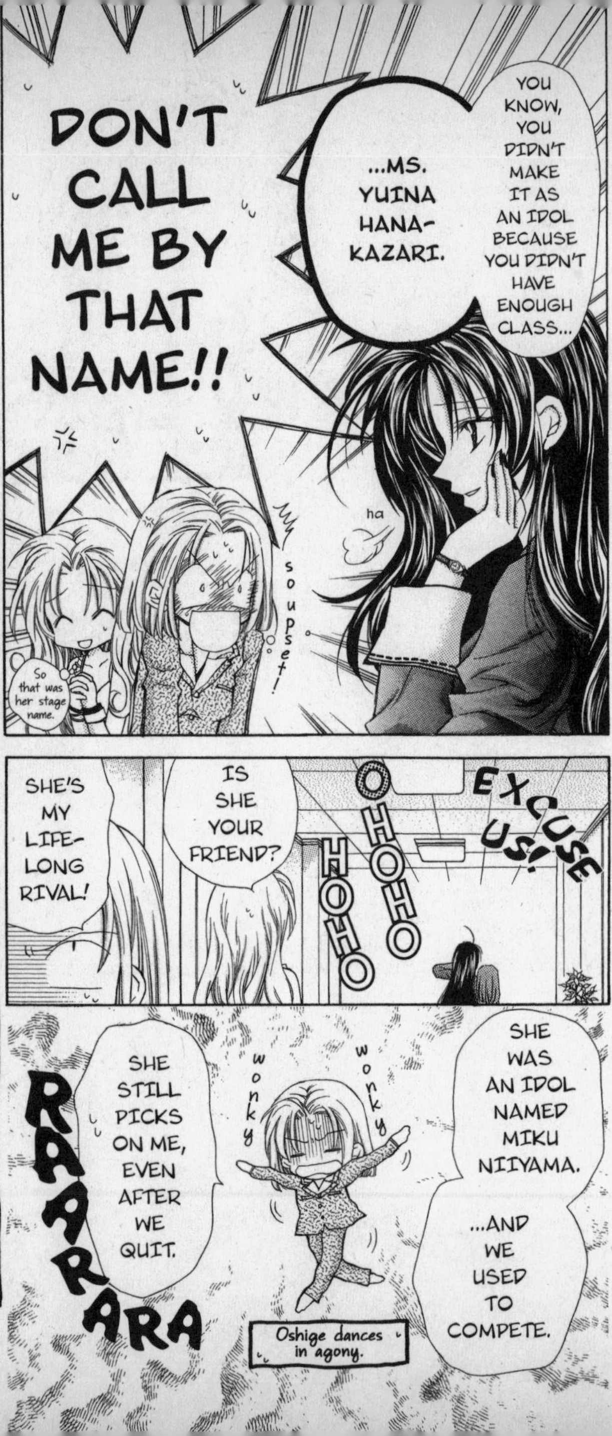

YOU KNOW, YOU DIDN'T MAKE IT AS AN IDOL BECAUSE YOU DIDN'T HAVE ENOUGH CLASS...
...MS. YUINA HANA-KAZARI.
DON'T CALL ME BY THAT NAME!!
ha
so upset!
So that was her stage name.
EXCUSE US!
OHOHO
HOHO
IS SHE YOUR FRIEND?
SHE'S MY LIFE-LONG RIVAL!
SHE WAS AN IDOL NAMED MIKU NIIYAMA.
...AND WE USED TO COMPETE.
wonky
wonky
SHE STILL PICKS ON ME, EVEN AFTER WE QUIT.
RAARARA
Oshige dances in agony.

Arina Tanemura's "Penchi de Shakiin Kiin",

it's here for the second edition!! ♡

Note: the first Japanese edition featured an ad for I-O-N. —Ed.

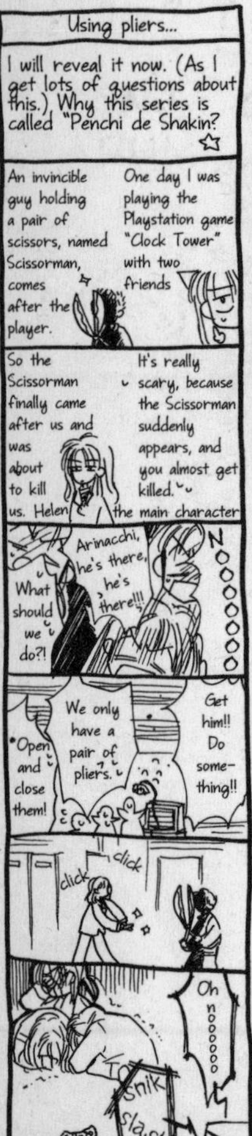

Using pliers...
I will reveal it now. (As I get lots of questions about this.) Why this series is called "Penchi de Shakin? ☆
An invincible guy holding a pair of scissors, named Scissorman, comes after the player.
One day I was playing the Playstation game "Clock Tower" with two friends
So the Scissorman finally came after us and was about to kill us.
It's really scary, because the Scissorman suddenly appears, and you almost get killed.
Helen
the main character
Arinacchi, he's there, he's there!!!
What should we do?!
NOOOOOOO
We only have a pair of pliers.
*Open and close them!
Get him!! Do something!!
click
click
Oh nooooooo
snik
slash

So the title was taken from this sad incident (what a memory).

*"Penchi de Shakin" in Japanese. —Ed.

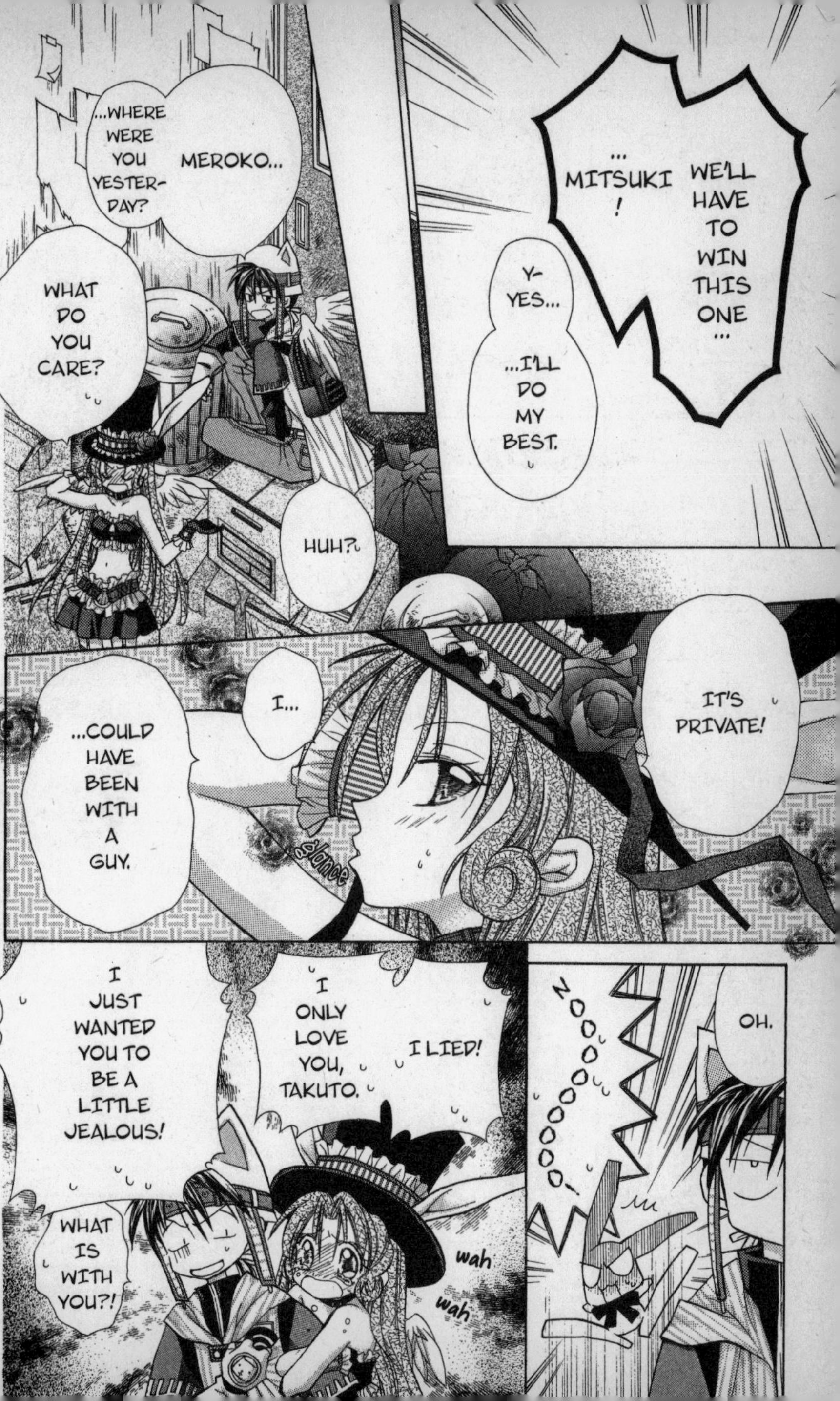
...MITSUKI! WE'LL HAVE TO WIN THIS ONE...
Y-YES...
...I'LL DO MY BEST.
MEROKO...
...WHERE WERE YOU YESTERDAY?
WHAT DO YOU CARE?
HUH?
IT'S PRIVATE!
I...
...COULD HAVE BEEN WITH A GUY.
glance
OH.
NOOOOOOOOO-!
I LIED!
I ONLY LOVE YOU, TAKUTO.
I JUST WANTED YOU TO BE A LITTLE JEALOUS!
WHAT IS WITH YOU?!
wah
wah

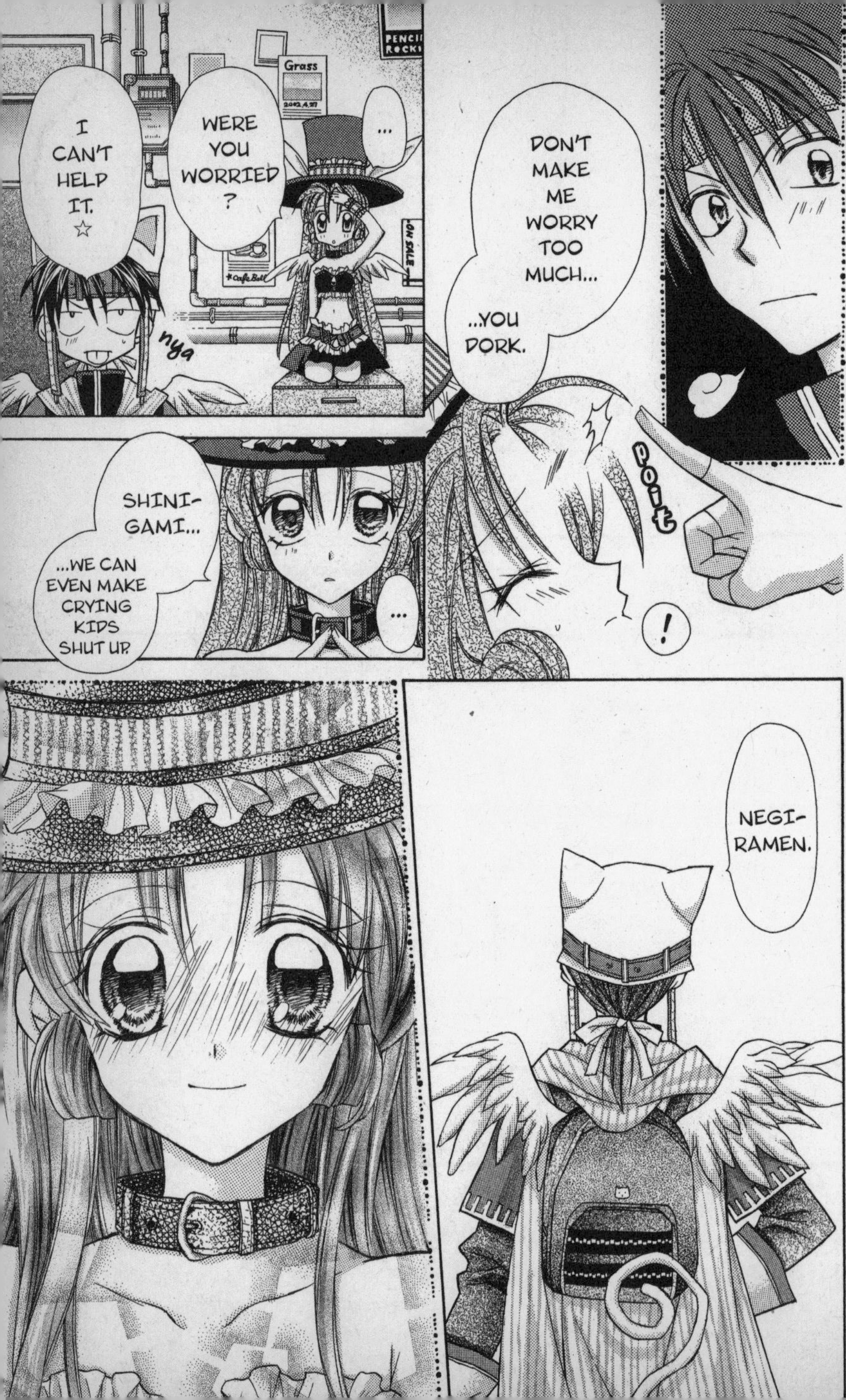
DON'T MAKE ME WORRY TOO MUCH...
...YOU DORK.
poit
!
...
WERE YOU WORRIED?
I CAN'T HELP IT. ☆
nya
Grass
ON SALE
SHINIGAMI...
...WE CAN EVEN MAKE CRYING KIDS SHUT UP.
...
NEGI-RAMEN.

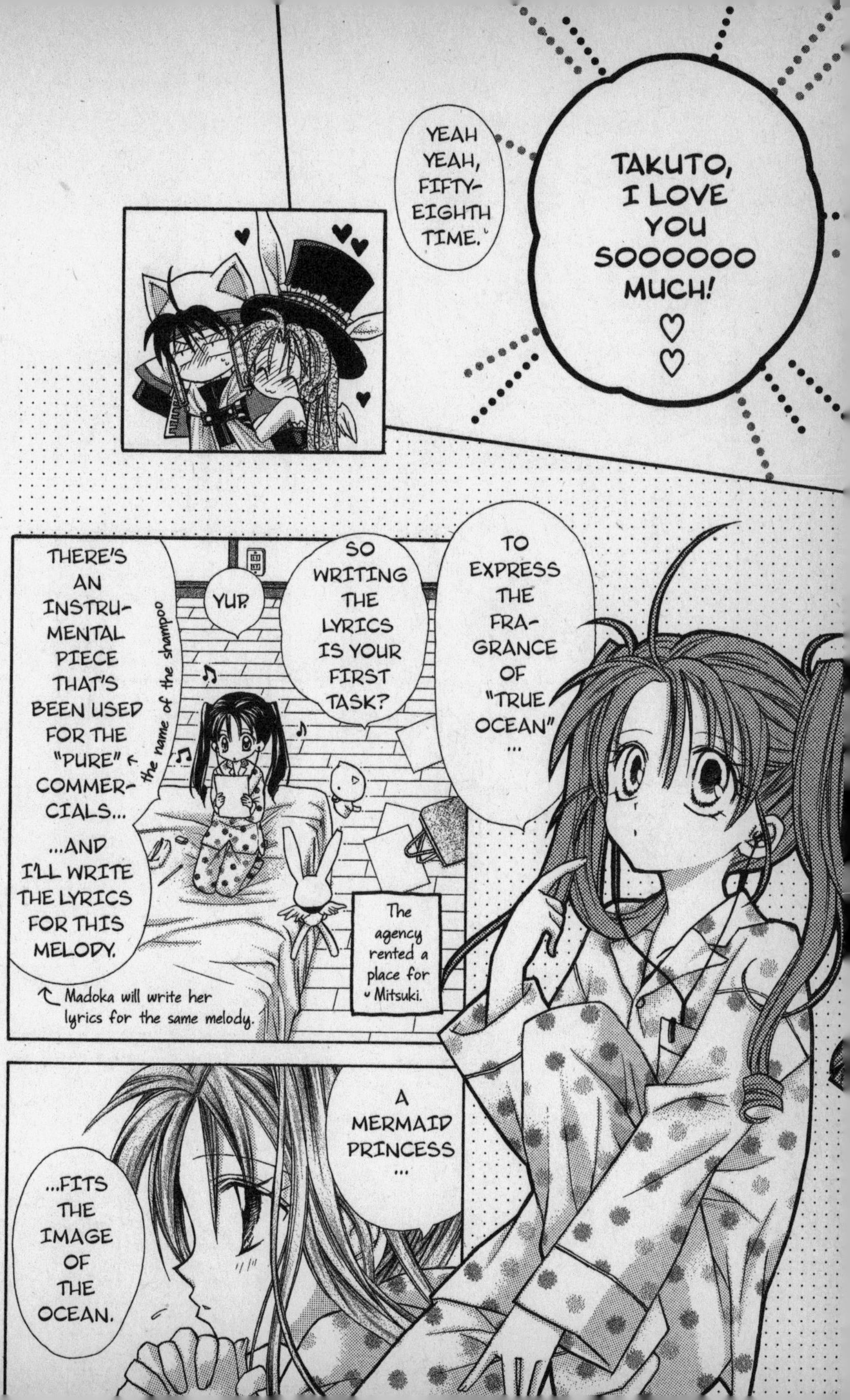
TAKUTO, I LOVE YOU SOOOOOO MUCH! ♡ ♡
YEAH YEAH, FIFTY-EIGHTH TIME.
TO EXPRESS THE FRAGRANCE OF "TRUE OCEAN"...
SO WRITING THE LYRICS IS YOUR FIRST TASK?
YUP.
THERE'S AN INSTRUMENTAL PIECE THAT'S BEEN USED FOR THE "PURE" COMMERCIALS...
the name of the shampoo
...AND I'LL WRITE THE LYRICS FOR THIS MELODY.
Madoka will write her lyrics for the same melody.
The agency rented a place for Mitsuki.
A MERMAID PRINCESS...
...FITS THE IMAGE OF THE OCEAN.

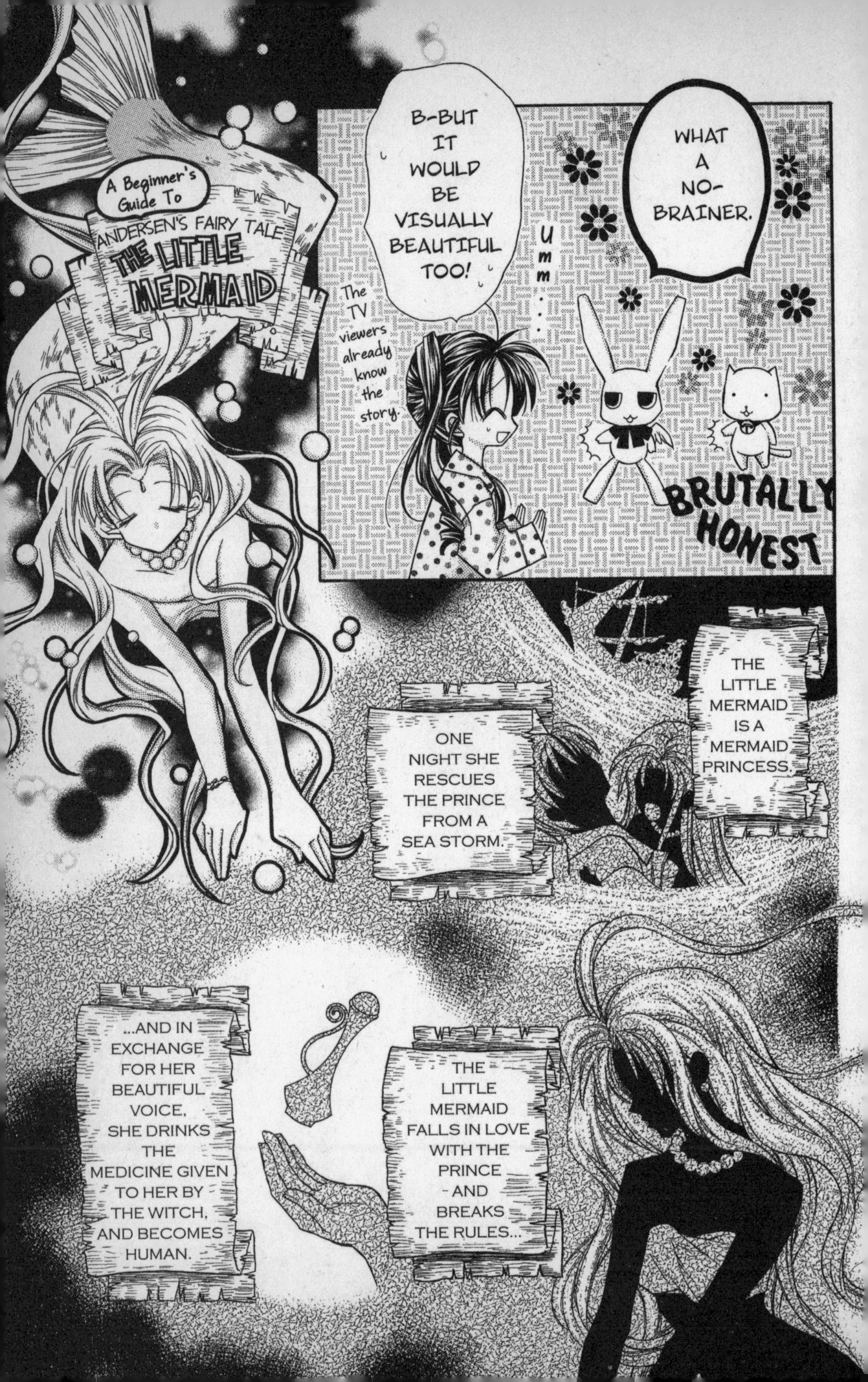
WHAT A NO-BRAINER.
BRUTALLY HONEST
Umm...
B-BUT IT WOULD BE VISUALLY BEAUTIFUL TOO!
The TV viewers already know the story.
A Beginner's Guide To
ANDERSEN'S FAIRY TALE
THE LITTLE MERMAID
THE LITTLE MERMAID IS A MERMAID PRINCESS.
ONE NIGHT SHE RESCUES THE PRINCE FROM A SEA STORM.
THE LITTLE MERMAID FALLS IN LOVE WITH THE PRINCE - AND BREAKS THE RULES...
...AND IN EXCHANGE FOR HER BEAUTIFUL VOICE, SHE DRINKS THE MEDICINE GIVEN TO HER BY THE WITCH, AND BECOMES HUMAN.

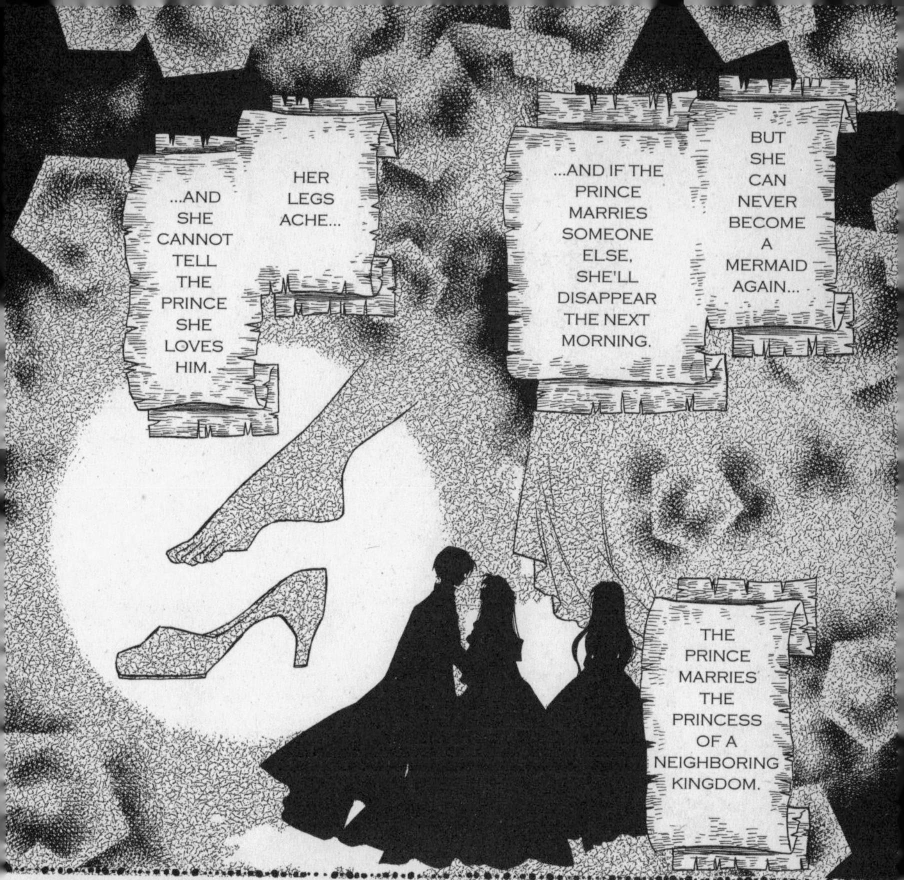
BUT SHE CAN NEVER BECOME A MERMAID AGAIN...
...AND IF THE PRINCE MARRIES SOMEONE ELSE, SHE'LL DISAPPEAR THE NEXT MORNING.
HER LEGS ACHE...
...AND SHE CANNOT TELL THE PRINCE SHE LOVES HIM.
THE PRINCE MARRIES THE PRINCESS OF A NEIGHBORING KINGDOM.

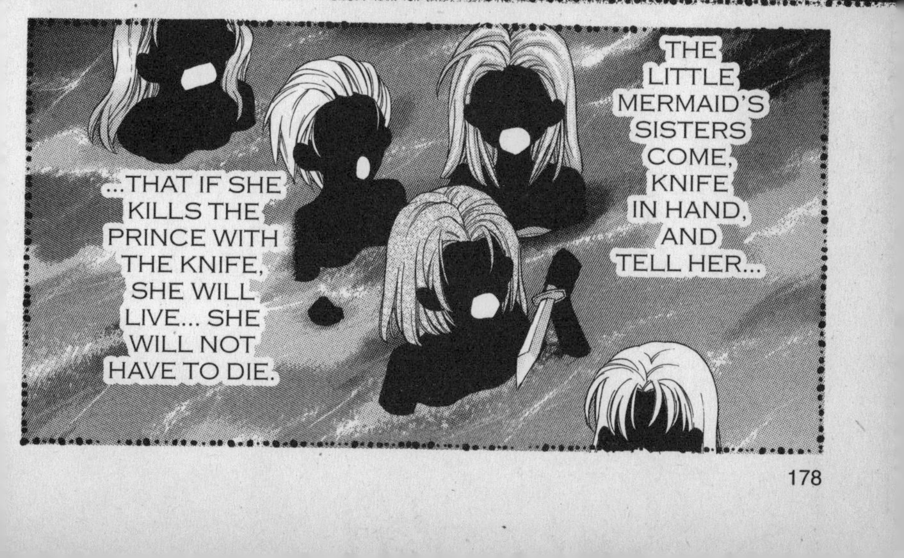
THE LITTLE MERMAID'S SISTERS COME, KNIFE IN HAND, AND TELL HER...
...THAT IF SHE KILLS THE PRINCE WITH THE KNIFE, SHE WILL LIVE... SHE WILL NOT HAVE TO DIE.

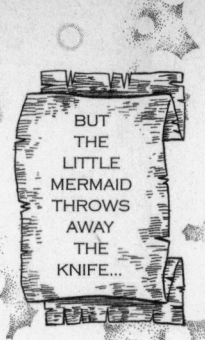

BUT THE LITTLE MERMAID THROWS AWAY THE KNIFE...
...AND THE NEXT MORNING...
...SHE TURNS INTO SEA FOAM.
WAAA
IT'S A SAD STORY, ISN'T IT.
IF SHE COULDN'T SPEAK, SHE SHOULD'VE WRITTEN A LETTER INSTEAD.
Lovin' You
I want that letter!
I DON'T THINK THE LITTLE MERMAID COULD WRITE.
I don't think she even knew the alphabet.
THAT'S RIGHT.
SHE HAS THE HEART OF BOTH A HUMAN AND A FISH.
SHE'S NOT HUMAN.
AND SHE GREW UP IN THE SEA...

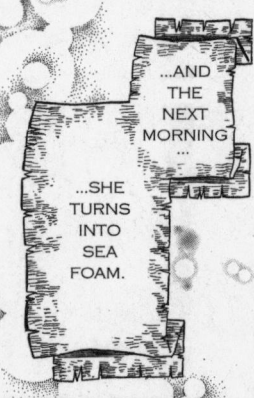

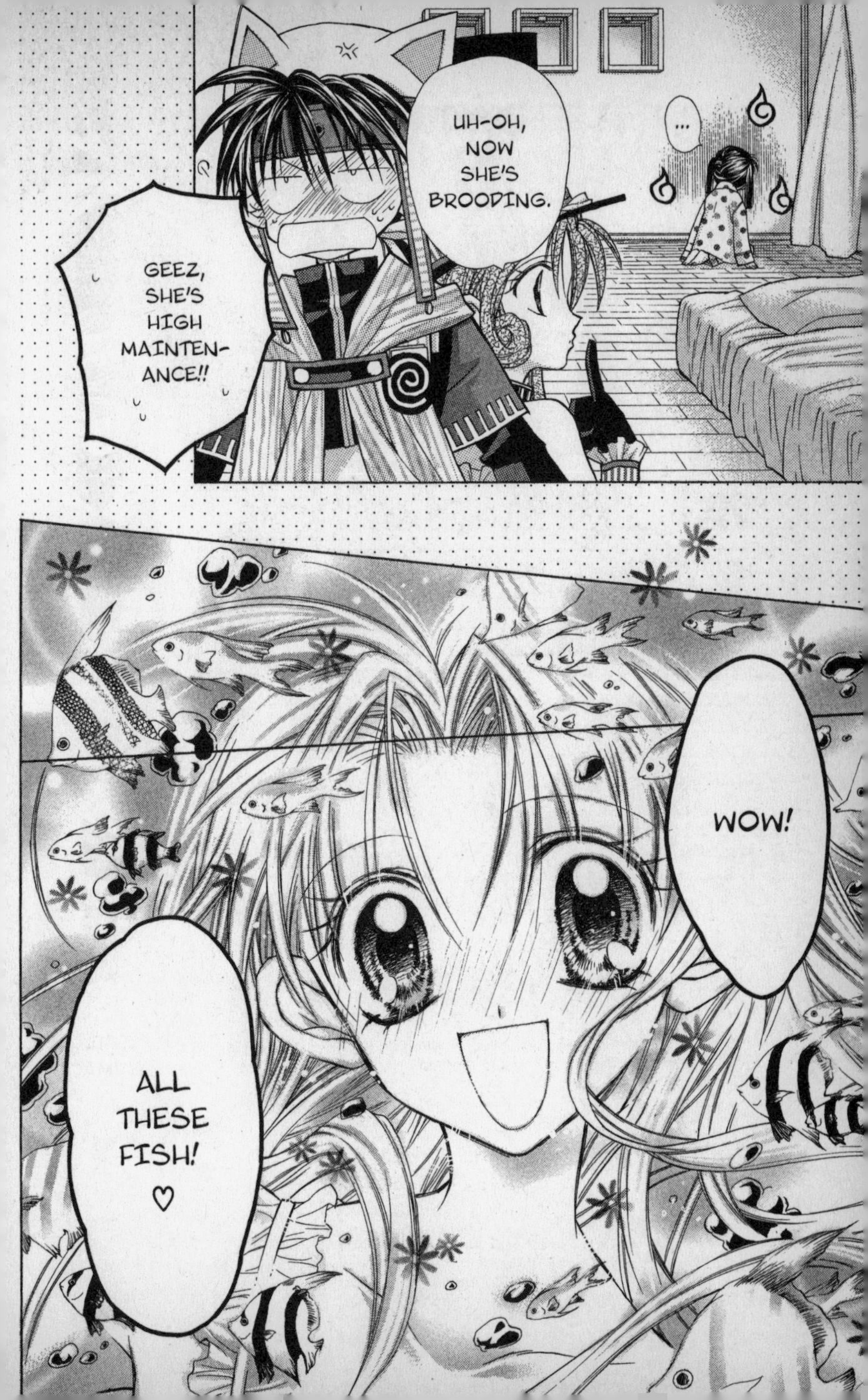
...
UH-OH, NOW SHE'S BROODING.
GEEZ, SHE'S HIGH MAINTEN-ANCE!!
WOW!
ALL THESE FISH! ♡

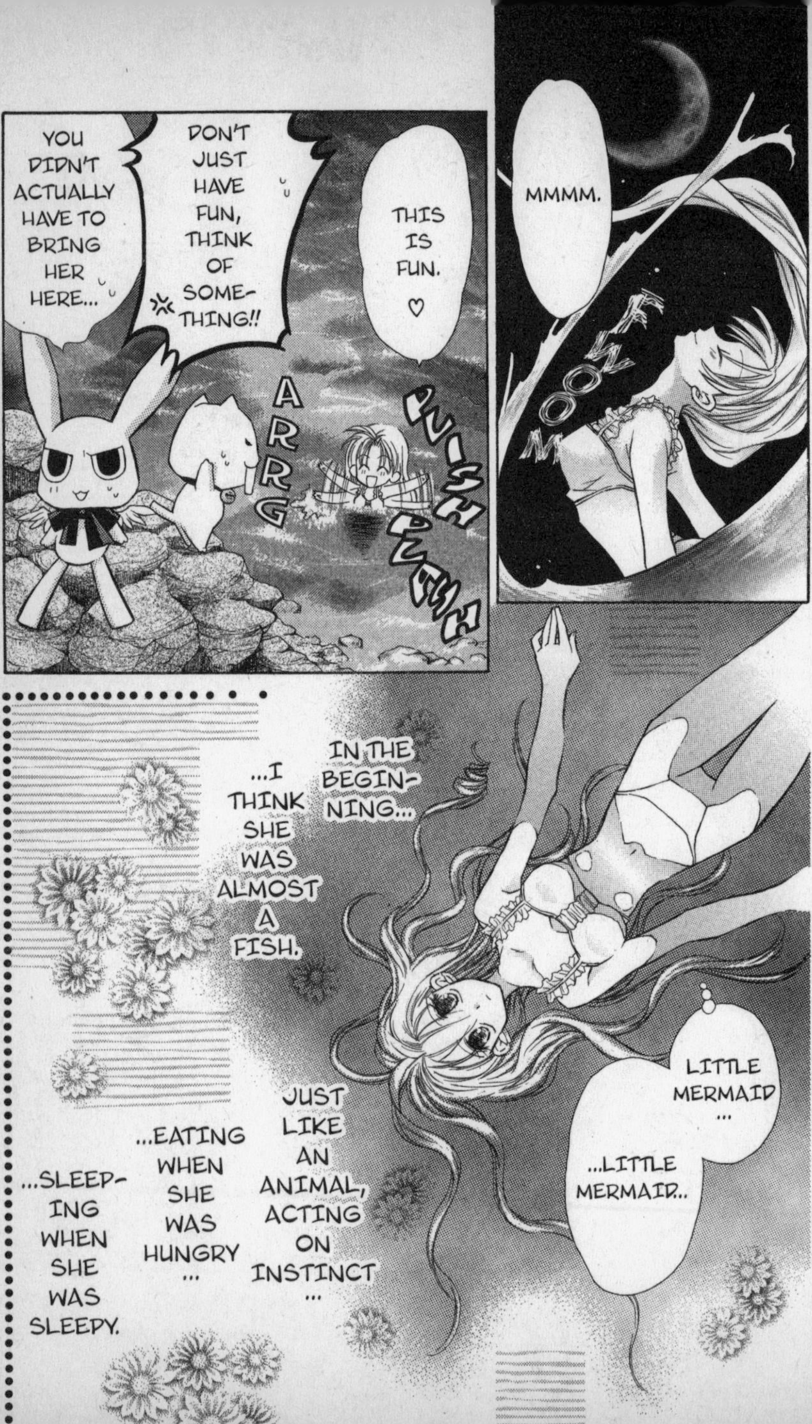
MMMM.
FWOOM
THIS IS FUN. ♡
DON'T JUST HAVE FUN, THINK OF SOME-THING!!
YOU DIDN'T ACTUALLY HAVE TO BRING HER HERE...
PLISH PLASH
ARRG
LITTLE MERMAID...
...LITTLE MERMAID...
IN THE BEGIN-NING...
...I THINK SHE WAS ALMOST A FISH.
JUST LIKE AN ANIMAL, ACTING ON INSTINCT...
...EATING WHEN SHE WAS HUNGRY...
...SLEEP-ING WHEN SHE WAS SLEEPY.

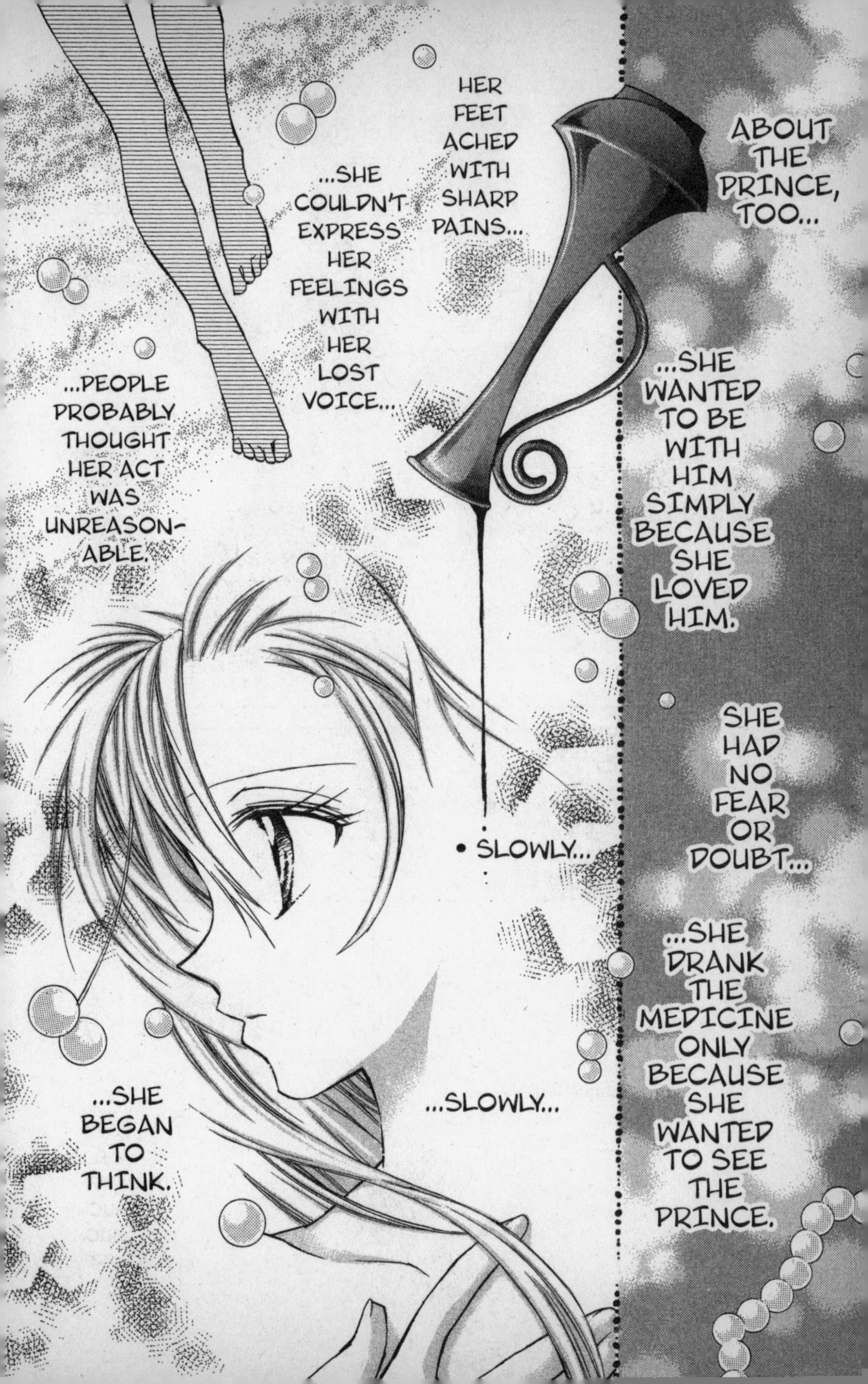

ABOUT THE PRINCE, TOO...
...SHE WANTED TO BE WITH HIM SIMPLY BECAUSE SHE LOVED HIM.
SHE HAD NO FEAR OR DOUBT...
...SHE DRANK THE MEDICINE ONLY BECAUSE SHE WANTED TO SEE THE PRINCE.
HER FEET ACHED WITH SHARP PAINS...
...SHE COULDN'T EXPRESS HER FEELINGS WITH HER LOST VOICE...
...PEOPLE PROBABLY THOUGHT HER ACT WAS UNREASON-ABLE.
SLOWLY...
...SLOWLY...
...SHE BEGAN TO THINK.

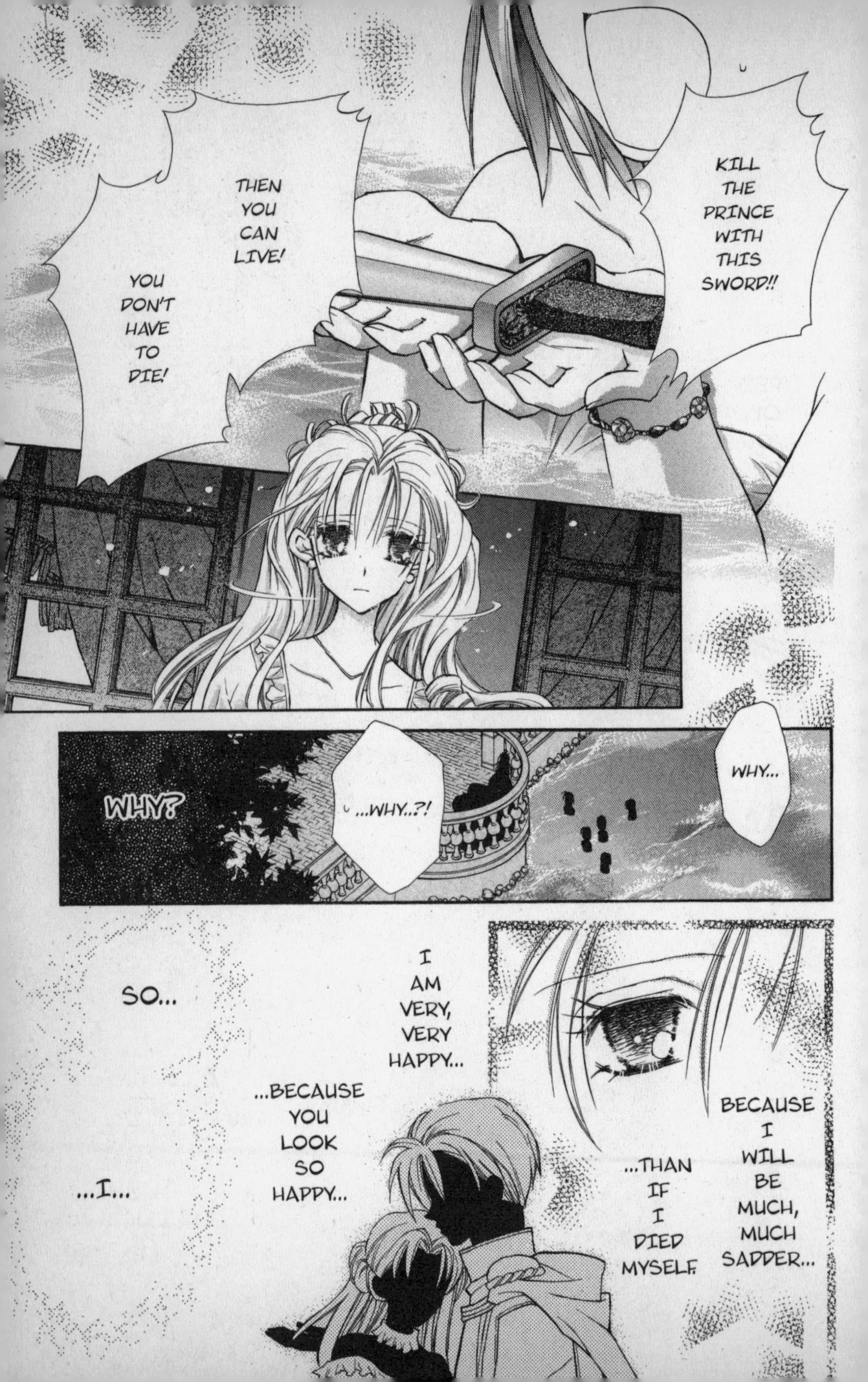
KILL THE PRINCE WITH THIS SWORD!!
THEN YOU CAN LIVE!
YOU DON'T HAVE TO DIE!
WHY...
...WHY..?!
WHY?
BECAUSE I WILL BE MUCH, MUCH SADDER...
...THAN IF I DIED MYSELF.
I AM VERY, VERY HAPPY...
...BECAUSE YOU LOOK SO HAPPY...
SO...
...I...

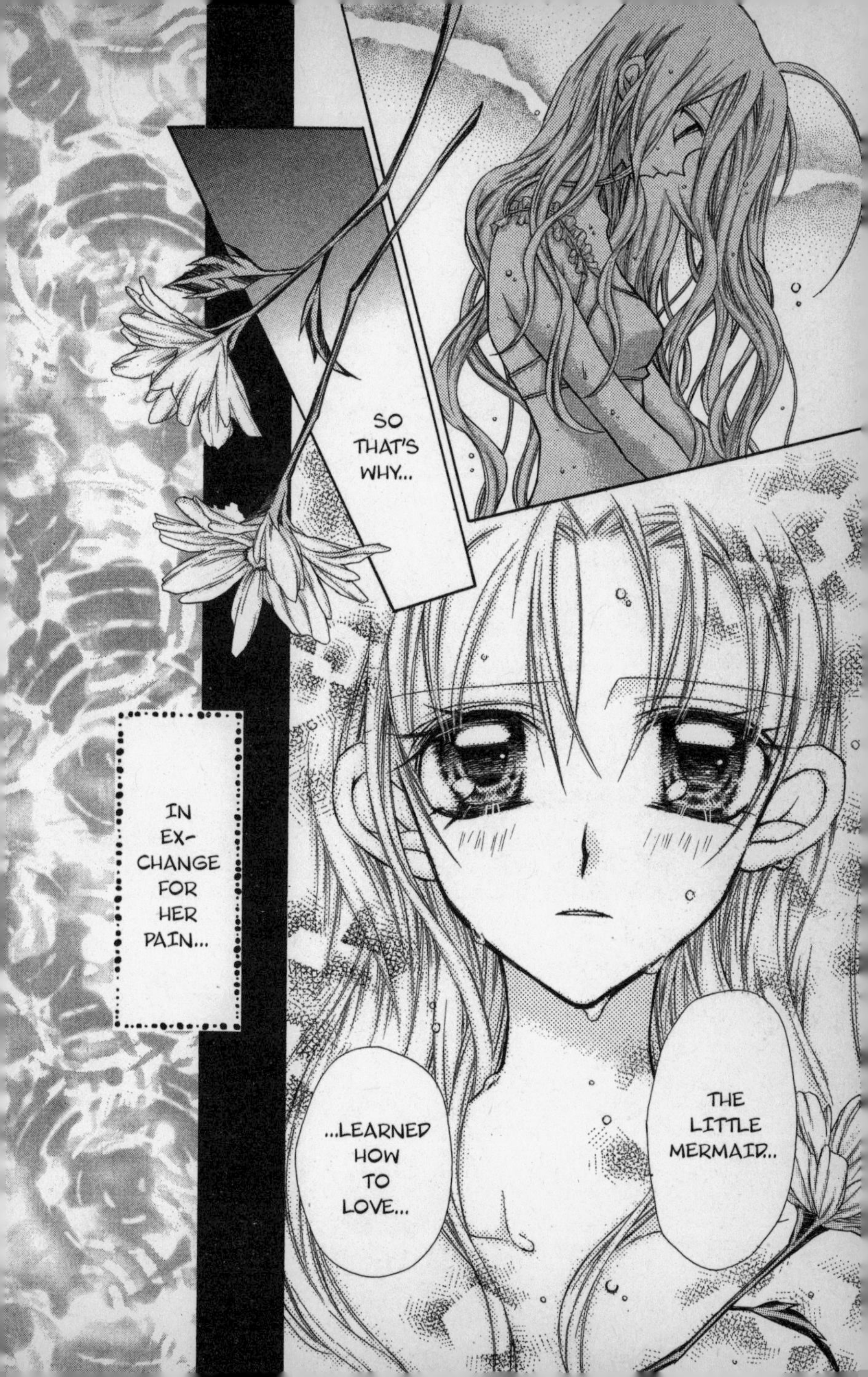
SO THAT'S WHY...
THE LITTLE MERMAID...
...LEARNED HOW TO LOVE...
IN EX-CHANGE FOR HER PAIN...

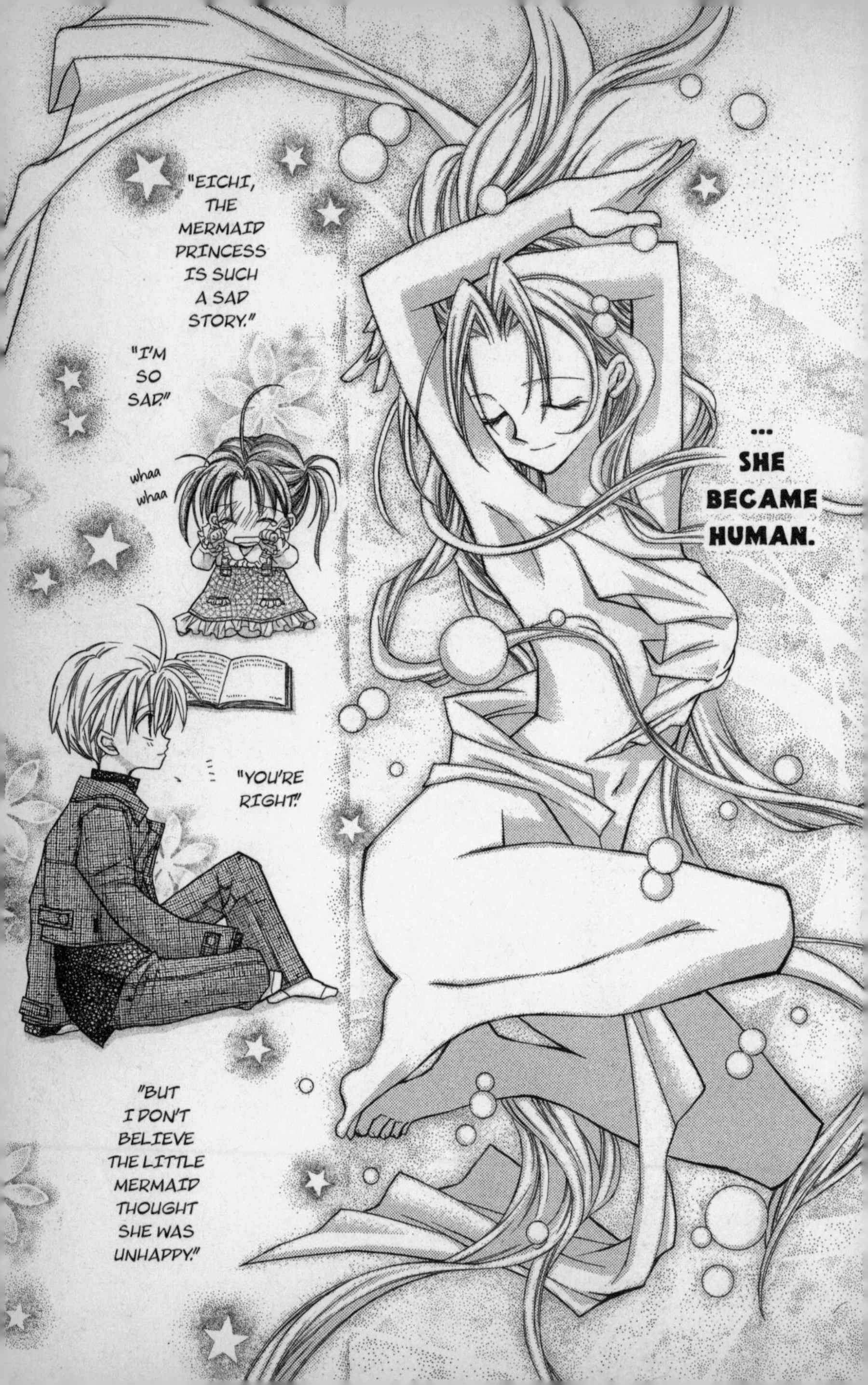

... SHE BECAME HUMAN.
"EICHI, THE MERMAID PRINCESS IS SUCH A SAD STORY."
"I'M SO SAD."
whaa whaa
"YOU'RE RIGHT."
"BUT I DON'T BELIEVE THE LITTLE MERMAID THOUGHT SHE WAS UNHAPPY."

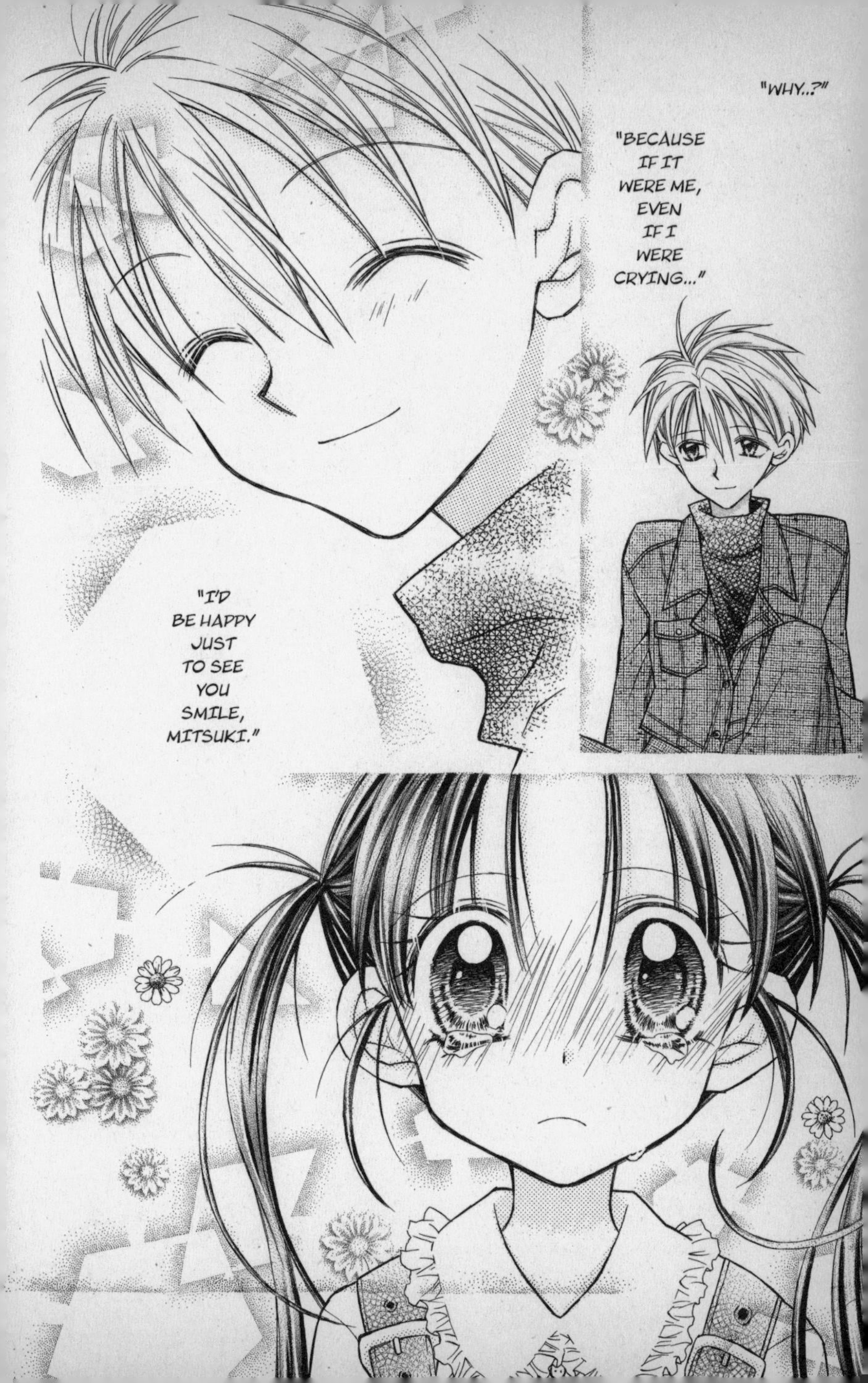
"WHY..?"
"BECAUSE IF IT WERE ME, EVEN IF I WERE CRYING..."
"I'D BE HAPPY JUST TO SEE YOU SMILE, MITSUKI."

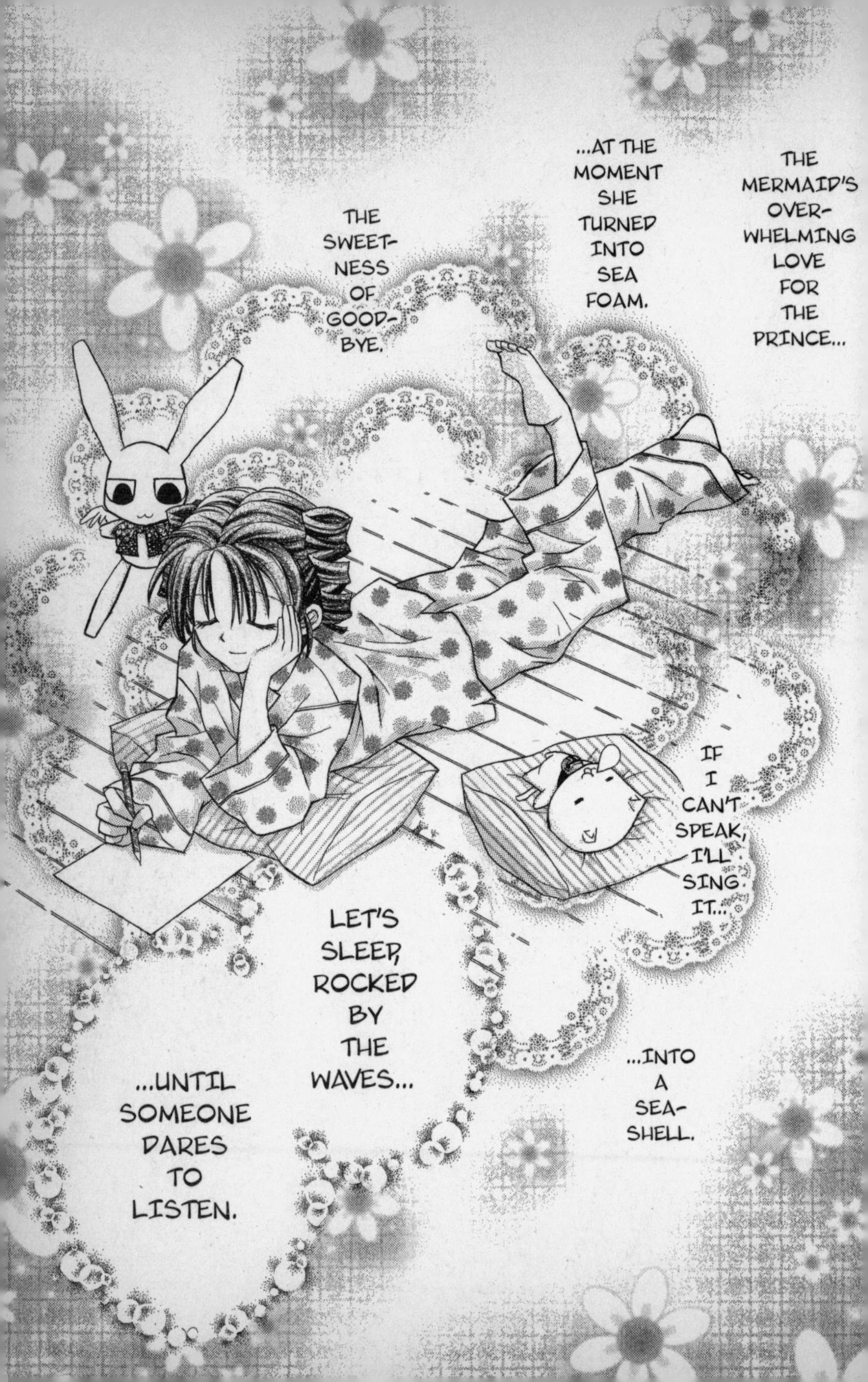
THE MERMAID'S OVERWHELMING LOVE FOR THE PRINCE...
...AT THE MOMENT SHE TURNED INTO SEA FOAM.
THE SWEETNESS OF GOODBYE.
IF I CAN'T SPEAK, I'LL SING IT...
...INTO A SEASHELL.
LET'S SLEEP, ROCKED BY THE WAVES...
...UNTIL SOMEONE DARES TO LISTEN.

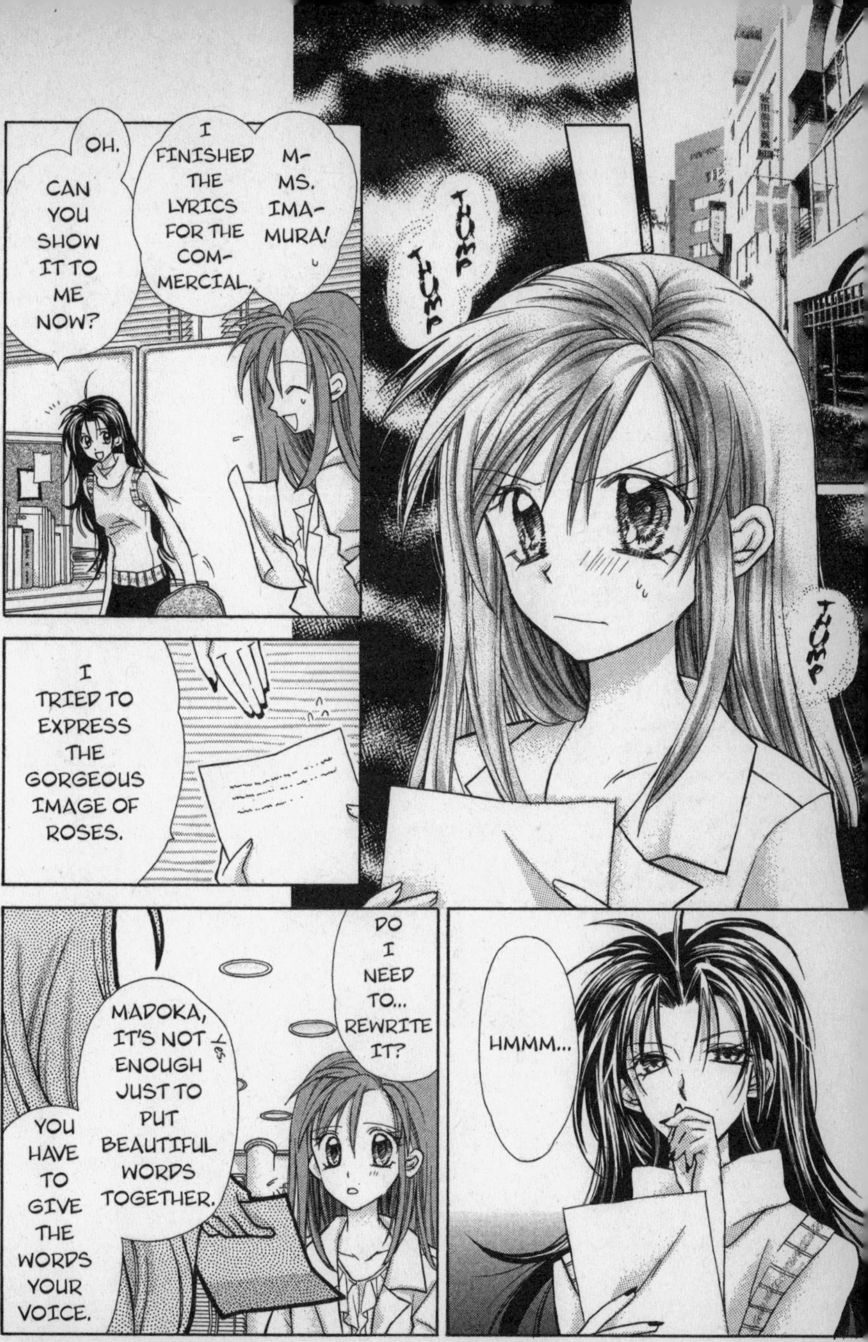
THUMP
THUMP
THUMP
M-MS. IMAMURA!
I FINISHED THE LYRICS FOR THE COMMERCIAL.
OH. CAN YOU SHOW IT TO ME NOW?
I TRIED TO EXPRESS THE GORGEOUS IMAGE OF ROSES.
HMMM...
DO I NEED TO... REWRITE IT?
YES.
MADOKA, IT'S NOT ENOUGH JUST TO PUT BEAUTIFUL WORDS TOGETHER.
YOU HAVE TO GIVE THE WORDS YOUR VOICE.

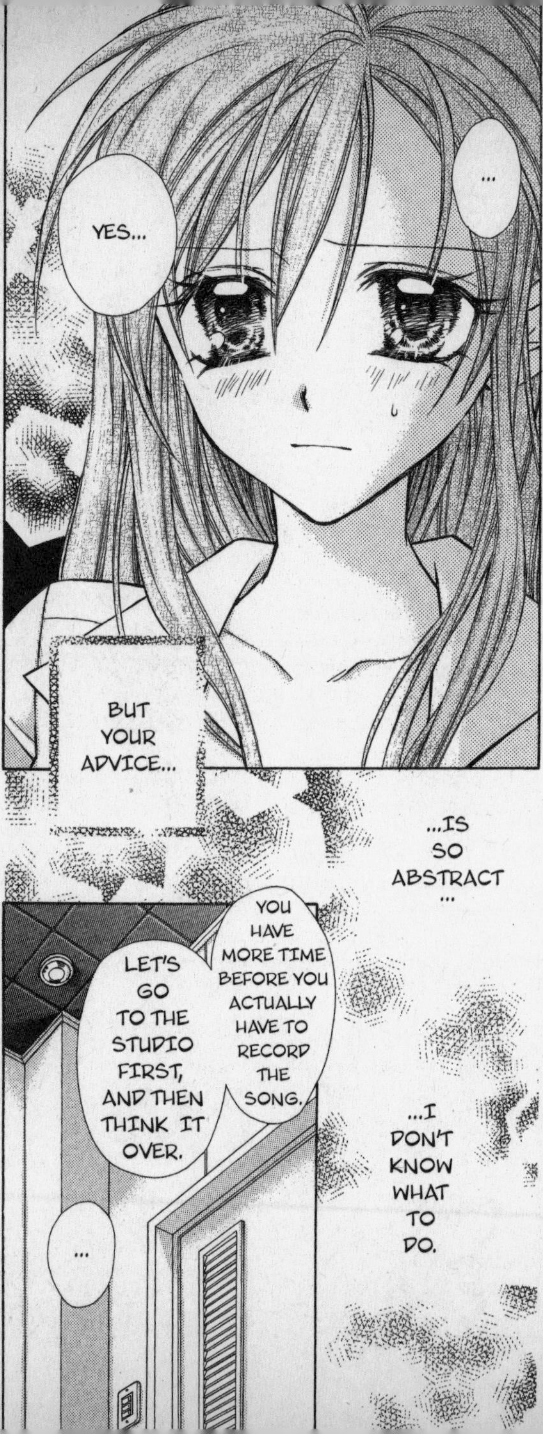
...
YES...
BUT YOUR ADVICE...
...IS SO ABSTRACT ...
YOU HAVE MORE TIME BEFORE YOU ACTUALLY HAVE TO RECORD THE SONG.
LET'S GO TO THE STUDIO FIRST, AND THEN THINK IT OVER.
...I DON'T KNOW WHAT TO DO.
...

② Please buy Volume Two, too! ♪

Man, you're being fresh, Arina.

Okay, here's the staff list, which sometimes I forget and people chide me for it. ^^;

Background Leader → Asano: (Please look at "The CM. Hana to Yume")

- Minase: (Screentone Leader. Some backgrounds.)
- Kaduki: (Screentone, backgrounds, all-rounder!)
- Niki: (Backgrounds. Beat Asano someday?)
- Konako: (Screentone, some backgrounds.)
- Kanan (Mariko): (Screentone)
- Airi: (Background, some screentone)
- Miwacha: (Background, some screentone)
- Rinarina: (Screentone)

Yay!

- Ammonite Limited: (Paperwork, accounting, miscellaneous tasks, responses to fan letters)
- Shueisha Ribon Department: (Furoku, magazine editing, typesetting)
- Mr. Koike (editor): (Checking the storyboards, page numbering, scheduling, final proofreading, coordinating with the anime staff, making Arina work(?), and many other tasks. ~~ ;)
- Arina Tanemura: (Furoku cuts, cover illustrations, story, a little bit of backgrounds, drawing small items, lettering, speed lines, starbursts, screentones, and others.)

Thank you everybody!

Fanletters to

Arina Tanemura C/O
FullMoon o Sagashite
P.O. Box 77064
San Francisco, CA 94107

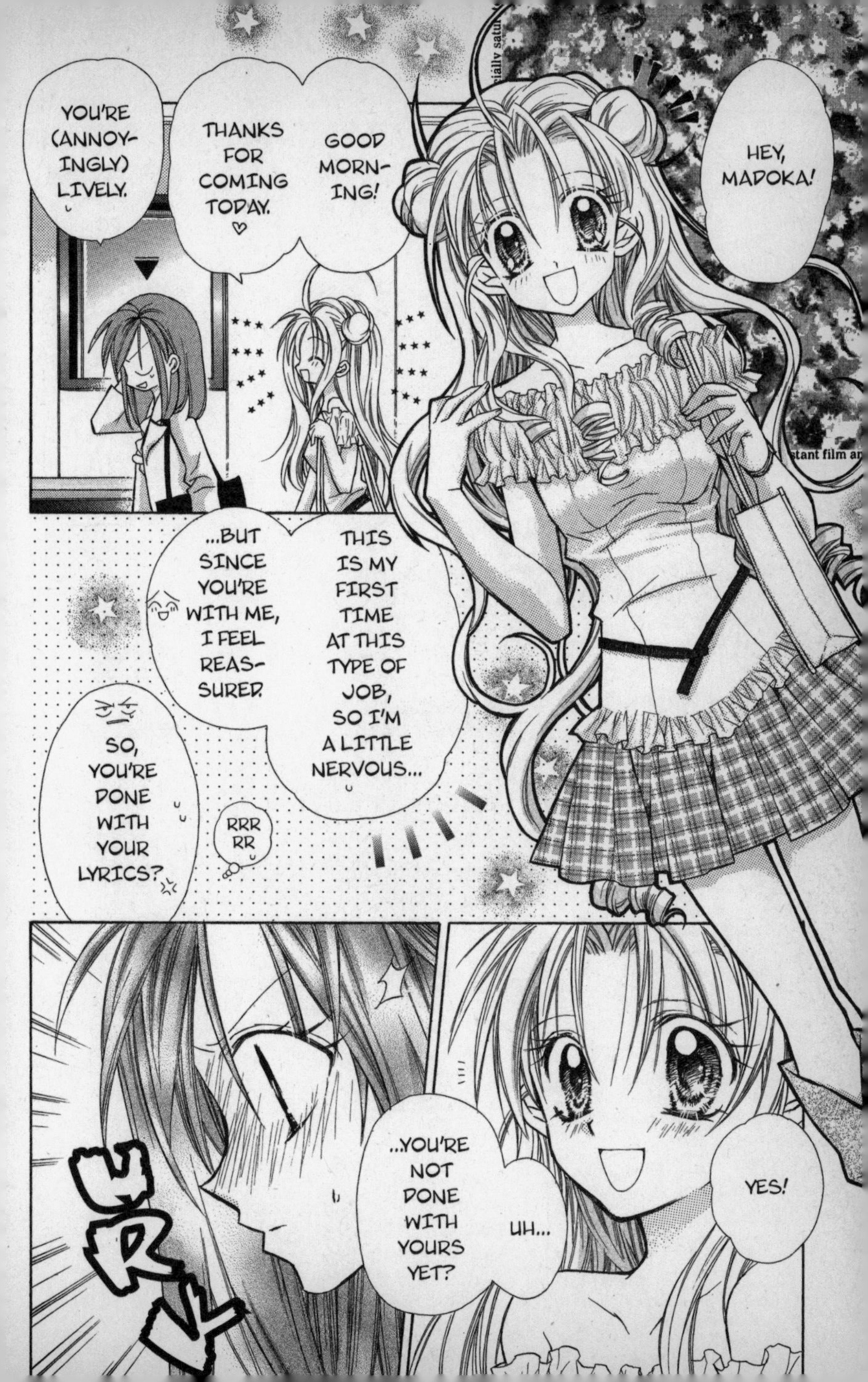
HEY, MADOKA!
GOOD MORNING!
THANKS FOR COMING TODAY. ♡
YOU'RE (ANNOYINGLY) LIVELY.
THIS IS MY FIRST TIME AT THIS TYPE OF JOB, SO I'M A LITTLE NERVOUS...
...BUT SINCE YOU'RE WITH ME, I FEEL REASSURED.
SO, YOU'RE DONE WITH YOUR LYRICS?
RRRRR
YES!
UH...
...YOU'RE NOT DONE WITH YOURS YET?
URK

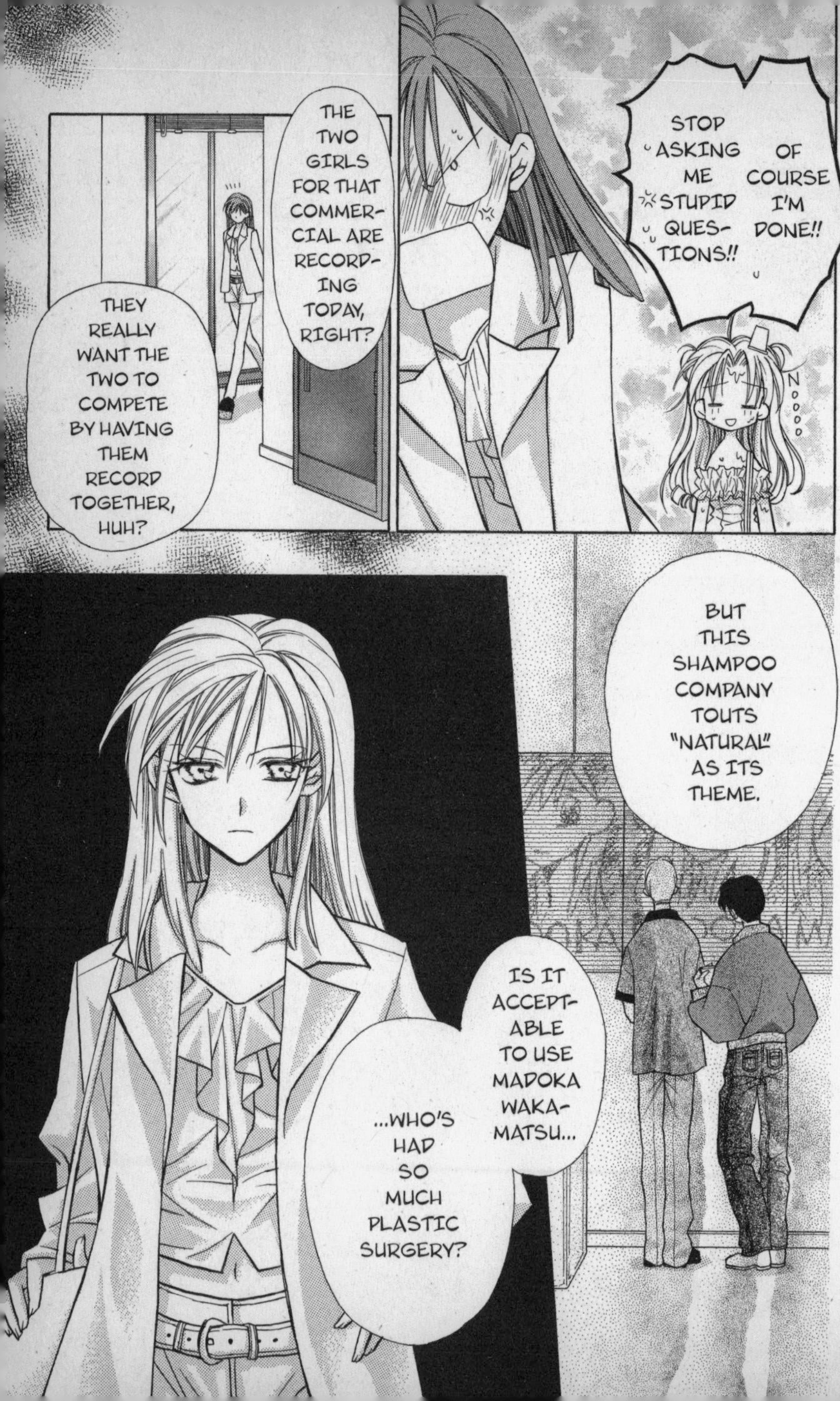

STOP ASKING ME STUPID QUESTIONS!! OF COURSE I'M DONE!!
NOOOO
THE TWO GIRLS FOR THAT COMMERCIAL ARE RECORDING TODAY, RIGHT?
THEY REALLY WANT THE TWO TO COMPETE BY HAVING THEM RECORD TOGETHER, HUH?
BUT THIS SHAMPOO COMPANY TOUTS "NATURAL" AS ITS THEME.
IS IT ACCEPTABLE TO USE MADOKA WAKAMATSU...
...WHO'S HAD SO MUCH PLASTIC SURGERY?

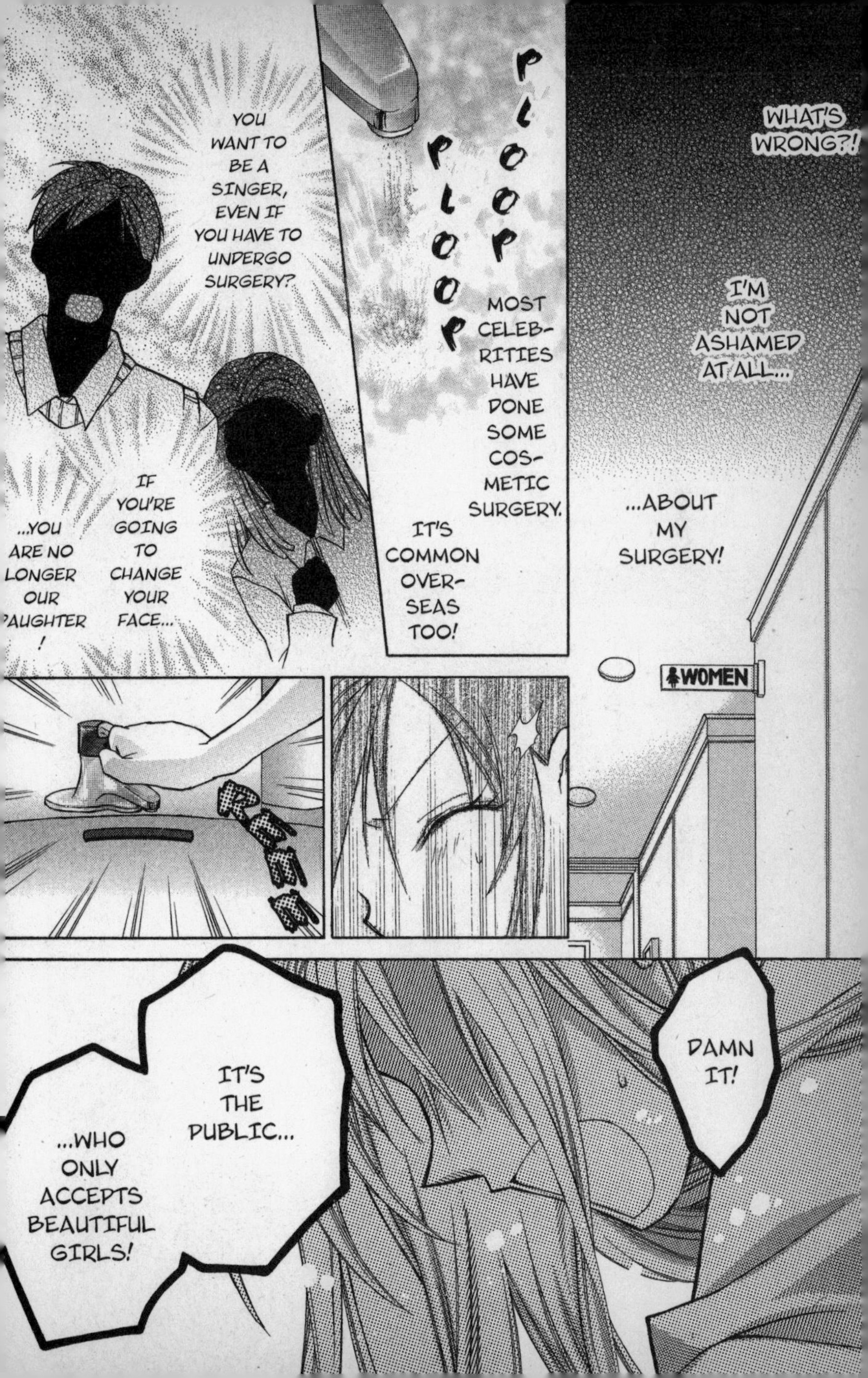
WHAT'S WRONG?!
I'M NOT ASHAMED AT ALL...
...ABOUT MY SURGERY!
WOMEN
PLOOP PLOOP
MOST CELEB-RITIES HAVE DONE SOME COS-METIC SURGERY.
IT'S COMMON OVER-SEAS TOO!
YOU WANT TO BE A SINGER, EVEN IF YOU HAVE TO UNDERGO SURGERY?
IF YOU'RE GOING TO CHANGE YOUR FACE...
...YOU ARE NO LONGER OUR DAUGHTER!
DAMN IT!
IT'S THE PUBLIC...
...WHO ONLY ACCEPTS BEAUTIFUL GIRLS!

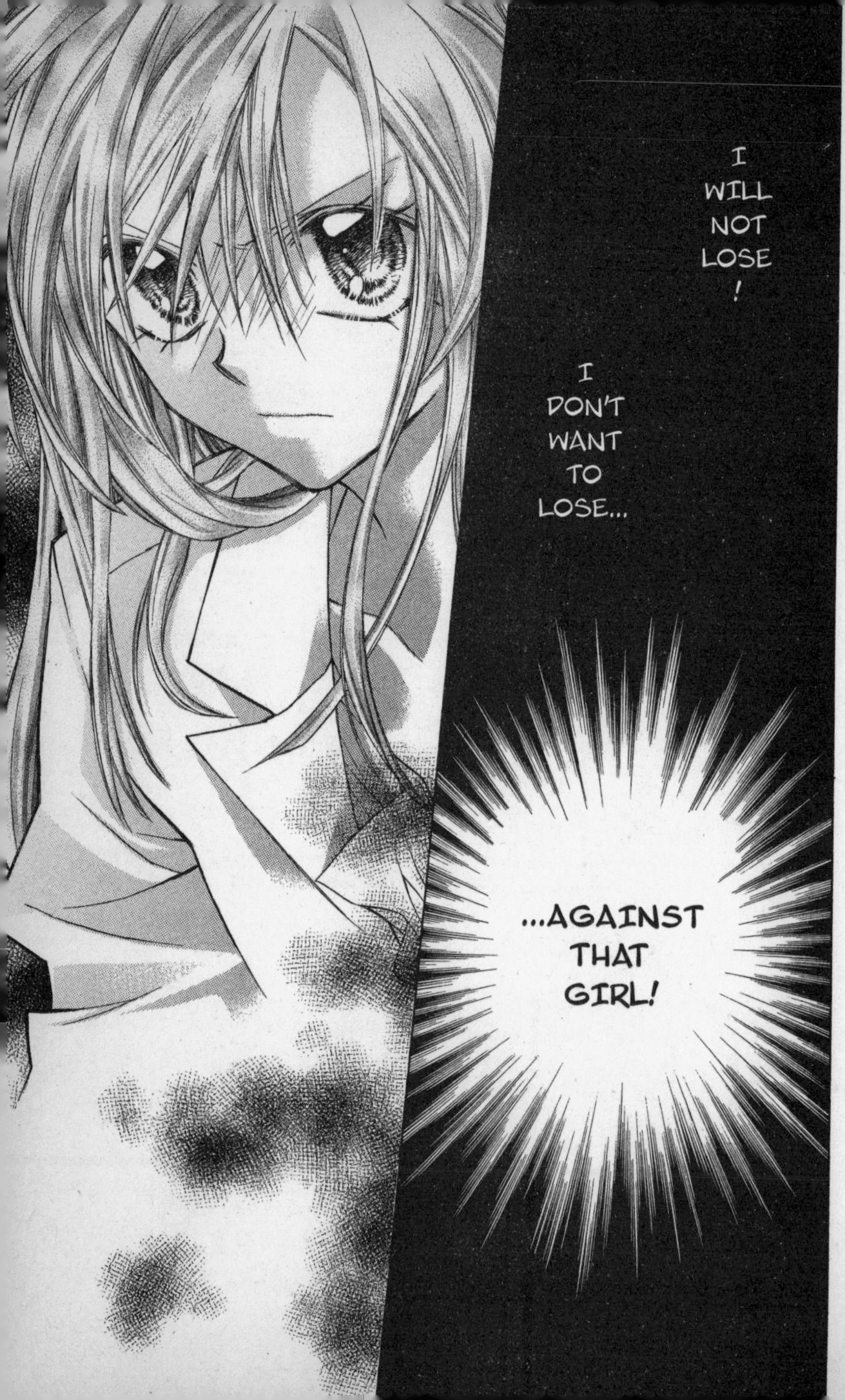
I WILL NOT LOSE!
I DON'T WANT TO LOSE...
...AGAINST THAT GIRL!

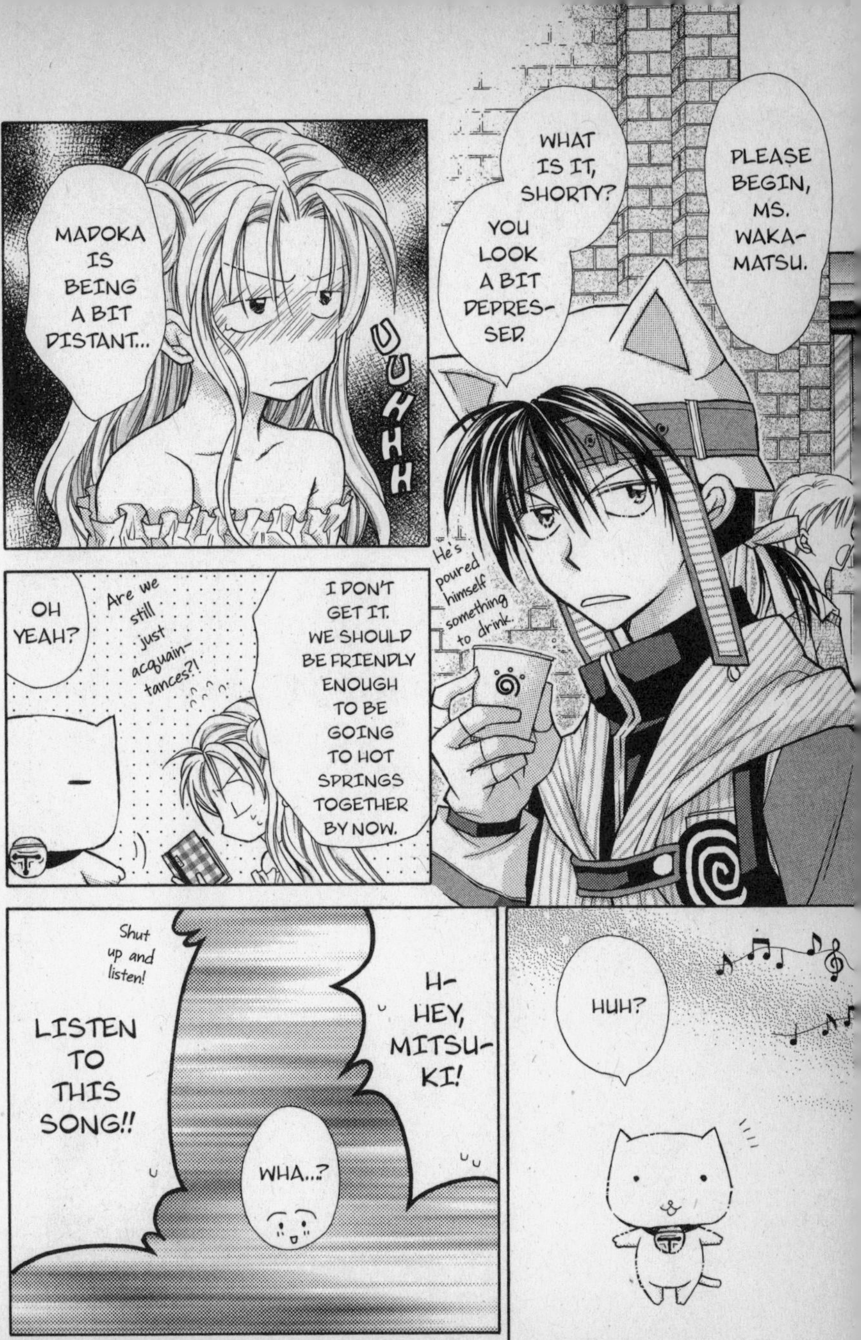
PLEASE BEGIN, MS. WAKAMATSU.
WHAT IS IT, SHORTY?
YOU LOOK A BIT DEPRES-SED.
He's poured himself something to drink.
MADOKA IS BEING A BIT DISTANT...
UUHHH
I DON'T GET IT. WE SHOULD BE FRIENDLY ENOUGH TO BE GOING TO HOT SPRINGS TOGETHER BY NOW.
Are we still just acquain-tances?!
OH YEAH?
HUH?
H-HEY, MITSU-KI!
WHA...?
LISTEN TO THIS SONG!!
Shut up and listen!

Oh, he's a bit paunchy.

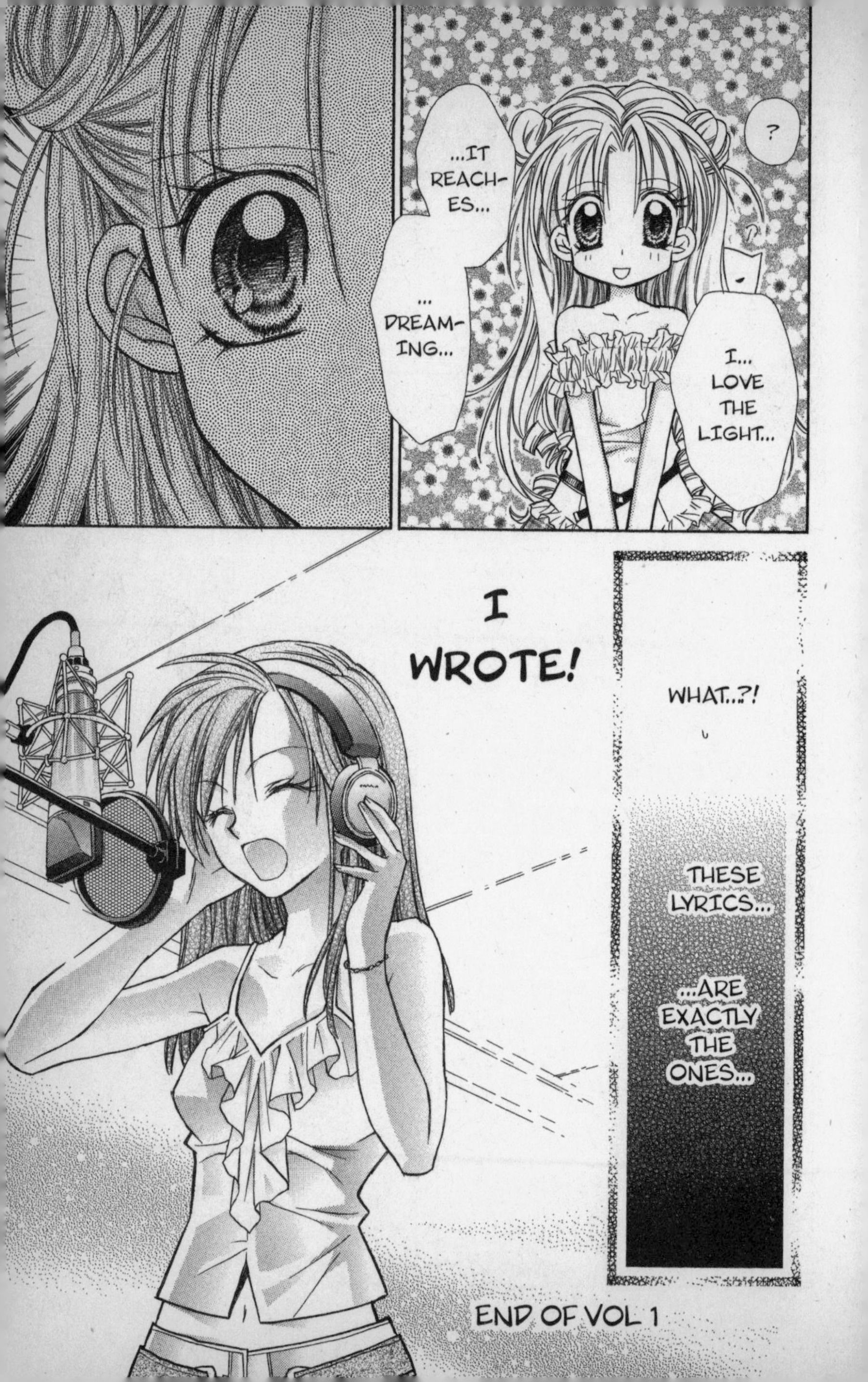

?
I... LOVE THE LIGHT...
...IT REACHES...
...DREAMING...
WHAT..?!
THESE LYRICS...
...ARE EXACTLY THE ONES...
I WROTE!
END OF VOL 1

FOUR-PANEL☆MANGA

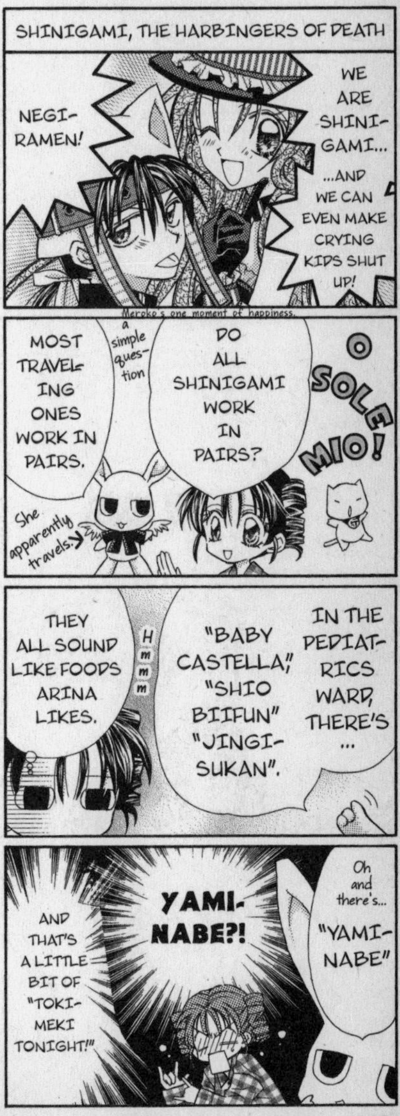
SHINIGAMI, THE HARBINGERS OF DEATH
WE ARE SHINIGAMI...
...AND WE CAN EVEN MAKE CRYING KIDS SHUT UP!
NEGI-RAMEN!
Meroko's one moment of happiness.
O SOLE MIO!
DO ALL SHINIGAMI WORK IN PAIRS?
a simple question
MOST TRAVEL-ING ONES WORK IN PAIRS.
She apparently travels.
IN THE PEDIAT-RICS WARD, THERE'S ...
"BABY CASTELLA," "SHIO BIIFUN" "JINGI-SUKAN".
Hmmm
THEY ALL SOUND LIKE FOODS ARINA LIKES.
Oh and there's... "YAMI-NABE"
YAMI-NABE?!
AND THAT'S A LITTLE BIT OF "TOKI-MEKI TONIGHT!"

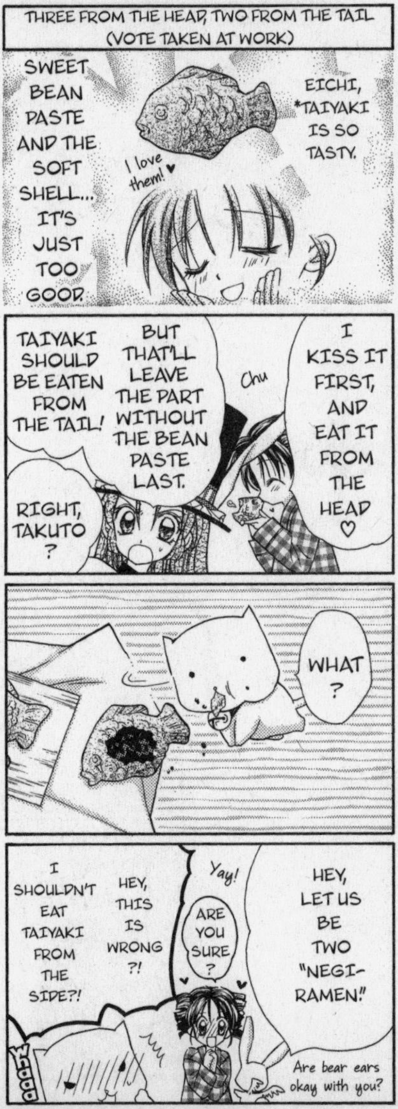
THREE FROM THE HEAD, TWO FROM THE TAIL (VOTE TAKEN AT WORK)
EICHI, *TAIYAKI IS SO TASTY.
SWEET BEAN PASTE AND THE SOFT SHELL... IT'S JUST TOO GOOD.
I love them! ♥
I KISS IT FIRST, AND EAT IT FROM THE HEAD ♡
Chu
BUT THAT'LL LEAVE THE PART WITHOUT THE BEAN PASTE LAST.
TAIYAKI SHOULD BE EATEN FROM THE TAIL!
RIGHT, TAKUTO?
WHAT?
HEY, LET US BE TWO "NEGI-RAMEN."
Yay!
ARE YOU SURE?
HEY, THIS IS WRONG?!
I SHOULDN'T EAT TAIYAKI FROM THE SIDE?!
Are bear ears okay with you?

*FISH SHAPED CAKE WITH SWEET BEAN PASTE.

Full Moon o Sagashite FOUR-PANEL!

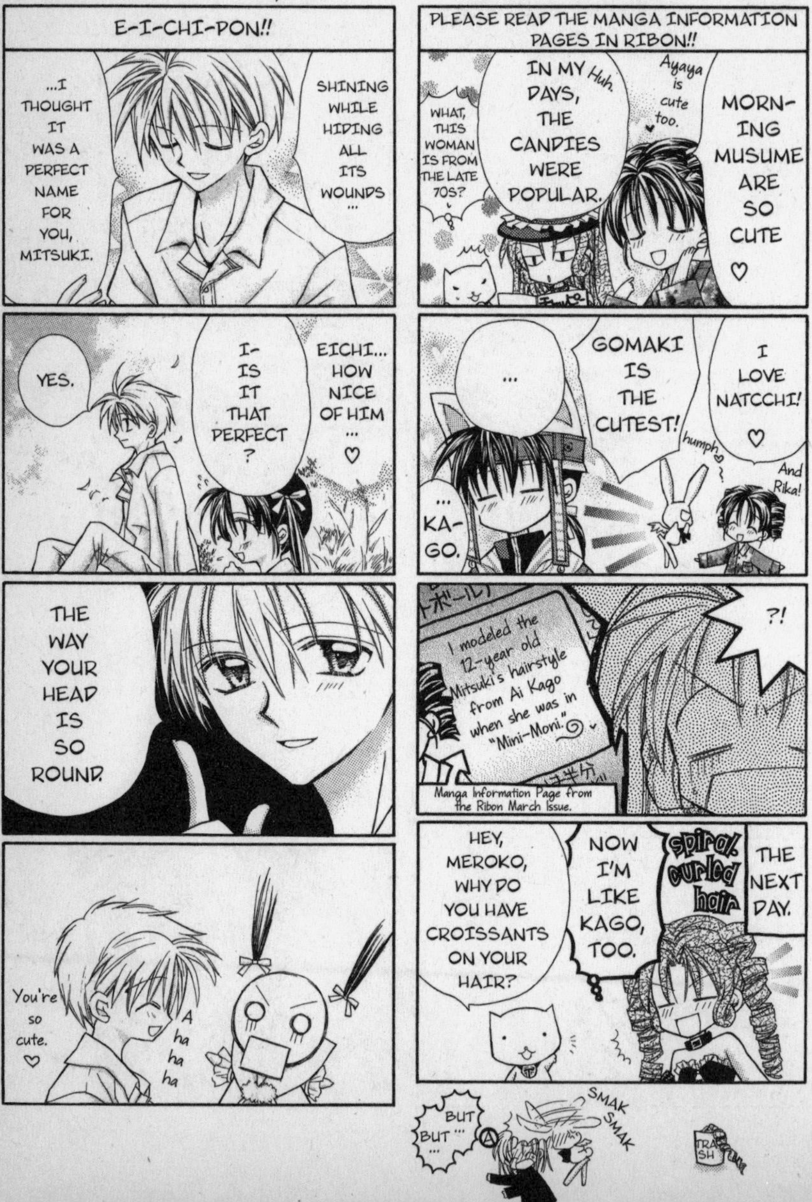
PLEASE READ THE MANGA INFORMATION PAGES IN RIBON!!
MORNING MUSUME ARE SO CUTE ♡
Ayaya is cute too.
Huh.
IN MY DAYS, THE CANDIES WERE POPULAR.
WHAT, THIS WOMAN IS FROM THE LATE 70S?
I LOVE NATCCHI! ♡
And Rika!
humph ?
GOMAKI IS THE CUTEST!
...
... KAGO.
?!
I modeled the 12-year old Mitsuki's hairstyle from Ai Kago when she was in "Mini-Moni."
Manga Information Page from the Ribon March Issue.
THE NEXT DAY.
spiral curled hair
NOW I'M LIKE KAGO, TOO.
HEY, MEROKO, WHY DO YOU HAVE CROISSANTS ON YOUR HAIR?
SMAK SMAK
BUT ... BUT ...
TRASH
E-I-CHI-PON!!
SHINING WHILE HIDING ALL ITS WOUNDS ...
...I THOUGHT IT WAS A PERFECT NAME FOR YOU, MITSUKI.
EICHI... HOW NICE OF HIM ... ♡
I- IS IT THAT PERFECT?
YES.
THE WAY YOUR HEAD IS SO ROUND.
A ha ha ha ha
You're so cute. ♡

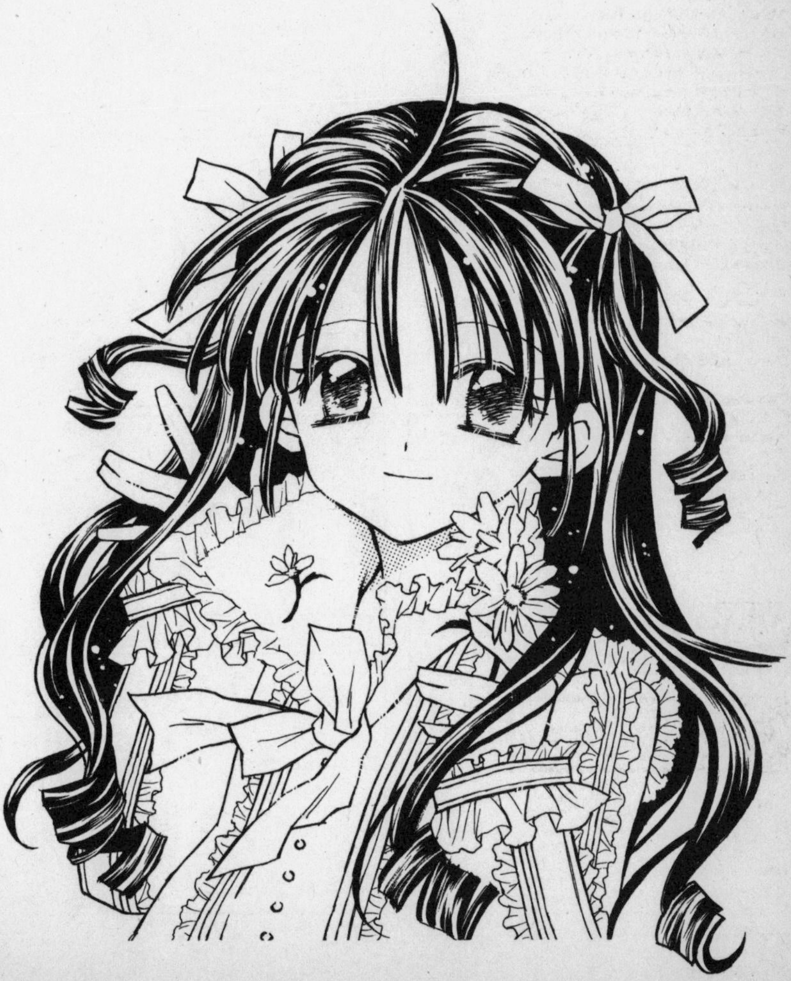

Full Moon o Sagashite
Vol. 1
The Shojo Beat Manga Edition

STORY & ART BY
ARINA TANEMURA

English Translation & Adaptation/Tomo Kimura
Touch-Up & Lettering/Elena Diaz
Graphics & Cover Design/Izumi Evers
Editor/Pancha Diaz

Managing Editor/Megan Bates
Director of Production/Noboru Watanabe
Vice President of Publishing/Alvin Lu
Vice President & Editor in Chief/Yumi Hoashi
Sr. Director of Acquisitions/Rika Inouye
VP of Sales & Marketing/Liza Coppola
Publisher/Hyoe Narita

Published by VIZ Media, LLC
P.O. Box 77064
San Francisco, CA 94107

Shojo Beat Manga Edition
10 9 8 7 6 5 4 3 2 1
First printing, June 2005

PARENTAL ADVISORY
FULL MOON is rated T. This volume contains themes of death. Recommended for teenagers 13 and older.

Author Bio

Arina Tanemura was born in Aichi, Japan. She got her start in 1996, publishing *Nibanme no Koi no Katachi* (*The Style of the Second Love*) in *Ribon Original* magazine. Her early work includes a collection of short stories called *Kanshaku Dama no Yuutsu* (*Short-tempered Melancholic*). Two of her titles, *Kamikaze Kaito Jeanne* and *Full Moon*, were made into popular TV series. Tanemura enjoys Karaoke and is a huge *Lord of the Rings* fan.

Author's Note

The girl I don't understand the most is Mitsuki. Takuto is my best friend. Meroko is beyond my control. (Eichi is my dream. A girl's dream-come-true!!) I,..like Madoka. I like characters that I can understand ☺. The manga was already an anime by the fourth episode, a real surprise, but I'd like to keep my own pace, and slowly get to know Mitsuki and company well.

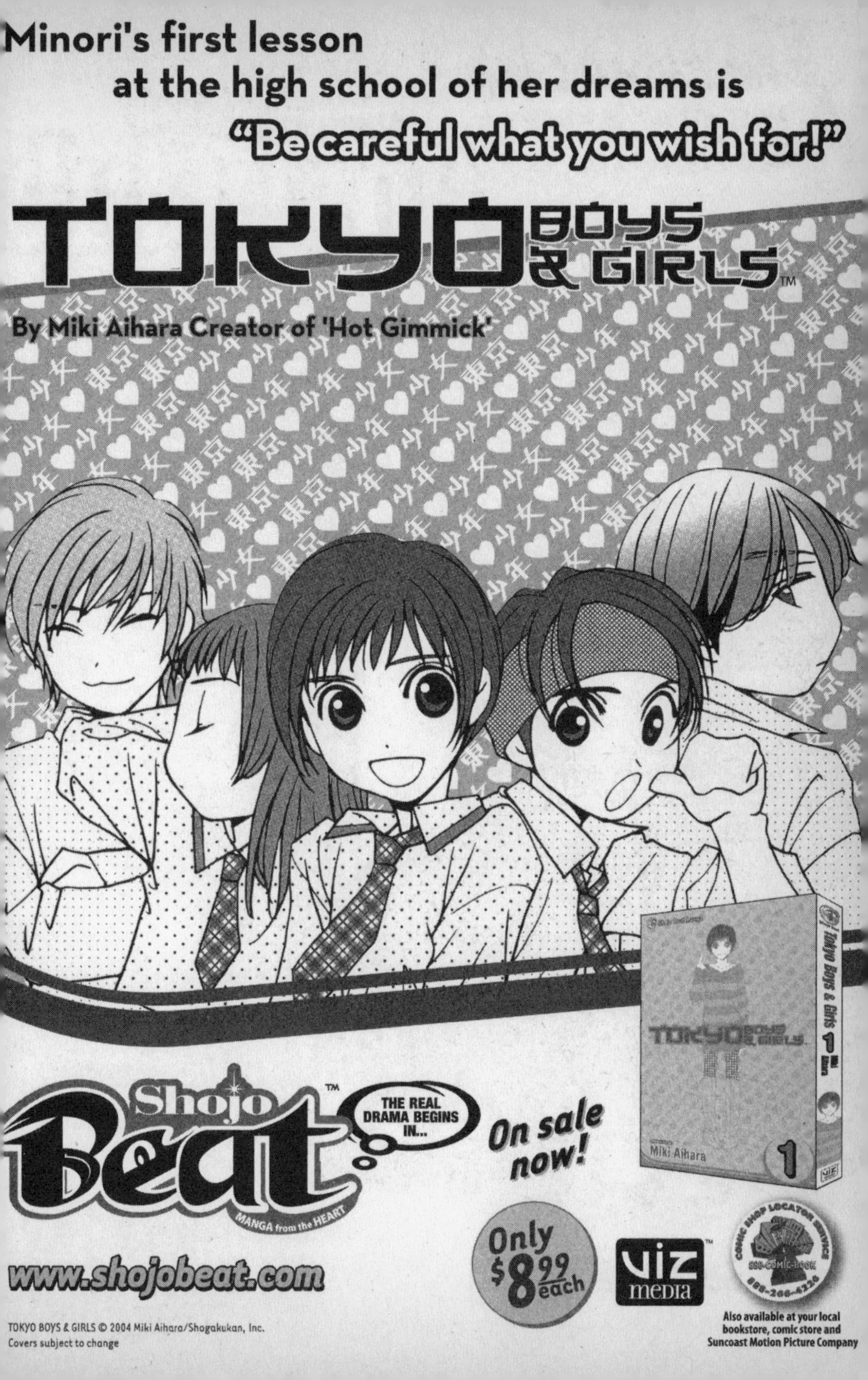
Minori's first lesson
at the high school of her dreams is
"Be careful what you wish for!"
TOKYO BOYS & GIRLS™
By Miki Aihara Creator of 'Hot Gimmick'
Tokyo Boys & Girls 1
Miki Aihara
1
Shojo Beat™
MANGA from the HEART
THE REAL DRAMA BEGINS IN...
On sale now!
Only $8.99 each
VIZ media
COMIC SHOP LOCATOR SERVICE
888-COMIC-BOOK
888-266-4226
www.shojobeat.com
Also available at your local bookstore, comic store and Suncoast Motion Picture Company
TOKYO BOYS & GIRLS © 2004 Miki Aihara/Shogakukan, Inc.
Covers subject to change

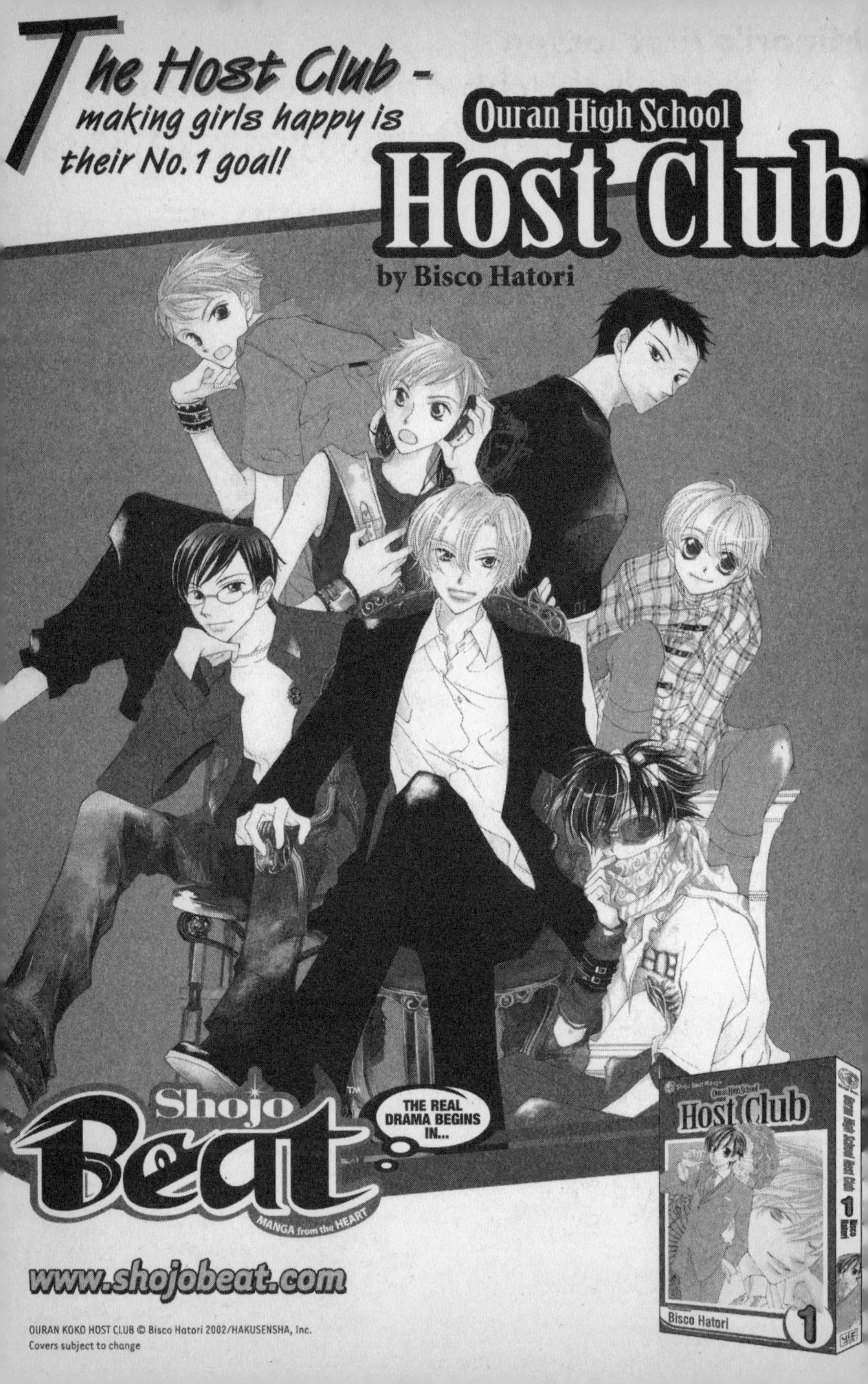
The Host Club - making girls happy is their No.1 goal!
Ouran High School
Host Club
by Bisco Hatori
Shojo Beat
MANGA from the HEART
THE REAL DRAMA BEGINS IN...
www.shojobeat.com
Ouran High School Host Club 1
Bisco Hatori
OURAN KOKO HOST CLUB © Bisco Hatori 2002/HAKUSENSHA, Inc.
Covers subject to change

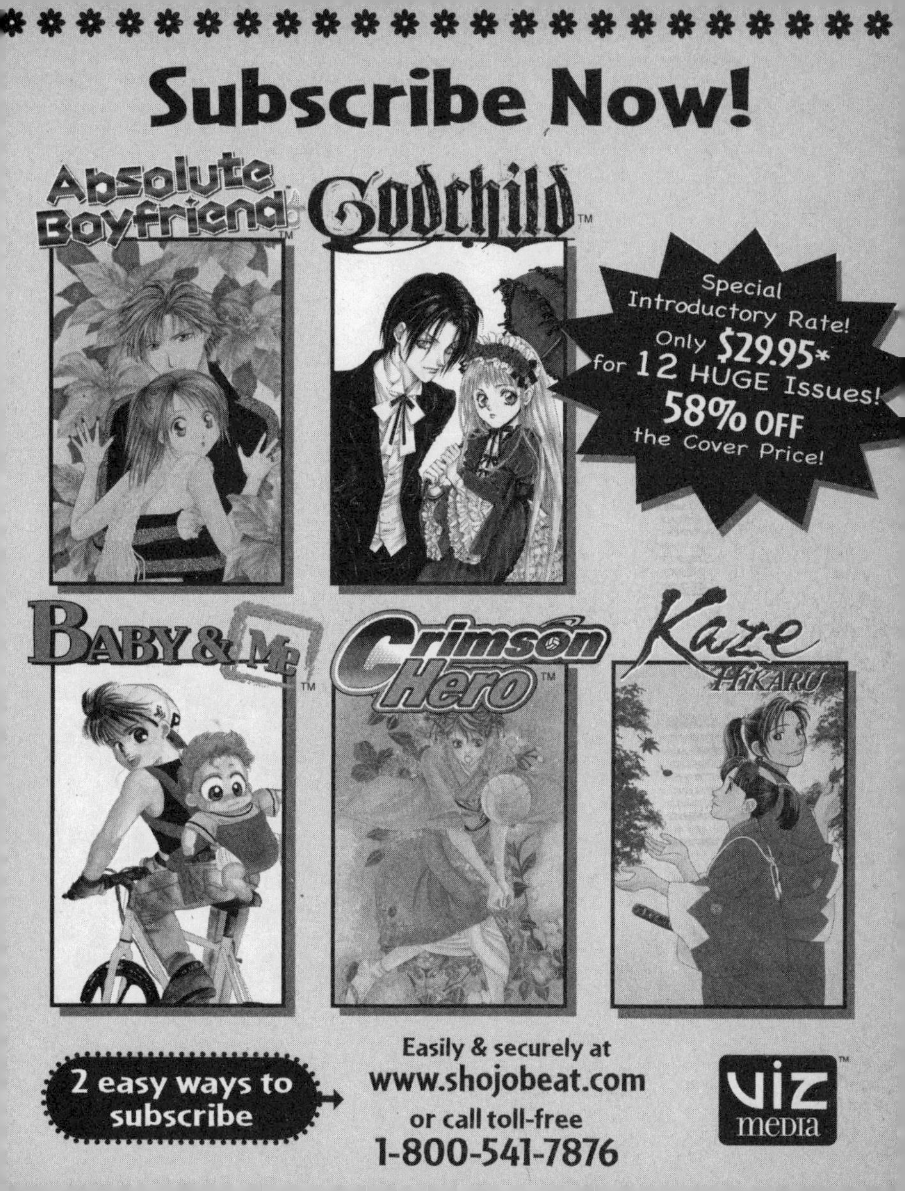
Subscribe Now!
Absolute Boyfriend™
Godchild™
Special Introductory Rate!
Only $29.95*
for 12 HUGE Issues!
58% OFF
the Cover Price!
BABY & ME™
Crimson Hero™
Kaze Hikaru
2 easy ways to subscribe
Easily & securely at
www.shojobeat.com
or call toll-free
1-800-541-7876
VIZ MEDIA™

Find the Beat online!
Check us out at

www.shojobeat.com!

P9 DTA-788